About the Authors

Richard Velleman is Professor of Mental Health Research at the University of Bath (UoB), a consultant clinical psychologist with the Avon and Wiltshire Mental Health Partnership NHS Trust (AWP), and Director of the AWP/UoB Mental Health Research and Development Unit. His previous books include *Clinical Handbook of Co-existing Mental Health and Drug and Alcohol Problems* (edited, with Amanda Baker, 2006).

Eric Davis is Visiting Senior Research Fellow at the University of West of England (UWE) and a consultant clinical psychologist with the Gloucestershire Partnership NHS Trust. He is the Trust lead, and the National Institute for Mental Health, England (NIMHE) southwest associate, for early intervention in psychosis and helped to set up the Integrated Approaches to Serious Mental Illness course at the University of Gloucestershire.

Gina Smith is a [illegible] nurse with the Avon and Wiltshire Mental Health Partnership NHS Trust and [illegible] lead for psychosocial interventions. She is a co-facilitator on the Integrated Approaches to Serious Mental Illness course at the University of Gloucestershire and is the Clinical Director of Studies for the postgraduate programme in mental health practice at the University of Bath.

Michael Drage is a carer who has been involved with the Family Work for Psychosis service in the Avon and Wiltshire Mental Health Partnership NHS Trust for many years, both as someone receiving help from the service and as a key participant in training and information courses about the family work service. He is now a lead carer-researcher with the AWP's Family Work for Psychosis service.

Changing Outcomes in Psychosis

Collaborative Cases from Users, Carers and Practitioners

Edited by Richard Velleman, Eric Davis, Gina Smith and Michael Drage

The British Psychological Society
BPS Blackwell

A BPS Blackwell book

BLACKWELL PUBLISHING
350 Main Street, Malden, MA 02148-5020, USA
9600 Garsington Road, Oxford OX4 2DQ, UK
550 Swanston Street, Carlton, Victoria 3053, Australia

First published 2007 by The British Psychological Society and Blackwell Publishing Ltd

1 2007

Library of Congress Cataloging-in-Publication Data

Changing outcomes in psychosis/edited by Richard Velleman . . . [et al.].
p. cm.
Includes bibliographical references and indexes.
ISBN-13: 978-1-4051-2641-0 (pbk.)
ISBN-10: 1-4051-2641-8 (pbk.)
1. Psychoses. 2. Psychoses—Treatment. 3. Outcome assessment (Medical care).
I. Velleman, Richard.
[DNLM: 1. Psychotic Disorders—therapy. 2. Socioenvironmental Therapy—methods.
3. Social Support. 4. Treatment Outcome. WM 200 C456 2007]
RC512.C45534 2007
616.89—dc22
2006029008

A catalogue record for this title is available from the British Library

Set in 10.5/12.5 pt Jenson Pro by The Running Head Limited, Cambridge, www.therunninghead.com
Printed and bound in Singapore
by Markono Print Media Pte Ltd

The publisher's policy is to use permanent paper from mills that operate a sustainable forestry policy, and which has been manufactured from pulp processed using acid-free and elementary chlorine-free practices. Furthermore, the publisher ensures that the text paper and cover board used have met acceptable environmental accreditation standards.

For further information on
BPS Blackwell, visit our website:
www.bpsblackwell.com

Contents

Contributors

Sean Adams was born in Guyana. He moved to the UK when he was 13, and later went on to study applied physics at university. He is currently working full-time in retail electrical goods. Sean is a very good sportsman and particularly enjoys badminton. He is interested in computers and IT and has recently registered for an Open University course to develop these skills. He hopes this will help him run his own business in the future. Sean was a user of the Gloucestershire Recovery in Psychosis (GRIP) service from the time of his discharge from hospital.

Jane Bellinger, RMN, RGN, BSc (Sports Science and Leisure Management), Dip Thorn, spends more time thinking about exercise than doing it. As a late convert to sport, she participates with more enthusiasm than skill, but believes it helps her cope better with life's stresses and frustrations. When not procrastinating about going to the gym, she works as a case manager/community development worker for an early intervention in psychosis service (EIS).

Lydia Bishop has managed to bring up three children as a single mum while juggling work commitments as a local councillor. She is the primary carer for her eldest son who is making a steady recovery from psychosis. Lydia has found that exercise helps her balance the demands of her caring role. She has contributed a great deal locally in promoting a positive message for those involved in helping someone recover from psychosis.

Sarah-joy Boldison, Dip COT, MSc, is an occupational therapist who has a rich tapestry of experience working in a range of mental health settings. She has a Masters in Management Development and Social Responsibility and is a graduate of the Common Purpose Programme (Bristol). She was a trustee of the Circles Network for 10 years. She now works for both the University of Bath and the National Institute for Mental Health in England. She is passionate about inclusion and human rights issues and the importance of whole systems work, alongside the leadership and team-working needed to bring about positive change.

Steve Brooks is 34 years old. He was born in Cheltenham and attended Grammar school and college and was employed in the Civil Service. When he was 19, he developed a serious psychosis. He had several admissions to hospital, firstly diagnosed as 'manic depressive' then 'schizo-affective', owing to the presence of voices and his beliefs about them. In the early years, medication and social therapy were offered. Ten years ago he was helped with individual and group cognitive behaviour therapy (CBT). Since that time he has developed the skills of working with others with psychosis and this includes part time work as a co-therapist and lecturer. He now lives independently in Cheltenham.

Frank Burbach, BSocSc, BA (Hons), MA (Clin Psych), Dip Mar and Fam Ther, C Psychol, is a consultant clinical psychologist with the Somerset Partnership NHS and Social Care Trust. As a family therapist and United Kingdom Council for Psychotherapy accredited cognitive-behavioural psychotherapist he has been involved in various training initiatives including the development, since 1995, of Somerset's family interventions services (with Roger Stanbridge). He established Somerset's assertive outreach services in 2000/1 and is currently the lead for early intervention in psychosis services. He is a member of the national NIMHE psychosocial interventions implementation group, convenor of the Division of Clinical Psychology family interventions network and previously chaired the Association for Family Therapy's ethics committee.

Jane Carter is now retired, following several years of working as a team leader in a Social Services department. In spite of this background, she was offered little assistance in attempting to gain help, advice and insight into her son's mental health problems. At a later date, the formation of a carers' training course, with the backup of an assertive outreach team, has proved invaluable in understanding and dealing with these serious problems. The continuity of the family support service has provided a solid base for recovery.

John Carter, BA, MA, started his career as a teacher, both overseas and in London. After the diagnosis of paranoid psychosis, he joined the family-run business which required less pressure. Later, following protracted mental health problems, the intervention of an assertive outreach team and the family support service became vitally important. These have helped him considerably on the way to recovery.

Matthew Carter is now retired, after having had a professional career in senior management, the last 20 years of which entailed operating his own business. During this time he has been very much self-sufficient, although it has been extremely difficult when the correct treatment for his son John could not be found. He was, however, able to provide stress-free employment for him. Subsequently, he has been able to help a mental health charity and the local mental health trust on a voluntary basis. The assistance given by the family support service has greatly helped John and himself in coming to terms with the dramatic changes in his son's life.

Nicola Cocks, BSc. Following a 10-year career in administration, Nicola returned to education and in June 2004 completed a psychology degree at the University of Bath. She then worked as an advocate for Bath Mind where she was responsible for running outreach advocacy projects at the local acute inpatient ward. Nicola has experience of carer research and is currently working on auditing and research projects for the Avon and Wiltshire Mental Health Partnership NHS Trust. She has also enrolled on a masters programme in Mental Health Practice.

Keith Coupland, RMN, BSc (Hons), Dip Thorn, was trained on the 1983 RMN syllabus. He has maintained an interest in working with psychosis throughout his career. He completed his nursing degree at the RCN and his Thorn diploma in working with psychosis from Manchester University. With Eric Davis, he set up a Thorn satellite course at the University of Gloucestershire; and was appointed to his present post of nurse consultant for psychosocial interventions in psychosis in 2001.

Tim Cuss trained to be a chemical engineer, but then began a decline into a family illness of schizophrenia. He was treated in hospital and became a long-stay patient, experiencing catatonia and complete withdrawal for many years. He steadily found recovery through the Milsom Street hearing voices group and received personal help for psychosis. Since then he has run a 'recovery' group for inpatients and has had a number of posts as a user consultant. He is also a bee-keeper with about 30 hives.

Rosie Davies, BSocSci, MSc, is research co-ordinator for a lottery-funded project based at Bristol Mind exploring access to services for people seen as 'hard to engage'. Rosie has bipolar disorder. Prior to diagnosis she worked in the voluntary sector and was training as a Gestalt psychotherapist. Since diagnosis, she has developed a keen interest in self-management. Rosie has been involved in other research projects as a service user researcher. Areas of work have included acute inpatient care and the impact of loss of occupation following mental health problems.

Eric Davis, BSc, MSc, PhD, Dip Thorn, Cert Management, C Psychol, is a consultant clinical psychologist and is Gloucestershire and NIMHE southwest lead for early intervention in psychosis services as well as being Visiting Senior Research Fellow with the University of West of England. As well as service development responsibilities, he remains an active clinical practitioner with children and young adults with first-episode psychosis, and their carers. He set up the GRIP early intervention in psychosis team which was featured in the CSIP/NIMHE document '10 High Impact Changes'. With Keith Coupland in 1996 he set up and lectured on the Thorn diploma course at the University of Gloucestershire. His research encompasses a range of interests including service effectiveness and the role of sport and exercise in recovery – this connects with his Senior Research Fellow role.

Jo Denney, MSc Dip COT, Dip Thorn, qualified as an occupational therapist in 1986 and has since worked in a variety of mental health settings. In collaboration with the University of Gloucestershire she has led the university diploma in Integrated Approaches to Serious Mental Illness for the past five years. She has a partner and two children.

Alison Drage, RGN. For the last 14 years Alison has worked as a theatre nurse at Royal United Hospital, Bath and is soon to retire. With the help of her husband, Michael, she brought up five children; the two youngest developed a severe mental disorder: the other three children continue unscathed from psychosis. With the help of Gina Smith, Alison started a carers' support group in Trowbridge; this group is now a registered Rethink (severe mental illness) group. Retirement from nursing will enable Alison to develop the support group further and give much needed private space and time to photography and growing vegetables.

Emily Drage is James' younger sister and is presently struggling in the grip of a severe and enduring psychosis. Though her future looks bleak she still perseveres against the odds. At rare times her warm sunny nature makes an all too brief appearance.

James Drage is Emily's older brother. He has spent the last six years battling with a severe mental disorder. He is now well on the road to recovery and living independently. He enjoys the guidance and benefits of an active support care network. Because of his experiences he feels that he is now in a position to help other service users and to warn against the dangers of drug abuse. He is a keen sportsman and his interests include motor-cycling, sailing, croquet and the importance of a good diet.

Michael Drage (Rev.), BA, MA Cantab, MSc Psych OU, is a lead carer-researcher with the Family Work for Psychosis service, Bath University, Avon and Wiltshire Mental Health Partnership NHS Trust. Married to Alison and father of five children, two inflicted with a mental disorder: the other three children continue unscathed from psychosis. Formerly lecturer/teacher in A level psychology and adviser in education, Canterbury diocese. He is interested in family intervention in cases of psychosis and the role of faith in brain chemistry.

Siobhan Floyd, BSc, is a researcher at the Mental Health Research and Development Unit, University of Bath. She has a particular interest in developing carer and service user led research collaborations and is committed to undertaking research which inspires change. Siobhan has certificates in both counselling theory and skills and is currently studying for an MSc in Mental Health Practice. She hopes to develop as a research-practitioner, aiming to bridge the practice–research gap within mental health services, while growing as a passionate, reflective and recovery-oriented practitioner.

Debbie Furniss, RGN, RMN, BSc (Hons), MBA, is the specialist services manager within Gloucestershire Partnership NHS Trust. This encompasses county-wide services for assertive outreach, rehabilitation, early intervention, prison inreach, criminal justice liaison and supported accommodation. Debbie is currently working with senior clinical colleagues to develop a psychological interventions strategy within specialist services and family work services within the Trust. A key aspect of her style is the integration of managerial and clinical knowledge and experience and she applies this approach in her role in commissioning and modernising services.

Hilary Hawkes, BSc (Hons), is an occupational therapist in a vocational service within a

Mental Health NHS Trust. She has 17 years experience in both the statutory and independent sector of supporting people into work who are disadvantaged in the workplace. She has previously published her experience of leading the conversion of a sheltered workshop to an individual support service. Additionally, Hilary periodically uses mental health services.

Annie Higgs, BSc (Hons) Community Studies, SRN, RMN, PGCEHE, Dip Thorn, is a clinical specialist for psychosocial interventions in the Gloucestershire Partnership NHS Trust. She is working with others to develop a local family work service and to develop psychosocial interventions for individuals and carers in the inpatient unit in Cheltenham. She delivers training for family work service on the local Thorn course. She has co-authored an article, in 2002, about the medication management dissemination project from the Institute of Psychiatry and awaits publication of a manual, co-authored, about working with families of those who experience psychosis.

Megan Jones had her first-episode of 'hypomania' at 18, while at university. During the rest of her studies, her employment and through becoming a mother of three children in her 30s, she was well. However in 1992 at the age of 42, she experienced a terrifying mental breakdown, with repeated episodes between then and the present, usually involving voice-hearing, and leading to a variety of diagnoses. She has given talks alongside Vicky MacDougall, both locally and internationally, on hearing voices, women and psychosis. She has co-facilitated focus groups for the NHS supporting people project and a group on recovery.

Karen Luckett is a student who developed serious mental health problems in her early 20s following the death of her mother. She began to hear voices and became paranoid. Eventually she was diagnosed with a schizo-affective disorder. For many months she was in and out of hospital. She is now well down the path of recovery. She attended a hearing voices group and she also received both CBT and psychotherapy. All of this together has made recovery possible.

Vicky MacDougall, MSc, Dip SW, is mental health development and project manager within the Gloucestershire Partnership NHS Trust. She has an interest in women's mental health and in particular women with self-harming behaviours, personality disorders, domestic violence and sexual abuse and women voice-hearers. She was involved with Keith Coupland and Eric Davis in setting up voice-hearing groups and self-harm groups in Gloucestershire. In addition to this, Vicky has also been involved in a number of research projects that include the employment of service users, and she teaches on a number of projects with service users.

John Mikeson had a career in local government and enjoyed sport and socialising until, at the age of 29, severe mental illness forced early retirement. His interests since then have included voluntary work, psychology and representing patients at user focus groups and forums. He has also had letters published on these issues in the national press. He created the Rainy Day plan to benefit others.

Willm Mistral, BSc, MSc, PhD, is general manager of the joint Avon and Wiltshire Mental Health Partnership NHS Trust/University of Bath, Mental Health Research and Development Unit. He manages a broad portfolio of research, and has published widely on mental health issues, substance misuse, young people, ethnic diversity and service evaluation. He is particularly interested in projects that make a positive impact on people's lives via collaboration, empowerment of participants and self-reflective inquiry.

Christiane Pacé is a practitioner in mental health. Her experience as service user and carer has made her passionate about the need for change and led her to become an advocate with Bristol Mind and train as a social worker. She had to stop both as she struggled with her mental health and the system. She is sure that her return to advocacy and involvement with user-led research projects have maintained her worth as 'person' v. 'patient' and led her back to work and 'social inclusion'.

Mandy Reed, RMN, RGN, MSc, Dip Thorn, has worked as a mental health nurse for most of her adult life, predominantly in community settings. She has always endeavoured to develop robust, collaborative relationships with clients and their carers, built around flexible models of care, and is passionately committed to developing proactive mental health services which promote social inclusion on all levels. Working with young people recovering from psychosis, their carers and social networks was therefore a natural progression in her career. She is the past UK chair of the Mental Health Nurses Association (MHNA). At the time of writing this chapter she was the specialist team leader for the Gloucestershire early intervention service (GRIP). She now works as a consultant nurse/senior lecturer in Acute Adult Care for Avon and Wiltshire Mental Health Partnership NHS Trust and the University of the West of England where she remains committed to developing best practice and implementing the Early Psychosis Declaration.

Lauren Samuels was born in London in 1971. She qualified as a health professional in 1993. Lauren experienced the mental health services as a service user at age 16, then again later as an adult in 1997. Lauren was diagnosed with bipolar disorder in 1998. In 2002 she started collaborative work on relapse prevention; since this work started she has remained relatively stable and not had a further nervous breakdown.

Ruth Sayers, BSocSc, PGCE, was a lecturer in sociology, and engaged in multi-cultural staff and curriculum development for further and higher education in the southwest. She became ill with a mood disorder aged 40. Retiring from teaching, she spent several years on courses, in voluntary and temporary work, and on benefit, before being awarded a grant by the Mental Health Foundation. This enabled her to research into the effects on individuals of losing work following mental health problems (2001–3). The published report, *Life's Labours Lost*, has led to other opportunities for research, training and development on issues of meaningful occupation and social inclusion, and related work, in the UK and Sweden.

Gina Smith, RMN, RGN, Dip Thorn, MSc, is known for her work on implementing family interventions in routine clinical practice, exemplified by an NHS Beacon award 1999–2002 granted to the family work service operating across the Avon and Wiltshire Partnership NHS Trust area. Her research interests include exploring the needs of families of forensic patients and developing meaningful outcome measures for family interventions.

Caroline Stevens was a mother of five children. She had not really had any contact with mental health services prior to her eldest son developing a psychotic disorder in the summer of 2003. She had always devoted most of her time to bringing up her children and was determined to help her son through this period of his life and support him in his recovery. She achieved this by devoting a lot of time and patience and working closely with the early intervention team members, in particular Mandy Reed, the co-author of her chapter in this book. She then resumed her full time work in the local resource centre and maintained a great relationship with her son and the rest of her children. Tragically, she then contracted lung cancer and died in the autumn of 2006, after completing her chapter, but before the book was published.

Roger Thompson, BSc, was an IT professional who developed bipolar disorder in his early 30s. Over a four-year period the resulting manic and depressive behaviour put his marriage under great strain, lost him his job and left him feeling worthless. Fortunately he was put on a family work programme, which has restored his health, his confidence, his relationship and his overall quality of life.

Guy Undrill, MB, ChB, PhD, MRCPsych, is a consultant psychiatrist at Gloucestershire Partnership NHS Trust and honorary senior lecturer at the University of Bristol. His previous research has been in psychoanalysis and performance aesthetics. His principal current interest is the ethics and politics of risk.

Richard Velleman, BSc, MSc, PhD, FBPsS, FRSS, C Psychol, is a consultant clinical psychologist, Professor of Mental Health Research at the University of Bath, and Director of the joint Avon and Wiltshire Mental Health Partnership NHS Trust/University of Bath: Mental Health Research and Development Unit. He has a keen interest in evidence-based service development, and has founded statutory addictions services, helped Gina Smith develop the families and psychosis service within their Trust, worked as an NHS Trust board director, undertaken many externally funded research projects and published very widely on a range of mental health topics.

Foreword

Lu Duhig, Laurie Bryant and Professor Antony Sheehan

This book presents an exciting and refreshing approach to supporting people with severe mental distress, giving a message of hope and encouragement to all.

Rather than being a dry manual for practitioners, the book combines living testimony underpinned by theory, in an easy-to-read and engaging style making it accessible for everyone with an interest in changing outcomes in psychosis.

It is compelling and dynamic in its ability to draw us in to the personal journeys but is always validated by the theory and research that we know is effective, but which is yet to be put fully into routine practice.

The book has been written in a collaborative style mirroring the style of working between the service users, carers and practitioners. By fully valuing and respecting each person's contribution to the journey, it endorses this partnership working, which can bring about such surprising and positive outcomes. Helping people to focus on every aspect of their lives in an holistic way must surely be the way to bring about the biggest improvements.

The overall theme is that the practitioners were able to convey an expectation that even for people experiencing severe distress, recovery is possible. They held the belief that even in seemingly hopeless situations, people could change outcomes and improve the quality of their lives.

We commend the book as a 'must read' for anyone who wishes to develop recovery in the life of someone experiencing severe mental distress. It is inspiring in its promotion of hope that people can build satisfying and meaningful lives.

Lu Duhig
National Service Development Team carer lead, carer lead for NIMHE MHIP Programme, carer lead for NIMHE Choose and Book Programme, and author of *A Carers' Information Pack* available on NIMHE southwest website

Laurie Bryant
National Service User representative for NIMHE, and the Service User lead for the Department of Health Service Improvement team

Foreword

Professor Antony Sheehan
Professor of Health and Social Care Strategy at the University of Central Lancashire, Director General for Health and Care Partnerships at the Department of Health with responsibility for a broad agenda on partnerships across central and regional government, responsibility for developing a voice for people within the Department and specific client group responsibilites including mental health, children, maternity and families.

Preface

Richard Velleman, Gina Smith, Michael Drage and Eric Davis

Changing Outcomes in Psychosis: Collaborative Cases from Users, Carers and Practitioners has been written because we want to change outcomes. For too long, people suffering with psychosis (and their families and loved ones) have been consigned to the dustbin. A diagnosis of psychosis was tantamount to a living death: no hope of reprieve, just a long slog, with at best 'stability', and at worst a deteriorating 'disease' course, with reduced intellectual, social and vocational functioning.

We know that it does not have to be like that, and this book collects together real examples of where outcomes have been changed, where there is hope, recovery and positive functioning. As chapter 1 outlines, the source of hope in many cases is not medication alone, although this may help. The sources of help are mainly psychological and social interventions (termed psychosocial interventions or PSI), often used in conjunction with medication to effect the best outcomes. This book draws on a broad range of experiences which demonstrate PSI in practice. We wanted to do this to help others learn from our experiences of putting government policy (which requires that more PSI are made available) into practice, and hence to share the lessons we had learned.

Format

All the chapters in this book other than the first and last follow a similar format: the chapter is organised around a case study, written collaboratively between a practitioner, and either a person with psychosis or their carer(s) or both. The style, where different 'voices' present the case from their perspectives, appears simple and seamless: in reality, it is extremely difficult to do well. This 'case study' takes centre-stage, but it is embedded in a brief review of the relevant research literature and of the policy background in which it was implemented. Each chapter in this book, therefore, is the product of extensive collaboration between the service user, and/or the family member, and/or the whole family, and one or more of the practitioners who cared for them, and in many cases still does care for them. Some of the later chapters look at overall service delivery, or management, or research instead of at individual therapeutic work: but we have tried to keep the same (or similar) format of using a central case study to demonstrate the points being made.

This is a 'how to do it' book. It is not a cookbook or a manual as such, but we hope that there is sufficient information and detail in each chapter that readers will be able to see and understand what the collaborations between service users, carers and staff have achieved and how they went about achieving this.

The ordering of the chapters in the book reflects three intentions, amongst others. The first was to follow a logical course: we move from first episode work, through relapse work, through longer term recovery; the second was to move from contributions having a larger evidence base, to those having a smaller one; the third was to move from more 'orthodox' PSI (family interventions, assertive outreach, etc.) to those slightly more unusual and even faintly 'heretical' (such as sports, employment, management and evaluation). It is also the case that some of the chapters cover centrally such overarching topics (e.g. gender and management) that they could have been placed almost anywhere in the book.

Anonymity

Some of the service users or carers or whole families have decided to use their real names; others have decided not to do so. In some of the chapters, authors discuss why they took these decisions; others do not, but we can know (and this is discussed in some detail in chapter 1 and returned to in chapter 14) that it is extremely difficult for people to 'come out' into open society as having had and sometimes still having serious mental health problems. There is immense stigma and prejudice against people with such serious mental health problems, and many of us can well understand why (for example in chapter 6) someone who is both a senior professional within NHS mental health services and also a user of such services, decided to remain anonymous, especially as they have chosen (as have many of the authors) to reveal some intensely personal information about themselves and their histories.

Terminology

We are dealing with psychosis in this book. There are many different models of psychosis, with accompanying differences in terminology. As editors we took the decision to reflect our psychosocial approach, and hence to use World Health Organisation terminology such as mental disorder as opposed to mental illness. We asked our contributors to do the same. We wanted to provide a guide to authors, not to overly constrain them, and hence we suggested that there were a range of possibilities of terms they could use: mental health problems, mental health difficulties, mental health issues, mental disturbances, etc. We decided that we were happy with any of these, but (as we were producing this book from a psychosocial perspective), the one term we asked people *not* to use was 'mental illness'. However, we also told authors that if any of them did wish to use the term 'mental illness', they should make explicit in their chapter their reasons for doing so. In the event, the authors of just one of the 14 chapters (chapter 3) felt that what they were dealing with was an illness, and that defining it as such fitted with both the service user's personal experiences and with his use of medication, and their own attributions for mental health disturbances, where they found biological explanations more useful.

In keeping with our decision not to adopt a medical viewpoint and not to use 'mental illness' terminology, we have used the term 'service user' rather than 'patient'. We also decided not to use the term 'consumers' as this is an aspirational statement: we might aspire to a situation where people with psychosis problems can pick and chose and select their mental health services as if they were consumers or customers, but this is not true (yet!).

We have also taken the decision not to have a glossary in the book; instead, we define each new or 'technical' term when it first occurs. Hence, by 'psychosis' we mean a general term used to describe a variety of experiences that indicate some loss of contact with reality, including hallucinations, false beliefs (delusions), confused thinking, changed feelings, and changes in behaviour. Schizophrenia and manic depression (bipolar affective disorder) are both included under 'psychosis'. Psychosis typically first affects people in young adulthood, causing disruption to social relationships, education and career plans. We also know that, unfortunately, many people will have been suffering from these experiences for one to two years before getting help. This is why early intervention in psychosis services (EIS) have started to be developed: these are NHS mental health services which aim to reach people early who are experiencing psychosis for the first time (i.e. who are suffering from first-episode psychosis (FEP)), and help them and their families cope and recover.

Acknowledgements

We would like to thank and acknowledge our organisations (the Avon and Wiltshire Mental Health Partnership NHS Trust, the University of Bath for RV, GS and MD; Gloucestershire Partnership NHS Trust for ED) not only for providing the support and encouragement to write and edit this book, and for the professional and personal relationships which they have led to, but also for their vision in enabling so many of the initiatives outlined in this book to occur. Thanks also to our colleagues within the Mental Health R&D Unit at the University of Bath for their ongoing interest and support. We would like to thank Debbie Masding, ED's secretary who did a wonderful job chasing up contributors, contracts and loose ends, making all of our lives easier.

We feel particularly privileged to have assembled such outstanding contributors to this book and have very much enjoyed working collaboratively, and with the chapter authors, to make the book come together. On our parts, we feel we have contributed our professional and personal expertise from having worked clinically, academically and managerially in services for people with psychosis, and having experienced these issues first-hand via family or friends. We hope that both new and experienced clinicians, and people suffering from psychosis, and their family members, find this book useful.

It is with deep regret that we heard just before the book was due to go to press that one of our authors had just died (Caroline Stevens, the co-author of Chapter 2 and a mother of and carer for someone with psychosis). Caroline put a great deal into the writing of her chapter, and it is extremely saddening that she did not live to see the book being published.

Richard Velleman, Gina Smith, Michael Drage and Eric Davis
January 2006

Chapter 1

Psychosocial Developments
Towards a Model of Recovery

Eric Davis, Richard Velleman, Gina Smith and Michael Drage

Key Points

There has been a paradigm shift, where recovery from psychosis is seen as possible.

- Although this shift started with the invention of neuroleptics, it has mainly involved psychological approaches. These have led to 'psychosocial interventions' (PSI), the core of this book.
- The 'recovery model' actually involves more than just the *possibility* of recovery: it concerns the development of a process of building a satisfying and meaningful life, despite having mental health problems; the promotion of hope; and the retaking of control of their lives by people with mental health problems.
- A major part of developing and encouraging 'recovery' involves stigma reduction.
- PSI and recovery each share both the ethos and the necessity of 'partnership/collaborative working'.
- If these ideas are blended and people (individuals, families, communities, institutions and organisations) all work together, then the future for people who develop serious mental health problems can be a positive one.

Introduction

Psychosis: incurable degeneration or treatable condition?

We are witnessing a major 'paradigm shift' (Kuhn 1970) in understanding and treating serious mental health problems in the UK. For many hundreds of years, people experienced serious mental health problems as lifelong and incurable disorders. In the Middle Ages people with these disorders were looked after informally, at home or in their own communities. Later, through more formalised religious, and then medical, interventions, care began to be concentrated within institutional settings (religious communes, hospitals); and the growing medicalisation of mental health problems meant that the drive for institutionalised care increased throughout the nineteenth and early twentieth centuries. But the underlying belief remained: that these were incurable or largely untreatable disorders.

This view started to change in the latter half of the twentieth century. There were many factors associated with this change: a realisation of the economic burden on the state of large-scale and long-stay institutions, a growing move towards a more humanitarian and anti-institutionalisation way of thinking, and a quasi-political movement – 'anti-psychiatry' – which started to question the tenets of 'mental illness'.

However, probably the main reason that these changes occurred was because some evidence began to appear suggesting that, possibly, these disorders could be helped, and that they were not necessarily lifelong and incurable (Harrison and Mason 1993).

Initially, the evidence was associated with new medications. The neuroleptics brought with them the chance that for some people, the most problematic symptoms of their mental health difficulties could be controlled, and that maybe they could start to retake their place within the wider society.

But the hope which was raised – that the new medications would change the picture entirely – did not materialise. Side-effects were experienced by up to 75 per cent of service users (Brennan et al. 2000) and, although this is only one reason for non-compliance, as many as 80 per cent of people with a diagnosis of schizophrenia did not take their medication as prescribed (Corrigan, Liberman and Engel 1990), or took it at a less than optimal dosage (Schooler 1993). And even when people did take medication in the prescribed manner, their problems were alleviated not 'cured'. Even today, with newer medications with less intolerable side-effects, it is the case that the pharmaceutical avenue alone has not led to the disappearance of serious mental health problems. Hegarty and colleagues (1994) demonstrated that although functional outcomes did improve with the advent of neuroleptics, the percentage of people deemed to be 'improved' at follow-up has never risen beyond 50 per cent, and by the early 1990s was falling once again. Singh (2004; Singh and Fisher 2005; Singh et al. 2000) has drawn attention to the ' paradox': that although 90 per cent of people who suffer a first episode of psychosis will be in remission (i.e. the psychosis disappears completely) at the end of one year of treatment, only one-third will have a good functional outcome. If anything, the disability which people with a diagnosis of psychosis suffer, seemed in the 1990s to be getting worse (Singh et al. 2000). Singh (2004; Singh and Fisher 2005) has drawn attention to the fact that there are at least four dimensions which are often seriously affected in people with a diagnosis of schizophrenia: *positive symptoms* (delusions, hallucinations, formal thought disorder); *negative symptoms* (amotivation, affective flattening, poverty of speech); *cognitive deficits* (impairment of attention, diminished executive functions); and *mood symptoms* (anhedonia, hopelessness, despair, disem-powerment, risk of suicide); all of which together define the extent of social, occupational and interpersonal disability or handicap that a person suffers. Singh makes the point that the psychotropic medications so far developed have reduced significantly the positive symptoms that people suffer, but have not reduced (and in fact have generally worsened) the other sets of symptoms. Although others claim that negative symptoms can be treated by atypical neuroleptics (Brennan et al. 2000), such claims are not made for their impact on cognitive or mood symptoms. As well as these four sets of psychological symptoms, there are a number of physical deficits that are well attested to in the literature, for example: weight gain, palpitations, high blood pressure, constipation, loss of sex drive, tremor, rigidity and menstrual disruption. All of these are highly debilitating neuroleptic side-effects and make medication compliance far from easy. According to Pratt (1998) 'most neuroleptics do produce a similar range of side-effects' (pp. 247–8, and see especially Box 11.4).

A second strand to the idea that these disorders need not be life-long came from the increasing questioning of what the disorders actually were. A major debate commenced, helped by the growth in the 'anti-psychiatry' movement, over whether or not they constituted diagnosable mental illnesses, with reliable and valid diagnoses (Bentall 1990, 2003). Some argued that entities such as schizophrenia did not actually exist. Szasz and others suggested that diagnosing someone with schizophrenia was a means of legitimising social control of deviants (Szasz 1976). Others argued that the diagnosis was a way of labelling those who are victims of a conspiracy between psychiatrists and their families (Laing and Esterson 1964).

Yet other arguments suggested that the whole notion of diagnosis in psychiatry is wrong or irrelevant. One version of this argument is based on the fact that classificatory systems necessarily discard information: the classification forces one to select certain salient dimensions along which people will be classified, and to discard information on other dimensions, in order to fit people into groups or categories. This does not matter if the information we discard is irrelevant; but the problem is that in the area of serious mental health problems, we do not know what is relevant and what is not, implying that (certainly at our current stage of knowledge) it is highly inappropriate to classify people. Another argument against the whole notion of diagnosis and classification states that people on all dimensions lie on continua, from adjustment to maladjustment, and therefore discrete judgements (this person is suffering from 'x'; this person is not) are inappropriate, and give a false impression of discontinuity between illness and wellness. It has been argued that this may be resolved by concentrating instead on individual symptoms (Persons 1986). Yet another argument along these lines suggests that, owing to the stigmatisation that arises once a diagnosis is made, psychiatric diagnosis always does more harm than good: even if diagnosis is (or could be) helpful, the stigmatisation is worse. We return to the problems of stigma again below.

These ideas above have demonstrated a view that holds that all psychiatric diagnosis is necessarily irrelevant or unhelpful. Others have accepted that diagnosis *could be* helpful (a position held by most of this book's editors), but have sought to question its current usefulness owing to its lack of validity and reliability (Bentall 1990, 2003). There have been a very large number of studies which have shown that psychiatric diagnoses are highly biased and unreliable. Some of these studies have become 'classics': frequently cited because they demonstrate the point so well. Among the best known are:

- Langer and Abelsen's 1974 study showing how labelling completely altered whether or not a diagnosis was made. A video tape of an interview between a young man in his mid-20s and a 'bearded professor' was shown to two groups of professionals, one who were told that the young man was a job applicant, the other that he was a psychiatric patient. The group who saw the video where the young man had the 'psychiatric patient' label were much more likely to rate his level of disturbance as 'very disturbed', and people read into his responses in the interview all kinds of meanings related to his 'psychiatric patient' label which the other group did not: people remarked on his 'tight defensive personality', 'impulsivity' and his 'conflict over homosexuality' (p. 8). The point of course is that all diagnosis is undertaken on people with an accompanying 'patient' label.

- Rosenhan's 1973 study 'On being sane in insane places' which again shows how people 'see' elements which fit their expectations of what mentally ill people are going to be like. Here 12 'sane' people went to different hospitals in the USA, complaining of only one symptom: of hearing voices that said – 'empty', 'hollow', 'thud'. Each person was given a clinical diagnostic interview, in which everyone properly reported their family history, current life circumstances (other than they were undertaking this experiment!), etc. Using the diagnostic categorisation in use at that time (the American Psychiatric Association's *Diagnostic and Statistical Manual* II or DSM-II), the diagnosing doctors should only have made a diagnosis of schizophrenia if there were (a) disturbances of thinking and affect (emotion), and (b) withdrawn or bizarre behaviour. Even in the early 1970s, schizophrenia should never have been diagnosed solely on the basis of someone having had an auditory hallucination. Yet all 12 were admitted to (different) hospitals, and all 12 were diagnosed as suffering from a psychotic illness: 11 schizophrenia; one manic-depressive psychosis. Immediately after admission all of them stopped talking about the voices and behaved in their usual ways. Interestingly, they remained as inpatients for an average of 19 days, and none were detected in that time as pseudo-patients by staff (though some were detected by other patients). Crucially, the circumstances of their past history were distorted to explain their 'disordered behaviour'. For example, one man accurately reported that as a child he had had a close relationship with his mother and a remote one with father; but that as he grew up, he got closer to father and became a bit alienated from mother. He also said he sometimes used corporal punishment with his children, and that he sometimes got angry with his wife/children. His discharge summary concluded: 'This white 39-year-old male manifests a long history of considerable ambivalence in close relationships, which begins in early childhood . . . Affective (emotional) stability is absent. His attempts to control emotionality with his wife and children are punctuated by angry outbursts and, in the case of the children, spankings. And while he says that he has several good friends, one senses considerable ambivalence embedded in those relationships also . . .' (Rosenhan 1973, p. 253). Finally, when these people were discharged, almost all were diagnosed again, usually with 'schizophrenia, in remission'. Very few were discharged with 'no mental disorder' on their records. All of this implies that people who make diagnoses (certainly in the 1970s in the USA) would take behaviour which is consistent with their model and fit that behaviour into their expectations so that the model is confirmed.
- Beck et al.'s 1962 study which showed very low levels of agreement and reliability between diagnosticians. Four very experienced psychiatrists diagnosed 153 patients within one week of admission, and all patients were diagnosed separately by two of the psychiatrists: each patient was interviewed twice in succession by two different psychiatrists. The four psychiatrists had met each other and discussed their diagnostic criteria, and all purported to use the standard diagnostic system of the time (DSM-I); yet their overall rate of agreement was only 54 per cent. Their agreements for different diagnoses are shown in Table 1.1.

Table 1.1 Agreements between psychiatrist for different diagnoses, from Beck et al. 1962

	Number of diagnoses	*% agreement*
Neurotic depression	92	63
Anxiety reaction	58	55
Sociopath	11	54
Schizophrenia	60	53
Involutional melancholia	10	40
Personality disturbance	26	38

And to add to all the issues over the reliability of diagnosis, there has been no consistency over time as to which symptoms should or should not be included to reach a psychiatric diagnosis. At two points in time, entirely different sets of symptoms have been used to reach what look like exactly the same diagnosis (Wing 1992).

Yet another issue with diagnosis relates to the significant problems which may arise once diagnoses are accepted, although these seem to be balanced in some cases by the relief that accompanied the greater understanding that it promoted:

- Karp and Tanarugsachock (2000) have discussed the guilt which commonly follows diagnosis, particularly in children of parents diagnosed with schizophrenia. They argue that this is apparently associated with having doubted their parent was ill. Consistently in their study, diagnosis led to (symptomatic) behaviours becoming understood within a medical framework, which promoted feelings of sympathy, love and understanding.
- Birchwood and colleagues (1993) found an acceptance of the diagnosis by patients with a psychotic disorder was then related to a lower sense of control over the illness. This perception of a lack of control was associated with an increased incidence of depression compared to those who did not accept their diagnosis. In one way, the patients who did not accept their diagnosis 'lacked insight'; in another, their refusal to accept the diagnosis contributed to their better psychological health!

Finally, it has been suggested that a diagnosis of schizophrenia could be seen as useful if it led to accurate predictions of who would respond positively to neuroleptic medication. Unfortunately diagnosis does not confer this benefit, with up to 50 per cent showing little or no response (Warner 1994), and with the 'factor structures of negative symptoms (being) similar with and without medication' (Kelley, van Kammen and Allen 1999, p. 406).

Psychological Approaches

The above discussion has outlined some reasons why the older 'permanent and deteriorating disease' picture changed: useful medications were discovered, and older ideas of the certainty of these diagnoses started to change. A further strand to this notion that these disorders need not be a lifelong disability arose from the huge growth in more psychological approaches which suggested that people with these serious mental health problems could in fact change and acquire control over their symptoms. These psychological approaches started to make inroads at around the same time as the pharmaceutical products were starting to appear.

Psychological approaches range from the token economies of the 1950s and 60s, through to belief modification (Milton, Patwa and Hafner 1978), social skills training (Liberman, DeRisi and Mueser 1989), and using a normalising rationale (Turkington and Kingdon 1996), up to the present day, where the psychosocial approaches with which this book is concerned are demonstrating their effectiveness.

There is increasing evidence of the value of these psychosocial interventions (PSI: that is, interventions which work with individual's social networks as well as with the individual on their own) in reducing relapse rates for schizophrenia sufferers by up to 50 per cent (Hogarty and Ulrich 1998). Many commentators now agree (and there is also much evidence to support this claim (Falloon, Boyd and McGill 1984; Nuechterlein 1987)) that, to be most effective, these interventions should not *replace* pharmacological treatments, but should work alongside them: that it is *in combination* that psychosocial and pharmacological interventions may work best and provide improved outcomes for service users and their carers.

This mix of psychological, social and pharmacological approaches often goes under the rather cumbersome title of a 'bio-psychosocial' approach, and this holistic approach or philosophy underpins this present book.

In a parallel approach, we have chosen to discuss schizophrenia and other serious mental health problems as 'disorders' rather then 'illnesses'. Some commentators would disagree with us here. It could be pointed out that the term 'disorder' may not always appear to fit well with certain forms of schizophrenia. For example, it has been argued that some neuro-scientific advances around the turn of the millennium support the existence of organic brain pathology in those sufferers who have a severe psychosis with predominant negative symptoms (Filbey et al. 1999; Mortimer and Spence 2001). A number of other studies (for example, Crow 1980; Johnstone et al. 1989; Gur et al. 1994) show considerable association between prominent and severe negative symptoms and an apparent irreversible pathological brain process; there was also the finding that the younger the age of onset, the greater was the presence and prominence of negative symptomatology. It can be argued that these findings do raise the possibility that some clients will be immune to psychosocial treatments; and indeed that for some of these service users, the term 'illness' or even 'disease' might be more accurate than the term 'disorder'. But findings of associations between psychiatric symptomatology and brain processes do not of course imply physical causation, only that there are strong relationships between events at a psychological level and events at a physiological level; and indeed, this understanding that there are such close relationships between physical, psychological and social processes lies at the heart of what we have described in this book as our holistic approach.

For many, the best enactment of this bio-psychosocial model is the stress-vulnerability idea. This is a development (also found in other areas such as depression and substance misuse treatment) of so-called 'two-factor' theories, which means simply that there are two sets of factors at work: vulnerability factors, and triggering, or precipitating, factors. These ideas suggest that everyone is vulnerable to or at risk of developing some problem or other. For some people, their risk is towards depression, for others anxiety, for yet others some physical problem such as cancer or coronary problems; and for some, psychosis. Vulnerability towards developing any of these problems will exist on a continuum from 'highly vulnerable' to 'very invulnerable'. Why some people are more at risk than others towards one problem rather than another is insufficiently understood at present, but probable factors relating to vulnerability include genetics, personality, patterns of upbringing and experience, and physiological factors.

The two-factor idea suggests that although everyone is vulnerable to one sort of problem or another (or maybe to more than one problem), even those people who are vulnerable will need some triggering factor(s) to push them towards developing a problem. The theory also suggests that a range of different factors could trigger or precipitate someone into developing a problem. Probable triggering factors include stress, other psychological factors, social factors, and (as far as psychosis or substance misuse problems are concerned) availability and patterns of consumption of alcohol and/or street drugs.

The most important of these two-factor theories is Zubin and Spring's (1977) stress-vulnerability model, which suggests that individuals respond and adapt to stress in various ways; and that although all individuals respond by breaking down if stress is sufficiently high, different individuals are more or less vulnerable at a given level of stress. Zubin and Spring also suggest that vulnerability has two components: an inborn/genetic/physiological one, and an acquired one, via the influence of trauma, disease, family experience, adolescent peer interaction, and so on. The stress-vulnerability model is examined in more detail in chapters 4 and 8.

Some (e.g. Velleman 2001) have also suggested that these two-factor ideas could be extended to three-factor ones, referring to 'the three Ps': the idea that there are 'predisposing', 'precipitating' and 'perpetuating' factors: predisposing factors include the 'vulnerability' ones listed above; precipitating factors again are those listed above; and perpetuating factors are those which maintain or perpetuate problematic symptoms and behaviour (relating to whatever the problem is: psychosis, substance misuse, etc.) once an episode begins.

All these strands: the development of better medications, the clarification that the actual diagnostic process may be flawed and unreliable, the growth in more effective psychosocial interventions, the development of the stress-vulnerability model and a more integrative bio-psychosocial approach, have laid the foundation for a view of *recovery* as opposed to lifelong disability and gradual decline.

A Recovery Approach

Borrowing from the physical health literature, Anthony (1993), one of the founders of the recovery approach, suggested that recovery from mental health problems can continue alongside impairment, dysfunction, disability or disadvantages. Recovery from any form of catastrophe does not negate the fact that it has happened, but it does suggest that successful recovery means that the person has changed.

There are all sorts of things which recovery *is* and *is not*. Recovery is about people with serious mental health problems seeing themselves (and the professionals working with them also seeing them in this way) as *capable of recovery* rather than as passive recipients of professional treatments. It is about people working out strategies and taking control of their own lives.

It is also the process of rebuilding a satisfying and meaningful life *even though* one has mental health problems. Recovery is certainly not necessarily about 'cure'. That is not to say that all people with serious mental health problems will always have them: 25 per cent of people *do* have a single episode of psychosis which does not recur (Aitchison, Meehan and Murray 1999). Even if this does not happen, there is considerable variation: for some people, difficulties last for only short periods of time; many others have difficulties that recur regularly and even frequently; and some have cognitive and emotional difficulties that are ever-present. But the fact that symptoms may continue or recur does not mean that people cannot live meaningful, satisfying and contributing lives. One definition of recovery is that it is: 'a personal process of overcoming the negative impact of a psychiatric disability despite its continued presence' (Took 2002, unpaged).

Anthony wrote that recovery is:

> a deeply personal, unique process of changing one's attitudes, values, feelings, goals, skills, and/or roles. It is a way of living a satisfying, hopeful and contributing life even with the limitations caused by illness. Recovery involves the development of new meaning and purpose in one's life as one grows beyond the catastrophic effects of mental illness.
>
> (Anthony 1993, p. 19)

It has been claimed that once someone has had a serious mental health problem, even if it were never to recur, it is simply not possible to go back to the way things were before the problems started. It can be argued of course that this is possibly no different from the situation that any person is in, having to deal with a life-changing experience (and there is no question that having even one episode of psychosis *is* a life-changing experience): one cannot simply forget that it happened and go back to the way that one was before. But the recovery approach suggests very strongly that even though one cannot go back, the fact of having had or continuing to have these problems does not have to mean the end of hopes and aspirations for that person's life (Allott and Loganathan 2003). The recovery approach is focused on the fact that many people with mental health problems have shown us that it is possible to move forward, and to recover meaning, purpose and value in life: 'recovery is about pursuing your ambitions whether or not your symptoms continue' (Perkins 2004, unpaged).

Within the recovery approach, individuals are encouraged to learn more about their experience, and find ways to *deal* with their mental health experiences. People are actively supported to acquire the skills, knowledge and strength to reduce the prevalence of harmful experiences in safe, simple and effective ways. Such ideas are a big change from traditional mental health services, and require a very different way of working from them.

A key element to recovery is about people taking control for themselves, and moving away from a negative mental health system:

> To me, recovery means I try to stay in the driver's seat of my life. I don't let my illness run me. Over the years I have worked hard to become an expert in my own self-care . . . Over the years I have learned different ways of helping myself. Sometimes I use medications, therapy, self-help and mutual support groups, friends, my relationship

> with God, work, exercise, spending time in nature – all of these measures help me remain whole and healthy, even though I have a disability.
>
> (Deegan 1997, p. 21)

Recovery is also about people working out ways of helping themselves, taking responsibility and having hope. Each person's recovery is an individual, personal and unique process, and hence everyone with a serious mental health problem recovers in a different way. Many factors influence a person's current stage of functioning within the recovery process, and consequently, movement is not linear: people frequently have to try and try again.

> Recovery . . . is not a perfectly linear journey. There are times of rapid gains and disappointing relapses. There are times of just living, just staying quiet, resting and regrouping. Each person's journey of recovery is unique. Each person must find what works for them.
>
> (Deegan 1996, pp. 96–7)

There are nonetheless also common themes and certain concepts or factors which are common to recovery. Some of these are:

- hope
- empowerment
- information and knowledge
- support
- employment/meaningful activity
- medication
- self-help
- spirituality
- humour
- enthusiasm.

Other themes are about challenging the belief that 'severe mental illness' must be chronic, and that stability is the best one could hope for. Indeed, low expectations on the part of mental health professionals can lead to a state of learned helplessness for service users, which can in turn delay an individual's recovery (Roberts and Wolfson 2004). There are actually multiple outcomes associated with severe mental health problems and many people do progress beyond a state of mere stability. It is also important to stress that recovery does not refer to an end product or a result: it is an ongoing process, a continuing journey. And finally, for a great many people, work is central to their recovery: meaningful and satisfying work which allows someone to participate in their society and feel valued and worthwhile. The issues of work and of other activity (such as sports participation) are considered in depth in chapters 9 and 10 in this book.

As more research has been undertaken which has demonstrated the importance of these ideas, the concept of recovery has begun to obtain greater legitimacy. Nevertheless, great obstacles still exist. There are major 'secondary difficulties' which arise from the consequences of suffering from a serious mental health disorder, over and above the disorder itself. Dysfunction, disability and disadvantages may present difficulties greater than impairment issues. The loss of a valid role and/or occupation, which often follows an episode of psychosis is often damaging to self-esteem. Being categorised as 'mentally ill' with all the stigma that surrounds that, can be very psychologically damaging. Such views can reinforce the maintenance of a 'sick role'. As Rachel Perkins states, herself both a senior clinician and someone with a recurrent psychotic disorder:

> recovery is about redefining your identity in a way which includes, but moves beyond, the limitations of 'illness'. We can and do develop a new sense of self, value, meaning and purpose in our lives in the face of continuing mental health problems and in the face of the discrimination and exclusion that exist.
>
> (Perkins 2004, unpaged)

The process of recovery seems to arise most often from talking to others, 'particularly to other service users rather than professionals' (Roberts and Wolfson 2004, p. 40). Central to this process appears to be an acceptance of the past alongside an optimism for the future. Care should be taken however: in the desire to see a recovery journey for all, it is important to acknowledge that for some service users, the journey does not appear to proceed very far. For some, basic abilities to learn, to remember short term, to sequence and even to hope, appear to be so muted by the mental disorder that all that seems possible after many years is a drug-induced stability. In these cases, professionals, and carers and families, could threaten this hard won stability by expecting too much too soon from both the service user and the psychosocial interventions which are so beneficial and effective for others. This is not to deny the importance of a hopeful and supportive atmosphere for all. It is, however, important to recognise the extent of the disability caused by some forms of severe and enduring psychosis, and hence to proceed carefully and at a pace appropriate to the individual. And even in the most severe cases, there is cause for optimism: in an experimental study of treatment-resistant schizophrenia, individuals showed significant improvement after recovery-focused psychotherapy compared with a control group (Randal, Simpson and Laidlaw 2003).

Stigma and Discrimination

It is very difficult to maintain a recovery approach when confronted by stigma and discrimination. A major part of developing and encouraging recovery involves stigma reduction, because the stigma involved in having (or having had) a 'psychiatric illness' is immense.

The issue of stigma is highly important for people with psychosis. This is because stereotypes, prejudices and discrimination can act, in concert, to reduce or deny users choices and life-chances, thereby contributing to and maintaining social exclusion. Angermeyer and Matschinger (2003) and Arboleda-Florez (2003) discuss these stigma components. Stereotypes represent rigid conceptions of groups of people. Prejudice is exhibited by people who endorse such negative stereotypes, and prejudice leads to social discrimination.

Goffman (1963) defined stigma as 'an attribute (which a person or people may have) that is deeply discrediting' (p. 13) which leads to discrimination owing to a belief that 'the person with a stigma is not quite human' (p. 15). The term may relate to race or religion, physical or psychological disability. And the stigma of having a serious mental health problem affects all areas of someone's life. It affects job prospects (Knight, Wykes and Hayward 2003), social relations (Mind 2004) and family life (Wahl and Harman 1989). Stigma has been shown to affect not only the person with a psychosis but also his or her family (Lefley 1987), which has been termed stigma by association (Ostman and Kjellin 2002).

The extent to which people hold stigmatising views about mental health problems is also affected by their model of these problems. Stigma is increased when people hold an illness model as opposed to viewing the condition as a response to overwhelming environmental stressors (Mehta and Farina 1997). A review by Read (2002) found people who embrace the medical model are more likely to reject schizophrenia sufferers, with less likelihood of forming friendships owing to concerns of unpredictable behaviour. It is likely that this increased stigmatisation is related to fear, with an illness model being associated with beliefs that 'mental patients' are not responsible for their actions. The consequent perceived risks of unpredictability and violence then lead to increased stigmatisation and consequently harsher treatment of service users (Read 2002).

An important source of information for the general public regarding psychosis and mental illness is from media representation. The link between dangerousness and mental illness is often reported, frequently in the most sensationalist ways: the archetypal 'mad axe murderers' from whom 'the public' need to be protected. This sensationalist approach is taken even with popular and favourite public figures, as occurred in the early 2000s when Frank Bruno (a former British heavyweight boxing champion) suffered from mental health difficulties. Such representations are highly unrepresentative, and very damaging for the clear majority of users, and for their carers. The media do not inform the public that only a very small minority of mental health users commit serious crimes, and that the percentage of violence attributable to mental illness as a proportion of the general violence in the community is also very small. Instead they generate a climate of fear and contribute to the negative stereotypes and stigmatising views which are held by so many of the wider population.

Unfortunately, it is not only the media who hold and promote these stereotyped and negative views: mental health professionals also contribute. Chadwick (1997) has noted that:

> even the briefest perusal of the current literature on schizophrenia will immediately reveal to the uninitiated that this collection of problems is viewed by practitioners almost exclusively in terms of dysfunction and disorder. A positive or charitable phrase or sentence rarely meets the eye . . . Deficit-obsessed research can only produce theories and attitudes which are disrespectful of clients and are also likely to induce behaviour in clinicians such that service users are not properly listened to, not believed, not fairly assessed, are likely treated as inadequate and are also not expected to be able to become independent and competent individuals in managing life's tasks.
> (pp. 11–12)

The possibility of a positive and optimistic future is central to the recovery model; a major part of developing and encouraging the recovery model therefore must involve stigma reduction; and a major part of that clearly needs to involve enabling professionals, as well as the general public, to see people with mental health problems in more positive ways.

Gaebel and Baumann (2003) attempt to capture some of the ways in which stigma can be reduced. They report in the Open the Doors Programme in Germany, suggesting that a package of strategies is used. First, improving media representation of people with 'mental illness', second, education of the public about psychological and psychiatric issues, and third the promotion of personal contact either with users or ex-users (it is known that 'Stigmatization may be reduced by promoting direct contact between the public and individuals with mental illness' (Penn et al. 1994, p. 572)).

Increasing personal contact with service users was recommended following the foundation of a public relations association in psychiatry. One initiative stemming from the association is the school project 'Crazy? so what!' (Schulze and Angermeyer 2003). Here a school project promotes direct contact between schoolchildren and service users as part of their health curriculum. The school children are encouraged to reflect upon their knowledge and attitudes regarding 'mental illness'. From contact with users, schoolchildren can explore their attitudes and develop an appreciation of the consequences of 'mental illnesses' and what life is like for a person who experiences such issues.

Another initiative designed, in part, to help combat stigma was started in the UK. The Early Psychosis Declaration (World Health Organisation 2004) is an aspirational charter of rights for users with psychosis and their carers (see chapter 2 for further detail). One of a number of targets is that all children aged 15 should have a working knowledge of psychosis. Given this age, the intention is to define accurate information via the health curriculum at schools, as Schulze and Angermeyer (2003) have done. Another reason for the genesis of the Early Psychosis Declaration is generally to drive up standards for the care of those with serious mental health problems. By advising service users and carers of what outcomes they should expect from an effective psychosis service, the World Health Organisation, through this charter, promotes an informed demand for evidence-based practice.

If a mental health service aims too low with regard to its aspirations for services users, then the system issues can become, indirectly, a potential source for stigma. Therefore, the design of modern mental health systems necessarily begins with clear attention to the importance of mental health promotion and employing staff with realistic/optimistic attitudes towards mental health. Organisational implementation of PSI service developments are discussed in a number of the chapters in this volume, and especially in chapter 11.

One important way to work to reduce stigmatisation and discrimination is for people who have had episodes of psychosis to present themselves as role models. Owing to the associated stigma, there is a temptation where people have recovered to minimise or deny their mental ill health; but those who have recovered, or are recovering, can serve as role models and as sources of inspiration to others.

Recovery and Psychosocial Interventions

PSI use many of the same ideas as the recovery approach; both attempt to place users and carers at the heart of service delivery. This means that services are designed around the needs of the service user (Repper and Perkins 2003), which requires (often) working with users' families or other carers, and also using community resources, either in terms of other (non-health) personnel and/or services.

One of the major differences in ethos between the recovery and PSI approaches as outlined above, and a more medicalised model of working as exemplified by the use solely of pharmacological interventions, is that in the latter model the primary therapeutic action is the drug-illness interaction. The 'person' and 'context' dimensions are less important in the medical philosophy, other than as an influence on whether or not people actually take the medication in the way prescribed for them (i.e. whether they are 'compliant' or 'in concordance' with their medication regime).

The more psychosocial ethos, however, sees the personal, family, community and cultural context as being completely central to the extent to which an individual with serious psychological problems can regain a significant role within his or her family and community. In a sense, both PSI and recovery ideas share the ethos and the necessity of 'partnership/collaborative working'.

The emphasis stressed within this book, on integrating both psychosocial and pharmacological interventions, and working with (as opposed to against, or at best in spite of) users, carers, and the wider community, means that PSI-plus-medication tends to be more holistic and person-centred. It is also an approach where a more developed partnership ethos is used, where clinical staff work alongside users and their carers.

Partnership working

The concept of recovery as outlined earlier in this chapter described it in individual terms: it was something that people with serious mental health problems did *in spite of* and *separately from* others: professionals, friends, colleagues.

However, recovery does not have to be like that, and indeed, if recovery can be linked into professional and personal support for that process, it is much more likely to be successful. Anthony (1993) linked recovery with the idea of a Community Support System (CSS), described by Turner and Shifren in 1979. He describes the CSS as:

> a network of caring and responsible people committed to assisting a vulnerable population to meet their needs and develop their potential without being unnecessarily isolated or excluded from the community.
>
> (p. 2)

In the mental health field, mental health professionals should be at the heart of such a CSS. Anthony (1993) describes a number of factors which such a recovery-focused mental health service should exhibit:

- Professionals should aim to assist in the recovery process. Both Deegan (1996) and May (2000) who are mental health professionals (and formerly service users) share this assumption. Deegan emphasises the centrality of seeing beyond limiting labels, and of the importance of a collaborative person-centred alliance. May (2000) also emphasises this view and sees that services can have a valuable role in recovery if they act as a safety net which contain a certain level of 'springiness' to enable users to 'bounce back'. The ability of staff to truly empathise and understand the persons lived experience, including that of psychosis, is suggested.

- Anthony includes the pivotal role of family, friends and other carers in promoting recovery. Also, and again in keeping with the emphasis of this text, non-mental health organisations and activities (such as sport and adult education) should be utilised to help. For some, a further path to recovery might rest on actively opting out of the mental health system.
- The centrality of an unwavering presence is suggested by Anthony. Such a person could be viewed as a mentor, coach or personal trainer (Roberts and Wolfson 2004): 'offering professional skills and knowledge, while learning from and valuing the patient, who is 'expert by experience' (p. 41). The abilities of both professional and user to trust and exhibit a non-judgemental attitude to each other are vital. The more extended in time the relationship between the helper and service user is, the greater the sense of unwavering continuity.
- Pragmatism is felt to be important. Rather than allowing theoretical differences over the cause of psychosis to obscure or hamper recovery-based intervention, a recovery-vision uses the best or most appropriate intervention deemed timely for a given individual. Recovery is possible whether or not psychosis is viewed as a biological illness. The recurrence of symptoms can still be managed; if greater periods of time of 'wellness' can be achieved, resulting in less distress and of less functional disruption, then this is a goal well worth aiming for. This relates back to the point that recovery is not a linear process or mechanistic in nature: personal growth can occur in unexpected and unanticipated ways.
- And for Anthony, a CSS should emphasise the centrality of a user- (consumer-)driven series of outcomes that would range from symptom relief, to being able to access valued services which help promote self-development, equal opportunity and choice.

Policy context

These ideas of partnership working, PSI, recovery, stigma reduction, and so on are closely connected to and strongly supported by UK policy initiatives in the 1990s and early 2000s, as exemplified by *The National Service Framework for Mental Health* (NSF) (Department of Health 1999), *Mental Health Policy Implementation Guide* (MHPIG) (Department of Health 2001) and the *NICE Guidelines* (NICE 2002).

Mental Health Promotion and a Recovery Approach

Stigma reduction is seen as central to the NSF (Department of Health 1999), especially in relation to Standard One, which addresses mental health promotion, stating that the NSF aims: 'to ensure health and social services promote mental health and reduce the discrimination and social exclusion associated with mental health problems' (p. 14).

The MHPIG (Department of Health 2001) further reinforced the importance of mental health promotion. A number of benefits of doing this are identified in the MHPIG which envisages that a more health-promoting approach would:

- improve physical health and well-being
- prevent or reduce the occurrence of some mental health problems, notably behavioural disorders, depression and anxiety and substance misuse
- assist recovery from mental health problems
- improve mental health services and the quality of life for people experiencing mental health problems
- strengthen the capacity of communities to support social inclusion, tolerance and participation and reduce vulnerability to socio-economic stresses
- increase the 'mental health literacy' of individuals, organisations and communities and
- improve health at work, increasing productivity and reducing sickness absence.

It is clear that such a stigma- and social exclusion-reducing approach would assist the recovery approach outlined earlier in this chapter.

Recovery-focused Mental Health Services

These ideas are closely connected to, and are informed by, the guiding values and principles which services need to have (or develop) for service users with mental health problems. These values are laid out in the NSF (Department of Health 1999); and again are further informed by the MHPIG (Department of Health 2001) and *NICE Guidelines* (2002).

The NSF external reference group (Department of Health 1999) developed 10 service values, stating that mental health services should:

- involve service users and their carers in the planning and delivery of care
- deliver high quality treatment and care which is known to be effective and acceptable
- be well suited to those who use them and be non-discriminatory
- be accessible so that help can be obtained when and where it is needed
- promote user safety and that of carers, staff and the wider public
- offer choices which promote independence
- be well co-ordinated between all staff and agencies
- deliver continuity of care for as long as this is needed
- empower and support staff and
- be properly accountable to the public, service users and carers.

Recovery-focused work can take place in a range of service settings, many of which are described in the chapters in this book. The MHPIG (Department of Health 2001) alludes to this:

> Our mental health strategy points the way . . . [taking] us forward to our ultimate goal of a society more sensitive to mental distress, where people with mental health problems do not have to suffer discrimination and where recovery based on service user and carer aspirations is a real possibility for the majority.
>
> (p. 3)

The MHPIG outlines how newer crisis, assertive outreach, early intervention and primary care services, in combination with well-established community mental health teams (CMHTs) and rehabilitation services, can help deliver effective service provision. Anthony (1993) posits that such a mental health system which is recovery-focused would be greater than the sum of its parts, where action in one domain would have a positive impact on others. For example, controlling a crisis would not only assure the personal safety of the individual, it would also mean that recovery opportunities would not be lost or destroyed by allowing such a crisis to continue.

One of the most exciting challenges is to link mental health services together with health promotion opportunities and anti-stigma action, via the formation (with a range of stakeholders) of creative local alliances; this is helpfully supported by the government policy focus on social inclusion from the Office of the Deputy Prime Minister (ODPM 2004). Thus local leisure operators may well be agreeable to the use of their facilities (and staff) by mental health services (as described in chapter 9). Also, non-statutory, voluntary and charitable and other 'third-sector' agencies may well be able to offer services and opportunities that are deemed either beyond the existing response of mental health services, or not part of their core business agenda. Existing mental health services may be able to reshape their operations (for example, CMHTs) by creatively reflecting on what they do. There is also ample opportunity for some of the newer services, in particular, to optimise their operations by recourse to creative partnership working.

If this can occur, mental health services should be able to identify what they can reasonably deliver, but also to maximise service delivery and range by working collaboratively with other organisations. Encouragingly, some of this seems to be occurring: Professor Louis Appleby, the National Director for Mental Health (Appleby 2004), has reported positively about what has been achieved in the first five years following the publication of *The National Service Framework for Mental Health*:

> In reviewing the impact of the NSF, I have been struck most of all by the huge amount of activity that it has generated, the benefits of which are now becoming apparent. An impressive range of policy initiatives has been triggered in an area of health care that was previously neglected. Services have become increasingly responsive to the needs and wishes of the people who use them. Specialist community mental health teams have been set up across the country, offering home treatment, early intervention or intensive support for people with complex needs. Staff numbers have substantially increased. Modern treatments are in widespread use. Most users of services report that their experience of mental health care has been positive. Suicide rates are at their lowest recorded level. It is a record of progress and achievement that I believe is unprecedented in the history of NHS mental health care.
>
> (p. 1)

He lists many examples of positive practices, drawn from throughout the seven standards within the NSF; but also suggests 'more is needed and some changes – improvements in the experience of patients from ethnic minorities, for instance – are needed urgently' (p. 1). He concludes that:

> the mental health NSF has had substantial benefits and has triggered a period of major change in the care that service users receive. The record of achievement has been impressive on services for severe mental illness (Standards 4 and 5), on suicide prevention (Standard 7), on research and on clinical guidance. It has been reasonably good on primary care and access (Standards 2 and 3), on finance and on workforce development, but there is much still to do. Less has been achieved on mental health promotion and social exclusion (Standard 1), on support for carers (Standard 6) and on information and IT.
>
> (p. 74)

He suggests (pp. 71–4) that the key challenges for the following five years (2004–9) are:

- patient choice
- the care of long-term conditions
- the improved access to services
- the broadening of focus from specialist mental health services to the mental health needs of the community as a whole
- the continued reform of specialist services, especially within inpatient care and an improvement to the ward environment, and within improved services for people with 'dual diagnosis' (i.e. people who suffer from both serious mental health problems and substance misuse): 'the most challenging clinical problem that we face' (p. 1)
- social exclusion in people with mental health problems, improving their employment prospects and opposing stigma and discrimination
- services for ethnic minorities, abolishing inequalities in care and earning the confidence of people from minority communities
- the care of long-term mental disorders, setting out a new model of mental health care in primary care
- much more help available to carers and family members
- much greater availability of and access to psychological therapies
- and he argues that the Social Exclusion Unit Report (ODPM 2004) will be 'central to future developments' (ODPM 2004, p. 71).

Many of the 'success stories' outlined by Appleby (2004), and many of the key challenges he identifies facing mental health services, are exemplified within the chapters in the rest of this book.

Conclusion

This chapter has outlined some of the central debates which have led us to write and edit this book. Many of the positive elements within mental health developments over the past decades which have been highlighted in this chapter have also infused the chapters in this book; it is our hope that this book will inspire further developments.

A central tenet of both the recovery approach and the more recent policy guidance has been to fully involve and collaborate with service users and carers; and there is a recognition that mental health services need to be shaped by, and be continually responsive to, users and their carers. This book reflects that an emphasis within each chapter of the book is one of implicit and explicit collaboration with users and/or carers to produce the chapter. To improve services, promote recovery, and reduce stigma, discrimination and social exclusion, users and carers will need to be involved in service delivery, training, supervision, evaluation and research; all areas where they have been involved in this volume. If users and carers are involved in this way, services will deliver meaningful choices, mental health promotion and social inclusion to suit the aspirations of those they serve better. In the same way, a range of service responses can best be delivered through partnership working between statutory health bodies and 'third-sector' agencies.

If these ideas are synthesised and people (individuals, families, communities, institutions and organisations) all work together, then we feel that the future for people who develop serious mental health problems can be a really positive one.

References

Aitchison, K., Meehan, K. and Murray, R. (1999) *First Episode Psychosis*. London: Martin Dunitz.

Allott, P. and Loganathan, L. (2003) *Discovering Hope for Recovery from a British Perspective: A Review of a Sample of Recovery Literature, Implications for Practice and Systems Change*. Birmingham: Mental Health Resource Centre, Centre for Community Mental Health, University of Central England in Birmingham. Published online at: *www.nuts.cc/almanack/lit/gov/nimhe/central/recovery.html* (accessed 2 January 2006).

Angermeyer, M. and Matschinger, H. (2003) The stigma of mental illness: effects of labelling on public attitudes towards people with mental disorder. *Acta Psychiatrica Scandinavica*, 108, 304–9.

Anthony, W. (1993) Recovery from mental illness: the guiding vision of the mental health service system in the 1990s. *Psychosocial Rehabilitation Journal*, 16, 11–24.

Appleby, L. (2004) *The National Service Framework for Mental Health – Five Years On*. London: Department of Health. Published online at: www.dh.gov.uk/assetRoot/04/09/91/22/04099122.pdf (accessed 10 March 2006).

Arboleda-Florez, J. (2003) Considerations on the stigma of mental illness. *Canadian Journal of Psychiatry*, 48, 645–50.

Beck, A., Ward, C., Mendelson, M., Mock, J. and Erbaugh, J. (1962) Reliability of psychiatric diagnosis: II. A study of consistency of clinical judgments and ratings. *American Journal of Psychiatry*, 119, 351–7.

Bentall, R. (1990) *Reconstructing Schizophrenia*. London: Routledge.

Bentall, R. (2003) *Madness Explained: Psychosis and Human Nature*. London: Penguin Books.

Birchwood, M., Mason, R., MacMillan, F. and Healy, J. (1993) Depression, demoralisation and control over psychotic illness: a comparison of depressed and non-depressed patients with a chronic psychosis. *Psychological Medicine*, 23, 387–95.

Brennan, G., Roberts, C., Gamble, C. and Chan, T. (2000) Chemical management of psychotic symptoms. In Gamble, C. and Brennan, G. (eds.) *Working with Serious Mental Illness*. Edinburgh: Bailliere Tindall, chapter 15, pp. 265–90.

Chadwick, P. (1997) *Schizophrenia: The Positive Perspective; in Search of Dignity for Schizophrenic People*. New York: Routledge.

Corrigan, P., Liberman, R. and Engel, J. (1990) From non-compliance to compliance in the treatment of schizophrenia. *Hospital and Community Psychiatry*, 41, 1203–11.

Crow, T. (1980) Molecular pathology of schizophrenia: more than one disease process? *British Medical Journal*, 280, 66–8.

Deegan, P. (1996) Recovery as a journey of the heart. *Psychiatric Rehabilitation Journal*, 19, pp. 91–7.
Deegan, P. (1997) Recovery and empowerment for people with psychiatric disabilities. In Aviram, U. (ed.) *Social Work in Mental Health: Trends and Issues*. New York: The Haworth Press, pp. 11–24.
Department of Health (1999) *The National Service Framework for Mental Health: Modern Standards and Service Models*. London: Department of Health.
Department of Health (2001) *Mental Health Policy Implementation Guide*. London: Department of Health.
Falloon, I., Boyd, J. and McGill, C. (1984) *Family Care of Schizophrenia*. New York: Guildford Press.
Filbey, F., Holcomb, J., Nair, T., Christensen, J. and Garver, D. (1999) Negative symptoms of familial schizophrenia breed true in unstable [vs. stable] cerebral-ventricle pedigrees. *Schizophrenia Research*, 35, 15–23.
Gaebel, W. and Baumann, A. (2003) Interventions to reduce the stigma associated with service mental illness: experiences from the 'Open the Doors Programme' in Germany. *Canadian Journal of Psychiatry*, 48, 657–62.
Goffman, E. (1963) *Stigma*. Reprinted (1990) in Harmondsworth: Penguin Books.
Gur, R., Mozley, P., Shtasel, D., Cannon, T., Gallacher, F., Turetsky, B., Grossman, R. and Gur R. (1994) Clinical subtypes of schizophrenia: differences in brain and CSF volume. *American Journal of Psychiatry*, 151, 343–50.
Harrison G. and Mason, P. (1993) Schizophrenia – falling incidence and better outcome? *British Journal of Psychiatry*, 163, 535–41.
Hegarty, J., Baldessarini, R., Tohen, M., Waternaux, C. and Oepen, G. (1994) One hundred years of schizophrenia: a meta-analysis of the outcome literature. *American Journal of Psychiatry*, 151, 1409–16.
Hogarty, G. and Ulrich, R. (1998) The limitations of anti-psychotic medication on schizophrenia relapse and adjustment and the contributions of psychosocial treatments. *Journal of Psychiatric Research*, 32, 243–50.
Johnstone, E., Owens, D., Bydder, G., Colter, N., Crow, T. and Frith, C. (1989) The spectrum of structural brain changes in schizophrenia: age of onset as a predictor of cognitive and clinical impairments and their cerebral correlates. *Psychological Medicine*, 19, 91–103.
Karp, D. and Tanarugsachock, V. (2000) Mental illness, caregiving and emotional management. *Qualitative Health Research*, 10, 6–25.
Kelley, M., van Kammen, D. and Allen, D. (1999) Empirical validation of primary negative symptoms: independence from effects of medication and psychosis. *American Journal of Psychiatry*, 156, 406–11.
Knight, M., Wykes, T. and Hayward, P. (2003) 'People don't understand': an investigation of stigma in schizophrenia using interpretive phenomenological analysis. *Journal of Mental Health*, 12, 209–22.
Kuhn, T. (1970) *The Structure of Scientific Revolutions*. 2nd edition. Chicago: The University of Chicago Press.
Laing, R. and Esterson, A. (1964) *Sanity, Madness and the Family*. Harmondsworth: Penguin Books.
Langer, E. and Abelson, R. (1974) A patient by any other name . . .: clinical group difference in labelling bias. *Journal of Consulting and Clinical Psychology*, 42, 4–9.
Lefley, H. (1987) Impact of mental illness in families of mental health professionals. *Journal of Nervous and Mental Disease*, 175, 613–19.
Liberman, R., DeRisi, W. and Mueser, K. (1989) *Social Skills Training with Psychiatric Patients*. New York: Pergamon Press.
May, R. (2000) Psychosis and recovery. *Openmind*, 106, 24–5.
Mehta, S. and Farina, A. (1997) Is being 'sick' really better? Effect of the disease view of mental disorder on stigma. *Journal of Social and Clinical Psychology*, 16, 405–19.
Milton, F., Patwa, V. and Hafner, R. (1978) Confrontation versus belief modification in persistently deluded patients. *British Journal of Medical Psychology*, 51, 127–30.

Mind (2004) *Not Alone? Isolation and Mental Distress*. London: Mind.
Mortimer, A. and Spence, S. (2001) *Managing Negative Symptoms of Schizophrenia*. London: Science Press.
NICE (2002) *NICE Guidelines: National Institute for Clinical Excellence Guidelines for Schizophrenia*. London: NICE.
Nuechterlein, K. (1987) Vulnerability models for schizophrenia: state of the art. In Hafner, H., Gattaz, W. and Janzarik, W. (eds.) *Search for the Causes of Schizophrenia*. Heidelberg: Springer Verlag, pp. 297–316.
ODPM [Office of the Deputy Prime Minister] (2004) *Mental Health and Social Inclusion – Social Exclusion Unit Report*. London: ODPM Publications.
Ostman, M. and Kjellin, L. (2002) Stigma by association. *British Journal of Psychiatry*, 181, 494–8.
Penn, D., Guynan, K., Daily, T., Spaulding W., Garbin, C. and Sullivan, M. (1994) Dispelling the stigma of schizophrenia: what sort of information is best? *Schizophrenia Bulletin*, 20, 567–78.
Perkins, R. (2004) *The Importance of Work to Recovery*. Paper presented at the Rethink conference: Get the Best! World Mental Health Day 2004, Bath, Saturday, 9 October 2004.
Persons, J. (1986) The advantages of studying psychological phenomenon rather than psychiatric diagnosis. *American Psychologist*, 41, 1252–60.
Pratt, P. (1998) The administration and monitoring of neuroleptic medication. In Brooker, C. and Repper, J. (eds.) *Serious Mental Health Problems in the Community*, London: Balliere Tindall, chapter 11, pp. 238–64.
Randal, P., Simpson, A. and Laidlaw, T. (2003) Can recovery-focused multimodal psychotherapy facilitate symptom and function improvement in people with treatment-resistant psychotic illness? A comparison study. *Australian and New Zealand Journal of Psychiatry*, 37, 720–7.
Read, J. (2002) The need for evidence-based destigmatization programmes. *ISPS Newsletter*, 5, 16–22.
Repper, J. and Perkins, R. (2003) *Social Inclusion and Recovery*. Edinburgh: Bailliere Tindall.
Roberts, G. and Wolfson, P. (2004) The rediscovery of recovery: open to all. *Advances in Psychiatric Treatment*, 10, 37–49.
Rosenhan, D. (1973) On being sane in insane places. *Science*, 179, 250–8.
Schooler, N. (1993) Reducing dosage in maintenance treatment of schizophrenia: review and prognosis. *British Journal of Psychiatry*, 163 (suppl.), 58–65.
Schulze, B. and Angermeyer, M. (2003) Subjective experiences of stigma: a focus group study of schizophrenic patients, their relatives and mental health professionals. *Social Science and Medicine*, 56, 299–312.
Singh, S. (2004) *Recovery from Psychosis: Helping People Rebuild Lives*. Paper presented at the Rethink conference: Get the Best! World Mental Health Day 2004, Bath, Saturday, 9 October 2004.
Singh, S. and Fisher, H. (2005) Early intervention in psychosis: obstacles and opportunities. *Advances in Psychiatric Treatment*, 11, 71–8.
Singh, S., Croudace, T., Amin, S., Kwiecinski, R., Medley, I., Jones P. and Harrison, G. (2000) Three-year outcome of first-episode psychosis in an established community psychiatric service. *British Journal of Psychiatry*, 176, 210–16.
Szasz, T. (1976) *Schizophrenia: The Sacred Symbol of Psychiatry*. New York: Basic Books.
Took, M. (2002) *Rethink Policy Statement 45: Supporting People in their Recovery from Severe Mental Illness*. London: Rethink. Rethink website: www.rethink.org/news+campaigns/policies/45-supporting-recovery.htm
Turkington, D. and Kingdon, D. (1996) Using a normalising rationale in the treatment of schizophrenic patients. In Haddock, G. and Slade, P. (eds.) *Cognitive-behavioural Interventions with Psychotic Disorders*. London: Routledge, chapter 6, pp. 103–115.
Turner, J. and Shifren, I. (1979) Community support systems: how comprehensive? *New Directions for Mental Health Services*, 2, 1–23.
Velleman, R. (2001) *Counselling for Alcohol Problems*, 2nd edition. London: Sage.

Wahl, O. and Harman, C. (1989) Family views of stigma. *Schizophrenia Bulletin*. 15, 131–9.
Warner, R. (1994) *Recovery from Schizophrenia*, 2nd edition. London: Routledge.
Wing, J. (1992) Differential diagnosis of schizophrenia. In Kavanagh, D. (ed.) *Schizophrenia: An Overview and Practical Handbook*. Chapman and Hall, London, chapter X, pp. 6–22.
World Health Organisation (2004) *Early Psychosis Declaration*. Geneva: World Health Organisation.
Zubin, J. and Spring, B. (1977) Vulnerability: a new view of schizophrenia. *Journal of Abnormal Psychology*, 86, 103–26.

Chapter 2

Shared Caring for a First Episode of Psychosis

An Opportunity to Promote Hope and Recovery

Mandy Reed and Caroline Stevens

Key Points

- The Early Psychosis Declaration (World Health Organisation 2004) is an extremely important policy initiative that is a highly relevant resource for young people with a psychosis as well as their friends and families.
- Local research into pathways by which young people experiencing a first episode of psychosis access services can highlight problems and hence stimulate service development.
- A first episode of psychosis, particularly during adolescence, is a scary experience for all concerned.
- Carers are usually searching for information about the disorder, medication and ways they can share the caring for their loved one with professionals.
- Early intervention in psychosis services (EIS) respect the strengths and qualities of young people with a psychosis, their families and communities. This approach helps to encourage ordinary lives and expectations, promoting hope and recovery.
- Routine services for families and carers are an integral part of any thorough EIS.
- A team caseload approach enables and enhances intensive support during the acute and recovery phase of psychosis.
- Collaboration between carers and service providers is key to EIS delivery.

Introduction

This chapter describes the collaborative work of an EIS within the Gloucestershire Partnership NHS Trust (GPT, a local specialist NHS mental health organisation) with Paul and his mother Caroline, which helped him to recover from a first episode of psychosis. During the acute phase of the disorder this involved intensive carer and family support alongside detailed assessments of Paul's experiences, risk management and careful use of medication. Individual work with Paul included cognitive behaviour therapy (CBT) and identifying his early warning signs (EWS) of relapse. Flexible ongoing support for Caroline to sustain her in her care-giver role and family interventions (FI) has helped them prepare for any ongoing difficulties should they arise as Paul recovers and gets on with his life. All members of a small, skilled EIS team have been involved in his care allowing for intensive contacts when needed, continuity of care, and the provision of an intensive treatment package over the last 18 months.

The Evidence

> Psychosis is a debilitating illness with far reaching implications for the individual and for his and her family. Without support and adequate care, psychosis can place a heavy burden on carers, family and society at large.
>
> (Department of Health 2001, p. 43)

EIS teams are a key part of government strategy to develop and improve mental health services (Department of Health 2001). Research shows that progress in the first few years following a first episode of psychosis is highly significant in determining the course of mental disorder (Birchwood 2000; Petersen et al. 2005), yet there are often long delays in people receiving treatment (Birchwood, Jackson and Todd 1998). 'Late intervention' can lead to young people presenting to services in crisis, having experienced several missed opportunities for detection and treatment. Individuals are then often hospitalised under the Mental Health Act (MHA) 1983 (Department of Health 1983) into stressful environments that can generate post-traumatic stress disorder in addition to the psychosis and an unwillingness to keep in contact with services after discharge from hospital (World Health Organisation 2004). This negative view of services, in turn reduces opportunities to work with the person and their family to promote recovery and minimise the potential for further episodes of psychosis. EIS teams are designed to target the period during and after a first episode of psychosis to reduce the impact of the disorder and promote recovery, to enable young people and their carers to lead a fulfilling life. They also aim to reduce the stigma associated with psychosis and improve professional and lay awareness of psychosis, including the need for early assessment, thus reducing the length of time young people remain undiagnosed and untreated.

A variety of reasons hamper early detection of psychosis and treatment (EPPIC 1996; IRIS 2000):

- The early signs ('prodromal period'[1]) of psychosis in young people are often difficult to differentiate from normal adolescent behaviours, making it hard for families and friends to recognise.
- Traditional mental health services often adopt a 'wait and see' strategy in the misguided interest of not wanting to bring people into services unless or until 'they are really needed'.
- There is a general lack of awareness by the wider community about how mental disorder affects individuals.
- There is the continuing stigma associated with mental disorder or having a family member suffering from psychosis.

Establishing Early Intervention in Psychosis Services in Gloucestershire

Although the setting up of EIS teams is prescribed in government policy (Department of Health 2001) there has been a reluctance to invest in them on the part of mental health services, and of Primary Care Trusts (PCTs) which commission and fund mental health services. To overcome this reluctance, a care pathway audit is recommended to highlight the unsatisfactory experiences of many first-time service users (Lincoln and McGorry 1999). It appears that even if there is good evidence for better services from randomised controlled trials, local evidence has a much larger impact on those who commission services (IRIS 2000).

Local research (Davis 2003) confirmed the findings of Lincoln and McGorry (1999); so, in line with national policy (Department of Health 2001), the Gloucestershire Recovery in Psychosis EIS team (GRIP) was established in April 2003 with the aim of assessing and treating people within Gloucestershire, between the ages of 14 and 35, experiencing and recovering from first-episode psychosis. Owing to pressure on other important clinical resources, initial funding for the team was secured through a grant from a local charity (The Barnwood Trust), with some additional support from one of the three PCTs, to start a pilot service. This money was paid to GPT with the proviso that the Trust would ensure that GRIP would continue and expand the following financial year and sever its initial reliance upon charitable sources. Had local EIS champions (led by Eric Davis, GRIP project lead) not applied for this money and received support from the Barnwood Trust (the largest individual grant they had ever made), it is likely that the service would have been delayed by at least another year owing to competing clinical demands and financial constraints locally.

In order to promote recovery and social inclusion, EIS teams employ a wide range of approaches. These include flexible and assertive engagement to build therapeutic relationships and maintain contact over time; practical support with daily living skills, housing, and benefits; and maintaining a normal lifestyle in the person's community of choice. This encompasses the principles first developed in America, known as assertive community treatment, for working with clients who did not respond to traditional services (Stein and Santos 1998).

Developing links with community based youth and leisure services helps to provide support to obtain/maintain employment, training or education. More specialised skills an EIS team should offer include CBT to assist with the positive symptoms of psychosis and secondary problems such as anxiety or depression that develop in response to the psychosis and its impact; assistance to individuals and carers so that they develop knowledge about EWS, relapse prevention strategies and crisis plans; information about medication and effective prescribing; and support and FI for carers. All of these approaches are routinely offered by GRIP.

Family Intervention in Early Psychosis

Between 60 per cent and 70 per cent of young people experiencing a first episode of psychosis are likely to be still living with their families. Research shows that the meaning attached by carers to the development of psychosis in a loved one has an impact on how they cope and adapt to the disorder (EPPIC 1997; Addington et al. 2003). These meanings, also known as attributions, are not fixed, but can alter as understanding increases (Barrowclough, Tarrier

Table 2.1 Goals for promoting well-being among family members and interventions with families of an individual experiencing psychosis (adapted from EPPIC 1996).

Focus 1 – The family system and key subsystems:
- Minimising the disruption to the life of the family throughout the phases of psychosis
- Maximising the adaptive functioning in the aftermath of acute psychosis

Focus 2 – Individual members of the family:
- Minimising the risk of long-term grief, acute stress, reactive depression and high levels of burden in individual family members in response to the psychosis
- Minimising the risk of the client becoming dependent on their family (as a result of their psychosis)
- Minimising the risk of the client becoming alienated from their family (as a result of their psychosis)
- Facilitating an understanding of psychosis and treatment across all members of the family

Focus 3 – Interaction between the family and the course of psychosis:
- Maximising communication skills, problem-solving skills and low expressed emotion (EE) responses
- Maximising the responsiveness of the family to early warning signs to facilitate relapse prevention
- Maximising the readiness of the family for dealing with crises associated with the psychosis

and Johnson 1996). The needs and issues for a family facing a first episode of psychosis are different from those whose relative has more enduring difficulties as targeted by traditional FI (Addington and Burnett 2004). Chapters 4 and 5 provide a description of the origins of FI and a critique of the early research.

With psychosis, the broad aim of FI is to reduce tension in the family environment in order to promote recovery and reduce the potential for further episodes of psychosis to occur (EPPIC 1996, 1997). EIS follow an evidence-based model developed by the pioneering work of the Early Psychosis Prevention and Intervention Centre (EPPIC) Service in Melbourne, Australia. This model, shown in Table 2.1, identifies three foci for intervention with families of clients: emotional, educational and practical support.

It is important to offer the client and family a clear explanation and rationale for offering FI. A non-judgemental attitude and involving an explanation of the principles of stress-vulnerability models[2] (Zubin and Spring 1977; Nuechterlein 1987) appears most useful. Families are advised that by learning more about the disorder and building on their existing strengths and problem-solving abilities, levels of stress may be reduced, thus reducing the likelihood of further relapses.

An important part of this process is an in-depth assessment of their perspectives and experiences as carers, using a semi-structured interview questionnaire such as the relative assessment interview (RAI) (Barrowclough and Tarrier 1992). This has been adapted for use with families experiencing a first episode of psychosis by EPPIC (1997). Of equal importance (in that it can lead to practical and financial support) is a carer's assessment, which should (and is within GPT) be undertaken as part of the care programme approach (CPA)

(Department of Health 1990). The opportunity to 'tell their story' is widely acknowledged to be of powerful benefit to carers who may have struggled to access appropriate help for their loved one (Addington and Burnett 2004; Drage et al. 2006). FI work best if they are part of a whole treatment package based on a model of psychosocial interventions (Fadden 1998).

In psychosis, the problem-solving component of FI is often the key to engaging families. However,

> it is vital for family workers to leave the responsibility for change with the client and their family, while offering themselves as a resource for the family as required. We must work with the family to help them learn to help themselves, not try to solve their problems ourselves.
>
> (Smith and Velleman 2007, p. 83)

Improving quality of life for families and clients through addressing specific difficulties caused by the disorder is intrinsic to FI (Gamble and Brennan 2000). By gaining an understanding of how individuals and their families are affected on a day-to-day basis, and identifying everyone's goals (which can be a positive way to reframe a problem), it is then possible to adopt a problem-solving approach within the family sessions.

The Case Study

Editors' note: This case study is about Paul and the service that he received, and about Caroline, his mother. It tells the story of the onset of Paul's psychosis at the age of 19, and of the ongoing work with the mental health services in Gloucestershire. The case study is written jointly by Caroline, and Mandy Reed, the specialist team leader for GRIP. Mandy undertook much of the work with Paul and Caroline, alongside Richard, another professional within the GRIP team.

Caroline says:

Paul is the eldest of my five children. He has one brother Michael (18), who is in the army, twin sisters Vikki and Louise (16) and a younger sister Sophie (6). They all live with me (Michael when home on leave); their father lives close by and sees them most days. I work part time, term time only, in the local community resource centre café.

Paul didn't particularly enjoy secondary school due to being bullied and he left school early, returning only to take his GCSEs. He then took up employment locally and enjoyed an active social life with friends. I rarely saw him as his spare time was spent either out clubbing with friends, or in his room playing computer games, watching science fiction/fantasy films or listening to music like most teenagers seem to.

At the age of 18, Paul moved to live with a boyfriend and some other people he knew in Coventry and got an office job there. He did not settle while living with this group of friends, so, although he liked his job, he decided to move back home to Cheltenham. Once back he did not really settle to looking for more work or sorting out college, and drifted for the next year before going on holiday with his friends from Coventry.

Mandy says:

Paul, aged 19, was not sure what he wanted to do, so had been out of work for about one year prior to his psychosis taking hold in summer 2003. A group of friends asked him to go to Spain on holiday with them in May for two weeks. It was his first time abroad and Paul was very excited but had been apprehensive before he left.

Once in Spain, he found being in a strange country stressful. His mates were all up for having a good time and much heavy drinking (over 100 units in the first few days) and clubbing took place. One evening they went along to a hypnotist show which Paul took part in. Although his memory of this evening has remained vague it would seem likely that he was made to do things while hypnotised that he would later feel uncomfortable and embarrassed about and added to some concerns he already had about being gay. He started to experience strange physical sensations and hearing voices criticising him. The remainder of the holiday was very stressful for Paul – he was scared and unhappy and a long way from home. All he wanted to do was get home and start feeling normal again. His thoughts felt strange; he was very paranoid and convinced there was something seriously wrong with him. When he got home things continued to feel weird and Paul asked his mum for help.

Caroline says:

On Paul's return it was immediately obvious that something was amiss; he looked and acted strangely and said he felt strange and needed to see a doctor for help. On making enquiries from his friends about the holiday I discovered that in the week before being taken ill they had been drinking heavily, clubbing late into the night and that Paul had taken part in a hypnotist show. Paul insisted he had not taken any street drugs knowingly (although much later told me he had used some cannabis).

I took him to see the GP the next day. He was then admitted to the medical ward at the local hospital for investigations and while there he saw a psychiatrist. Tablets were prescribed but we didn't understand what they were for – I wasn't there when he was seen and Paul wasn't making much sense at the time. He was only in there overnight and given a follow-up appointment two weeks later. I didn't get a chance to speak to anyone, so I got a friend to look them up and found out they were for psychosis. The tablets made Paul exhausted – if he wasn't awake worrying, he was asleep for long periods. We went back to see the GP who said the tablets were too strong and decreased the dose.

Mandy says:

The psychiatrist first assessed Paul as an emergency in the local general hospital. His impression was that Paul was experiencing psychosis, possibly triggered by excessive alcohol use on holiday. He started him on Risperidone (2 mgs to increase after a few days to 4 mgs) and made an appointment to see him as an outpatient two weeks later. This medication regime was in line with the National Institute for Clinical Excellence guidelines (NICE 2002) which advise that for young people not used to taking such medications, a low starting dose to reduce side-effects and increase the likelihood of them continuing to take them is recommended. Paul experienced side-effects even at this dose, so his GP advised to delay the increase to 4 mgs allowing him to adjust to the smaller dose. By the time the psychiatrist saw Paul again he was taking 4 mgs of Risperidone with fewer side-effects and reported that his voices were not quite so bad. However, he said that the television was talking to him and that he felt like he had 'lost the plot'. The psychiatrist made an appointment to see him again four weeks later and made a referral to GRIP, which had been operational for a few months on a pilot basis with two full-time and two part-time members.

An extract from GRIP Operational Policy (Reed 2005) demonstrates its assessment process:

- The timescale for assessment will be determined by the source of referral.
- If a client is not known to adult services, the full assessment period can take up to two months. This will allow for a number of contacts to take place and careful liaison with carers and services known to the person where appropriate.
- If the route of referral is through statutory services, in particular inpatient or forensic routes, the assessment period will normally take no more than two weeks. This will include liaising with the existing team and carers where possible.

The policy includes specialist assessments:

- A KGV assessment (Krawiecka, Goldberg and Vaughan 1977) will be undertaken by the team as part of the initial assessment and screening process. The results will determine suitability for acceptance and help signpost which service is most appropriate if the referral is not appropriate for the GRIP caseload.

Mandy says:

The team psychologist, Eric Davis, and a colleague on placement with GRIP met with Paul at home two weeks later. Meeting people in their own environment is part of assertive engagement as it is likely to make them feel more at ease talking about their experiences. It is also an opportunity to meet with other family members and carers, although, in this instance, Caroline was not present. Paul reported at the time of this first meeting that he was feeling a little more settled; he described his strange experiences more in the past tense during the semi-structured interview (Krawiecka, Goldberg and Vaughan 1977). He scored highest for anxiety with some depressive transient suicidal thoughts, hallucinations and delusions. An initial risk screen (part of the CPA core assessment) indicated that Paul was at low risk for self-harm, violence and neglect. The information Paul gave was consistent with psychosis although the relatively rapid development of symptoms initially led us to believe that things would improve with medication and short-term input from GRIP. At this point he was taking anti-depressant and anti-psychotic medication.

Our care plan at this stage was to involve two team members in an extended assessment period, offering education and support to Paul and his mother to enable him to get back on track with his life as quickly as possible. Unfortunately, before the team could meet Paul again things deteriorated

Caroline says:

After Paul started to take medication things got worse, with voices in his head often telling him to kill himself and depression causing withdrawal from all his social activities. He would not go out alone, could not watch television, listen to music or play computer games. Paul could not stand any noise at all. This was very different from how he is normally – he became very clingy and dependent on me. It felt like he was a baby again and I just took care of him like any parent would. That meant the rest of the family had very little attention from me. I used to spend hours in his bedroom quietly lying down with him waiting for him to fall asleep before I could escape to do what I needed to do with the others. They were all expected to keep quiet, so after a while everybody in the family apart from me kept their distance from him. Fortunately, I could talk to my friends about what was happening as they all knew Paul and would often ask me how he was doing.

After a few weeks like this Paul became more desperate and didn't feel safe at home. He went around to his Dad's and took a lot of his Dad's blood pressure medication. His Dad took him back to the general hospital from where he was admitted to the local psychiatric hospital. I'd never been there before but found it to be a friendly place, even though some of the other patients were a bit odd at times and seemed to upset Paul.

I spent a lot of time with Paul, visiting every day. He was very quiet at this time and I would often sit for long periods in silence with him. The nurses were friendly but we could see he wasn't getting any better for the first few weeks. His Dad used to visit at a different time of the day and would take him out for a few drives. He was prescribed Valium to help him relax when he was anxious. His tablets were watched closely and an anti-depressant was added again after a few weeks. He remained there for four weeks altogether. Towards the end he was able to go out for short periods, but seemed to feel safer in hospital and was always keen to get back. I didn't really know who else was seeing him or what else was being done for Paul at this stage, because he was vague with us and we were only invited to a meeting with the doctor when they said he was ready to be discharged. I didn't realise at the time that they would have been having regular meetings about Paul, so we tended to rely on how we found him and how he told us he was feeling.

A further extract from GRIP operational policy (Reed 2005) describes its relationships with other services:

- The team will endeavour to work with their clients during all aspects of care for those clients not involved with other statutory services.
- Robust relationships with other services in the community and hospital will be essential to provide seamless care for GRIP clients who are under the care of community mental health teams (CMHTs).
- For people known to the service whose crisis plan indicates intensive home treatment, a joint assessment with an assessor from the appropriate Crisis and Home Treatment team (once established) will facilitate additional out of hours input. Wherever this is indicated in a person's relapse prevention and crisis plan, a copy will be sent to the crisis team for information.

- Until the establishment of a local crisis service, the inpatient unit at Charlton Lane Centre will provide out of hours support and hold copies of relevant CPA/crisis plans.

Mandy says:

The next the team heard was that Paul had taken an overdose six days after our initial assessment. Although the risk screen had failed to highlight any thoughts of self-harm, assessment in first-episode psychosis is more difficult due to the lack of information to base predictions upon. His voices had been telling him he was useless and to harm himself – he felt like he was a burden to his family and could not see any way of getting better. We knew the medication was taken impulsively out of desperation, but it could have caused permanent harm. We therefore arranged to visit him in hospital to continue our assessment of his experience of psychosis and to begin to develop a relationship with him. This is known as 'inreach' and is an important part of the engagement work of an EIS; it aims to provide a link between different periods of a person's care and to manage high-risk situations more effectively. It was also an opportunity to evaluate the effectiveness of his prescribed medication through liaison with the ward and consultation with the medical team.

Due to GRIP's limited resources at this time we were only able to visit him in hospital once a week, so had little opportunity for joint working with staff there; we weren't there for the weekly ward rounds. This was not an ideal situation as it gave us little opportunity to be involved in decisions about his care and was not dissimilar to the experience that Caroline had in that she only met the doctor when discharge arrangements were being made.

During his admission Paul's main experiences were of anxiety and low mood in reaction to his psychotic experiences. These were treated with anxiolytics initially and later on another anti-depressant alongside his anti-psychotics. His voices became less troublesome as were his feelings of déjà vu when watching the television. Although he was able to spend periods of leave at home before discharge he had begun to experience headaches, which was possibly a further side-effect of medication.

Caroline says:

On his return home from hospital Paul deteriorated again, trying to self-harm and overdose most days. I had to hide all the knives and take over responsibility for his tablets, which I kept in my handbag. I was afraid to leave him and I used to phone GRIP most days for support and advice. He used to be awake most of the night and asleep a lot in the day, so if I went out I would hope he stayed asleep and safe. The voices were telling him every tea-time onwards to kill himself and neither he nor I felt he was safe during this time of the day. Sometimes he was able to get out to the shops to buy tablets, which he would then tell me he had taken and even cut himself on a few occasions, which he said was to find out if he was still alive.

Mandy (the co-author with me of this chapter) and Richard (another worker from the GRIP team) visited him several times a week, showing concern about his safety and my ability to keep looking after him. I was exhausted by this time, so it helped to know that they were sharing the responsibility for Paul with me and to hear their suggestions about how to deal with him.

Mandy says:

The team and consultant psychiatrist decided that more input from us was indicated, including a carer's assessment and FI. I first met Paul and Caroline, at home, after Paul had been out of hospital a few days, aware that things were not going well. He complained of headaches and seemed very changeable in his mood, again distressed and bothered by his voices telling him that he was worthless and should kill himself, although only during certain periods of the day. Caroline was understandably having difficulty leaving Paul on his own.

The meetings at this stage generally focused on identifying coping strategies with Paul to help him feel safer, and enlisting Caroline as an ally to reduce the risks in his home environment. She had already taken responsibility for his medication and felt that she could mostly keep him safe by her presence and vigilance. Unfortunately, Paul still managed to find ways to harm himself on several occasions and seemed to become increasingly hopeless that anything would take his voices away. When he couldn't get hold of any tablets he started to cut himself with sharp implements. By mid-August a suicide risk assessment (GPT's standard tool as part of their CPA documentation) confirmed our fears that Paul was high risk, although the tool (as previously stated) is probably more accurate with someone with more of a history than he had. Caroline was becoming exhausted from her efforts to keep him safe, often staying up most of the night with him while still trying to run the home. She was not working in the café as it was the school holidays, but still had Sophie and the twins to take care of, and virtually no time for herself or for us to complete the formal carer's assessment.

Caroline says:

Mandy, the consultant psychiatrist and I all felt that hospital admission would be a good idea to keep him safe and to sort his medication out but Paul was ambivalent. We persuaded him to go but then he tried to leave and was sectioned for a few days before returning home. He was still complaining of a lot of headaches, which we were told were tension, although they could have been side-effects of his medication, which was adjusted frequently. His GP prescribed yet another medication for the headaches, but the psychiatrist stopped them, saying they could be dangerous if he took another overdose. All I had wanted was for the headaches to stop because they made Paul really upset.

Paul carried on trying to harm himself and, on one occasion, took a whole month's worth of a new anti-depressant but refused again to go to hospital. All I wanted was for him to be well and happy again, if he wanted to come home that was fine with me. I couldn't bear to see him so upset and wanted what ever he wanted.

Mandy says:

This was a difficult period in Paul's care. An increasingly exhausted Caroline was looking after him, trying to keep watch on him twenty-four hours a day. Paul's sleep pattern was reversed so that he was awake from late afternoon to early morning; the only time she could catch up with the other children, shopping and the housework was when Paul slept during the day. This was not always reliable and Paul harmed himself on several occasions when she was out at the shops, once cutting his arms in front of his sisters who were upset by his behaviour. Caroline was in daily contact with GRIP to update us on what was happening with Paul, often acting as the point of liaison between all concerned. We were visiting several times a week, attempting to help Paul and Caroline by offering support, assessing symptoms and self-harm risk, closely monitoring his medication and trying to discover effective strategies Paul could harness to cope with his symptoms.

Medication was having little effect and after discussion with the consultant psychiatrist we decided to offer to admit Paul again to the local hospital for fuller assessment, to see if any other medication would help and to give Caroline a break from the burden of keeping Paul safe. At the time of writing there are no respite houses nor a Crisis and Home Treatment team within Cheltenham, and GRIP was not able to offer more than two or three visits per week plus telephone support. This did not feel like enough contact from us to share the caring of Paul with Caroline and to manage his risky behaviours positively.

Paul reluctantly accepted admission, but had to go to a busy, unfamiliar ward so then didn't wish to stay. Caroline did not feel being there would help keep him any safer than she could and that it was too distressing for Paul, so he came home again. Had there been a specific inpatient facility for young people with psychosis (Davis 2003) it is possible he would have felt more able to accept hospital admission.

The team felt that his high levels of anxiety and desperate wish to feel better were leading Paul to look for immediate benefit from any change in medication. Part of our work was to explain the time needed to see benefit from either of his main medications and encourage him to continue to use the Diazepam for a short while longer to manage his anxiety while the others were taking effect (NICE 2002; McGorry 2004). Caroline expressed concern about the possible addictive nature of this drug and, with our support, gradually reduced his dose over the next few weeks. The use of benzodiazepines is very effective during the acute phase of psychosis but is most effective when prescribed for four to six weeks with a reducing regime to prevent chemical dependence and the creation of a secondary problem for the person concerned.

Formal FI began at the end of August with Eric Davis and myself as the workers. The first session focused on reviewing the events of the previous few months and establishing some goals for the next few weeks. Caroline had already received some informal education about psychosis during GRIP's earlier contacts and wanted to feel Paul was safe to leave when she was due to start back at work, while Paul was describing being caught up in the moment of wherever his mood and voices took him. A mood diary had already been suggested on several earlier occasions and this was talked through again within FI. The idea was for Paul to monitor his mood twice daily scoring out of 10 (with 0 being the worst and 10 the best) each time and noting what else was happening at the time, in particular if he was hearing voices and what they were saying. It was expected this would be useful for both his individual and family meetings with the team. To help Paul complete this we worked through an example of a mood diary during the session to ensure both he and Caroline fully understood the nature of the task.

The next family session two weeks later saw the beginnings of the benefit of a structured agenda, with a review of the previous homework. Caroline had been able to get back to work by popping home (the Community Centre is across the road from their house) to keep an eye on Paul and using his reversed sleep pattern to her advantage. She, on the other hand, was still getting very little sleep. The mood diary helped to clarify the times of day difficult for Paul and that some days were getting a little better, although his mood remained depressed and hopeless. The structure of this meeting allowed me to book some time with Caroline for a carer's assessment and to get a fuller background history of the family background through a family genogram and RAI (Barrowclough and Tarrier 1992). These confirmed that there was little indication apart from a slight deterioration in Paul's functioning prior to the holiday that he was at risk of developing psychosis and that Caroline was getting very little time to herself. Also highlighted was a family history of bipolar disorder (Caroline's mother) and that Caroline had coped ably with other stressful periods in her life. Paul in the meantime had started individual CBT sessions with Richard, which reinforced our plan for him to keep a mood diary and explored Paul's beliefs about the power his voices had over him and how much he had over them. It is surprisingly common for people to hear voices but generally they only prove problematic when malevolent like Paul's (Chadwick and Birchwood 1995).

In response to our concerns about his low mood and Paul's perception that none of his medication was helping, his anti-depressant medication was changed again by the consultant psychiatrist at the beginning of September. Paul seemed to interpret this decision in a negative way (that nothing was going to help) and the next day took a whole months supply of his new anti-depressant tablets. Fortunately he was very sick afterwards, as he remained determined not to go back into hospital.

Paul's mood diary was beginning to link the headaches to stress from when his voices were bad, as opposed to side-effects of medication. Paul had observed this when he was in hospital the first time but had been forgotten in the distress of the ensuing few weeks. He also identified that when the voices were bad he could see and smell things, which he found scary. Discussion with the consultant psychiatrist led us to decide to continue with the current regime for at least several months and resist adding or changing anything, in line with the recommendation (NICE 2002) that a period of six to eight weeks' trial is required to determine the effectiveness of any anti-psychotics or anti-depressants. This would we felt give Paul the best chance to stabilise and develop more positive coping strategies through both his individual CBT session with Richard and the FI with Eric and me.

Caroline says:

By early September he gradually started to improve. The headaches subsided and GRIP were visiting him regularly as well as FI with Eric and Mandy. It was helpful to know I could phone and ask for advice and talk through what ever was the problem of the day. I knew they couldn't make Paul do things any more than I could (for example, force him to go to hospital if he'd harmed himself), but it was helpful to share the responsibility with others who understood and supported my decisions.

By the time Paul started to feel better he hadn't been able to socialise for many months. In October he started going out with another GRIP member for coffee and then started attending a social group, which helped his confidence. This was the main social thing he did for a while. It was introduced as he was getting better and became the highlight of the week for some time. Getting used to going out again in the evening also took a while – he went out with his brother or me initially and then his friends. Paul soon found that his friends' heavy drinking didn't agree with him and he would end up looking after them instead of the other way around. He started to look at going back to college, but was limited because he didn't like using local buses.

Mandy says:

Over the next few months GRIP kept in frequent contact as things gradually stabilised with Paul. The medication worked well alongside the FI and CBT. As a result, the voices gradually became less powerful and later stopped altogether. Paul's mood improved and he stopped feeling impulsive urges to harm himself as his voices subsided.

Caroline continued to phone us regularly and I met with her on several occasions to look at developing her own care plan. Like many mothers, the care and time she gave Paul was instinctive and she had had years of putting her children's needs above her own. In order to continue effectively in her caring role we focused on her being able to take up opportunities for a social life when they arose. GRIP had been struck by her calm accepting attitude towards Paul's difficulties and her determination to help him get better. FI became a forum for problem-solving, reviewing the CBT and for Caroline to hand responsibility back to Paul.

A link was established between his voices and the bullying that he had received at school. This was also linked to a loss of confidence and lack of interest in occupying his time, which became the focus for the next stage of GRIP's intervention.

Paul has gradually built up his social networks again and became a founder member of GRIP's social group, which helped rebuild his self-confidence. He has talked about his experience of psychosis with family and friends and they have been accepting and supportive of him in return. He is now in a stable relationship and sees less and less of his mother as he has continued to recover. Caroline feels her bond with Paul is closer as a result of the disorder and that he has mostly returned to a normal lifestyle. The family meetings take place less frequently and the individual work is focusing on early warning signs and a planned reduction in medication.

It is likely that GRIP will discharge Paul later this year once he has successfully stopped medication and started some kind of employment or training. By then he will have had approximately two years contact with GRIP and will be discharged back to primary care, recovered and feeling in control of how to deal with any possible EWS should they occur in the future.

Caroline says:

After over 18 months we still have regular contact with GRIP, whose help has been invaluable. It's good to talk to someone who can see reason in what's going on and understands. I know that Paul finds this as well – he still gets some bad dreams but talks to Richard who helps him to stop worrying that he is getting ill again. He has joined a local employment project and has a better understanding of the things that happened and what to look out for

Table 2.2 Paul's early warning signs work

Paul's EWS	*His stress triggers*	*His coping strategies*
Feeling more energetic Feeling more talkative and outgoing Feeling like playing tricks and pranks Getting less sleep Having restless sleep	Going on holiday (first time abroad) Increased consumption of alcohol, not sleeping/ having reversed sleep patterns Sunstroke Being hypnotised on stage	Drinking moderately Using breathing techniques Regularising sleep patterns Avoiding stage hypnosis Challenge thinking Listening to calm music Increasing or starting medication Contacting GRIP/GP

in the future through the EWS he has done with Richard (see Table 2.2). From my point of view he is not exactly the same person he was before this happened and still has times when he worries about things. On the whole he seems to have recovered and is able to enjoy his life again. He is in a supportive relationship, is out a lot of the time and has resumed his hobbies. I don't know if he will become ill again, and obviously I hope he won't, but I do know that I would understand and be there for him again. I would be more frightened if he was out of my care and would want to be involved, as I would know the things that helped this time and feel that my caring was a big factor in him recovering so well.

What Went Well and Why

Although Caroline and Paul had not had any previous contact with mental health services, Caroline was already involved with her local community through her work and contacts with the neighbourhood project. Paul was asking for help and was able to explain what was happening to him to his local GP. Both of these factors probably helped Paul to get access to specialist service quickly. Once Caroline and Paul had got into contact with GRIP, they were able to remain in close contact during the acute phase of his psychosis. GRIP discussed Paul's care regularly with Caroline, which helped support her in looking after Paul. Their close emotional bond was a significant factor for managing the potential risk of serious self-harm during this time and kept his contact with inpatient services to a minimum. This in turn helped to normalise his experiences and to keep him at home with his family and remain included with his friends and the local community.

By operating a team caseload approach, intensive support was offered to them in the form of FI, individual CBT, carer, telephone and social support during the acute phase of the disorder. Close communication with the consultant psychiatrist was helped by a good working relationship, easy access for discussions about changes in Paul's presentation and close liaison to manage the frequent medication changes needed to find the right combination for Paul. Had this range of treatment not been available, it is possible that Paul might have spent much longer in hospital and been more frequently detained under the 1983 Mental Health Act. He may have had a longer period of the acute phase of his disorder and could even have succeeded in killing himself.

Although GRIP was small and newly formed at the time of Paul's referral, all four team members were highly skilled practitioners. The team caseload enabled GRIP to provide intensive support during the acute phase of Paul's difficulties and a wide range of interventions. A single EIS worker, even with a protected caseload, would not have been able to offer this and there would have been gaps in the service needed if they were on leave or off sick. Paul eventually worked with all four members of the team and several post-registration students on placement, who helped with increasing his social functioning once he was past the acute phase of his disorder. It would have been impossible for a standard CMHT to offer this intensive amount of support over the period of time GRIP had worked with Paul and Caroline. At the time of writing there is a Crisis and Home Treatment service being planned for the locality. Had one been in place during the acute phase of Paul's disorder, GRIP would have worked closely with them to provide additional home treatment and support for both Paul and Caroline (Department of Health 2001; NICE 2002).

The National Policy Context

Prompt and effective interventions for young people with early psychosis, and for their families, close friends and other carers, are embodied in an individual's rights to citizenship and social inclusion (Early Psychosis Declaration (World Health Organisation 2004); *Social Exclusion Report* (ODPM 2004)). The Early Psychosis Declaration arose out of the work of the Initiative to Reduce the Impact of Schizophrenia (IRIS 2000) which, in turn, evolved following the difficult experiences Dr David Shiers experienced when his teenage daughter developed psychosis. As a GP he had had only a professional relationship with mental health services, but as a carer he was appalled by the lack of cohesion and negative attitudes of the services involved in his daughter's care. His wish was to have a declaration (like that developed for people with diabetes) which would inform those using services what outcomes they could and should expect. Comprehensive programmes for the detection and treatment of early psychosis and in supporting the needs of young people with early psychosis, carry the important function of promoting recovery, independence, equity and self-sufficiency while facilitating uptake of social, educational and employment opportunities for those young people. The Early Psychosis Declaration has been adopted by the World Health Organisation (World Health Organisation 2004). Table 2.3 shows the main principle of this declaration.

Specialist mental health services have increasingly been unable to allocate resources to people who may be developing psychosis, focusing instead on people with longer histories and serious risk issues. Child and adolescent mental health services (CAMHS) are traditionally clinic based and under resourced, with long waiting times for new referrals. Transfer between CAMHS and adult mental health services is often problematic and arbitrary when a young person reaches the age of 18. EIS are key to developing mental health services (Department of Health 2001) and address these issues by focusing on the young person, and on their symptoms, and not waiting until after a diagnosis is made before intervening. The transfer period between CAMHS and adult services is addressed by EIS teams by removing the service boundary for a young person with psychosis and covering the years from 14 to 35 (Department of Health 2001, 2004). Research in Gloucestershire has confirmed the

Table 2.3 Key principles of the Early Psychosis Declaration

- To respect the right to recovery and social inclusion and support for the importance of personal, social, educational and employment outcomes.
- To respect the strengths and qualities of young people with a psychosis, their families and communities, encouraging ordinary lives and expectations.
- To be entitled to services that actively partner young people, their families and friends to place them at the centre of care and service delivery, at the same time sensitive to age, phase of disorder, gender, sexuality and cultural background.
- To use cost-effective interventions.
- To respect the right for family and friends to participate and feel fully involved in the care of their loved one.

problematic transfer between CAMHS and adult services (Davis 2003) and the improved user and carer satisfaction since the inception of GRIP (Davis and Morgan 2004).

Another issue within Gloucestershire is the lack of an adolescent inpatient unit. Children under the age of 18 generally have to go to Swindon, Oxford or Bristol if they need admission. If they are admitted locally, the only option is a generic adult ward that tends to be mostly populated by much older adults. This is not 'youth friendly' and often compounds the trauma of the psychosis for both the person and their carers if admission is needed. As can be seen in this case study, for both Paul and Caroline the atmosphere and environment were significant negative factors in both of his admissions. In particular, Caroline felt she could keep Paul safer than the ward could at the time of the second admission, which contravenes the notion of hospitals as a 'place of safety'. One of the recommendations of local research (Davis 2003), which links with both the adult and children's national service frameworks (Department of Health 1999, 2004), is the development of a young persons' (14–25 years) psychosis unit within the county.

People experiencing a first episode of psychosis will be generally medication naive and require smaller doses of anti-psychotic medication (NICE 2002; McGorry 2004). The policy guidance indicates that atypical anti-psychotics should be considered at the earliest possibility, starting at the lowest end of the prescribing range and building up gradually. It also states that during an acute phase, where symptoms of anxiety and agitation are prominent, the use of benzodiazepines is indicated for limited periods (NICE 2002).

It is not uncommon for medication to need to be adjusted, especially during psychosis when the right combination and dosage is not known. However, users and families have not always been given enough information to help them keep trying different alternatives, which often precipitates a more serious crisis. Caroline was not present when Paul first saw the psychiatrist so was not consulted or informed about the original prescription. She had to get a friend to look it up on the Internet even to discover her son had been put on anti-psychotic medication. The issue of confidentiality and age is of note on this point. As Paul was 19, he was regarded as an adult and therefore there was no automatic legal requirement to consult with Caroline. However, he was living at home under her care and clearly distressed and psychotic at that first meeting, putting his capacity to understand explanations about medication and its effects into question. An important aspect of GRIP's operational policy is to collaborate closely with families and carers from as early a point as possible, in order to foster the notion of shared caring. If a carer is on board with the need for medication and other interventions, they will be more likely to be allies and partners in the young person's care as demonstrated in this care study.

Implications and Conclusion

Eighteen months down the line Paul continues on his way to making a full recovery. His medication is gradually being reduced and he has started a supported back-to-work scheme locally. His relationship is going well and he is looking to leave home to move in with his partner in the near future. Caroline sees very little of him and has been able to take the opportunity of working more hours which she would not have been able to do during the acute phase of his disorder. She feels she is now in a position to offer support herself to other parents whose son or daughter is at an earlier stage of recovery than Paul's, or to be involved in the training initiatives that the GRIP team are involved in to promote best practice.

If Paul were referred to GRIP now he would probably receive a very similar service. Although his initial assessment indicated that Paul had had some thoughts of harming himself, at the time he was seen he described these as being in the past and he felt that the medication was helping. Given that his mood was fluctuating along with his psychosis, the first overdose may not have been prevented. However, relationships between GRIP and the wards and the psychiatrist have developed and we are now routinely involved in a person's care and plans for discharge. The team run regular study days with CAMHS staff for inpatient colleagues aimed at helping them to understand the needs of a young person with psychosis in hospital. This includes input from other GRIP carers about their experiences and tackles the issue of 'need to know' confidentiality, promoting reflective discussions among the delegates each time. The local Crisis and Home Treatment team will be operational in the near future; GRIP is involved in the steering group for that service. Caroline would have found the support of an out-of-hours service when Paul was in crisis very helpful. We have only expanded slightly this year but should have a fuller complement of staff come the next financial year, which will allow for the team to work with a greater number of young people with psychosis and their carers in the future.

Notes

1 'Prodrome' refers to the early symptoms and signs that someone experiences before a full blown syndrome becomes evident.

2 More detail on this topic can be found in chapters 1, 4 and 8.

References

Addington, J. and Burnett, P. (2004) Working with families in the early stages of psychosis. In Gleeson, J. and McGorry, P. (eds.) *Psychological Interventions in Early Psychosis*. Chichester: Wiley, chapter 6, pp. 99–116.

Addington, J., Coldham, E., Jones, B., Ko, T. and Addington, D. (2003) The first episode of psychosis: the experience of relatives. *Acta Psychiatrica Scandinavica*, 108, 285–9.

Barrowclough, C. and Tarrier, N. (1992) *Families of Schizophrenic Patients: Cognitive Behavioural Interventions.* London: Chapman and Hall.

Barrowclough, C., Tarrier, N. and Johnson, M. (1996) Distress, expressed emotion and attributions in relatives of schizophrenia patients. *Schizophrenia Bulletin*, 22, 691–702.

Birchwood, M. (2000) The critical period for early intervention. In Birchwood, M., Fowler, D. and Jackson, C. (eds.) *Early Intervention in Psychosis: A Guide to Concepts, Evidence and Interventions.* Chichester: Wiley, chapter 2, pp. 28–63.

Birchwood, M., Jackson, C. and Todd, P. (1998) The critical period hypothesis. *International Clinical Psychopharmacy* 12, 27–38.

Chadwick, P. and Birchwood, M. (1995) The omnipotence of voices II: the beliefs about voices questionnaire (BAVQ) *British Journal of Psychiatry*, 166, 773–6.

Davis, E. (2003) *Mental Health Service Response to First-episode Psychosis in Gloucestershire.* Gloucester: Gloucestershire Partnership NHS Trust. Available online: www.gripinitiative.org.uk (accessed 16 Ocotober 2005).

Davis, E. and Morgan, J. (2004) *Mental Health Service Response to First-episode Psychosis in Gloucestershire.* Gloucester: Gloucestershire Partnership NHS Trust. Available online: www.gripinitiative.org.uk (accessed 16 October 2005).

Department of Health (1983) *Mental Health Act.* London: HMSO.

Department of Health (1990) *The Care Programme Approach for People with a Mental Illness Referred to Specialist Psychiatric Services* (HC(90)23). London: HMSO.

Department of Health (1999) *The National Service Framework for Mental Health: Modern Standards and Service Models.* London: HMSO.

Department of Health (2001) *Mental Health Policy Implementation Guide.* London: Department of Health.

Department of Health (2004) *National Service Framework for Children.* London: Department of Health.

Drage, M., Floyd. S., Smith, G. and Cocks, N. (2006) *Evaluating Family Interventions: A Qualitative Investigation.* Bath: Mental Health R&D Unit, University of Bath.

EPPIC (1996) *The Australian Clinical Guidelines for Early Psychosis.* Parkville, Melbourne, Australia: Early Psychosis Prevention and Intervention Centre (EPPIC). Usually available online, but guidelines under review; see www.eppic.org.au/mhp/resources/clinical_guidelines.htm (accessed 28 September 2005).

EPPIC (1997) *Working with families in Early Psychosis*, no. 2 in a series of early psychosis manuals. Parkville, Melbourne, Australia: Early Psychosis Prevention and Intervention Centre.

Fadden, G. (1998) Family intervention. In Brooker, C. and Repper, J. (eds.) *Serious Mental Health Problems in the Community – Policy, Practice and Research.* London: Balliere Tindall, chapter 8, pp. 159–83.

Gamble, C. and Brennan, G. (2000) *Working with Serious Mental Illness. A Manual for Clinical Practice.* London: Balliere Tindall.

IRIS [Initiative to Reduce the Impact of Schizophrenia] (2000) *Early Intervention in Psychosis: Clinical Guidelines and Service Frameworks and Tool Kit.* www.iris-initiative.org.uk

Krawiecka, M., Goldberg, D. and Vaughan, M. (1977) Standardised psychiatric assessment scale for chronic psychiatric patients. *Acta Psychiatrica Scandinavica*, 55, 299–308.

Lincoln, C. and McGorry, P. (1999) Pathways to care in early psychosis: clinical and consumer perspectives. In McGorry, P. and Jackson, H. (eds.) *The Recognition and Management of Early Psychosis: A Preventative Approach.* Cambridge: Cambridge University Press, chapter 3, pp. 51–80.

McGorry, P. (2004) An overview of the background and scope for psychological interventions in early psychosis. In Gleeson, J. and McGorry, P. (eds.) *Psychological Interventions in Early Psychosis.* Chichester: Wiley, chapter 1, pp. 1–22.

NICE (2002) *Guidance of the Use of Newer (Atypical) Antipsychotic Drugs for the Treatment of*

Schizophrenia – Provisional Appraisal Determination. London: National Institute for Clinical Excellence.

Nuechterlein, K. (1987) Vulnerability models for schizophrenia: state of the art. In Hafner, H., Gattaz, W. and Janzarik, W. (eds.) *Search for the Causes of Schizophrenia.* Heidelberg: Springer Verlag, pp. 297–316.

ODPM (2004) *Mental Health and Social Inclusion – Social Exclusion Unit Report.* London: ODPM Publications.

Petersen, L., Jeppesen, P., Thorup, A., Maj-Britt, A., Ohlenschalaeger, J., Christensen, T., Krarup, G., Jorgenesen, P. and Nordentoft, M. (2005) A randomised multicentre trial of integrated versus standard treatment for patients with a first episode of psychosis *British Medical Journal,* 331, 602–16.

Reed, M. (2005) *GRIP Team Operational Policy.* Gloucester: Gloucestershire Partnership NHS Trust. Available online: www.gripinitiative.org.uk/pdf/operationpolicy05.pdf (accessed 28 September 2005).

Smith, G. and Velleman, R. (2007) Family intervention for co-existing mental health and drug and alcohol problems. In Baker, A. and Velleman, R. (eds.) *Clinical Handbook of Co-existing Mental Health and Drug and Alcohol Problems.* Hove: Brunner-Routledge, chapter 5, pp. 74–94.

Stein, L. and Santos, A. (1998) *Assertive Community Treatment of Persons with Severe Mental Illness.* New York: W.W. Norton and Co.

World Health Organisation (2004) *Early Psychosis Declaration.* Geneva: World Health Organisation.

Zubin, J. and Spring, B. (1977) Vulnerability: a new view of schizophrenia. *Journal of Abnormal Psychology,* 86, 103–26.

Chapter 3

Integrating Family and Individual Approaches with People Who Experience Bipolar Disorder

Annie Higgs and Roger Thompson

Key Points

- 'Real' recovery from bipolar disorder is possible with the 'right' combination of treatments, understanding and support.
- It is useful to use structured frameworks that take us beyond early warning signs (EWS) and to use psychological techniques such as cognitive behaviour therapy (CBT) to tackle core problems (of sexual abuse during childhood in this case).
- Managing the psychosis was a small but important step in preparing the way for this ultimately deeper and vastly more effective work.
- Equally important to the overall success of this work were the personal qualities of all parties involved, particularly maintaining a positive attitude, believing in 'miracles', tenacity and hope for the future.
- The work required wide-ranging knowledge and skills, appropriate supervision and a supporting network of relevant professionals.
- A worker without specialist training with regard to abuse issues, can still employ CBT techniques very successfully, drawing on material from self-help manuals while harnessing the expert knowledge that the service user has of their experience.

Introduction

The term illness is used within the chapter to reflect the severity of the impact of the psychosis on Roger[1] and his family. Along with the terms bipolar disorder and psychosis, it reflects the terminology used within the mental health services who offered care to Roger. It also reflects the biological component that contributed to the bio-psychosocial concept that underpinned the work undertaken as detailed below.

This chapter will briefly discuss the evidence base for interventions that were found to be effective in managing psychotic illness for this husband and wife, also referred to as the service user and carer. In a chronological way, we will set the scene prior to work commencing, give the rationale for work undertaken and offer reflections (collated collaboratively) about the work we shared. This will include introducing family and individual work, through to using assessments and interventions, and evaluating their effectiveness. It highlights what seemed to work well and identifies some obstacles to using these approaches within our NHS Trust setting.

The purpose of our writing was to understand better what we had experienced. We wanted to identify what had gone well in order to guide our interventions in the future. With the benefit of hindsight, we could identify and modify what had 'slowed' us up, so that in future we could take the simplest route to recovery. This we aim to share, to promote others' understanding.

The Evidence

There are a number of strands of evidence underpinning this integrated approach.

Stress-vulnerability model

All interventions described within this chapter are founded on Zubin and Spring's stress-vulnerability model (1977), which conceptualises how psychosis may develop. It also offers hope for changing the outcomes of psychosis through relapse prevention, using a range of approaches including biological, psychological and social interventions.[2]

Relapse prevention

Intervening early by noticing the EWS and taking immediate action, either very early in the onset of a first or subsequent psychotic episode, or even before the episode has actually taken hold, has been shown to reduce the severity and duration of psychosis (Birchwood, Fowler and Jackson 2000). The prevention or minimisation of relapse reduces interference to social and vocational functioning and hence promotes recovery. Mueser et al. (1992) found patients expressed a strong interest in learning about early signs of illness and relapse, identifying that a person's perception of their level of control is important to recovery. Acting on recognition of signs of reduced well-being, with use of a plan to manage symptoms, promotes this feeling of control (Birchwood 1996). Involvement of carers in the process of monitoring EWS can provide useful information and practical suggestions to reduce the risk of relapse, through sharing perspectives on health and by using problem-solving techniques (Birchwood, Fowler and Jackson 2000).

CBT for anxiety and low self-esteem

Beck and colleagues' (1979) cognitive theory of emotional disorders asserts that a thinking disorder maintains emotional disorders, i.e. distortions in thinking accompany anxiety and depression. The therapies which have resulted from this theory – cognitive-behaviour therapy (CBT) and cognitive therapy (CT) – have been shown to be very effective in enabling people to learn to manage anxiety, depression and low self-esteem (Padesky and Greenberger 1995). For example, Padesky and Greenberger (1995) describe CBT as a very effective way to learn to manage anxiety, by assessing thoughts, mood, behaviour, biology and the environment, and the relationship between these five components (in that each is viewed as having an influence on the others). Most commonly, change is effected by focusing on evaluating thoughts and changing behaviour. Greenberger and Padesky (1995) have also produced a simple-to-use self-help manual (*Mind over Mood*), designed for people to understand their anxiety and its impact on mood. It provides practical directions for individuals to use CBT to change the way they may be thinking, their beliefs about themselves and/or others, what evidence this is based on and how this influences how they are feeling.

CBT has also been used to overcome problems associated with low self-esteem (Fennell 1999). Fennell (1999) defines self-esteem as 'the overall opinion we have of ourselves, how we judge or evaluate ourselves and the value we attach to ourselves as people' (p. 6). She notes that self-esteem is linked to the conclusions one makes about oneself, based on past experiences. She asserts that negative experiences will generate a negative self-evaluation, thus demonstrating a likely link between (for example) childhood sexual abuse and low self-esteem. Of course, low self-esteem may be a consequence of other problems, such as long-standing anxiety; and/or may contribute to a range of other problems, including suicidal thinking and depression (American Psychiatric Association 2004).

Psychosocial interventions for mood swings

There are a range of effective psychosocial interventions that help deal with mood swings (Scott 2001, 2002), which are based on clinical techniques shown to be effective. For example, Scott (2001) in her self-help book, combines information about bipolar disorder with specific strategies that use CBT to manage better the mood swings from depression to mania. The aim is to treat emotional disorders by changing negative patterns of thought and behaviours likely to exacerbate mood disorders, thus regaining stability. Relapse prevention techniques are suggested, developing these through awareness-raising for self or others, as well as implementation of practical self-management techniques. This book makes CBT techniques that have been clinically proven to be effective more widely available (Scott 2002). It also discusses combining CBT with medication use, thus broadening options to minimise the likelihood of relapse.

Early and individual interventions for bipolar disorder

The idea that service users with bipolar disorder can recognise and then act upon emergent or 'prodromal' signs of illness to better manage their outcome receives support from the extant literature. Lam, Wong and Sham (2001) found that users could report bipolar prodromal symptoms reliably. Depressive prodromes were more difficult to predict for 25 per cent of users, owing to a mix of behavioural, cognitive and somatic symptoms. For mania, identification of prodromes was comparatively easier. For both depression and mania, behavioural coping strategies helped prevent relapse.

Scott and Gutierrez (2004) also report that psychological treatments resulted in fewer relapses and recommended therapy length of between 10 and 20 hours over 6 to 9 months. Lam et al. (2005) demonstrated that cognitive therapy significantly reduced bipolar episodes when medication compliance was controlled for. They also showed that relapse prevention was most effective in the first year of treatment: for the last 18 months of the 30-month study, no significant beneficial effects were reported. Lam et al. (2005), suggest that the effect of booster sessions or maintenance therapy deserves future research.

Family intervention for bipolar disorder

A number of systematic reviews (for example, Pharoah et al. 2003) have shown that family work with people suffering from psychosis decreases the frequency of relapse and hospitalisation. The National Institute for Clinical Excellence (NICE 2002) guidelines recommend family work as a core intervention in the treatment and management of schizophrenia; and family work has been adapted to also work with bipolar disorder (see below).

The family intervention described in this chapter follows the integrated family work model recommended by Smith and colleagues (Smith, Gregory and Higgs 2007). The aim is to integrate knowledge of biological mechanisms, psychological processes and social influences and join with the family who are viewed as the experts of their experience (Falloon, Boyd and McGill 1984). Families are seen as being able to influence the course of the illness and not as the cause of it, there being no single cause (Barrowclough and Tarrier 1997). The model has been adapted for working with bipolar disorder by Miklovitz and Goldstein (1997). There remains a focus on accepting, understanding and managing the effects of bipolar disorder; and the work is also underpinned by a model of stress-vulnerability (Zubin and Spring 1977). Management includes sharing information about the nature of bipolar disorder, the use of medication, and improving communication and problem-solving skills. Family relationships and coping are also enhanced through developing contingency plans to reduce the likelihood of relapse to mania or depression.

Combining individual and family work

Combining individual and family work may reduce the likelihood of relapse for those who experience bipolar disorder (Miklovitz et al. 2003). The exact nature of this relationship needs further research, although preliminary findings (Miklovitz et al. 2003) indicate there are benefits in combining two approaches which in themselves have proved helpful to improving mental health.

Medication management

An approach termed Medication Management, combines cognitive behavioural techniques with motivational interviewing. Collaborative working is fostered by structuring sessions with a jointly set agenda, which involves asking for service user feedback to elicit their viewpoint. The service user is encouraged to engage in a process of guided discovery, in which the worker listens carefully and summarises the information shared to check that he/she has understood, so that together they may develop alternative views for consideration. Shared decision-making, reviewing medication used and those available, side-effect management, and relapse prevention planning, are key components of this (Gray 2001).

Links between childhood sexual abuse and psychosis

There is a known causal link between abuse suffered in childhood and the experience of mental health problems (including anxiety, depression and post traumatic stress disorder) in adult life (Read, Mosher and Bentall 2003, 2004). These authors demonstrate that there is a strong correlation between childhood abuse and psychotic conditions that had not been recognised previously. A specific and significant link has also been found between adults diagnosed with bipolar disorder and child abuse in their past (Hammersley, Burston and Read 2004).

A determinant of whether survivors of childhood abuse will experience psychosis is 'whether the individual encounters further traumas in later life' (Read, Mosher and Bentall 2004, p. 238). It appears too that having been abused as a child leads to an ongoing hyper-sensitivity to threat. One can see how, within a stress-vulnerability model, this could become a vicious cycle, linking childhood abuse to psychosis.

With particular reference to sexual abuse, the worse the abuse, the greater the likelihood that mental health problems will ensue (Mullen et al. 1993). Psychiatric patients with a history of sexual abuse have more and longer hospital admissions, receive more medication, have higher global severity of their symptoms and are at increased risk of self-harm and suicide than non-abused patients (Read, Mosher and Bentall 2004).

A review of the literature linking childhood abuse to psychosis by Read and colleagues (2003) is recommended to those wishing to explore this subject further.

The Case Study

Editors' note: this case study is about Roger and the service that he received, from the time he developed bipolar disorder in his early 30s, until the present time some eight years later. The case study is written jointly by Roger and Annie Higgs, a Clinical Specialist for Psycho-social Interventions within the Gloucestershire Partnership NHS Trust. Annie undertook much of the work with Roger from about 2001 onwards, although he was also helped by his care co-ordinator, Jane Mather, a community psychiatric nurse (CPN) within the community mental health team.

Annie's Background

Annie says:

What I brought to the work was my professional training (undertaken as a result of my long-standing interest in people) and a working knowledge of some of the evidence base about managing a variety of serious mental illnesses, including bipolar disorder. My involvement in the Training the Trainers Medication Management initiative from the Institute of Psychiatry (Gray 2002) allowed me to develop skills relating to compliance issues. This built on my experience of using motivational interviewing techniques and cognitive behavioural interventions with psychotic disorders, introduced to me on the Diploma in Integrated Approaches to Serious Mental Illness, known as the Thorn course.

An overview of the framework, which I use to guide my work, can be found in Appendix 1.

My training, experience, role as clinical specialist for psychosocial interventions and personal qualities lead me to work collaboratively, focusing on the service user while aiming to integrate this work with others relevant to the recovery process. The structure offered by individual and family work uses small steps to long-term goals relating to basic and more complex needs being met. I work with the service user and carer priorities to encourage engagement while considering psychological, emotional, social, vocational, physical and physiological need. Guided discovery (Padesky and Greenberger 1995) maintains a service user focus while offering alternative perspectives in a non-confrontational way. I aim to work at the appropriate pace of those involved, towards maximum independence. My stance as a worker is probably best described as 'approachable, purposeful, flexible and ordinary' (Gamble 2000, p. 116). I can be tenacious and hold a sense of hope for change over time. To promote this approach I use regular clinical supervision.

Roger's Background

Roger says:

To appreciate the near miraculous effect of our work on my mental health, it is important to understand just how much I used to suffer from bipolar disorder. I had my first manic and depressive episodes in my early 30s (in 1998). I was voluntarily admitted to hospital for a period of approximately six weeks, which felt like a lifetime of emptiness.

Being released from hospital to recover at home brought about a slight lift in spirits but my life still seemed to be a vacuum. I spent nearly five months 'recovering', but the days just dragged and I couldn't seem to remember how I used to fill my time. Time was now an enemy, something that had to be filled rather than something that most people don't have enough of. My confidence was also shot to pieces and I was certain I wasn't capable of doing my job ever again. I did manage to return to work, although walking into the office that morning seemed like the hardest thing I'd ever done. Without the support and encouragement of my wife, I would never have reached the door.

Over a period of six months at work, I built myself steadily back up to the level I had reached before the onset of illness. On the surface, I was back to where I had been before the episode but the reality was starkly different. For the whole of 2000, time was still very much the enemy and my days seemed empty and unfulfilling.

At the start of 2001, my mental health dived to new lows after I was told that I was unfit to do my job, should consider demotion and was not performing anywhere near the standard for my grade. Within days, I had completely fallen apart and this time the damage to my mental health seemed irreversible. For 18 months I stumbled between manic and depressive episodes (five in all) trying different mood stabilisers to stem the tide. I eventually had to leave work due to the poor state of my health and resigned myself to life as a 'social outcast'.

Life now seemed very pointless and I slept for large parts of the day. I felt a useless failure and suicidal thoughts occasionally flitted through my mind. I hung onto the love I had for my two-year-old, refusing to give up on him, even though I had long since given up on myself.

Fortunately, by this stage my wife and I had built up a lot of respect for Jane Mather, my community mental health nurse (CMHN), and our trust in her meant that we were prepared to give family work a go.

Why Roger got referred for family work

Kuipers, Leff and Lam (2002) suggest criteria for family work for those with a diagnosis of schizophrenia. The aim is to reduce stress within the environment, as well as in any acute form, in order to reduce the likelihood of psychotic relapse. Given that the experience of any long-term illness, such as bipolar disorder, can generate stress within the family's environment (Leff 1998), we utilised these same criteria (but relating them to bipolar disorder instead of schizophrenia) to guide appropriate interventions for Roger's care. Hence:

- The family and the care co-ordinator requested it, aiming to control the illness better and to promote all round recovery.
- The illness was causing stress at home, impacting on roles, on relationships, and on the health and well-being of the carer (in this case Roger's wife), and creating an increased risk of relapse for the service user.
- Multiple mood swings (five in 18 months) suggested the need for alternative ways of managing the illness.
- Roger's recent retirement from work increased the likelihood of increasing contact with his wife. Leff (1998) identified that those who had less than 35 hours contact time per week demonstrated less frequent relapse rates.
- The impact on his social and vocational roles.

Annie says:

At the time of referral Denise Hall (the ward manager in the acute ward within the Gloucestershire Partnership NHS Trust, who became one of the two staff who undertook the family work) was a student on the Thorn course, actively looking for families with whom to work. As a colleague, Jane Mather (Roger's care co-ordinator) knew this and contacted Denise. I was co-teaching the family work module of the Thorn course and was able, on this occasion, to act as a 'co-ordinator' for family work, based on the family work service model in Bath (Smith and Velleman 2002). As suggested in this model (Smith 1999), I became the second family worker, thereby demonstrating the value of family work without the need to request any extra resource from the community mental health team (CMHT). Supervision for this work was offered through the course.

Early stages of family work

Annie says:

We gave verbal and written information about family work, about why it can help, its likely structure and underlying philosophy, and agreed to meet at home due to their child-care commitments. We also planned individual support for Roger and Michelle through which alliances could develop.

Notes of meetings were shared, and feedback invited throughout and after each session. The agenda was negotiated at each meeting.

Both Roger and Michelle identified the need to better manage stress. The stress-vulnerability model (Zubin and Spring 1977) was shared, as it underpins both individual and family work and guides interventions.

Roger says:

Our first two months of family work seemed to be about the family workers getting to understand our situation/problems better. This was done in two very different ways: filling out some standard sections in an 'early warning signs pack' (Smith 2000); and trying to help us deal with the day-to-day arguments that were proving very stressful for both of us. I felt that the underlying cause of those arguments was the instability and lack of trust that the illness had brought into the relationship. The family workers spent the first two months helping us to learn to communicate more effectively with each other, reach joint decisions and build more confidence/trust in each other. While this may sound simple, it was very hard work, as some of the decisions were significant ones. This practical help built a foundation of trust and respect on which the subsequent sessions flourished.

Annie says:

The family work focused on the priorities set by Roger and Michelle to promote engagement. Once the work had acknowledged the different problem-solving styles and frameworks used by them, we built on their suggestions for compromise in terms of ways to problem-solve: consequently their communication improved.

Acknowledging emotions generated by their experience was important in enabling them to be able to move on to problem-solving, rather than being held back by these various emotions. They seemed 'spurred on' to further work as fewer arguments arose. Much of our success in getting started and achieving what we did was down to Roger and Michelle's efforts between sessions, as well as their honesty and courage within them. To gain a better insight into the difficulties Roger and Michelle were experiencing, we used the following assessment tools:

- *The relative assessment interview* (Barrowclough and Tarrier 1997), a semi-structured interview that allows the carer the opportunity to give information about psychiatric symptoms, behaviours and social functioning. The conversational style is designed to elicit the carer's responses towards the service user and the illness. It covers behaviours, beliefs, thoughts and feelings; and elicits positive and successful coping responses and resources as well as difficult areas. It encourages carers to assess the consequences of the illness on themselves and any 'significant others'.

- *The knowledge about psychosis interview*, adapted locally from the knowledge about schizophrenia interview (Barrowclough et al. 1987) by merely substituting the word 'schizophrenia' with 'psychosis' on the front page. This assesses carer's knowledge about psychosis, and explores their beliefs and attitudes. (In its original format the relative's responses can be scored, giving an indication of areas where education is needed. Although our adaptation obviously affects its validity in terms of scoring, the change did not impact on its ability to pick up how Michelle was able to make use of her knowledge of Roger's disorder, which is its main function and my reason for using it.)
- *The general health questionnaire* (Goldberg and Williams 1988) assesses potential distress within four dimensions: somatic symptoms, symptoms of anxiety, and of depression, and social functioning. (This assessment was licensed through the Thorn course and is not in the public domain.)

As the framework for our individual sessions we used *Early Warning Signs: A Self Management Training Manual for Individuals with Psychosis* (Smith 2000). I chose this pack as I thought it would suit Roger, it being logical, analytical and sophisticated. Certain steps are suggested within it:

- assessing awareness of, and also attitude to, relapse
- identifying relapse signs
- compiling a timeline
- monitoring early signs for four weeks to obtain an 'average' score
- identifying stress triggers and coping strategies
- involving medication and others
- compiling, using and evaluating an action plan
- reassessing awareness of, and also attitude to, relapse.

Our individual sessions focused on management of illness, making relapse prevention documentation more explicit and appropriate to a changed lifestyle. It gave the opportunity to develop a shared understanding of Roger's psychosis so that I might offer new information or perspectives to him as regards managing it.

Roger says:

My initial reaction to the EWS pack was to see it as a form-filling exercise and I didn't appreciate its full potential until much later. The baseline assessments I had to complete seemed to be stating the obvious, namely, that I feared relapse.

We used a 'card-sort' of commonly experienced early signs of psychosis to help identify my 'relapse signature' in more detail, or to put it another way, the pattern of behaviour I would exhibit that would eventually result in a psychotic episode. The cards provided by the pack were very useful to help get us started; eventually I added a lot of my own additional signs as well as those that could only be observed by my wife.

At the end of the second month, we had developed a fairly basic self-management plan that highlighted some actions I could take to counteract any signs of the illness trying to get a foothold. This was combined with the EWS monitoring where I scored myself against a number of key questions each week, to establish whether I was showing any signs of illness. I felt a lot more confidence knowing that this plan was in place, and it made me feel that I finally had some control over the psychosis rather than the other way round (Mueser et al. 1992).

Annie says:

Even after the card-sort I did not know the specific subtleties of the signs, for example, frequency, severity, duration of each sign, that make psychosis individual to the person. I accepted that Roger was very proficient at identifying his early signs of psychosis.

From my previous clinical experience I understood that compiling a timeline can be upsetting, so beforehand we planned how best to cope with any distress generated by this exercise. This involved support from Michelle.

We used the timeline of significant events from the beginning of difficulties with Roger's mental health as part of the pack (Smith 2000) and the medication management structure (Gray 2001). Together these interventions can help to get to know the person and the impact of their psychosis. In particular it helped us acknowledge difficulties with treatment, especially the use of medication in the past. Circumstances of good times were also highlighted for future use.

As our work progressed the timeline evolved as more detail of the past emerged.

Roger says:

I found the production of my timeline a real emotional 'roller coaster'. Writing it was like reliving the pain of each event. After many tears there was a slight feeling that this would help put the past behind me, and also relief that the family workers would understand how difficult it had been for us. By the time I had written all of it, I had to take some of my self-administered medication to settle down. This was very much the pattern of the next few months, with every positive break-through causing significant emotional stress and threatening my recovery. Fortunately my determination to win back my health for the sake of my family kept driving me on.

During months three to six, the self-management plan really took off and started turning into a comprehensive medical encyclopaedia about me. We had identified six escalating categories of behaviour that demonstrated how I would slip slowly but surely from 'well' to needing hospital treatment.

Our efforts were concentrated on preventing occurrence of the first categories, which we called green and reducing the risk of escalation into the next two, which we called amber and red.[3] Use of this plan made me feel much more in control of my health and developing it gave me great insights to my behaviour and how it affected the family.

What this early work told us

Annie says:

Following the assessments carried out with Roger and Michelle individually, Denise and I met to identify specific problem areas which we then shared with Roger and Michelle. These they agreed, prioritised and decided what they wanted to do about each problem. Some were worked on in sessions as a group or as pairs, and others they dealt with by themselves at home together.

The assessments gave us a list of problems which we discussed alongside strengths and needs. Their common needs were for:

- hope of change
- emotional and psychological support
- identifying a shared problem-solving framework
- practical suggestions for managing the illness, sharing knowledge about psychosis and treatment
- understanding the impact of illness on roles and health.

We built up trust by exchanging ideas through spending time together regularly, using the structure for individual and family sessions. Our approach to any lapses was to look for triggers, exploring any change to thought patterns, behaviour, physical well-being and socialisation. We developed our use of the pack, documenting specifics: e.g. although the pack suggests the use of medication if the score for early signs (ES) rises to a level which is 10 points above the average ES score, as Roger's mental health improved, and his average ES score fell, so he chose to work to a slightly higher average score, thus 'tolerating' more ES on a daily basis; he did this by coping with changes to his routine rather than 'running the risk' of using medication more regularly (as suggested in the pack if the score rises by 10).

The frequency, duration, severity and impact of early signs were developed and the impact of coping strategies evaluated. These included strategies other than using medication, as Roger did not wish to use this over the long term owing to side-effects.

What I learned was: Roger's thought patterns reflected significant anxiety, and he seemed to think that using medication was a 'black mark'. The possibility of relapse induced fear, which increased early signs scores. Over time we evaluated the not-so-good and good things about using the medication, and explored their effects (Bazire and Branch 2001). Roger became more pragmatic about the use of medication, using one 200 mg Sulpiride tablet daily, until he felt the sedating effects of it. This seemed to offer him the best effect of the medication in its shortest use.

The major breakthrough

Roger says:

Despite getting many benefits from self-management for these four months, it soon replaced the illness as the albatross around my neck. My days felt very restricted and as a free spirit

I found this very depressing. I seemed to be constantly announcing that I was 'green', which resulted in disruptions to the family's plans. I can best describe it as living in a trench during the war; it offers tremendous safety from flying bullets but also boredom, solitude and the feeling of imprisonment. Then came a major turning point when I had four weeks of generally poor mental health where I was almost constantly 'green'. I was set to throw in the towel and return to mood stabilisers when we discovered that my 'green state' was due to the side-effects of taking self-administered medication for more than a few days at a time. We pressed on with our work and the next six months saw a dramatic recovery.

Annie says:

I think Roger was relieved that there was a way of trying to differentiate side-effects from early signs. Using the Liverpool University neuroleptic side-effect rating scale (LUNSERS) (Day et al. 1995), and his increasing knowledge of his early signs, made this possible.

Roger was clearly frustrated with the self-management approach. He had worked so consistently hard to complete this work and still the early signs appeared, often without apparent reason. I decided to offer more information about how others have managed their illnesses to see if this helped.

Among other resources, I gave Roger the self-help book *Overcoming Mood Swings* (Scott 2001). We had discussed the benefits of being high as well as the down side of the illness and I wanted Roger to consider how else he could achieve these apparent illness 'benefits'. I was surprised by how important this book turned out to be for his recovery process.

After reading this book (Scott 2001), Roger asked about the relevance of sexual abuse to his psychosis. He had not previously raised this issue within family or our individual work, although he had discussed (after his first episode of psychosis) being sexually abused as a child. He had discussed this with his wife, and his parents, and the CMHT. Although Roger knew that I was not an 'expert' in this field, he appreciated our working relationship and my links to others who could support exploring its implications, so we agreed I would undertake this work. I thought that a better understanding of anxious thinking and self-esteem issues might allow him to get beyond 'maintenance'.

The effect of his abuse on thinking and self-esteem was explored with me, supported by supervision. A completed written relapse plan, shared with Michelle, the CMHT and their GP was essential in terms of reducing risk of relapse while these issues were worked on. Our relapse prevention work took on a whole new importance.

To complete the work, more books were shared, the first being *Overcoming Low Self-esteem* (Fennell 1999). This is a self-help book that offers a framework to understand the development of low self-esteem, relating this to early experience, and what perpetuates low self-esteem; introducing Roger to this framework greatly increased his understanding of his symptoms.

Another book written for service users: *Mind over Mood* (Greenberger and Padesky 1995) was used to deal with the thinking errors caused by anxiety, by using thought diaries and further exploring the links between thoughts, emotions and behaviour.

This work allowed Roger to understand what from his early experience was impacting on his 'here and now'. This meant that we were able to identify that, to engender change, we had a 'cycle' to break. Once activated, negative judgements about himself led to negative predictions and anxious thoughts, which further generated negative predictions, leading to unhelpful behaviour. This then confirmed the negative judgements about himself, led to self-criticism and low mood, and thereby activated more negative judgements about himself. This is depicted by Fennell (1999) as a map of the territory (p. 27), which became our map to the road to recovery.

Roger says:

During the earlier work on self-management, my family worker had given me a book that explained how childhood trauma could lead to mental health problems in later life (Scott 2001). Particularly helpful to me was its explanation of low self-esteem and how this could make people think 'dysfunctionally', causing them unnecessary anxiety. The book's basic premise was that how we perceive ourselves, affects the way we interpret life's events. Very negative self-perception can turn the most innocent event into a major trauma and this has a cumulative effect, reducing esteem further. The book could have been written about me as I had been sexually abused as a child and I suddenly realised what a huge impact this had had on the way I perceived myself as an adult.

Fennell's book (1999) was another huge breakthrough. The family workers had already identified anxious thinking as the main trigger of my psychosis and now I had a potential root cause for it. Somehow knowing that this kind of anxiety was an understandable outcome of sexual abuse rather than a personality defect helped me feel more positive about the situation. I told my family workers about the sexual abuse and they were incredibly supportive and helpful. We worked on re-balancing my thinking with the help of CBT techniques called 'thought plans' (Greenberger and Padesky 1995), which are a way of checking your thinking to correct the negative connotations your esteem will tend to put on things. When I got anxious over something I would write out a thought plan explaining what had triggered the anxiety, what I was thinking and why I was thinking it. This was a good start but the clever bit was when you had to produce evidence to justify those negative thoughts and suggest alternative, more positive, conclusions, with alternative evidence. After just six months, I had successfully used thought plans to bust anxiety (instead of needing ad hoc medication) and the repeated use of the plans in this way had corrected and re-balanced my thinking.

My day-to-day life is now full of positive examples of the benefits of my new balanced thinking. Situations that would have traumatised me and triggered the illness, pass me by like the morning breeze, rebuilding my esteem in the process (a true virtuous circle). Also gone are the days when small positive events would lift me so much that I would start to go high, again this is easily related to the restoration of my esteem. When you feel a worthless failure inside and something actually goes well, its not surprising you get a bit carried away!

While I remain susceptible to real rather than imaginary stress, I have my self-management plan to fall back on when this bites. Most importantly, because I don't blow everyday events out of proportion, my off days are so few and far between that the self-management is no longer the huge negative factor it used to be. To sum up the impact of the family work, the before/after comparisons in Table 3.1 are very useful.

Table 3.1 Comparisons in my life, before and after family work

Before family work	*After family work*
Five mood swings in 18 months	No mood swings in 19 months
Mood stabilisers all the time	No mood stabilisers for 19 months
Several EWS a week	EWS less than once a month
Three ad hoc tablets a week	Only nine tablets in the last eight months
Unable to work	Significant community responsibilities
Cycle of depreciating health	Cycle of improving health
Marriage at breaking point	Marriage very strong/new baby
My wife off work with stress	My wife able to enjoy life again
Felt continual relapse inevitable	Feel relapse to psychosis is not even a remote possibility

Annie says:

It would be easy for us to get carried away by the success of this work until you look overall and consider the degree to which luck played a part. ('Luck' because there was in our Trust no system of referral for family work, or for workers to be found to deliver it: Denise and I were able to respond solely due to time we could allocate to the Thorn course.)

Implications of the Work We Shared

Family intervention is congruent with recent government policy and legislation regarding mental health care. The *National Service Framework for Mental Health* (Department of Health 1999) recommends involving carers, promoting engagement, reducing crisis, fostering independence for service users, and medication management as described earlier. We have embraced all of these 'ideals'. Annie was able to act as a co-worker and a co-ordinator of family work in her role as Thorn tutor. The requirements of the Thorn course allowed Denise to work outside of the inpatient services to practice family work. Annie's role as clinical specialist for psychosocial interventions (PSI) meant that she had a range of skills required for family and individual PSI. However, without the following service changes, this may not be accessed equitably across the trust:

- There has to be one person specifically nominated to co-ordinate family work, linking family workers to families in need across the CMHTs. Without this, the majority of staff once trained on the Thorn programme return to their original caseloads, which are not usually organised to facilitate offering family work. Given the competing demands from a generic caseload, a family work 'champion' can help to keep this on the agenda (Smith and Velleman 2002). There is also a shortfall of locally accessible appropriate supervision for family work, further hampering skill development (Smith and Velleman 2002), although for our work, supervision was available for family work through Denise's attendance at the Thorn course.

- There needs to be an awareness of family work and its co-ordination in practice, so that it can be discussed with carers, and referral be made promptly if appropriate. A range of skills is necessary within the staff group to allow access to this work (Smith 1999).
- Family work should be an integral part of the integrated care programme approach (Department of Health 1999), the framework adopted by staff to provide services for people with health and social need. Co-ordination and continuity of care between family work and overall interventions is essential (Department of Health 1999). The link between individual and family work needs further research (Miklovitz et al. 2003).
- What it is that carers find most useful about family work also needs further research to ensure 'key ingredients' are highlighted in training programmes.
- Services to support people who have been abused should be easily accessible in non-stigmatising settings, for example, within primary health care. A range of treatment options should be available to those who experience psychosis, which might include access to CBTs and support from employers (see chapter 10, this volume). Awareness of such services should be raised within society to promote uptake as soon as is necessary.

We also would argue that, given what we consider to be the astounding success of our work, research into childhood sexual abuse and related mental health problems in later life, and proper assessment of this relationship, should be given high priority (Hammersley 2004). Read and Fraser (1998) recommend inpatient staff be trained about how and when to ask about abuse.

Conclusions

Annie says:

Despite the support from the local CMHT, particularly the CMHN described as 'excellent', endeavours had not been sufficient to reclaim 'normal life' over psychosis. Roger needed to manage his disorder differently. This was a cornerstone in terms of the foundations on which his recovery was based. He needed to consider a new structure for EWS work, so that he could then develop a better understanding of his symptoms. Having done this he was able to work on his self-esteem issues and then could look to wider, quality-of-life issues.

Various structures were key to this process, including those of family work (Smith 1999), the early signs pack (Smith 2000), and medication management (Gray 2001). The regular meetings also offered a structure which helped within a previously somewhat stressful home environment.

Overall I feel we succeeded through combining these structures with our personal qualities, including the ability to engage with each other, listening to people's perspectives and at times offering alternative perspectives in a non confrontational way. Knowing when to 'back off' was as important as gauging when additional information was needed or new issues needed to be tackled. Being 'ordinary', consistent and persistent have helped the working relationship (Gamble 2000). All this needed to be undertaken while simultaneously considering specific and wide issues, working logically through a plan of intervention, while remaining flexible with the plan.

Networking occurred, sessions were planned, delivered and reviewed, communication took place through conversation and documentation. Most importantly we kept our focus on people and the psychosis, worked towards change and looked beyond simply using the structures known to us.

Roger says:

The trust, improvement in health, and coping strategies, were all necessary foundation stones that enabled me to face and resolve my inner demons caused by the sexual abuse. I finally really like myself, and the effects of that are indeed miraculous. Most importantly, I could still see a life worth fighting for, a life that offered the love of my wife and children: without that I could not have found the strength and resolve to overcome all the hurdles in the illness.

I think being successful in a variety of ways bred success, new hope bred new hope, and energy became available for living rather than 'fire fighting' signs of illness. The optimism for change from the family workers was refreshing to us, as we had for so long struggled to get 'on top' of the illness. Their ability seemingly to deal with any problem we came up with inspired us to move on as a family.

We appreciate good luck but do not want to rely on its fickle nature and therefore suggest service configurations that offers timely, equitable access to a range of approaches in order to support those who suffer this illness.

We would support our Trust in developing local services by adopting the model for a family work service developed in Bath (Smith and Velleman 2002). Their service configuration was designed to overcome the barriers commonly experienced in developing family work services. Since there are competing demands within the organisational environment, identifying one person to 'champion' family work offers benefits to carers, service users and staff. The appointment of a 'champion' for family work allows liaison with the CMHTs. This has several benefits including raising awareness of the service, appropriate referral, and use of family work potentially to reduce other current demands on the teams, by, for example, relapse prevention work. This champion works as co-worker if no one is available within the CMHT and offers supervision at local venues at appropriate times. These sessions also offer the family work service a structure, while supporting clinical work. Given the skills and knowledge necessary for this role, the champion is also an ideal person to offer formal training relating to family work for psychosis (Smith and Velleman 2002).

Finally, further exploration into the inter-relationship between family work and individual work, and what it is that recipients of these interventions most value, would help to define service development.

Notes

1 A note on authorship: the name of the service user has been changed to provide anonymity. Written contributions are not made by the service user's wife (who will be known as Michelle), Denise Hall (who works as the ward manager in an acute ward within the Gloucestershire Partnership

NHS Trust) or Roger's care co-ordinator, Jane Mather. Discussions with everyone involved have, of course, shaped reflections, and we appreciate that without these key players the work would not have been possible. Although they have not directly contributed to the writing of this chapter we hope that the reader will remain able to consider how individual and family work with Roger and Michelle has been combined to promote recovery from bipolar disorder. The resources in terms of time and energy of all those involved were, and remain, precious.

2 This model is discussed in chapter 1, and underpins many of the approaches used within this book.

3 Editor's note See chapter 6 for an example of a completed EWS grid with green, amber and red categories. The use of these colours here are not synonymous with 'traffic lights' colours: in these EWS grids, having *no* colour means that there are no EWS: green denotes that there *are* problematic signs, although green ones are the mildest of these signs: hence the task is to stop even 'greens' from arising, but if they do, ensure that they do not lead on to amber or red signs.

References

American Psychiatric Association (2004) *Practice Guidelines for the Treatment of Psychiatric Disorders*. Arlington, VA: American Psychiatric Association.

Barrowclough, C. and Tarrier, N. (1997) *Families of Schizophrenic Patients: Cognitive Behavioural Intervention*, 2nd edition. Cheltenham: Stanley Thornes.

Barrowclough, C., Tarrier, N., Watts, S., Vaughn, C., Bamrah, J. and Freeman, H. (1987) Assessing the functional value of relatives' knowledge about schizophrenia. A preliminary report. *British Journal of Psychiatry*, 151, 1–8.

Bazire, S. and Branch, S. (2001) *Drugs Used in the Treatment of Mental Health Disorders: Frequently Asked Questions*. Salisbury: APS Publishing.

Beck, A., Rush A. Shaw, B. and Emery, G. (1979) *Cognitive Therapy of Depression*. New York: Guildford Press.

Birchwood, M. (1996) Early intervention in psychotic relapse: cognitive approaches to detection and management. In Haddock, G. and Slade, P. (eds.) *Cognitive Behavioural Interventions with Psychotic Disorders*. London: Routledge, pp. 171–211.

Birchwood, M., Fowler, D. and Jackson, C. (2000) *Early Intervention in Psychosis: A Guide to Concepts, Evidence and Interventions*. Chichester: Wiley.

Day, J., Wood, G., Dewey, M. and Bentall, P. (1995) A self-rating scale for measuring neuroleptic side-effects. *British Journal of Psychiatry*, 166, 650–3.

Department of Health (1999) *The National Service Framework for Mental Health: Modern Standards and Service Models*. London: HMSO.

Falloon, I., Boyd, J. and McGill, C. (1984) *Family Care of Schizophrenia*. New York: Guildford Press.

Fennell, M. (1999) *Overcoming Low Self-esteem. A Self-help Guide Using Cognitive Behavioural Techniques*. London: Robinson Publishing.

Gamble, C. (2000) Using a low expressed emotion approach to develop positive therapeutic alliances. In Gamble, C. and Brennan, G. (eds.) *Working with Serious Mental Illness. A Manual for Clinical Practice*. Edinburgh: Bailliere Tindall and RCN, chapter 8, pp. 115–24.

Gamble, C. and Brennan, G. (2000) (eds.) *Working with Serious Mental Illness. A Manual for Clinical Practice*. Edinburgh: Bailliere Tindall and RCN.

Goldberg, D. and Williams, P. (1998) *A User's Guide to the General Health Questionnaire*. NFER-Nelson, Windsor.

Gray, R. (2001) *Medication Management. Working to Improve the Health of People with Schizophrenia. A Randomized Control Trial of Medication Management Training for Community Psychiatric Nurses*. London: Institute of Psychiatry, King's College.

Gray, R. (2002) Medication management for people with a diagnosis of schizophrenia. *Nursing Times*, 98, 38–40.

Greenberger, D. and Padesky, C. (1995) *Mind Over Mood: Change How You Feel by Changing the Way You Think*. New York: Guildford Press.

Hammersley, P., Burston, P. and Read, J. (2004) Learning to listen: childhood trauma and adult psychosis. *Mental Health Practice*, 7, 18–21.

Kuipers, E., Leff, J. and Lam, D. (2002) *Family Work for Schizophrenia*, 2nd edition. London: Gaskell.

Lam, D., Hayward, P., Watkins, E., Wright, K. and Sham, P. (2005) Relapse prevention in patients with bipolar disorder: cognitive therapy outcome after 2 years. *American Journal of Psychiatry*, 162, 324–9.

Lam, D., Wong, G. and Sham, P. (2001) Prodromes, coping strategies and course of illness in bipolar affective disorder – a naturalistic study. *Psychological Medicine*, 31, 1397–1402.

Leff, J. (1998) Needs of the families of people with schizophrenia. *Advances in Psychiatric Treatment*, 4, 277–84.

Miklovitz, D. and Goldstein, M. (1997) *Bipolar Disorder: A Family-Focused Treatment Approach*. New York: Guilford Press.

Miklovitz, D., Richards, J., George, E., Frank, E., Suddath, R., Powell, K. and Sacher, J. (2003) Integrated family and individual therapy for bipolar disorder: results of a treatment development study. *Journal of Clinical Psychiatry*, 64, 182–91.

Mueser, K., Bellack, A., Wade, J., Sayers, S. and Rosenthal, K. (1992) An assessment of the educational needs of chronic psychiatric patients and their relatives. *British Journal of Psychiatry*, 160, 668–73.

Mullen, P., Martin, J., Anderson, J., Romans, S. and Herbison, G. (1993) Childhood sexual abuse and mental health in adult life. *British Journal of Psychiatry*, 163, 721–32.

NICE (2002) *Core Interventions in the Treatment and Management of Schizophrenia in Primary and Secondary Care. Clinical Guideline 1*. London: National Institute for Clinical Excellence.

Padesky, C. and Greenberger, D. (1995) *Clinician's Guide to Mind Over Mood*. New York: Guildford Press.

Pharoah, F.M., Rathbone, J., Mari, J. and Streiner, D. (2003) *Family Intervention for Schizophrenia (Cochrane Review)*. The Cochrane Library, Issue 3. Oxford: Update Software.

Read, J. and Fraser, A. (1998) Abuse histories of psychiatric inpatients: to ask or not to ask? *Psychiatric Services*, 49, 355–9.

Read, J., Mosher, L. and Bentall, P. (2004) *Models of Madness: Psychological, Social and Biological Approaches to Schizophrenia*. Hove, East Sussex: Brunner-Routledge.

Read, J., Agar, K., Argyle, N. and Aderhold, V. (2003) Sexual and physical assault during childhood and adulthood as predictors of hallucinations, delusions and thought disorder. *Psychology and Psychotherapy: Theory, Research and Practice*, 76, 1–22.

Scott, J. (2001) *Overcoming Mood Swings. A Self-help Guide Using Cognitive Behavioural Techniques*. London: Constable and Robinson.

Scott, J. (2002) Cognitive therapy with patients with bipolar disorder. In Morrison, A. (ed.) *A Casebook of Cognitive Therapy for Psychosis*. London and New York: Routledge, pp. 236–64.

Scott, J. and Gutierrez, M. (2004) The current status of psychological treatments in bipolar disorders: a systematic review of relapse prevention. *Bipolar Disorders*, 6, 498–503.

Smith, G. (1999) Linking theory with practice. *Mental Health Care*, 3, 133–5.

Smith, G. and Velleman, R. (2002) Maintaining a family work for psychosis service by recognizing and addressing the barriers to implementation. *Journal of Mental Health*, 11, 471–9.

Smith, G., Gregory, K. and Higgs, A. (2007) *Integrated Approaches to Family Intervention: A Manual for Practice*, London: Jessica Kingsley Publishers, in press.

Smith, J. (2000) *Early Warning Signs. A Self-management Training Manual for Individuals with Psychosis*. Worcestershire Community and Mental Health Trust.

Zubin, J. and Spring, B. (1977) Vulnerability: a new view of schizophrenia. *Journal Abnormal Psychology*, 86, 103–26.

Appendix 1: Medication Management Overview

Compiled by Annie Higgs based on work by Gray (2001) and Gamble and Brennan (2000) (see key to abbreviations at end of chart)

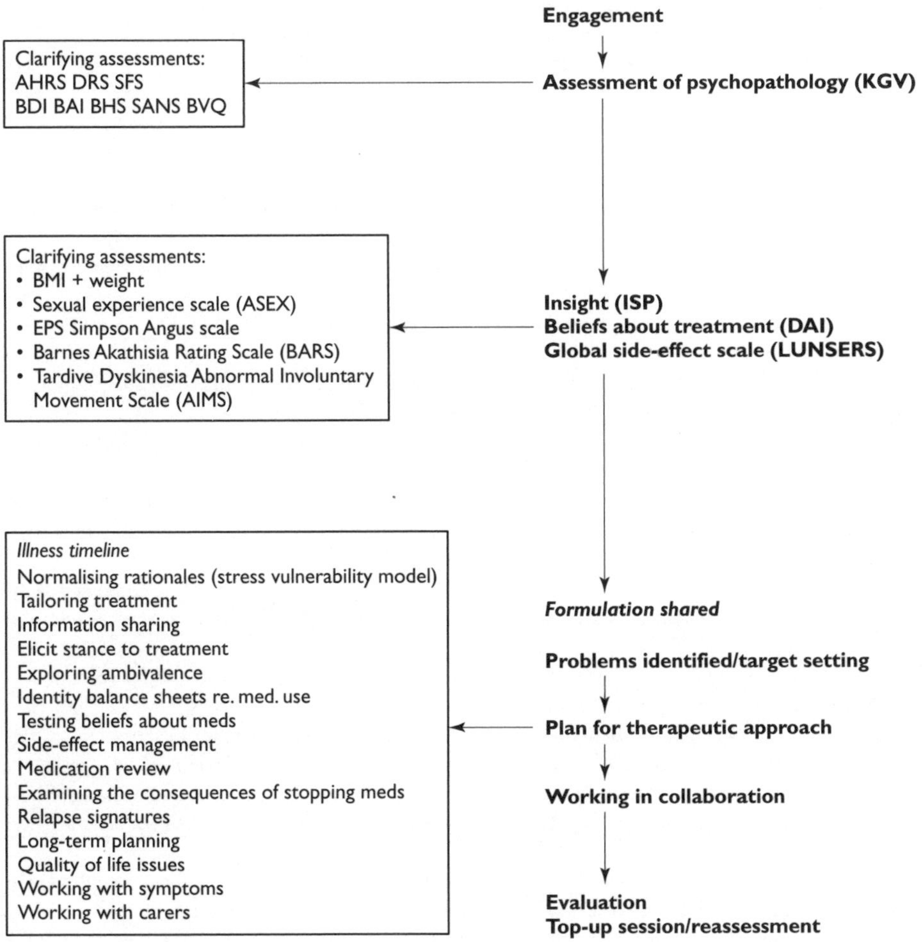

Key to abbreviations:

(A)HRS	Auditory hallucinations rating scale – Haddock et al. (1999)
AIMS	Abnormal involuntary movement scale – Wiener and Lang (1995)
BARS	Barnes akathisia rating scale – Barnes (2003)
ASEX	Arizona sexual experience scale – McGahuey et al. (2000)
BAI	Beck anxiety inventory – Beck and Steer (1990)
BDI	Beck depression inventory – Beck and Steer (1987)
BHS	Beck hopelessness scale – Beck and Steer (1988)
BMI	Body mass index – weight in kilograms divided by (height in metres) squared

BVQ	Beliefs about voices scale – Chadwick and Birchwood (1995)
DAI	Drug attitude inventory – Hogan, Awad and Eastwood (1983)
DRS	Delusion rating scale – Haddock et al. (1999)
EPS	Extrapyramidal symptoms – Simpson and Angus (1970)
ISP	Insight scale for psychosis – Birchwood, Smith and Cochrane (1994)
KGV	Manchester scale – Krawiecka, Goldberg and Vaughan (1977)
LUNSERS	Liverpool University neuroleptic side-effect rating scale – Day et al. (1995)
SANS	Schedule for the assessment of negative symptoms – Andreasen (1982)
SFS	Social functioning scale – Birchwood, Smith and Cochrane (1990)

References for Appendix 1

Andreasen, N. (1982) Negative symptoms in schizophrenia: definition and reliability. *Archives of General Psychiatry*, 39, 784–8.

Barnes, T. (2003) The Barnes akathisia rating scale revisited. *Journal of Psychopharmacology*, 17, 365–70.

Beck, A. and Steer, R. (1987) *Beck Depression Inventory Scoring Manual*. San Antonio Texas: Psychological Corporation.

Beck, A. and Steer, R. (1988) *Manual for Beck Hopelessness Scale*. San Antonio Texas: Psychological Corporation.

Beck, A. and Steer, R. (1990) *Manual for Beck Anxiety Inventory*. San Antonio Texas: Psychological Corporation.

Birchwood, M., Smith, J. and Cochrane, R. (1990) The social functioning scale: the development and validation of a new scale of social adjustment for use in family intervention programmes with schizophrenic patients. *British Journal of Psychiatry*, 157, 853–9.

Birchwood, M., Smith, J., Drury, V., Healy, J., Macmillan, F. and Slade, M. (1994) A self-report insight scale for psychosis: reliability, validity and sensitivity to change. *Acta Psychiatrica Scandinavica*, 89, 62–7.

Chadwick, P. and Birchwood, M. (1995) The omnipotence of voices II: the beliefs about voices questionnaire (BAVQ). *British Journal of Psychiatry*, 166, 773–6.

Day, J., Wood, G., Dewey, M. and Bentall, R. (1995) A self-rating scale for measuring neuroleptic side-effects: validation in a group of schizophrenic patients. *British Journal of Psychiatry*, 166, 650–3.

Haddock, G., McCarron, J., Tarrier, N. and Farager, E. (1999) Scales to measure dimensions of hallucinations and delusions: the psychotic symptoms rating scales (PSYRATS). *Psychological Medicine*, 29, 879–89.

Hogan, T., Awad, A. and Eastwood, R. (1983) A self-report scale predictive of drug compliance in schizophrenics: reliability and discriminative validity. *Psychological Medicine*, 13, 177–83.

Krawiecka, M., Goldberg, D. and Vaughan, M. (1977) A standardised psychiatric assessment scale for rating chronic psychotic patients. *Acta Psychiatrica Scandinavica*, 55, 299–308.

McGahuey, C., Gelenberg, A., Laukes, C., Moreno, F. and Delgado, P. (2000) The Arizona sexual experience scale (ASEX): reliability and validity. *Journal of Sex and Marital Therapy*, 26, 25–40.

Simpson, G. and Angus, J. (1970) Drug-induced extrapyramidal disorders. *Acta Psychiatrica Scandinavica*, 45 (supplement 212), 11–19.

Wiener, J. and Lang, A. (1995) (eds.) *Behavioural Neurology of Movement Disorders: Advances in Neurology*, vol. 65. New York: Raven Press.

Chapter 4

Positive Risk-taking within Family Intervention

Gina Smith, Alison Drage, Emily Drage, James Drage and Michael Drage

Key Points

- Family intervention (FI) is effective.
- Stress-vulnerability models can lead to a culture of avoiding stress for fear of exacerbating symptoms of schizophrenia.
- Family members who are unable to find a way to work with clinicians for the good of their loved one are likely to become either very withdrawn or angry.
- Individual cognitive behavioural therapy (CBT) offers the service user some privacy to explore the meaning of his experiences before sharing them with his relatives.
- FI provides an opportunity for a person diagnosed with schizophrenia to explain to his relatives how his symptoms are affecting him.
- A family worker can continue to work with a family for a number of years, providing ongoing support, without creating a sense of over-dependence.
- Families and clinicians working together can create a climate for positive risk-taking. Within this the service user should always maintain some sense of control.

Introduction

This chapter describes the collaborative work which was undertaken between two siblings, James and Emily, who were both diagnosed as having schizophrenia, their parents Michael and Alison, and two family workers. The chapter will explore how this collaboration helped James to leave hospital to live independently in his own flat. This involved individual CBT to help him gain a greater understanding of the experiences that led to his diagnosis, as well as family meetings with his parents, facilitated by the two family workers. In these meetings James explained his difficulties to them, which enabled them to pool their resources and work together towards recovery. To a lesser extent, Emily's experience of schizophrenia and its impact on the family will also be discussed.

The notion of vulnerability to schizophrenia being exacerbated by stress (Zubin and Spring 1977) underpinned the family work. For example, it offered an explanation for the ways that James appeared to manage his symptoms initially by avoiding activities that he found stressful. Gradually his parents were able to use the understanding gained through FI to help him see the difference between 'good' and 'bad' stress, and through this he and his sister Emily are learning the value of trying new things, or 'positive risk-taking' as the authors have come to define it. A transactional model of stress (adapted from Goetsch and Fuller 1995) is included as a means to begin to explain why carers become overwhelmed.

This chapter provides an opportunity to see in action the policies relating to FI and to meeting the needs of carers. The authors hope that their reflections will prove helpful to others.

The Evidence

During the late 1950s, Brown, Carstairs and Topping (1958) were monitoring the progress of patients leaving hospital. As predicted, those going to large, impersonal hostels coped badly, but unexpectedly so did some returning to live with spouses or parents, while those with siblings or landladies fared best. Further investigation (Brown et al. 1962) led to a realisation that the emotional climate of the home environment influences outcomes in schizophrenia. From this, the term 'high expressed emotion' was introduced (Brown and Rutter 1966) to describe the emotionally charged environments, characterised by high levels of criticism and hostility or over-involvement which were associated with an increased risk of relapse for a person suffering from schizophrenia. Consequently, a number of intervention models were devised, based on the hypothesis that the course of schizophrenia could be improved by reducing expressed emotion (EE). However, changes in EE are not merely dependent on intervention (Falloon et al. 1985): sometimes a spontaneous move from high to low EE is found when a patient's condition stabilises. This indicates that EE is a representation of the relationship and not a personality trait of the relative concerned (Kuipers and Bebbington 1988).

It appears that high levels of criticism are associated with higher levels of burden (Jackson, Smith and McGorry 1990) and that there is a relationship between high EE, disturbed behaviour and greater subjective burden, as carers perceive themselves as not coping effectively (Smith et al. 1993). Scazufca and Kuipers (1996) found some correlation between high EE and burden, suggesting critical comments or emotional over-involvement are outward signs of burden.

The correct use of EE, as a means to measure a carer's emotional response to the service user (Leff and Vaughn 1985), is sometimes lost. The consequent lack of understanding can lead to a label of high EE being employed pejoratively (Hatfield 1997). The following quotation provides an example to demonstrate such misuse, attaching EE to the person rather than the relationship: 'a significantly higher number of patients living with high EE relatives relapse than patients living with low EE relatives' (Barrowclough, Tarrier and Johnson 1996, p. 691). And even when the term is used appropriately, families may still feel blamed (Johnstone 1993). Therefore EE does not appear to be a useful concept to share with families without a link to attributions.

A criticism of the EE theory is that it does not provide a means to understand the complexities of family life. This is because it does not account for other sources of stress (such as financial problems or other family members in need of particular attention) that may occur in addition to caring for a relative with serious mental health problems (Rungreangkulkij and Gillis 2000).

Ways to provide assistance to families coping with schizophrenia were explored through well-crafted 'first generation' FI studies over two decades ago (for example Falloon, Boyd and McGill 1984; Tarrier et al. 1988). These interventions, which became known as family work, adopted a psycho-educational approach (Gamble and Midence 1994). They aimed to help the family to develop a shared understanding of the disorder, and appropriately attribute what may previously have been thought of as awkward behaviours that the service user can easily control, to attempts to cope with schizophrenia (Kuipers, Lam and Leff 2002). Although there is some concern about how these studies defined and used relapse as a measure for failing or effective intervention, there remains continued uncertainty about what the 'active ingredients' exactly are in these interventions (Lam 1991). However, it is widely agreed that FI is effective (Pitschel-Walz et al. 2001; Pharoah et al. 2003).

Despite the evidence of its effectiveness, most workers who have undergone training to work with families encounter difficulties using their skills in routine clinical practice (Fadden 1997). The situation was no different in Bath until Gina and a few other interested practitioners approached their Trust Director of Research and Development (Richard Velleman) for assistance. Together they devised a strategy that engaged the Trust board (Smith 1999), who then invested in trying to find a solution to the common problem. Their finding that FI needs a 'service champion' to promote and sustain their delivery (Smith and Velleman 2002) is becoming more widely accepted (Burbach, personal communication 2004; Kelly and Newstead 2004).

In practice, psychological treatments, including FI, require the clinician to have a theoretical understanding of the presenting problem (Clements and Turpin 1992). For this, a stress- vulnerability model (Zubin and Spring 1977; Nuechterlein 1987) is particularly useful, suggesting possible contributing factors from the individual and the environment, and the bearing they may have on each other (see chapter 1 for a more complete explanation). It is easily understood by clients owing to its face validity, thus facilitating a therapeutic relationship, while having the flexibility to encompass all professions. This brings together workers within a multi-disciplinary team through a common understanding, leading to a clear plan for the service user. This is especially valuable for a sufferer with schizophrenia, who may otherwise continue to struggle while professionals focus on the reliability and validity of the diagnosis, rather than the client's real concerns.

However, the stress-vulnerability model can be criticised for presenting an implicit message that stress should be avoided because it increases the risk of acute symptoms for someone vulnerable to illness. This can then cause a problem if the service user or their carers see them as unable to take on any new challenges for fear of becoming unwell. In practice, this pitfall can be avoided by ensuring that carers' attributions are explored during the initial stages of FI. (It is beyond the scope of this chapter to describe and discuss attribution theory, which is conspicuously absent from most family work literature. Exceptions are the excellent descriptions found in Barrowclough, Johnston and Tarrier 1994 and 1996 and the EPPIC guidelines for working with families (EPPIC 1996.)

The Case Study

Editors' note: this case study is about four members of the Drage family: Michael and Alison, the parents, and the two youngest of their five children, James and Emily. It tells the story of the last eight years, from when first James, and then Emily, developed what was later diagnosed as schizophrenia, through the initial interactions with mental health services, and then the subsequent work with the Families and Psychosis service. The case study is written jointly by all four of these family members, alongside Gina Smith, the founder of the Families and Psychosis service within the Avon and Wiltshire Mental Health Partnership NHS Trust, who undertook much of the work with the family, collectively and individually.

Family History

Michael says:

At the present moment my family seem to be almost OK. But schizophrenia is a condition that rarely disappears completely, although containment through the proper use of medication and psychosocial support networks is usually effective in most cases. However we are constantly aware that the long shadowy fingers of this illness can reach out and grasp again, almost it seems at the drop of a pin. The scary edge of psychotic relapse is never too far away.

Eight years ago the Drages had no real idea what was about to hit them. For nearly 20 years, they had lived a largely secure and happy family life in a lovely old country house in Wiltshire. Alison had brought up five children, as well as working as a nurse in a variety of settings including the role of school nurse; Michael enjoyed a secure job teaching in a state comprehensive and then in further education, teaching A level psychology, specialising in psychopathology. The house had six bedrooms and two sets of stairs and a pleasant back garden and yard: heaps of room for them and the usual addition of ducks, rabbits, dogs and cats. By 1996 the two eldest boys, Alexander (28) and Jasper (25) had moved away; this left in descending order of age, Louise (21), James (18) and Emily (15). Michael was keen on boats and the family boat 'Dragonfly', a converted 17-foot fishing boat, when not dry-moored in the yard, was the vehicle of many exciting family holidays on the Thames. It could be said with some truth that 'things were set pretty fair'. However, they were not to know what lay ahead of them.

Illness strikes

James was the first to go.

Michael says:

He began to change and disappear about eight or nine years ago. Physically present most of the time, the personality we thought we knew gradually slipped away and was replaced by a stranger, a semi-violent, suspicious, deceitful stranger, that was haunted and hunted down by a thousand voices, delusions and hallucinations. His family was the enemy and his world was peopled with armies, spies, gangs, bombs and plots. James became the target of a vicious, unrelenting storm of reality distortion that is referred to as paranoid psychosis. That part of his personality that was kind, affectionate, gentle and trusting had been almost replaced with a deep psychotic mess diving down through inner space. There appeared to be no rational mind left, no learning, no affection, no insight and no morality. It seemed that there were three tools left in his engagement with the normal world: anger, suspicion and distrust. Every material possession was destroyed, every family relationship mostly faded away. We seemed to have lost him. Who was next?

Alison says:

For some years we saw James through many crisis situations and felt powerless in our attempts to help him through what we believed was a very difficult adolescence. We failed at every turn. I felt as his mother a mixture of emotions from worry and anger, to feelings of deep hurt and exasperation. On the journeys from work I would reluctantly return home, full of trepidation. How long as a family could we go on lurching from crisis to crisis? It seemed that our reasonable expectations for James were gradually disappearing from sight. I had a real sense that James could soon end up in prison. How would he cope given his fundamental over-sensitive nature? James was then an adult so perhaps for him to move into a flat could help him grow up and become responsible for his own actions. With hindsight this was just wishful thinking on my part.

Very soon after James' move it became evident that he was suffering from paranoid schizophrenia and needed a psychiatric assessment. This eventually happened with our help, including an important letter from us to our doctor. James was then formally diagnosed with schizophrenia, although I think we'd already guessed, but not allowed ourselves to admit it; this made sense of some of his childhood and most of his adolescent years. Looking back, although I thought I had some knowledge about mental illness, in reality it was like discovering a parallel universe and not a very nice one at that.

James says:

Looking back at that time I was feeling that everything was OK, but clearly my parents knew something was wrong. I remember that my parents were trying to tell me about the local street gang and how they were using me. I thought the gang was OK and were my friends and that my parents had got it all wrong. I didn't want to believe what my parents were saying. Everything was a big dangerous game really.

James was diagnosed with schizophrenia in July 1997 when he was 19; three months later, under the strong grip of paranoia, he entered the mental health system. In 2002 he was sufficiently recovered to take on the responsibility of a small flat. Wondrously and to the delight of James and parents, he is still there and 'getting a life'. What was the nature of this recovery and how did it happen?

Treatment and recovery

Prior to James being admitted to an acute psychiatric ward, he and his family experienced a horrifying 'roller-coaster' of suffering, conflict and despair, drugs, gangs, police helicopters, courts, debts and minor infringements of the law. All this culminated in James' diagnosis and eventual admission to hospital under section three of the 1983 Mental Health Act (Department of Health 1983). There were many difficult times during this hospital admission for all the family, but very gradually, changes for the better set in. Both family and professionals attribute this change to the following:

1 The willingness of professionals and family to stand back and give James space to re-engage the world in his own time.
2 Allowing James to realise his options as he sees them and make his own choices, including medication; this enabled him to set-up small risk-taking ventures that revealed the evidence about his world he needed to know.
3 Ongoing one-to-one CBT sessions with a skilled worker (Gina) who took the time to learn how to work collaboratively with James.
4 The whole family enjoying the support network of a flexible, tailor-made intervention service that has no set end date.
5 James and family members learning to work together with members of the care team to resolve problems as they arose.

Alison says:

While James was on the acute ward and later in the hospital rehabilitation unit it was traumatic to see him suffer not only the symptoms of his illness, but also the side-effects of the various medications. I am not sure which was worse for him at times.

I tried to make sense of events and feelings in my way, while Michael did the same in his way. I tended then to withdraw into myself and become inaccessible; my husband became even more extroverted and wanted constant communication. As we reacted to similar events in an opposing way, it caused much conflict and misunderstanding.

I believed from the beginning when James was on the acute ward that it would be totally unrealistic for us to take on the main responsibility for his care. Michael was busy drawing up a care plan for James and getting frustrated with staff, for no one in the rehabilitation unit seemed to be interested in implementing it!

Michael says:

The 'drawing up of a care plan' for James is a good example of my ignorance, anxiety and unrealistic expectations about James' true condition at that time!

In January 1998 the mental health trust which included the hospital where James was an inpatient began to invest in trying to implement FI within routine clinical practice; Gina was the project manager.

Gina says:

In spring 1998 James and his parents were referred to me for FI. Interestingly, although in my role to promote family work I had been trying to help staff understand how such interventions can benefit service users, I think this referral was generated by the staff's difficulty in not knowing how best to communicate with Michael.

I had met Alison and Michael some months previously at a workshop about family work run by Julian Leff, an international expert in this field. Despite their obvious distress, their wish to work together to help their son shone through. This insight helped me in our future work together, even when they appeared quite disparate.

Although the drive from staff was for me to tame Michael, I chose to speak to James first, to explain family work to him. He was still very guarded at this point so I merely said that most people in his situation benefited from support from their families, and that families could be more supportive if they understood more about the individual's experience of schizophrenia. He agreed it would be useful if we worked together to help them understand, so I arranged to visit Alison and Michael at home.

Individual assessments

Michael says:

I have to say how very difficult it was at first to 'deal' with Gina on a one-to-one basis. Being well informed about mental disorders was no shield against the shame and stigma I felt; I thought she saw me as shamed, frightened and angry, clutching at the falling pieces of pride and knowledge, pathetically trying to maintain control. Indeed there were times when I felt we could cope on our own! I did not even see the suffering of my wife, or that I was adding to this suffering.

Gina? Who was she? She had a nice face I remember, but so did some of the other professionals who had been out of their depth. What did Gina have that was so special? What did she really know about psychosis close to? I guess I wanted a big row and to get really nasty, but she was so nimble witted and unpretentious that there was no steady target to aim at!

Alison says:

I was surprised and encouraged by James' acceptance of Gina's help. Over the following months I felt that Gina's optimism was misplaced and I believed at times that she must be from another planet! These ideas of mine were confirmed when James relapsed a number of times while in rehabilitation. I felt the need to protect myself by not hoping. But I had to trust Gina as a professional. It is true that I know my son but I had no experience of someone recovering from a severe mental illness.

Gina says:

I found the structured approach to FI advocated by Barrowclough and Tarrier (1992) extremely valuable at this point. The loose structure of the relative assessment interview (Barrowclough and Tarrier 1992) followed by the knowledge about schizophrenia interview (Barrowclough et al. 1987) provided the framework I needed to elicit both strengths and areas of need.

My approach was also informed by the concept of accurate empathy (Rogers 1959), which I hope I achieved through empathic warmth and reflective listening; my aim was to understand, without judging individual's feelings and perspectives. The rationale for this respectful stance comes from the work of Miller (1983), who found that an accepting attitude built a therapeutic alliance that supported clients' self-esteem, a prerequisite for change.

I was very aware of Michael's anger and Alison's sadness. I tried to convey my own optimism that their situation could improve through my experience of working with other families. I was also interested in what they both knew and what they had found useful in the past, which I hope, at some level, reminded them of their strengths.

I am aware that investing in the hope that things can get better may present a risk of feeling vulnerable (Deegan 1996), and that for Michael this could exacerbate his anger. At all times I tried to avoid confrontation by providing clear information and encouraging discussion.

Based on this information gained from these assessments, I began formal family intervention with James and his parents, co-working with his primary nurse from the hospital rehabilitation unit to ensure that the family work was well integrated with the rest of the treatment plan.

Education

Providing information about schizophrenia for relatives when a family member has received this diagnosis is a well recognised means to 'increase the family's understanding and tolerance of the patient, and improves their ability to set limits appropriately' (Anderson, Hogarty and Reiss 1980, p. 493). But in this case the family were in some ways already very well informed, Alison through her training as a nurse and Michael as a lecturer in psychopathology.

Gina says:

What I felt we lacked was the deeper knowledge of what James was experiencing. So what my co-worker and I tried to do was to help him to try to be clear about how schizophrenia was affecting him and to encourage him to recognise himself as 'the expert' (Falloon, Boyd and McGill 1984, p. 140). He was then able to be clearer about what he found helpful, thereby enhancing the constructive support that his parents and the rest of the care team could offer.

I also tried to ensure that James received a consistent message about being 'the expert'. He talks now about how frequently he felt his views were devalued or dismissed as symptoms, particularly when he disagreed with his psychiatrist. Sadly it appears that this type of oppression is not uncommon (Repper and Perkins 2002). Initially I think this experience did compound James' feelings of paranoia, but as it became possible to talk about it in family meetings he saw that others recognised what was happening and we were able to make plans to overcome it. At first this involved his parents or me speaking on his behalf, but gradually James did gain the confidence to speak up for himself and by the time he left hospital he had achieved a truly collaborative relationship with his psychiatrist.

As well as the family work, I also worked with James individually, using cognitive behavioural therapy to help him explore issues that were too personal to work on in family meetings. He used these sessions to make sense of his own experiences, devise ways to check the beliefs he had about what others thought of him, develop coping strategies to manage symptoms of schizophrenia not controlled by medication, and decide how much to share with other people. When he felt the individual work was complete, James summed it up as helping him to see the bigger picture.

Over many months James helped everyone involved in his care to understand his difficulties and how they could best support him to move things forward at his own pace. For me this can best be described as a process of guided discovery, which entailed setting up experiments and sometimes taking risks, to gather the information necessary to make plans. I believe learning 'to see the bigger picture' through individual CBT helped him to take bigger 'risks', such as going on holiday to Cornwall, while still an inpatient.

Managing stress

As noted earlier there is an implication within the stress-vulnerability model that all stress is bad and therefore should be avoided by the vulnerable person. A useful counter-argument to this is provided by *The Capable Practitioner* (SCMH 2000), which describes some of the skills a worker should demonstrate under the heading 'positive risk-taking'. This provided a framework for Gina's work alongside the belief held by Alison, Michael and herself that learning takes place and confidence grows by trying things out (or 'behavioural experiments' as it may be called in the CBT literature). A good deal of time was spent both in family meetings and in conversations with his parents, helping James to feel prepared to cope with the effects of stress that would accompany trying new things. The authors of this chapter have since come to talk about 'good' and 'bad' stress and define stress in general terms as 'emotional tension'. 'Good stress' describes the feelings of hope and excitement that accompanies new experiences, and is ideally of short duration; whereas 'bad stress' is generated when feeling out of control and angry for long and continuing periods of time; this concept was informed by Goleman (1996) and the work of Selye (1956). Indeed, Selye (1956) argues that (perceived) moderate stress can be beneficial, and the authors of this chapter would maintain that this remains true for someone recovering from psychosis.

James says:

Eventually my life at the rehabilitation unit became calmer . . . it became a safer place to be. I started to lose the feelings of powerlessness and a kind of control over things began to be mine. I began to realise who I was and where I was and how I got there.

A particular source of stress for Alison and Michael was James' use of street drugs, which they could see was hindering his recovery. It was noticeable however that initially James did not share their view. This could be explained theoretically as them being at different stages of the change model developed by Prochaska and DiClemente (1986). This model describes various stages of readiness to change that an individual may experience, ranging from pre-contemplation (no acceptance of a problem), through contemplation (considering the pros and cons of change) and action, to maintenance of the desired change.

Gina says:

I was very aware of James' use of street drugs as a source of great conflict between him and his parents. This was most evident in one of the first family meetings, when James' behaviour seemed to be influenced by a stimulant. I could see that he did not want to accept advice from his parents and was not ready to change. Although we did not discuss the Prochaska and DiClemente model explicitly, it underpinned my interventions at this point. In practice, my co-worker and I steered Alison and Michael away from trying to persuade James to change and instead guided them to work with the rest of the care team to increase his motivation to change (Miller and Rollnick 1991).

This strategy worked well. James began to make a connection between his street drug misuse and his inability to process information effectively and within a year he stopped using them completely. Some months later he gave up cigarettes too because, he says, the voices told him to. This suggests that voices in some instances can be helpful, although James says it is difficult to know when they can be trusted.

James says

I stopped smoking in August 1999 and hid the money in my wardrobe. When a member of staff told me about a place in Cornwall, I realised no one knew me there and that I could go for a holiday. I did . . . for two weeks and spent my cigarette money!

Returning to rehab. I felt different; I could live a life outside hospital! The nurses were different; they trusted me. I felt more alive, in control and could even manage my medication.

A few months earlier I had tried a Princes Trust venture . . . not my idea. Things went wrong . . . it was a government thing . . . too like school and hospital where I had no choice . . . my voices told me that 'they were watching and that this was a set-up to get me'. I panicked and left on the first day, although part of me wanted to stay. What saved me was having the choice to back out.

Now, so long as I get real choice, things are much easier. Like getting a motorbike. Having my own flat is a big plus but I wish I had my own front door!

Around the time James was admitted onto an acute ward Alison became aware that her youngest daughter Emily was experiencing difficulties; she subsequently developed schizophrenia too.

Alison says:

With hindsight, perhaps Emily's existing difficulties became more evident at college, because more was expected of her. Gradually her thought processes became more muddled. She appeared to be lying constantly, but I believe now that her muddled thinking caused her to say whatever came into her mind at a given time.

Over the next seventeen months Emily became psychotic and was admitted on to an acute ward under section three of the Mental Health Act (Department of Health 1983). We had given her a huge amount of help over these months but nothing worked. I became unwell with a stress-related depression and believed I would have to give up work indefinitely.

Coping with guilt

Alison says:

Up until Emily's admissions into hospital, James and our family had been receiving FI for 10 months. We had come to a difficult decision not to have James home but to help and support him from a distance. It was with great heartache that we came to the same decision with Emily. As a mother, I felt extreme guilt. This guilt was compounded by some of the ward staff making it known to us that they thought that we should have Emily home. Gina was able to liaise with the ward staff on our behalf to explain our decision. This intervention made our visits to Emily more comfortable.

It was during Emily's second psychotic episode (at a different hospital) that her psychiatrist had told Emily that she could go home. This was without any prior consultation with us. I felt so sorry for Emily when we explained, yet again, our reasons for not having her home.

Gina says:

I was very aware of how much pressure both Alison and Michael were under from the hospital staff to have Emily back to live with them, but I thought this would overwhelm them, despite their considerable resources. By this time I felt my relationship with Alison and Michael was strong enough to have a very frank conversation about Emily; with encouragement, Alison was able to agree it would not be fair on any member of their family for Emily to leave hospital to live with her parents again.

During this time I would quite often ring Alison, as I felt she would need a great deal of support to stick to the painful decision she had had to make.

Alison says:

Gina helped me to see that Emily's needs could be best served by involving different professionals in day-to-day care alongside our support. We needed then, and still need now, to keep strong so as to enable our very vital support for James and Emily to be there when required. I knew that if I took on day-to-day care it would be detrimental for all concerned. But as a mother I wanted to protect James and Emily; here enters the guilt and therefore a real emotional conflict.

Emily did not return to live with her parents, but with a great deal of help from Alison and Michael she was able to move into a residential home that has staff available 24 hours a day.

Seven months later she is able to reflect on the episode described above concerning this psychiatrist and his staff team.

Emily says:

When I was at this hospital I was asked by the doctor to recover at home because there were not enough beds on the ward. I automatically said 'yes'. But deep down inside I knew it was not possible. This doctor did not even call my parents about all this. Thinking about this I should have stood up for my parents' wishes. I feel a bit ashamed of myself really. [These are not her exact words, but her parents' interpretation of her spoken sentiments at the time.]

Michael says:

This incident was a horrid experience for all concerned. There was no prior consultation with ourselves and our perception was that it was a fait accompli. It caused weeks of distress and clouds of guilt. To our mind, what had been strongly suggested to Emily and more or less agreed upon without any attempt at home assessment or consultation, was unprofessional and extremely damaging. In the event, it did destroy hard won collaborative relations with key staff. The psychiatrist in question hotly denied that sending Emily home 'in his clinical judgement' had anything to do with running out of beds. I do not think anyone present at that last meeting with the team and family believed this denial. Of course bed-blocking entered into the equation, for the way things are in our mental health services, it had to. It was the way it had been handled that was totally unacceptable.

This transactional model of stress shown in Figure 4.1 appears to explain the high stress experiences of Michael and Alison at this time.

The model shows that when perceived demand rises (in this instance both children diag-

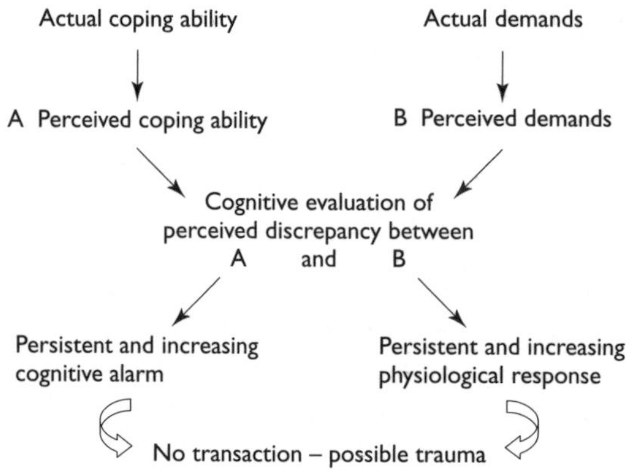

Figure 4.1 A transactional model of stress (adapted from the work of Cox (1975) and Goetsch and Fuller (1995))

nosed with schizophrenia, accompanied by a lack of adequate services) then the perceived inability to meet that demand also rises. The demand and the need to meet it, at this point, is made even more intense as it is fuelled by the basic instinct of parental care. For both parents it was the perceived demand and the perceived inability to meet the demand that caused their levels of stress to reach such heights. They could not 'pay the price' to save their loved ones. No transaction was apparently possible.

Alison and Michael write:

Our perceived inability to pay the price and to meet the demands, though longing to do so, rendered us close to despair. This is the nature of the carer burden when it first descends. We became like moths driven to immolation on the twin furnaces of psychosis and instinct.

It seems paramount to the authors that mental health services at all levels (but especially at acute ward level) should become aware of the forces in operation here, and do nothing to fuel the flames. This sadly remains a crucial training issue.

Goal setting

Gina says:

We never used a formal process of goal setting or problem-solving as described in the literature (for example, Falloon, Boyd and McGill 1984; Barrowclough and Tarrier 1992) in the family meetings, because this was already the way Alison and Michael operated. We did, however, discuss possibilities, made plans, and carefully recorded the things any of us intended to do between sessions, so that we could discuss them at the following meeting. This allowed us all to begin to understand what worked and how to build on everyone's strengths.

I think the main task for me and my co-worker was to help the family realise their skills and to help them pace themselves for the long journey towards recovery.

Alison says:

Gradually, the family work for psychosis service came to our rescue and slowly created a collaborative partnership with Michael, James and myself, and eventually with the whole family including Emily, in a more indirect way.

Maintenance and ongoing support

Recovery for James was slow, painful and is still not yet complete. However, given a suitable medication which he chooses to take, an alert support network, and a not-too-close accepting and understanding family nexus, he should continue to take the right risks at the right time and so gradually increase his ownership of his life. The risk of relapse remains, but James is learning, step by step, to keep that risk low in all that he does. When an event threatens his stability, he now recognises the unwelcome symptoms and calls for a family/support network meeting at once. This is his 'red button', which he trusts. This ongoing family intervention service response for James and his parents is a crucial ingredient in the maintenance of recovery (Drage et al. 2006).

James says:

This chapter is really about taking risks; and through CBT sessions with Gina, family meetings, and working with Dad on a project about the Thames, I gradually came to realise that taking moderate risks (moderate for me that is) was a good way to begin to recover.

For a long while I had been living in a big jumble, not knowing what was reality and what was fantasy, what was real and what was not. Risk-taking was and is 'experimenting', a way of collecting evidence. In this way I could become more confident about the decisions I came to, the things I was seeing and the things I was feeling. For example: riding my motorbike, taking on a flat, flying a radio controlled model airplane, fixing a holiday in Cornwall for me and my sister, trusting my parents . . . and respecting my psychiatrist, who gradually changed in my head from a stubborn arrogant sort of beast who always saw my opinions as part of my psychosis, to almost a trusted friend who saw me as a normal person with important insights. When he eventually left I almost missed him!

I like people to treat me as a normal person for I believe I am becoming so. We've all got something wrong with us, we all have ups and downs. I know I will have to live with my illness and medication probably forever . . . but so what. I can do it and it helps a lot if others see *me*, not just the illness I have.

Just recently I have agreed to work voluntarily with Mind and get some training so that I can befriend and help others who are in this jumble, perhaps for the first time. I can do this . . . I have been there . . . on the *inside* and it is very scary. So, there's something good I can do . . . a life to live. I should be able to do it.

Emily says:

I feel that people like me with mental health problems should take risks in their lives because that's how they're going to find more confidence in themselves. It's a way of putting the past behind me and overcoming my boredom. I took an Open University part time course recently. Ok I didn't finish it but I've learned a lot about myself and there's always another time. It was too big a risk to take and I can think of other things I want and should be able to do . . . with one-to-one support. [As before, this is her parents' interpretation.]

Alison says:

Being realistic, I do not believe I will ever completely come to terms with the fact that both James and Emily have a severe mental illness. The deep grief that I felt has been partially healed by James' gradual recovery and therefore the return of our son and a more stable married life for us.

Michael says:

I believe we all have our mental prisons to cope with, though for those who live with psychosis the prison bars and walls are so much stronger and the walls so much thicker and the normal escape mechanisms we employ simply do not work. James suffers still from paranoid schizophrenia. He and those who suffer like him, who want meaningful occupation beyond eating, sleeping and watching television, desperately need a hope-inspiring professional to take them through. This journey into risk experimentation is hazardous and needs very careful expert management. Medication alone is not enough. In the long run, individual CBT and FI should be cost effective in many cases of psychosis, to help people get to and stay on their individualised recovery roads.

James says:

One thing is for sure, I owe much to my family, to Gina, and to my support network. I was lucky; if it's just the patient against the system with no support network and intervention, then the patient doesn't stand a chance of walking that recovery road. That's what I think anyway. There should always be room for the patient's insights to be considered by the professionals, in order to further recovery. People like me speak from the inside and this will often clash with what the professionals outside of the illness want to do. When I want to do something that my voices say I shouldn't, then I need time, support, space and additional medication perhaps to help me get through that door and stay long enough on the other side. This way, risk-taking can be viewed as a safe experiment and not the road to a relapse. I know it won't be easy. But I know that if I stay the other side of the door long enough, then my tension and voices will grow less and then more ground to live will be mine. I know I need to keep on trying if I want to do something, I don't mean doing a performance for others, but if I am in control, there's a good chance of staying in control for myself. With support, I can stay on the other side, I've stayed there before and I can do it again if it is at my pace.

The National Policy Context

At first glance it could appear that the work between Gina, James and his parents was merely a response to *The National Service Framework for Mental Health* (NSF) (Department of Health 1999) or the NICE guidelines for schizophrenia (NICE 2002), in that it comprised evidence-based interventions for both James as an individual and for the family as a whole. It included assessments of carers' needs and although these were never formalised into a 'carer's care plan', services were organised through the care programme approach (Department of Health 1990) to try to meet the identified needs, which included setting up a local carers' support group, plus family work.

In reality this work preceded the publication of the NSF (Department of Health 1999) by over a year. It was in fact enabled, not by a national policy document, but a local project with Bath Mental Health Care Trust (see Smith 1999; Smith and Velleman 2002 for details) and was founded through a wish to provide a service to families, based on interventions that were known (even at that time) to be effective (Mari and Streiner 1994; since updated a number of times, see Pharoah et al. 2003).

The family work project in Bath was so successful in establishing family interventions in routine practice that it received a government Beacon award in 1999 and was mentioned by name within the NSF as an example of good practice. The service held 'open days' which encouraged many visitors to come to discuss its development with those providing the service, as well as with people who had received it. Although Gina had responsibility for the overall co-ordination of the open days, James, Alison and Michael all played a vital role in helping people who came, to understand some of the essence of what made the service work. Gina benefited too from hearing their reflections and was consequently inspired to seek funding for a small-scale research project to explore how the effectiveness might really be measured in practice. The bid was successful and now Michael works as a part-time researcher with Gina at the University of Bath on this project (see Drage et al. 2006). Without the Beacon award and the general focus now on clinical governance (Department of Health 1997), it is probable that none of this later work would ever have taken place.

A review of research evidence and services provided to support carers of people with mental health problems (Arksey et al. 2002) suggests four principles on which services should be delivered. 'They should be:

- positive and inclusive – mental health professionals should have a positive attitude to carers, involve them in decision-making and recognise them as 'partners' or 'co-experts'
- flexible and individualised – services should be person-centred, reflecting the diversity of carers rather than being picked off a menu of what happens to be available locally
- accessible and responsive – services should be available at all times, including outside office hours, and able to offer a rapid response
- integrated and co-ordinated – services should be 'joined up'; carers' services should be embedded within mainstream mental health services'.

(NHS 2002 (SDO R&D Programme) p. 2)

These principles neatly capture the philosophies of care shared by the authors of this chapter. However, the ways in which this collaboration has evolved (and continues to evolve), as described in this case study, have been exceptional, and even greater than might have been expected. Indeed, being able to write together in this way provides a true example of their partnership.

Conclusion

The spirit of reflection that is ever present, has allowed the Drage family and Gina to consider not only the day-to-day effectiveness of their work together, but also to think about how things might have been different if FI had been available sooner. It is generally accepted that early intervention is a good thing (Birchwood 2003), nevertheless, the grounds on which to intervene are not always clear. Having given this a great deal of consideration it remains unclear whether James' behaviour, which is so easily defined in terms of psychosis, with hindsight, could really have been recognised as such by professionals at the time. This highlights the importance of IRIS guidelines (IRIS 2000) and the Early Psychosis Declaration (WHO 2004) to help raise awareness of recognising the earliest possible signs of schizophrenia and listening to relatives who are able to detect subtle changes in a family member's behaviour (see chapter 2). It is almost certain that James and his parents could have been spared some suffering had there been a greater willingness to accept that families really are *expert by experience*, and it remains a great testament to the Drage's resilience as individuals and as a family (Marsh et al. 1996) that they are here together to tell their tale.

References

Anderson, C., Hogarty, G. and Reiss, D. (1980) Family treatment of adult schizophrenic patients: a psycho-educational approach. *Schizophrenia Bulletin*, 6, 490–505.

Arksey, H., O'Malley, L., Baldwin, S., Harris, J., Mason, A., Newbronner, E. and Hare, P. (2002) *Overview Report: Services to Support Carers of People with Mental Health Problems.* London: National Co-ordinating Centre for NHS Service Delivery and Organisation.

Barrowclough, C. and Tarrier, N. (1992) *Families of Schizophrenic Patients.* Cheltenham: Stanley Thornes.

Barrowclough, C., Johnston, M. and Tarrier, N. (1994) Attributions, expressed emotion and patient relapse: an attributional model of relatives' responses to schizophrenic illness. *Behaviour Therapy*, 25, 67–88.

Barrowclough, C., Tarrier, N. and Johnson, M. (1996) Distress, expressed emotion and attributions in relatives of schizophrenia patients. *Schizophrenia Bulletin*, 22, 691–702.

Barrowclough, C., Tarrier, N., Watts, S., Vaughn, C., Bamrah, J. and Freeman, H. (1987) Assessing the functional value of relatives' knowledge about schizophrenia. A preliminary report. *British Journal of Psychiatry*, 151, 1–8.

Birchwood, M. (2003) Is early intervention in psychosis a waste of valuable resources? *British Journal of Psychiatry*, 182, 196–98.

Brown, G. and Rutter, M. (1966) The measurement of activities and relationships: a methodological study. *Human Relations*, 19, 241–63.

Brown, G., Carstairs, G. and Topping, G. (1958) Post-hospital adjustment of chronic mental patients. *The Lancet*, 2, 685–9.

Brown, G., Monck, E., Carstairs, G. and Wing, J. (1962) Influence of family life on the course of schizophrenic illness. *British Journal of Preventive and Social Medicine*, 16, 55–68.

Clements, K. and Turpin, G. (1992) Vulnerability models and schizophrenia: the assessment and prediction of relapse. In Birchwood, M. and Tarrier, N. (eds.) *Innovations in the Psychological Management of Schizophrenia.* Chichester: Wiley and Sons, pp. 21–47.

Cox. T. (1975) The nature and management of stress. *New Behaviour*, 25, 493–5.

Deegan, A. (1996) Recovery is a journey of the heart. *Psychiatric Rehabilitation Journal*, 19, 91–7.

Department of Health (1983) *Mental Health Act.* London: HMSO.

Department of Health (1990) *The Care Programme Approach for People with a Mental Illness Referred to the Specialist Psychiatric Services.* London: DoH health circular. HC(90)23/LASSL(90)11.

Department of Health (1997) *The New NHS: Modern, Dependable.* London: Department of Health.

Department of Health (1999) *The National Service Framework for Mental Health: Modern Standards and Service Models.* London: Department of Health.

Drage, M., Floyd. S., Smith, G. and Cocks, N. (2006) *Evaluating Family Interventions: A Qualitative Investigation.* Bath: Mental Health R&D Unit, University of Bath.

EPPIC (1996) *The Australian Clinical Guidelines for Early Psychosis.* Parkville, Melbourne, Australia: Early Psychosis Prevention and Intervention Centre (EPPIC). Usually available online, but guidelines under review; see www.eppic.org.au/mhp/resources/clinical_guidelines.htm (accessed 28 September 2005).

Fadden, G. (1997) Implementation of family interventions in routine clinical practice following staff training programmes: a major cause for concern. *Journal of Mental Health*, 6 6, 599–612.

Falloon, I., Boyd, J. and McGill, C. (1984) *Family Care of Schizophrenia.* New York: Guildford Press.

Falloon, I., Boyd, J., McGill, C., Williamson, M., Razani, J., Moss, H., Gilderman, A. and Simpson, G. (1985) Family management in the prevention of morbidity of schizophrenia: clinical outcomes of a two-year longitudinal study. *Archives of General Psychiatry*, 32, 887–96.

Gamble, C. and Midence, K. (1994) Schizophrenia family work: mental health nurses delivering an innovative service. *Journal of Psychosocial Nursing*, 32, 13–16.

Goetsch, V. and Fuller, M. (1995) Stress and stress management. In Wedding, D. (ed.) *Behaviour and Medicine*, 2nd edition. St. Louis, MO: Mosby Year Book, pp. 289–302.

Goleman, D. (1996) *Emotional Intelligence.* London: Bloomsbury Publishing, chapter 11, pp. 164–72.

Hatfield, A. (1997) Working collaboratively with families. *Social Work in Mental Health: Trends and Issues*, 25, 77–85.

IRIS (2000) *Early Intervention in Psychosis: Clinical Guidelines and Service Frameworks and Tool Kit.* Available online: www.iris-initiative.org.uk/guidelines1.pdf (accessed 30 September 2005).

Jackson, H., Smith, N. and McGorry, P. (1990) Relationship between expressed emotion and family burden in psychotic disorders: an exploratory study. *Acta Psychiatrica Scandanavia*, 82, 243–49.

Johnstone, L. (1993) Family management in 'schizophrenia': its assumptions and contradictions. *Journal of Mental Health*, 2, 255–69.

Kelly, M. and Newstead, L. (2004) Family intervention in routine practice: it is possible! *Journal of Psychiatric and Mental Health Nursing*, 11, 64–72.

Kuipers, L. and Bebbington, P. (1988) Expressed emotion research in schizophrenia: theoretical and clinical implications. *Psychological Medicine*, 18, 893–909.

Kuipers, L., Lam, D. and Leff, J. (2002) *Family Work for Schizophrenia*, 2nd edition. London: Gaskell.

Lam, D. (1991) Psychosocial family interventions in schizophrenia: a review of empirical studies. *Psychological Medicine*, 21, 423–41.

Leff, J. and Vaughn, C. (1985) *Expressed Emotion in Families: Its Significance for Mental Illness.* New York: Guildford Press.

Mari, J. and Streiner, D. (1994) An overview of family interventions and relapse on schizophrenia: a meta-analysis of research findings. *Psychological Medicine*, 24, 565–78.

Marsh, D., Lefley, H., Evans-Rhodes, D., Ansell, V., Doerzbacher, B., LaBarbera, L. and Paluzzi, J. (1996) The experience of mental illness: evidence for resilience. *Psychiatric Rehabilitation Journal*, 20, 3–12.

Miller, W. (1983) Motivational Interviewing with problem drinkers. *Behavioural Psychotherapy*, 1, 147–72.

Miller, W. and Rollnick, S. (1991) *Motivational Interviewing: Preparing People to Change Addictive Behaviour.* New York: Guildford Press.

NHS (SDO R&D Programme) (2002) *Briefing Paper: Services to Support Carers of People with Mental Health Problems.* National Co-ordinating Centre for NHS Service Delivery and Organisation.

NICE (2002) *Core Interventions in the Treatment and Management of Schizophrenia in Primary and Secondary Care. Clinical Guideline 1.* London: National Institute for Clinical Excellence.

Nuechterlein, K. (1987) Vulnerability models for schizophrenia: state of the art. In Hafner, H., Gattaz, W. and Janzarik, W. (eds.) *Search for the Causes of Schizophrenia.* Heidelberg: Springer Verlag, pp. 297–316.

Pharoah, F.M. Rathbone, J. Mari, J. and Streiner, D. (2003) *Family Intervention for Schizophrenia (Cochrane Review).* The Cochrane Library, issue 3. Oxford: Update Software.

Pitschel-Walz, G., Leucht, S., Bauml, J., Kissling, W. and Engel, R. (2001) The effect of family interventions on relapse and rehospitalisation in schizophrenia: a meta-analysis. *Schizophrenia Bulletin*, 27, 73–92.

Prochaska, J. and DiClemente, C. (1986) Towards a comprehensive model of change. In Miller, W. and Heather, N. (eds.) *Treating Addictive Behaviours: Processes of Change*. New York: Plenum, pp. 3–27.

Repper, J. and Perkins, R. (2002) *Social Inclusion and Recovery*. Edinburgh: Balliere Tindall.

Rogers, C. (1959) A theory of therapy, personality and interpersonal relationships, as developed in the client centered framework. In Koch, S. (ed.) *Psychology: A Study of a Science. Volume 3*. New York: McGraw-Hill, pp. 184–256.

Rungreangkulkij, S. and Gillis, C. (2000) Conceptual approaches to studying family caregiving for persons with severe mental illness. *Journal of Family Nursing*, 6, 341–66.

Scazufca, M. and Kuipers, E. (1996) Links between expressed emotion and burden of care in relatives of patients with schizophrenia. *British Journal of Psychiatry*, 168, 580–7.

SCMH (2000) *The Capable Practitioner*. London: The Training and Practice Development Section of the Sainsbury Centre for Mental Health.

Selye, H. (1956) *The Stress of Life*. New York: McGraw-Hill.

Smith, G. (1999) Linking theory with practice. *Mental Health Care*, 3, 133–5.

Smith, G. and Velleman, R. (2002) Maintaining a family work for psychosis service by recognising and addressing the barriers to implementation. *Journal of Mental Health*, 11, 471–9.

Smith, J., Birchwood, M. Cochrane, R. and George, S. (1993) The needs of high and low expressed emotion families: a normative approach. *Social Psychiatry and Psychiatric Epidemiology*, 28, 11–16.

Tarrier, N., Barrowclough, C., Vaughn, C., Bamrah, J., Porceddu, K., Watts, S. and Freeman, H. (1988) The community management of schizophrenia: a controlled trial of behavioural intervention to reduce relapse. *British Journal of Psychiatry*, 153, 532–42.

WHO (2004) *Early Psychosis Declaration*. Geneva: World Health Organisation.

Zubin, J. and Spring, B. (1977) Vulnerability: a new view of schizophrenia. *Journal of Abnormal Psychology*, 86, 103–26.

Chapter 5

Assertive Outreach and Family Work

Frank Burbach, John Carter, Jane Carter and Matthew Carter

Key Points

- Assertive outreach (AO) services have been established throughout England as a result of a large evidence base and following their inclusion in *The National Service Framework for Mental Health* (NSF).
- AO is a model of service delivery in which teams work intensively with people with severe mental health problems and complex needs and includes their care-givers.
- If provided in a collaborative, flexible and holistic manner, AO is an effective vehicle for the delivery of psychosocial and medical interventions.
- Family intervention (FI) is highly effective in reducing relapse in people with severe mental health problems and also has benefits in terms of improved social functioning, reducing family stress/burden and a reduction in overall treatment cost.
- Despite the establishment of numerous FI training courses, relatively few FI services have been established in routine clinical settings.
- The literature contains very few reports of the integration of AO and FI, although logically integrating them can maximise the benefits of both services.
- In Somerset FI and AO services have been successfully developed in each of the four Primary Care Trust (PCT) areas.
- 'John's' parents were critical of the mental health services offered in the first 10-year period following John's initial presentation, and did not feel valued as partners in care.
- The 'Carter' family valued the collaborative approach of the AO and FI services, which helped to reduce misperceptions and miscommunication and develop coping strategies within the family.

Introduction

I (Frank Burbach) have drawn this account together to demonstrate the value of integrating family interventions (FI) and assertive outreach (AO). As a founder of the Somerset Family Support Service (FSS) and consultant to and originally the manager who established AO locally, I regularly train and supervise workers in these services. It is from that overview position that I write my reflections on the work carried out with this family.

This chapter is the product of extensive collaboration between the 'Carter' family and the first author. 'John Carter' decided he preferred to remain anonymous as it enabled him to be remarkably open and honest.[1] We are using the names 'Matthew' and 'Jane' for John's parents and 'Linda' for his sister.

Although initially concerned that the process of writing this chapter might be stress-inducing, it soon became clear that the careful retelling of the story was also therapeutic for John and his parents.

John acknowledges that although we 'covered fresh ground in writing this chapter, a lot of the intimate things had already been talked about in the family sessions'. He felt that seeing it in print was 'helpful . . . a declaration . . . recognising that I am possibly unwell'.

Matthew described the process as 'mentally stocktaking . . . it enabled us to look at the whole'. Jane found it 'quite shocking to read the first draft . . . horrible to see it written down', but felt that ultimately she 'really valued it', and felt like saying 'eureka' when John began to revise some of his long-standing beliefs as a result of our detailed exploration.

Writing this chapter is thus part of John's recovery. It describes the mental health services experienced by the Carters: the traditional psychiatric services which were experienced as unsupportive over many years and, more recently, the AO and FI services. It also provides a brief overview of these two services and argues that integrating them is essential if mental health services are to maximise their effectiveness.

The Evidence – Assertive Outreach and Family Intervention

Although there is a growing evidence base for a range of psychosocial interventions (PSI) for schizophrenia and other psychoses, reviews agree that, to date, only FI and AO (or assertive community treatment – ACT) have unequivocal evidence of efficacy (Lehman 1999). These approaches would appear to have much in common. Both have a recovery philosophy – assuming that people with severe mental health problems can live satisfying lives in the community as long as they have appropriate medical treatment, develop adaptive coping strategies for ongoing symptoms, acquire community living skills and have appropriate social support from family and friends. It is surprising therefore that there are few published reports of the integration of these two evidence-based approaches.

Assertive outreach

AO originated in the USA in the late 1970s when multi-disciplinary teams moved into the community, providing intensive, comprehensive services to people who were at high risk of hospital readmission and who could not be maintained by more usual community-based treatment (Stein and Santos 1998). Randomised trials have consistently shown that 'assertive community treatment' leads to a reduction of inpatient admissions and promotes continuity of outpatient care (Marshall and Lockwood 2005). However, later studies did not demonstrate the same effect in reducing the need for hospital care as the earlier US studies, which led to considerable debate about the 'essential ingredients' for AO (Burns 2002). Nonetheless, there is substantial agreement about the nature of AO.

AO provides high levels of input for people who present a risk to themselves or to others and who tend to be difficult to engage in standard services; most have experienced many relapses in the past. It is distinct from other mental health services in that the qualified staff members have small caseloads (10–12) and are able to maintain daily contact, if necessary, for seven days a week. Other distinctive features are that the team members go out to see clients (for example, at home, in local cafés) and the use of a team approach – caseloads are managed jointly by clinicians rather than being assigned to individuals. The (largely USA) research evidence led to the inclusion of AO in the UK *The National Service Framework for Mental Health* (NSF) (Department of Health 1999). Major investment in the new model of service followed the publication of *The NHS Plan* (Department of Health 2000) and AO services were established throughout England based on the service specifications published in the *Mental Health Policy Implementation Guide* (Department of Health 2001).

In Somerset, following a four-week training programme, four dedicated AO teams (one in each PCT area) began delivering this new service in April 2001. In order to emphasise the particular philosophy and clinical approach of the new service, following discussions with service user representatives, we adopted a different name for the Somerset AO service – the Enhanced Community Support (ECS) service. It indicates that the service works closely with the existing mental health services, providing additional (community-based) input for this particular group of clients. It also reflects our collaborative, holistic approach which includes PSI and medical interventions. The service name is also appropriate in that all clients are on *enhanced* integrated care programmes.

Family interventions

Following a number of randomised controlled trials in the 1980s, which indicated that the addition of FI to standard care significantly reduced relapse rates for people with schizophrenia, the UK government specifically recommended the establishment of FI services in 1993 (Department of Health 1993). The importance of involving families/carers in routine mental health treatment was further recognised throughout the NSF (Department of Health 1999), with its revolutionary focus on the 'rights of carers' (see Stanbridge and Burbach 2004).

Robust research studies indicate a four-fold reduction in relapse rates one year after FI; relapse rates increase in the second year but are still only half what they are when only medication is provided. There is also evidence of improved social functioning, a reduction in family burden and a reduction in overall treatment cost (see Fadden 1998). Recent reviews of the trials of FI throughout the world (Bustillo et al. 2001; Dixon, Adam and Lucksted 2000; Mari and Streiner 1996; Pharoah et al. 2003; Pitschel-Waltz et al. 2001) has led to FI being recommended as a routine treatment for schizophrenia in the 2002 NICE guidelines (NICE 2002).

Despite substantial efforts to train the workforce in FI, at the time we were developing our services, relatively few FI services had been established in routine clinical settings (Brooker 2001). Studies at that time (for example, Kavanagh et al. 1993; Brennan and Gamble 1997; Fadden 1997) found that difficulties in the implementation of FI were due both to trainees returning to unsupported work environments and to a difficulty in meeting the range of needs presented by families.

In this context we decided to develop an in-situ, whole-team training approach to promote multi-disciplinary and multi-agency partnerships, transcending existing training structures (Burbach, Donnelly and Stanbridge 2002) to try to establish sustainable FI services in Somerset. We combined cognitive-behavioural and systemic family intervention approaches within a one-year university accredited course and between 1996 and 2001 successfully trained staff in each of our four PCT areas (see Burbach and Stanbridge 1998, 2006). We have since trained further FI workers to 'top up' the teams. Two AO team members conducted the FI described in this chapter; they began working with the family during a FI training course, and continued after completing their training.

The Case Study

Background information

Childhood and early adulthood

John describes himself as having been 'quite a spirited child' and found it quite easy to make friends, which he says 'is a contrast to how I am now'.

Jane describes his early years:

I look back on John's childhood and early teenage years as times of great fun and happiness. [We] had two children in our middle twenties; Linda is only fourteen months the senior and they were almost like twins. We moved around southern England with Matt's work. I worked part-time, school-terms only, so life was pretty good. Linda was an extremely hard-working girl and did very well indeed at school and university. John always seemed to make it by the seat of his pants, but using his charm and good luck did reasonably well at school and university. He travelled in his teens quite extensively with school friends, always keen to visit new countries. He returned home full of enthusiasm, always broke financially. [He] worked in local shops and factories to repay loans.

He was close to his sister and proud of her career in advertising. In retrospect he did not appear to be carving out a career himself, [instead doing] various jobs for local people and agencies.

Despite 'indifferent' A level results at the local boys' grammar school, which John ascribes to 'laziness', he achieved a BA in American Studies. Although he had been drinking heavily, it was not until the age of 21, when he spent a year living and studying in the USA, that he began using cannabis. Following graduation John decided to work in the Sudan, teaching English. He says he enjoyed his work and the experience of such a different culture, but reports that he 'lacked maturity'. He and the three other young men with whom he shared a house all drank heavily, 'smoked a lot of pot', and 'consorted with prostitutes', which resulted in John contracting sexually transmitted infections (STI).

It was during a second period of work in the Sudan that his parents noticed changes in his behaviour.

In the words of his mother:

We were dismayed when he returned for another period to continue this work. We did not know about the cannabis and heavy drinking until several years later, [but] at this time his personality and loving attitude changed. He did not correspond from Africa for such a long time that Matthew contacted the Foreign Office. Eventually he returned to the UK, worked part-time for 18 months teaching English to immigrants and applied for a place at university for a MA in Development Studies. Obviously we all thought that everything was going to be all right.

John remembers that on his return from Africa he felt 'worried/anxious because I feared I had STIs' and that this 'got in the way' of a relationship with Jackie who he had met at work.

His parents hoped that John would 'settle down' following the successful completion of his MA degree. However, this was not to be.

Onset of psychosis

When he had completed his MA, John returned to London and his relationship with Jackie became sexual. This resulted in John becoming 'very worried' and he 'broke down'. Within two months, John (aged 29) unexpectedly returned to Somerset to live with his parents for three months. He was depressed and vulnerable, went for long solitary walks, and needed a lot of emotional support. He wanted to discuss past relationships and, as a result of his concerns about sexually transmitted disease, his parents arranged for private tests for STIs, and although these were negative he continued to believe he was infected. When Matthew rang Jackie at John's request her mother told Matthew of their concern: 'We are praying for John every day but he needs professional help'. Their local vicar showed his concern by giving Matthew and Jane a copy of a book about mental health problems.

Jane recalls thinking that 'John had overdone it – doing his MA in one year', but also 'thought he might have AIDS'. He would come back from job interviews saying that the interviewer 'wouldn't look at me', and when he started a part-time job he soon left, reporting that colleagues 'were talking about me'. In retrospect his father regards this as the 'start of a persecution complex'.

John appeared delighted when they decided to start a family business, which would provide him with employment. However, shortly afterwards, he became agitated and returned to London. Thereafter John's parents became increasingly concerned for his mental health. When they met in the summer of 1990 (John aged 29), his father was struck by John's 'grubby appearance'. He refused to change into a suit for the MA graduation ceremony and showed no pleasure on being awarded the degree. Jane remembers feeling 'horrified . . . his trousers were dirty and he refused to change'.

John's parents described an agonising 18-month period of 'isolation' for John on his return to London.

Jane recounts:

He slowly deteriorated into a life of drinking, some occasional work, no communication with family, not eating. We attempted to visit but he was always angry and abusive or never turned up to arranged rendezvous. He phoned once or twice, saying people were against him. We became quite desperate, not knowing what to do . . . living in Somerset became problematic. Mental health [problems] were something we had no experience of . . . Samaritans were kind but not really practical. John's GP said if we could persuade John to visit him he would let us know. We contacted the Maudsley Hospital – same response really.

Eventually we visited in person the local Social Services department in south London . . . we thought they were going to make it all okay but we came right up against the 'rights of the individual' . . . it had to be [John's] decision to make contact. There was no one at the time to really talk to.

After several awful scenes in London we slowly realised that sectioning could be looming. Matthew and myself did all this intervention on our own, finding out facts, helped by an acquaintance working in Bristol Social Services. Fortunately John agreed at the eleventh hour to go for treatment voluntarily. In our ignorance we hoped he would recover and return as the lovely boy that he once was.

John's account of the onset of psychosis includes many factors described by his parents, particularly moving house in childhood, alcohol and cannabis misuse and worries about STIs:

John says:

My college days (1980–4) were characterised by heavy drinking and cannabis abuse. I grew up during that time, living independently in the USA for a year, aged 21 to 22 . . . I decided to work in Africa on graduation, where I consorted with prostitutes and struggled to cure venereal infection. The alcohol and cannabis abuse persisted on my return to England. A friend in London suggested that I was trying to impose Africa on Europe. I think this attempted transition from England to Sudan and from Sudan to England was really the root of my slowly developing schizophrenia. Although I went back to college I could no longer stop events unravelling.

I care-took a flat in London but there was no escaping the fact that my family was suppressing the knowledge that I had five illegitimate children. I don't think they had the courage to talk to me about it. As a consequence I isolated myself for a year. During the summer of 1990 I was involved in two violent incidents and I began to see people as a threat. On neither occasion was anyone badly hurt.

Reflections

With many people it is notoriously difficult to pinpoint precisely when someone's mental health problems began. John was an intelligent, happy-go-lucky person who drifted into heavy alcohol and cannabis use. His lifestyle was not particularly unusual and mental health problems were not suspected by his parents until the age of 28/29 when he spent three months with them, apparently depressed. At this time he also expressed some paranoid ideas and in retrospect this appears to have been the 'prodrome' (referring to the early symptoms and signs that someone experiences before a full blown syndrome becomes evident – see also chapters 2 and 6) of his psychosis.

Following his return to London on completion of his MA, John became increasingly withdrawn and socially isolated, and in the summer of 1990 lost his job following a serious assault on a colleague whom John thought had turned his girlfriend against him. During this time John also thought that a person on television was telling him what to do and he gave his sister's boyfriend a black eye because 'they were managing knowledge I had a right to know'. The clinical notes from that time record that John believed he had fathered five children, whom he knew by 'metaphorical' means. He severed contact with his family because he believed that his parents and sister were communicating 'metaphorically' and were keeping information regarding his children from him. He believed he was being followed by the colleague he had assaulted, and continued to believe that he had sexually transmitted diseases despite investigations proving negative. He felt symbols and noises had special meanings and experienced auditory hallucinations.

During this time his parents became increasingly concerned about John but as Matthew reports: 'It took until November 1991 before we could get regular treatment for John. We had no offer of support; in fact we were dealt with throughout as interfering parents.'

Although John's parents experienced difficulties 'getting into the system' as described by other families (Howe 1998), it should also be acknowledged that it is often difficult to ascertain whether someone is experiencing psychotic symptoms, particularly if they are bright and socially skilled. In June of 1991 a letter from John's consultant psychiatrist to his GP notes that 'information from John's family indicates that he is clearly psychotic' but that in her consultation he was 'polite, reasonable, pleasant and did not say anything unequivocally delusional or psychotic.'

Treatment phase 1

Once John agreed to accept medication his symptoms appeared to lessen, although he says he still heard voices after a year on anti-psychotic medication. Mental health professionals recorded that medication was effective and a subsequent forensic review (November 2001) noted that John's three relapses over the previous 10 years had all been linked to changes or cessation of medication.

However, it was John's family who provided the 'psychosocial interventions' that enabled him to achieve a reasonable quality of life; these included meaningful work, support, housing and structure. Possibly the most important of these was his parents taking him on as an employee in the family business. John worked for his father for seven years, initially staining, waxing and lacquering furniture, and later doing administrative tasks such as organising deliveries and producing invoices on the computer.

Matthew reports:

[Initially] he was only able to do manual jobs . . . As John improved [he] became less inhibited; I gave him more and more responsible jobs till it reached the stage where he could stand in for me. He managed 10 employees.

Although John had improved substantially working with me, and I believe that we had created an environment in which he could work and find satisfaction, this was probably due to good luck, which ran out in 1999/2000. I decided to merge the business with another and John would not come.

Following his redundancy John tended to stay longer in bed, remained alone in his flat and drank more heavily. His father reports that John was offered little help or support by the community mental health team (CMHT); he (John's father) found their attitude 'appalling': 'We made numerous requests to his support worker and psychiatrist for help, none was forthcoming. John voluntarily went to hospital in June 2001'.

John generally learned not to discuss his long-standing beliefs, but his ongoing symptomatology continued to cause difficulties. For example, in 1996 he had an altercation with a colleague, Martin, over a remark that John believed he made regarding sexual attraction towards Jane. Five years later John committed a serious assault on Martin, who he was convinced was hounding him, was affecting his sleep and wished to do 'obscene' things to him.

After his admission in 2001 to a psychiatric inpatient unit and despite medication, John continued to experience psychotic symptoms, repeatedly absconded, was detained under the 1983 Mental Health Act, transferred to the psychiatric intensive care unit and was assessed by the forensic team owing to ongoing paranoid ideas. During this nine-month period of inpatient treatment he had a number of violent altercations with male patients. He was finally stabilised on Clopixol 400 mg weekly (having previously been prescribed Sulpiride, Risperidone and Prozac) and transferred to Brook House, a rehabilitation unit (24-hour nursing staffed house in the community). However, he continued to experience delusional ideas regarding Martin while living there. John was finally discharged to his parents' home after three months at Brook House, with the hope that he would be rehoused nearby in due course. Referrals were made at this point to the AO and FI services.

Reflection on events leading up to the relapse

The family reported feeling 'totally let down' by the services prior to his admission to hospital . . . the monitoring of John was abysmal'. They felt that more appropriate help might have prevented traumatic experiences such as being arrested and sectioned under the Mental Health Act.

Tracing the sequence of events leading up to this relapse it is clear that services did not respond well. After leaving the family firm in September 1999 he remained unemployed for many months and when he gained employment at a garden centre in September 2000, he soon began misinterpreting events, feeling certain people were against him. John's increasingly concerned parents eventually met with his psychiatrist in January 2001, armed with information provided by Rethink (a mental health charity) regarding medication, and it was agreed that he should try Risperidone. Thereafter, his parents noticed that he became increasingly withdrawn, was drinking more heavily and was preoccupied with thoughts of his 'children'. They returned to the psychiatrist in June 2001 to report that the 'medication was not working' and the psychiatrist telephoned John and arranged for him to take a higher dose. A week later Martin telephoned John's parents to complain that John had been bothering him. They in turn contacted the mental health services and a community psychiatric nurse (CPN) went to visit John later that afternoon. By this time John had made repeated visits to see Martin and had been arrested. As John put it: 'I asked him what he had been doing, bothering me at night . . . I went back a few times and then there was a fight'. When the police took John home to get his medication his CPN was there. Jane remembers that the CPN 'waved goodbye to him in the police car and didn't even tell us'. This was an extremely traumatic experience for John and his parents. Jane continues: 'It was a nine-month period with us floundering . . . [but] we never thought that John would assault anyone'.

His parents were left uninformed again when six weeks later John left the inpatient unit in order to find Martin, was arrested, spent the night in police cells and was subsequently sectioned. Poor communication clearly added to the traumatising effects of the situation and they all agree that it was 'an awful time'.

Treatment phase 2 – enhanced community support (ECS) service

John and his parents clearly recognised the benefits that the ECS offered and contrasted it with the service received prior to this.

Matthew notes:

For the first time we started to have confidence that a structured support system had been put in place . . . Until the ECS team came along we did not feel involved as partners and from time to time felt shabbily dealt with.

John remembers:

They were more thorough, friendlier, more human. Matthew considered them to be a vital support to assist in his recovery programme.

At the time of considering discharge from hospital, an intensive service appeared to be appropriate, owing to John's unstable mental state and concerns about risk. He was one of the first clients to be taken on by the ECS.

During the year that the ECS team worked with John and his family, the team focused on some jointly determined goals: independent housing, developing a larger social network, work/meaningful occupation, finance/benefits and medication management. Team members helped John to complete housing application forms, accompanied John and Matthew to meetings with housing officials, arranged for him to attend walking and yoga groups, and helped him to find work in an internet café. Although these objectives are not significantly different from those found on CMHT care programmes, they were carried out in a more intensive, supportive manner, both on a regular, planned basis as well as in response to crises. For example, an ECS support worker would regularly provide John with transport to and from his supported employment and would sometimes have lunch with him.

ECS workers took a cognitively orientated reality-testing approach to help John to cope with ongoing psychotic symptoms (auditory hallucinations or misinterpretations and delusional beliefs). For example, John believed that Martin was outside his new flat when he heard noises outside. By gently exploring his understanding of these situations John was able to reassure himself that alternative explanations were more likely. His responses were also normalised in terms of a stress-vulnerability model (Zubin and Spring 1977, and see chapter 1) by exploring the context in which John had these worrying experiences, for example, when he was tired and concerned about family matters.

Jane summed up the ECS team's input:

The team visited regularly – helped to maintain benefits, etc. The support worker and the CPN became well known to all of us, they were like friends. This was the first time in our son's long illness that help and advice was at the end of the phone, and also visits in person could be requested and acted upon almost immediately.

Reflections

The ECS team members were able successfully to deliver cognitively oriented interventions because they were people with whom John had developed an open, trusting relationship, who responded quickly and spent the required time with him, and had the skills to help John develop his own coping strategies. This work was complemented by more formal FI sessions within which similar cognitively orientated coping strategy enhancement was undertaken. The formal, regularly scheduled FI sessions and the more flexible support provided to John and his family by the ECS thus provided an effective package of support.

Family support service

John summarised the purpose of the FI sessions as being 'to perpetuate the harmony between the three of use . . . to smooth things over'. Matthew agreed: 'if we three are a motor, they are the lubricant to make sure we work harmoniously together'. Jane felt that the sessions had been helpful because each person's views were elicited and taken on board: 'We blossomed in that room with them . . . it was during these regular meetings we first were able to listen to John explaining much of his fears, and the terrible thoughts he had endured. I feel this was due to skilful questioning by the team and total privacy'.

John remembers that sessions often focused on his fears: 'They asked about my stress levels when I go past Martin's house'.

As a result of these conversations Jane acknowledges: '[We have] more respect for John – he states his case so succinctly, so well . . . we see a flash of the old John . . . [They taught] us a lot about how to deal with John's stress'.

John agrees: 'They deal with me better as a result of the sessions. They understand my fears and how to cope with my fears'.

They contrasted these sessions with the 'noncommittal' responses or unclear/contradictory information previously provided by professionals. Matthew states that: 'For ten years we sought professional advice on how to react to different aspects of John's illness and no one gave us any straight answers'

Jane agrees: 'One said don't agree with John, challenge him and another said don't challenge him, be sympathetic'.

Reflections

The two clinicians conducted the FI sessions using a model that is both cognitive behavioural and systemic (Burbach and Stanbridge 1998, 2006). While focusing on ways people construe one another and their actions (as is the case with most family intervention in psychosis services), our approach also focuses on the interactional patterns in which people have become 'stuck'. In the early sessions it was soon apparent that this family had experienced a high burden of care over the years; they needed to express their justifiable frustration and anger with the mental health services to date. This had to be balanced with the need to facilitate more open dialogue between John and his parents, as John tended to be somewhat withdrawn and silent in the sessions. The pattern that had been established over the years could be summarised as in Figure 5.1.

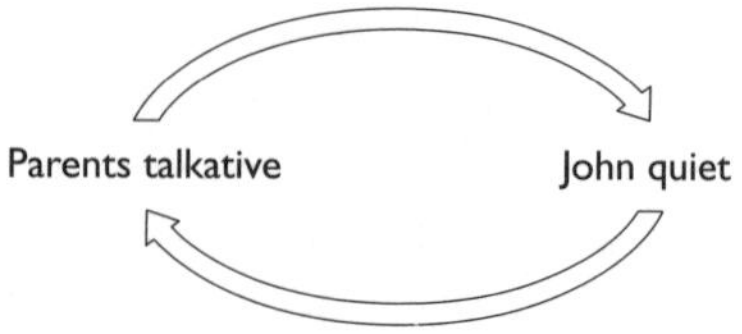

Figure 5.1

Understanding behaviour as part of an interactional pattern is helpful because it provides a non-blaming perspective based on the notion of circular causality, rather than linear causality. We can hypothesise that the pattern between John and his parents had arisen over many years for understandable reasons. As is common in such situations, John appears to have learned, over the years, not to discuss his beliefs with others, as disclosure was met by a range of dismissive reactions. Like many other sufferers of severe and enduring mental health problems, John has tended to become less active, more withdrawn, and dependent on others. Simultaneously, his parents had to take on increasingly active roles in supporting him, but did not know how to react to John when he occasionally shared some of the psychotic experiences which were preoccupying and troubling him (see Figure 5.2). Their understandable responses to one another have thus been mutually reinforced, with the

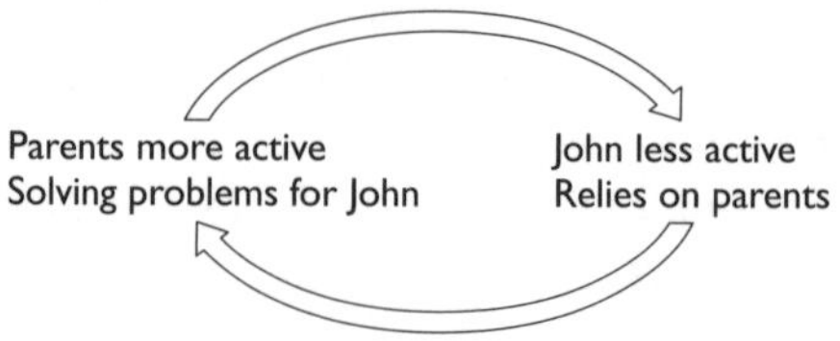

Figure 5.2

result that they have become locked in a repeating pattern. Such patterns have a major effect, with people acting 'automatically', having come to expect a particular behaviour of the other.

This dynamic was most apparent when considering the relationship between John and his father. Matthew, a forceful man who was used to running a business and solving problems, confirmed that he was 'a bit intolerant' as he did not understand John's difficulties. Until John had received his diagnosis he tended to 'dismiss/ignore his fears . . . used to feel he should snap out of it'.

Exploring this interactional cycle in relation to the family members' goals in the FI sessions provided helpful ways of normalising and de-catastrophising, and enabled them to begin practising alternative ways of being with one another. Because increasing withdrawal was an indicator of impending relapse, John's parents would sometimes become concerned and consequently become more watchful. In turn, this would be associated with John withdrawing further – another interactional cycle which resulted in a self-fulfilling prophecy.

An example of reframing that took place after such interactional cycles were explored was when John had explained to his parents that he withdrew to his room in the evenings to 'give his parents time together'. It was extremely reassuring for his parents to realise that John was being 'considerate' rather than 'ill/relapsing'.

This technique, known as cognitive interactional analysis (Burbach 2000, see Figures 5.3 and 5. 4), provided a means to explore and elucidate 'vicious circles' (for example, John not talking about his symptoms led to increased stress and therefore resulted in more symptoms).

Exploring current difficulties from a cognitive interactional perspective promotes a revision of attitudes and beliefs as well as facilitating behavioural change. It is possible to reverse 'downward spirals' or 'vicious cycles' which maintain problems and to establish 'virtuous cycles' in their place, by 'tracking' the sequence of actions and the associated constructions

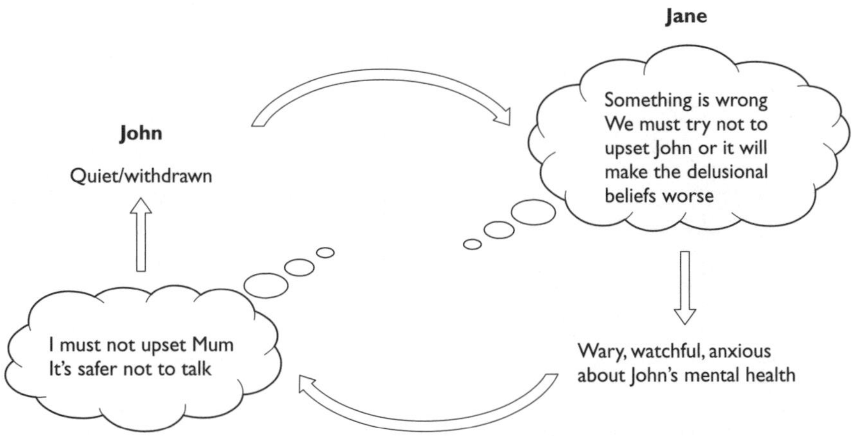

Figure 5.3 An example of a cognitive interactional analysis which indicates both the link between each individual's beliefs and behaviour, as well as the mutual reinforcement which maintains/exacerbates these behaviours.

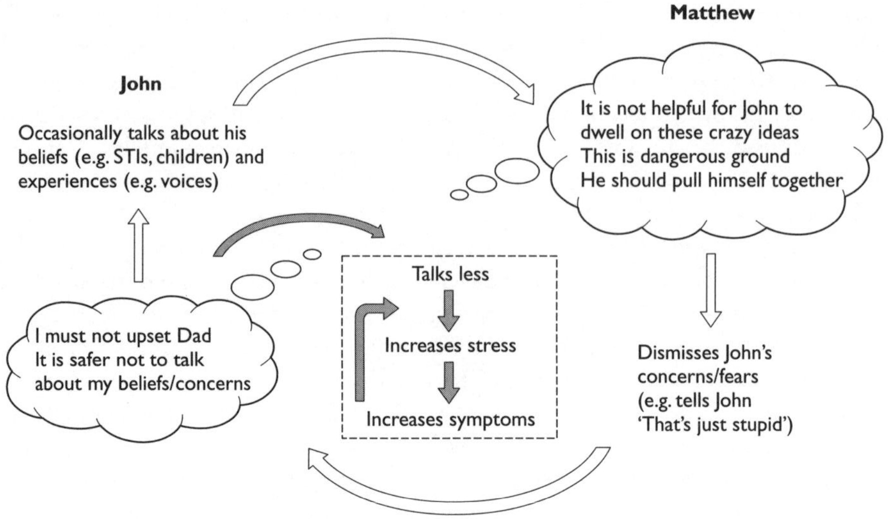

Figure 5.4 Another cognitive interactional analysis which also indicates the possible link between this interactional cycle and the maintenance/exacerbation of symptoms.

of each other and by using techniques such as goal setting (see Figure 5.5). Exploration of cognitive interactional cycles led to more positive perceptions of John, which enabled some of this family's initial goals, such as John becoming increasingly independent, to be focused on; significant achievements included his parents going away for long walks, weekends and longer holidays together, John going away (for example, visiting his sister in the city in which she lives) and John moving into his own flat. These behavioural goals were achieved in a gradual step by step manner.

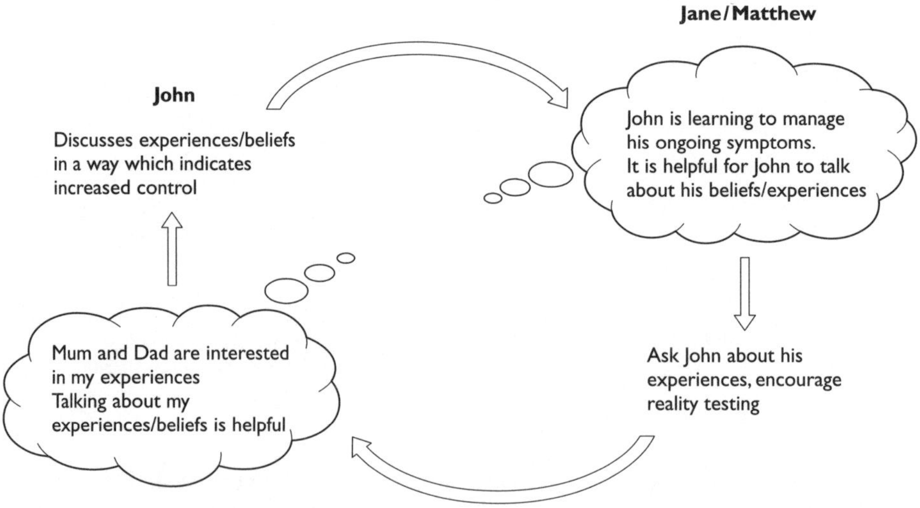

Figure 5.5 A 'virtuous' cognitive'-interactional cycle

Others issues focused on in FI sessions included John's ongoing positive symptoms and concern about his alcohol and tobacco use. Indicators of relapse included John trying to stop smoking and his increased alcohol use. By scaling the level of distress caused by various symptoms, or concern about John's alcohol use at various times, on a 1–5 scale, it was possible to track stress levels and develop coping strategies. This exercise also revealed that Matthew was much more concerned about John's alcohol use than Jane and John and that he feared relapse whenever John drank. Open discussion reassured Matthew that John had some control over his drinking and this helped to change the watchfulness–withdrawal cycle.

The symptom-focused work largely consisted of exploring John's anxiety-provoking beliefs to enable him to develop more neutral 'reality based' perspectives. These CBT based techniques (see Chadwick, Birchwood and Trower 1996) were combined with a normalising/psychoeducational approach. For example, in the ninth session John revealed that he had been 'hearing voices for the past three weeks'. His parents had been unaware of this and described this as a 'bombshell'. Besides normalising the increase in symptoms as probably relating to John's impending move to his own flat (utilising a stress vulnerability model) the therapists modelled how to explore John's experiences. His parents observed how the therapists calmly accepted his symptoms (rather than interrogating him about them or dismissing them), focusing on his coping strategies and beliefs about the voices. In subsequent sessions it became apparent that both auditory hallucinations and misinterpretations of noises such as voices from the street could trigger John's paranoid beliefs regarding Martin. With encouragement, John began to test the reality of his beliefs by checking outside to develop alternative explanations, rather than remaining inside the flat, becoming increasingly anxious. As the CBT was conducted in the context of FI, rather than in individual therapy, Jane and Matthew were able to provide ongoing support between therapy sessions and enable the ongoing practice of CBT techniques.

More recently John became concerned about a man who moved in nearby. John reported his increasing preoccupation and thoughts of assaulting this man to his psychiatrist, so was admitted as a voluntary patient for six days. At this admission John's medication was changed to Clozapine and Sulpiride, which was 'helpful' and it was reported that John 'appears less robotic'. In the subsequent FI session his parents began by reporting the hospitalisation had been a 'major set back'. The therapists positively reframed it as John successfully recognising and talking about these escalating thoughts, seeing his psychiatrist and spending only six days in hospital, a marked contrast to previous admissions. This new perspective – a blip handled well rather than a disastrous relapse – was extremely helpful to the family.

Outcome of FI

Although the FI sessions are ongoing at the time of writing this chapter, the family is moving into a maintenance phase. Sessions are likely to end by mutual agreement relatively soon, with the proviso that, as stated in the FSS operational policy, any member of the family may contact their FSS therapists at any time in the future if they would like further sessions.

The focus on interactional cycles has resulted in significantly altered family dynamics.

This is reflected in their contributions within the FI sessions. Matthew remarked: 'John takes control in meetings sometimes now . . . we realise John is better able to fend for himself and we don't have to say things for him'.

Although John still experiences auditory hallucinations and delusional beliefs, he has developed his coping strategies and he now tends to have shorter 'blips' rather than extended periods where he is overwhelmed with fear. His parents' new attitudes have played a crucial part in this. Prior to FI they believed it was safer not to talk about John's symptoms, and especially his beliefs about Martin; now they encourage him to talk about his experiences in order to reduce his distress. They help him to examine a particular experience in detail and encourage reality testing and the generation of alternative perspectives.

Initially John's parents, and especially his father, were very angry at the mental health services. They had hoped he would be given the right medication and (as a result of this medication) simply stop being preoccupied with Martin. As a result of the open discussion engendered by FI and their increased understanding of his difficulties, they now accept that John's recovery will be slow and steady. They know that their role will continue to be crucial, and hope that further progress may also be made through additional CBT sessions.

Discussion

This case study highlights a number of important issues related to the nature of AO, service design and organisation, training approach and family intervention models.

The nature of AO

One way of making sense of the differing research findings with regard to AO/ACT is that some of the services appear to have simply provided a more intensive 'treatment as usual', focusing on medication compliance. The finding in the large multi-site randomised controlled trial, the UK700 study – that smaller caseloads were not associated with better outcomes – could be partially explained in this light (Burns 2002). On setting up the services in Somerset I (Frank Burbach) was mindful of what Len Stein (one of the originators of ACT) has repeated on numerous occasions – AO is a *vehicle* for the delivery of effective treatments. Although services need to be provided in a collaborative, flexible and holistic manner in order to establish and maintain engagement, the frequent community-based contacts simply enable the delivery of a more sophisticated range of interventions. Staff in AO services are uniquely well placed to provide PSI, including maximising medication adherence, and where these are provided, they are likely to contribute significantly to the improved clinical outcomes reported in many studies.

It is noteworthy that, despite research evidence for both the AO/ACT and FI, it appears that the two are not often provided to service users in combination. This is despite the clear recommendations in the MHPIG (Department of Health 2001) that 'assertive outreach services should provide family/carers and significant others with support and intervention' (p. 31). That there are so few reports of a combination of the two approaches no doubt reflects the widespread difficulty experienced by mental health services in establishing FI in routine clinical practice. It is also possible that the development of AO out of 'rehabilitation' services has led to many staff still holding traditional beliefs that a patient's contact with their family may hinder successful treatment.

A notable exception to the dearth of information in the literature about the combination of the two approaches is a report by McFarlane and colleagues (McFarlane and Deakins 2002) about the combination of psycho-educational multi-family groups with ACT in New York. They report that:

> The merger of these two treatment methodologies formally integrates the family as a partner in the ongoing treatment and rehabilitation work being conducted by the ACT clinicians. It combines the unique efficacies of each approach, potentially enhancing outcomes additively or perhaps synergistically.
>
> (p. 176)

Psycho-educational programmes for groups of families who are caring for people with ongoing positive and negative psychotic symptoms provide an additional benefit over individual family sessions in that family members not only learn new coping strategies from one another but also develop a new supportive social network.

Service design and organisation

John and his parents clearly benefited from the recent establishment of these two services in Somerset and, in this particular case, the benefits of the two services have been maximised by their integration. This has been enabled by the organisation of both services according to PCT boundaries, with some AO staff devoting part of their working week to the delivery of FI. Although some FSS teams do not at present contain a representative of the local AO team, the effective integration of the work with the Carters illustrates the benefits of our FI service development strategy. We select staff to attend our one-year FI course on the basis of their formal contracting of at least one half day per week to the FSS. We specifically attempt to maximise representation from all the local teams and try to achieve a wide multi-disciplinary spread (see Burbach and Stanbridge 1998 and 2006 for more details). Not having a stand-alone team of full-time FI practitioners has proved to be an effective, natural method of ensuring that FI is well integrated with the local services.

Training and clinical approach

Our in-situ whole team training approach has been an effective way of developing FI services. A study we conducted in 2000 (Bailey, Burbach and Lea 2003) found that graduates from our one-year FI course had fewer difficulties in applying the approach than trainees from other courses. This is illustrated by this case study, in that the two therapists started work with the family with live supervision while on the course (nine sessions in six months) but subsequently successfully continued to work with the family on their own (with routine monthly supervision discussions with colleagues). In addition, the integration of psycho-educational and systemic approaches as taught on our FI course has been effectively demonstrated in the sessions with this family. We would argue that our integrated approach offers significant advantages over a purely psycho-educational one, in that the systemic (interactional) view of causality as circular enables a non-blaming exploration and resolution of family dynamics which may be maintaining problems. This non-linear view of causality is combined with a postmodern therapeutic stance which enables an integration of the various FI models within a more open, collaborative therapeutic relationship (Burbach and Stanbridge 2001). Therapy based on these concepts is particularly valued by families who have used our service (Stanbridge et al. 2003) and therapists trained in Somerset have found it much easier to engage families than clinicians trained in more prescriptive psycho-educational family intervention models (Bailey, Burbach and Lea 2003).

Final Comments

This family benefited from responsive, flexible support from an AO team as well as more specific skilled FI, and receiving it from people who worked in *both* services, ensured a consistent approach. As the services develop in Somerset we hope that the integrated package of care offered to the Carters will increasingly become the norm rather than the exception.

Note

1 Accordingly, all names of people (other than my own) or local services have been changed to ensure confidentiality.

References

Bailey, R., Burbach, F.R. and Lea, S. (2003) The ability of staff trained in family interventions to implement the approach in routine clinical practice. *Journal of Mental Health*, 12, 131–41.

Brennan, G. and Gamble, C. (1997) Schizophrenia, family work and clinical practice. *Mental Health Nursing*, 7, 12–15.

Brooker, C. (2001) A decade of evidence-based training for work with people with serious mental health problems: progress in the development of psychosocial interventions. *Journal of Mental Health*, 10, 17–31.

Burbach, F.R. (2000) Combining psychoeducational family work and systemic approaches. Paper presented at the Working with Families: Making it a Reality conference, Stratford-upon-Avon, 20–1 March 2000.

Burbach, F.R. and Stanbridge, R.I. (1998) A family intervention in psychosis service integrating the systemic and family management approaches. *Journal of Family Therapy*, 20, 311–25.

Burbach, F.R. and Stanbridge, R.I. (2001) *Creating Collaborative Therapeutic Relationships with Families Affected by Psychosis.* Paper presented at the International Society for the Psychological Treatments of Schizophrenia and Other Psychoses conference, University of Reading, 13–14 September.

Burbach, F.R. and Stanbridge, R.I. (2006) Somerset's family intervention in psychosis service: an update. *Journal of Family Therapy*, 28, 39–57.

Burbach, F.R., Donnelly, M. and Stanbridge, R.I. (2002) Service development through multi-disciplinary and multi-agency partnerships. *The Mental Health Review*, vol. 7, 27–30.

Burns, T. (2002) The UK 700 trial of intensive case management: an overview and discussion. *World Psychiatry*, 1, 175–8.

Bustillo, J.R., Lauriello, J., Horan, W.P. and Keith, S.J. (2001) The psychosocial treatment of Schizophrenia: an update. *American Journal of Psychiatry*, 158, 163–75.

Chadwick, P., Birchwood, M. and Trower, P. (1996) *Cognitive Therapy for Delusions, Voices and Paranoia.* Chichester: Wiley.

Department of Health (1993) *Health of the Nation Key Area Handbook: Mental Illness.* London: Department of Health.

Department of Health (1999) *National Service Framework for Mental Health: Modern Standards and Service Models.* London: Department of Health.

Department of Health (2000) *The NHS Plan.* London: Department of Health.

Department of Health (2001) *Mental Health Policy Implementation Guide.* London: Department of Health.

Dixon, L., Adam, C., and Lucksted, A. (2000) Update on family psychoeducation for schizophrenia. *Schizophrenia Bulletin,* 26, 5–20.

Fadden, G. (1997) Implementation of family interventions in routine clinical practice following staff training programs: a major cause for concern. *Journal of Mental Health,* 6, 599–612.

Fadden, G. (1998) Research update: psychoeducational family interventions. *Journal of Family Therapy,* 20, 293–309.

Howe, G. (1998) *Getting into the System: Living with Severe Mental Illness.* London: Jessica Kingsley.

Kavanagh, D.J., Piatkowska, O., Clarke, D., O'Halloran, P., Manicavasgar, V., Rosen, A. and Tennant, C. (1993) Application of cognitive-behavioural family intervention for schizophrenia in multidisciplinary teams: what can the matter be? *Australian Psychologist,* 28, 181–8.

Lehman, A.F. (1999) Improving treatment for persons with schizophrenia. *Psychiatric Quarterly,* 70, 249–72.

Mari, J., and Streiner, D. (1996) The effects of family intervention on those with schizophrenia. In C. Adams, J. Anderson and De Jesus Mari (eds.) *Schizophrenia Module, Cochrane Database of Systematic Reviews* (updated 23 February 1996) London: BMJ Publishing.

McFarlane, W.R. and Deakins, S.M. (2002) Family-aided assertive community treatment. In W.R. McFarlane (ed.) *Multifamily Groups in the Treatment of Severe Psychiatric Disorders.* New York: Guilford Press.

Marshall, M. and Lockwood, A. (2005) *Assertive Community Treatment for People with Severe Mental Disorders (Cochrane Review).* The Cochrane Library, issue 5. Oxford: Update Software.

NICE (2002) *Schizophrenia: Core Interventions in the Treatment and Management of Schizophrenia in Primary and Secondary Care. Clinical Guideline 1.* London: National Institute for Clinical Excellence.

Pharoah, F.M. Rathbone, J. Mari, J. and Streiner, D. (2003) *Family Intervention for Schizophrenia (Cochrane Review).* The Cochrane Library, issue 3. Oxford: Update Software.

Pitschel-Walz, G., Leucht, S., Bauml, J., Kissling, W., Engel, R.R., (2001) The effect of family interventions on relapse and re-hospitilization in schizophrenia: a meta-analysis. *Schizophrenia Bulletin,* 27, 73–92.

Stanbridge, R.I. and Burbach, F.R. (2004) Enhancing working partnerships with carers and families: a strategy and associated staff training programme. *The Mental Health Review,* 9, 32–7.

Stanbridge, R.I., Burbach, F.R., Lucas, A.S. and Carter, K. (2003) A study of families' satisfaction with a family interventions in psychosis service in Somerset. *Journal of Family Therapy,* 25, 181–204.

Stein, L.I. and Santos, A.B. (1998) *Assertive Community Treatment of Persons with Severe Mental Illness.* New York: W.W. Norton.

Zubin, J. and Spring, B. (1977) Vulnerability: a new view on schizophrenia. *Journal of Abnormal Psychology,* 86, 103–26.

Chapter 6

Relapse Prevention in Bipolar Disorder with Staff Who Are also Service Users

Eric Davis, Guy Undrill and Lauren Samuels[1]

Key Points

- Relapse in bipolar disorder can be reduced and better managed by use of detailed early warning signs (EWS) psychological work.
- Combining cognitive behavioural therapy (CBT) for psychosis and motivational interviewing regarding the taking of medication will help in EWS work.
- EWS work is aided by a detailed understanding of a person's life history, so the use of a timeline is recommended.
- Providing previous examples of EWS work with former users, in terms of completed EWS 'grids' is usually of practical benefit.
- Where possible, and with user consent, the views of a person/people who know the user well can help identify further useful EWS.
- Any EWS work should be considered as part of a dynamic, evolving process, whereby new EWS can be identified and added to a 'relapse drill' in a collaborative spirit.
- Spiritual and religious beliefs are important, and may need to be incorporated into EWS work.
- Mental health professionals who have experienced psychosis can develop extra insight and sophistication when delivering services in the role of a 'wounded healer'.
- However, the stigma which surrounds serious mental health problems also affects staff; revealing to other staff that one suffers from bipolar disorder is very difficult, owing to fear of possible judgemental and discriminatory attitudes.

Introduction

This chapter explores relapse prevention with a staff member who experiences bipolar disorder. Relapse prevention developed from work in the addiction field where people frequently relapse into their older, problematic, ways of behaving. But relapse can be prevented, or better managed if it occurs, by undertaking detailed planning work. This involves looking at a person's EWS and formulating a response, known as a 'relapse drill'.[2] This work is usually most successful in dealing with mental health problems when medication is also taken – so 'medication compliance' is an important component of relapse prevention. This work connects to policy guidance and also to an evidence base, both of which are briefly explored below. The bulk of the chapter is concerned with the actual clinical work that was conducted – CBT to inform a relapse prevention strategy including judicious medication use – and of how this work fits in with the authors' organisational context. 'Lauren's' views on her interaction with the mental health service are examined, along with her views upon receiving intervention as a staff member.

The Evidence – Policy and Research

Mental health policy guidance

At least three publications give policy direction and provide clinical guidelines when considering relapse prevention work with users: *The National Service Framework for Mental Health* (Department of Health 1999), *Mental Health Policy Implementation Guide* (Department of Health 2001) and *Early Intervention in Psychosis* (IRIS 2000). Such policy direction recognises that service users and their carers, working collaboratively with mental health professionals, can maximise the chances of preventing a psychotic relapse. The aim of this chapter is to demonstrate that coherent and collaborative work between Eric, Lauren and Guy was essential in forming a shared understanding of the difficulties faced by Lauren. A pooling of shared expertise is necessary to devise a system based on focused identification of Lauren's EWS associated with relapse. Policy recognises that such EWS work is useful, so that clinicians are now expected to undertake this work with users and carers.

IRIS (2000, pp. 53–8 also discusses relapse prevention measures. For each service user, changes in thoughts, feelings and behaviours (and other domains – see Denney and Davis 2006), can reliably precede psychotic relapse. The combination of emotional and early psychotic change (known as a prodrome) can signal, with some reliability, the onset of later psychosis (Birchwood, Spencer and McGovern 2000). The highly individualised set of changes for a given service user can be carefully tracked and documented, as an individual's 'relapse signature'. By remaining vigilant, clinicians, service user and carers/family can use the 'relapse signature' to prompt a more rapid response in the user, and potentially avert relapse. Such a response could involve increasing or decreasing their activity levels, or resuming or increasing medication.

Relapse prevention evidence and bipolar disorder

An early study (Smith and Tarrier 1992) demonstrated that 20 users with bipolar disorder could identify symptoms of depression or of increased energy or speeding up of thinking process with some reliability (85 per cent for depressive symptoms and 75 per cent for manic symptoms). The majority of users could identify a time sequence for the length of time that insight was retained during their prodromes and could also identify idiosyncratic symptoms. This early work suggested that structured cognitive behavioural work showed promise in managing relapse.

Perry and colleagues (1999) conducted a randomised controlled trial in which users with bipolar disorder recognised symptoms of manic relapse and sought prompt treatment. They discovered that early detection leading to prompt treatment was associated with important clinical improvements, which delayed manic relapse, and to improved social functioning and employment.

Lam, Wong and Sham (2001) and Lam et al. (2005) found that while depressive prodromal symptoms were harder to detect than symptoms of mania, nevertheless psychological treatments could prevent or ameliorate relapse. Scott and Gutierrez (2004) state that such psychological treatments require at least 10 hours of treatment over a six to nine-month period, but that more research is required to determine the most effective type of psychological therapy.

Asking carers to contribute to the identification of EWS can help. Denney and Davis (2006) using this approach showed that the construction of an EWS grid can not only help to clarify the type of early symptoms that are experienced, but also the timescale, suggesting that clinical intervention can be targeted at specific points in time most advantageous to users and carers. That work was completed with a young user in receipt of a diagnosis of schizophrenia but, in keeping with the identified research for bipolar disorder, such clinical techniques are transferable.

Miklowitz and colleagues (2003) demonstrated that combining family and individual therapy with medication management in bipolar disorder may protect episodic bipolar disorder sufferers from early relapse and ongoing depressive symptoms. Colom and others (2003) aimed to assess psycho-education and its efficacy in helping bipolar disorder users to remain medication compliant, so as to prevent relapse. However, while they found that psycho-education showed efficacy in preventing bipolar disorder relapse, they made further observations: that the action of psycho-education was not sufficient, by itself, to avert relapse; and that adopting a vigilant stance, the incorporation of healthy lifestyle habits (such as exercise), and remaining medication compliant, all helped keep people well.

The Case Study – Collaborative Working between Lauren, Eric and Guy

Editors' note: this case study describes the actual clinical relapse prevention work conducted between Lauren, Eric and Guy. Lauren is a senior health professional who has periodically experienced bipolar disorder since the age of 16 (she is now 35). Eric is a consultant clinical psychologist and Guy a psychiatrist: they have all worked collaboratively to help Lauren.

The main aspects of the work took the following order:

- engagement and psycho-education
- assessment
- treatment adherence work
- timeline development
- development of the early warning signs grid (EWSG)
- development of a relapse drill
- revisiting and refining the EWSG and relapse drill.

The orientation of Eric's work was cognitive behavioural therapy (CBT), given its efficacy and clinical effectiveness with bipolar disorder. The importance of good medication compliance to complement the CBT is underscored.

Engagement and Psycho-education

The attitude adopted by Eric and Guy towards Lauren is that she is an 'expert through experience'. The philosophical stance is that recovery and the *process* of recovering are possible. Guy's approach to the medical component of the care of a patient with bipolar disorder is substantially drawn from motivational interviewing (MI) and its adaptations. MI is a client-centred approach; it differs from other client-centred approaches both because it is overtly directive, and because it has a strong empirical evidence base (summarised in Miller and Rollnick 2002). The aim of interactions is to enhance the user's own intrinsic motivations to change by exploring and resolving ambivalence (Rollnick and Miller 1995).

From the point of view of the service user, the main problem with much of the drug treatment of bipolar disorder (as with many treatments in psychiatry) is often that the drugs are inherently unpleasant to take. The personal costs of drug treatment are real and immediately apparent, in terms of side-effects such as weight gain, sedation, cognitive dulling and feeling slowed down, among many others. In contrast the benefits can seem more abstract (a good chance of reduced frequency, severity and length of relapse in the future compared with typical users not taking medication). Usually these benefits take months or even years to produce real pay-off in terms of a more stable life, with all that brings: employment, relationships, financial security.

MI provides a framework for allowing the service user to address this difficult cost-benefit analysis. Zweben and Zuckoff (2002) divide this in to two phases. The first phase is an empathic assessment, aimed at getting to know the service user in a broader perspective, in particular focusing on their values and how these relate to the disorder. This has the secondary aim of creating a safe atmosphere in which to explore the service user's thoughts and feelings about treatment. In this first stage, reviewing past treatment (both successful and unsuccessful) is important. Discrepancies can then be explored between the users values and goals, and past treatment plans. This may entail reviewing what has brought the person to treatment and eliciting what problems they have had with treatment before, without jumping to explain these problems away. Sometimes problems may be generated by previously unmet expectations, for example, 'I took the medication but still got ill'. It also involves eliciting discrepancies about current treatment plans – for example the belief that talking about the past is fruitless in someone embarking on psychodynamic therapy. These discrepancies are viewed as early warning signs for non-adherence and are reflected back to the person.

In Guy's first session with Lauren they discussed her ongoing difficulties with her ex-husband and the contact arrangements he had for their daughter. Lauren's role as mother was clearly an important one to her. Her ex-husband had used information about her illness to discredit her in the family court. This had understandably affected Lauren's confidence about her ability in a key area of her life and self-concept. In this session they did not discuss medication; Guy's interventions at that time were primarily educational and supportive. First, Guy encouraged Lauren to read *An Unquiet Mind* by Kay Redfield Jamison (1997). This is an excellent first hand account of bipolar disorder by a sufferer; but it is also a nuanced, informed and optimistic account of the illness by a professor of psychology with academic expertise in the field of bipolar disorder. Jamison writes eloquently about her own struggles with accepting a diagnosis of bipolar disorder and accepting a need for medication, in particular about the upfront cost of medication and the deferred pay-off. Second, Guy suggested Lauren got in touch with the Manic Depression Fellowship. This is something that many users find invaluable, in terms of support, education and normalisation of their experiences. Guy's third intervention was to refer Lauren to the team social worker for low key support during a stressful time with her contested custody. The social worker was available for Lauren at short notice while the legal process unfolded.

Guy's second session with Lauren focused on a recent period of insomnia. For many sufferers from bipolar disorder, insomnia is a danger sign for relapse. Lauren knew this herself and was anxious that she might be becoming unwell again. Guy made a minor adjustment in her medication, switching some of her sodium valproate from morning to evening for the extra sedative effect; but Guy's major intervention at this session was to work with Lauren's own curiosity and anxiety about early signs of relapse, and to refer her to Eric for some specific work on relapse prevention (discussed below). It may seem obvious, but the best time to do work on relapse prevention is when the user is engaged with the idea of relapse.

Over the next few sessions, Guy's own work with Lauren switched to phase 2 of the Zweben and Zuckoff model, which explores ambivalence to taking medication. Key interventions at this stage emphasise personal choice in forming a treatment plan and the practice of what has been termed 'autonomy support' (i.e. supporting Lauren in enabling her to feel that she had the ability to exercise these choices). Negative aspects of treatment are actively logged and addressed, typically by providing information about drugs and emphasising that there is always a degree of choice in medication regimes. Where possible, Guy aimed to present a 'menu' of options that Lauren could choose from, using an approach of 'collaborative empiricism' where, with Guy's advice and help Lauren could adjust dosages and timings of medication until they could find a system she was happy with. In Lauren's case, one of the key determinants was to have enough sedation but not too much. Decisions around this implicitly referred back to Lauren's values of wanting to be a good mother: 'too much' sedation was sedation that impinged on child-care, for example, by making it difficult to wake when her daughter got up in the night, or by having such a medication hangover that she could not get up with and care for her daughter in the morning. Had this core value not been identified in phase 1, there may have been a risk that Lauren would simply have stopped medication because it was interfering with her ability to look after her daughter.

During the second phase it is important to continue to work with ambivalence around treatment: in particular, it is important to expect problems and to take a 'non-perfectionistic' attitude. Guy and Lauren were able to try various medications because Lauren was confident that if one combination was unacceptable, Guy would prescribe something else, and that she would stay in control. A position between realism and optimism was taken which embraces the fact that Lauren has strengths and coping resources as well as identified problems and needs. An integrated biopsychosocial model of functioning, the stress-vulnerability model (Nuechterlein and Dawson 1984), was also used to emphasise that a combination of biomedical, psychological and social factors can interact, to influence a given outcome for

Lauren. By developing a sophisticated 'early warning signs' system, enhanced levels of control are made possible with help from family as well as Eric and Guy. Potential 'vulnerability factors' could involve various negative, unhelpful and overlearned cognitions or thought patterns (schemas). Identifying these schemas helped Lauren to identify, evaluate and modify negative thoughts, thereby returning a sense of control to her.

Eric was able to achieve 'schema identification' (highly overlearned ways of seeing the world) by rigorously assessing Lauren' psychological status. This was accessed through a combination of Lauren's timeline (see Figure 6.1 below, which gave a clue as to Lauren's habitual patterns of thinking, feeling and behaving in the past), and cross-referencing this with information derived from clinical interviewing and careful questioning, combined with information that Lauren provided in her 'EWSG' (see Table 6.1). For example, Lauren does not like conflict and will seek to avoid it. However, Lauren's thoughts that she will not be able to deal effectively with conflict situations means that she does not get an opportunity to actually test this out and so the problem is maintained. And yet behavioural experiments can only be devised to challenge this belief once it has been identified. This process of identifying and challenging negative thinking patterns, leading to potential feelings of being more in control, were central to the CBT work undertaken by Eric and Lauren.

Lauren says:

Both Eric and Guy have respected my views as a person. If they ask questions, they wait for the answer. I know they are listening to what I am saying. I know they try to build on my observations both in terms of psychology and medicine. We discuss strategies that might be more and also less helpful. Talking about my earlier experiences with the mental health services has helped, because you get to know each other.

My first experience was when at the age of 16 I met a psychiatrist who recommended a 10-day hospital stay. I recall him stating that the people would not be my age and I had a notion they would be younger so agreed to go to hospital. The reality was they were all older and experiencing mid life crises or breakdowns following divorce. I however, did not feel I belonged there with my adolescent issues: I now believe I needed to be seen as a part of a specialist children's service.

Another part of the work was completing the timeline (Figure 6.1) with Eric. This was useful and it allowed me to think about my earlier life some more and of how I think about things more generally, and that I have currently remained well for over three years.

Eric says:

The timeline was an essential part of early assessment. This gave an understanding of the life difficulties that Lauren had faced but also gave insight into her routine appraisal and belief systems. For example, two highly overlearned but unhelpful views of the self (schemas) had emerged:

Schema 1 revolved around considerable self-sacrificial behaviour 'I gain my own sense of self-worth by constantly doing things for other people' and Schema 2 was strongly related to conflict-avoidance: 'I cannot deal with conflict – the only way to do so is to avoid it'.

Figure 6.1 Lauren's timeline

1971	Born in London.
1972	Twin brother and sister born.
1974	Family move.
1982	Family move. Finished primary and started secondary school; happy at school.
1985	Moved to a rural county town.
1986	First boyfriend and sexual relationship (strong parental disapproval).
	Achieved 7/9 O levels (perception of self as failure).
	Father went away to study. Brother went to boarding school. Parents relationship under pressure (strong feeling of stress).
1987	First breakdown (felt was a failure owing to 'only' obtaining 7/9 O levels).
1987/8	Attending day hospital in the rural county.
1988	Returned to school to study for 2 A levels.
	Left school for college to do 3 A levels.
	Raped at the Freshers Ball (guilt and shame. Did not report incident. Aware of issues of how I relate to men in relationships).
1990	First long-term boyfriend.
	Entered professional training.
1993	First job in Midlands (poorly trained and supervised, so stressful).
1996	Attended course at an Evangelical church (caused great personal conflict owing to history and current sexual behaviour. Comfort from worship, but stress owing to God's laws).
	Plastic surgery breast augmentation.
	(Time off and grieving for loss of six-year relationship.)
1997	Clubbing in Ibiza. Studying for Masters degree. (Stressed and tired. Jealous of sister marrying in summer.)
	Religious outreach mission in Somerset. (A shaking wreck – woman praying for a devil to be removed from me.) Admitted to psychiatric hospital two days later under Section 3. (Thoughts of possessing supernatural powers. Reading meaning into everything. Feeling persecuted. Hearing voices. Feelings of utter chaos and losing my mind. Smashed a mirror because I didn't want to look at myself. Felt demonic.)
	Sister married. Attended the wedding while on Section. (Delusion of parents arranging a marriage to my ex. And of being pregnant.)
	End of the year. Taking Depixol and still very depressed.
1998	Brother married. Still unwell.

	Second opinion. Bipolar disorder felt a burden to the family and had suicidal thoughts diagnosed. Prescribed mood-stabiliser and anti-depressants.
	Returned to work. Met Jim.
1999	Relationship with Jim.
	Summer. Third breakdown (trying to sort out Jim's problems and mine).
	Discovered I was pregnant. Attending Relate to shore up relationship with Jim prior to the birth of the baby.
2000	Alison born by emergency Caesarean.
	Trauma caused a lack of sleep leading to a fourth breakdown.
	Left hospital to stay with parents (when facing conflict, e.g. with Jim, the pattern of my life has been to run away, in this case to my parents).
	Returned to Jim in time for Christmas.
2001	Decided to leave Jim.
	Invited Jim to Alison's first birthday and relationship recommenced.
	Winter. Relationship with Jim formally ended.
2002	Upped work to full-time but experienced fifth breakdown. Admitted to hospital for two months.
	Jim filed claim to become resident parent. I moved to live in a rural county with Alison to be with my parents. (Joined Church which helped practically and emotionally.)
	Attended a resource centre for emotional support/friendship.
	Summer. Parents bought a house for me. A real Godsend.
	Series of court cases to determine guardianship. Custody granted to me, but Jim is also allowed substantial access to Alison.
	Met Dr Guy Undrill.
2003	Referral to Dr Eric Davis.
	Spring. CBT work commenced.
	New job.
2004	Wrote to Jim suggesting reconciliation.
	Helping at church with youth work – enjoying it.
2005	Summer. Remaining well – since 2002.

Table 6.1 Early warning signs grid[3]

	Early		Late
	Green	*Amber*	*Red*
Somatic	Tension in body, especially shoulders/back Jerky movements of hands: uncontrolled Increased energy levels – more get up and go Can be more clumsy as rushing about	Back stiffens up, can't bend or sit for long Body movements feel as if controlled by thoughts outside my body ('implanted') Restlessness: inability to relax, sleep disturbed as unable to 'switch off', awake 2–3 hours at night	Increasing tension leads to aching back Jerky movements of hands/arms and head: more intense and uncontrollable Inability to sleep heightened: can be awake all night for days on end
Interpersonal	Talkative and enjoy social contact, need people's company, generally dislike being alone for long periods	Over-identify with other people's problems and take them on as if my own. Try to 'rescue people' Over-assertive at times Can appear vacant – preoccupied[1]	Empathy: becomes judgemental and can be insensitive to others Lack of regard to authority as believe in God's laws
Situational	Loss of interest in upkeep of house Always out with daughter versus time at home to play ↑ creative energy – enjoy art, gardening	Neglect house-work especially ironing as need to be still Attend groups as much as possible for support and social contact[1] Pre-occupation with new projects, e.g. gardening	Pre-occupation with tidiness and order Cleaning can become a focal point Unable to cope with Alison's needs – have to get help from family
Behavioural	Generally drink more alcohol to relax/aid sleep Start to smoke at any stage early on in an attempt to calm myself Increase in general spending Lose interest in TV/Radio – become very selective Lose interest in reading	Drinking can increase from ½ bottle to bottle of wine per night Give gifts/possessions away to people Purchase lots of unnecessary items, e.g. CDs Avoid news and become very selective in TV viewing[1] Stop reading books (except Bible); may dip into a magazine[2]	May avoid alcohol: desire to purify body Usually stop again to be pure/clean in body May decide to re-carpet the house! May not watch any TV or listen to radio. Play CDs only No reading at all of books/magazines: can't concentrate

	Green	*Amber*	*Red*
Cognitive	Generally worrying about things more Over-personalise people's problems and think they are my responsibility Listening to music, radio, CDs, etc. Over-identifying with lyrics Feel I am being watched – either as if I'm special like an example to society or as I've failed (late green)	Tendency to becoming very negative and assume worst – may make irrational decisions I believe that I can make a difference and 'solve' problems. Can be very intrusive and insensitive Excessive Bible reading and talk about religion and personal conflicts[1] Believe that there is a special message for me Feel as if people are plotting against me Flavour (i.e. an intuition, based on past experience) that something is wrong[2]	Over-react to worries which get blown out of proportion. It is difficult to put incidents into bigger picture as it's a fuzzy mess Believe that I have God-given gift of insight to see into the heart of the problem and therefore solve it. Can be very tactless at this stage I am: Jesus, God's Healer, Heart of God. Meant to be with Jim – God's will Music/TV can be avoided as I believe that there are 'messages': some positive to boost me up, others persecutory This is never more real than when in hospital and I want to go home
Mood	Low mood – try to avoid tears and empty feeling by keeping busy – ↓ concentration	Mood elevation with ↑ energy and ↓ sleep[1] ↑ irritability and restlessness[1]	Extreme mood swings tears and tantrums Get angry
Sensory-perceptual	Poor focus, e.g. TV and talking: can't channel it Heightened awareness, e.g. fridge buzzing can be annoying	Dislike a lot of hustle and bustle, e.g. towns TV/radio on together High pitched noises are unbearable See faces and remind me of people from the past (old friends or relatives) Objects in peripheral vision take on more importance Onset of voice–hearing, connected to distortion of self, especially with regard to self-grandiosity[1,2]	Prefer social isolation – nights are best as quiet – no one to annoy me Distorted perception of facial images; feel possessed Other people give messages to me from the devil See things shadows, etc. when not there

1 Key sign – Lauren   2 Key sign – parents

Simply identifying that these dysfunctional assumptions were in routine operation allowed Lauren the opportunity to stand back and re-appraise potential ways forward, including purposely 'acting against' such assumptions and noting the results.

Assessment

The second major aspect of more formal assessment was to use the KGV or Manchester scale (Krawiecka, Goldberg and Vaughan 1977; revised by Lancashire 1994). This is a semi-structured assessment tool that asks the user about affective and psychotic difficulties and requires the interviewer to rate the user for behavioural domains and also levels of co-operation with the interview process.

Development of the EWSG

Lauren and Eric comment:

Lauren was asked by Eric to examine her attitude to a possible relapse, which highlighted ongoing concerns. Eric provided a grid (see Table 6.1) which acted as a prompt for Lauren to identify factors associated with her becoming increasingly unwell. To help this process, Eric examined with Lauren the link between anxiety being expressed through tension in the body, for example in the neck and back, and the possibility for Lauren of a link between her anxiety and paranoia – something that Lauren had not really considered. They looked at the idea that paranoia can be thought of as heightened anxiety, as might be experienced in the context of an extreme threat to self (e.g. perceiving that you were being watched), but also that it may be a defence mechanism against depression. Lauren found these new concepts helpful and useful.

The next task was to address the possibility of there being three stages to Lauren's disorder: the first stage being the early signs, then the middle stage where Lauren becomes slightly hypomanic (e.g. thoughts beginning to race, more energy becoming available), and then the final stage, where Lauren becomes very disturbed and develops full-blown mania. Eric provided a completed EWSG (with permission) from a previous user, a young man who was a student. This formal grid involved putting the three sections of early to late signs and symptoms into a grid of green, amber and red, representing early, middle and late signs respectively. They were then further subdivided into the areas of somatic, interpersonal, situational, behavioural, mood, cognitive and sensory-perceptual. Lauren found this very easy to follow because it was logical and systematic.

The EWSG was collaboratively devised by Lauren and Eric using information from the KGV and supplemented by information from Lauren's timeline. Her parents also suggested early warning signs they had noticed. A comprehensive array of EWS, with key signs identified by Lauren and her parents, is presented in Table 6.1.

Development of the relapse drill

A relapse drill is an action plan that is to be activated once a certain number of relapse indicators have been experienced. The relapse drill usually involves contacting the workers involved in delivering care, so in Lauren's case this was Eric or Guy. Alternatively Lauren's parents could make contact if they were sufficiently concerned.

Key early warning signs and Lauren's relapse drill

Eric worked with Lauren to clarify which key mental health indicators were associated with potential relapse. They came up with the following:

1. The presence of disturbed sleep (at least two to three hours awake at night lying in bed) and an increased inability to 'turn in' at the appropriate bedtime.
2. Increasingly over-identifying with other people's problems and a tendency to offer friends who may be perceived as depressed more help and ignore those friends who appear to be well.
3. Increased irritability (owing to decreased sleep and heightened sensory awareness).
4. The onset of voice-hearing as connected to distortion of self, especially with regard to self-grandiosity or grandiose ideas.
5. Heightened sensory awareness in terms of being much more bothered by external sensory stimulation than usual.
6. Stopping reading books except for the Bible.

They agreed that the presence of three out of six of these factors meant that Lauren would activate the relapse drill. Eric and/or Guy would respond quickly. Helpful responses would be to examine the level of activity that Lauren was undertaking (for example the number of hours being spent at work), and reviewing Lauren's psychological interpretation of events. Also, medication timing and dosage could be reviewed with Guy.

Revisiting and refining the EWSG and relapse drill

Eric and Lauren both view the EWSG and relapse drill as 'work in progress'. Careful assessment will continue, with the views of Lauren and her parents continuing to be used and incorporated into the EWSG, which will be modified as necessary. Personal coping strategies remain under review, and where needed pragmatic changes will be made to the relapse drill as appropriate.

Lauren's reflection on the work with Mental Health Services in Gloucestershire particularly with Guy and Eric

Lauren says:

Guy

Guy is able to listen to his patients and is very like the Carl Rogers client-centred approach in his attitude and manner. Guy takes the attitude that his patients know themselves best and by taking the approach he does he is able to gain further insight into their illness. When seeing Guy at the clinic or for review he is very thorough, always taking a full mental state examination. He will ask about medication, sleep, appetite etc. Guy is very aware of the necessity for balance in everyday life and also enquires about activities like leisure and hobbies. Guy's approach to medication using a client-centred attitude is a new concept for me and one I have not experienced with other psychiatrists. Guy has encouraged me personally to titrate my medication according to how I feel. This has been closely monitored with work I am doing with Eric. The combination of the early warning signs management plan and medication management has helped to keep me relatively stable for three years now. This concept of allowing the patient to believe that they are in control of their medication helps with concordance. In the past I did not have a lot of faith in the drugs and actually believed they didn't work: consequently I would not take them or if I did this was sporadically. This led to extreme mood swings and ultimately a nervous breakdown.

With the current treatment regime, I have regular outpatient clinic appointments with Guy and with Eric which has changed my belief system about the drugs. I now take my medication daily and I am less fearful of lack of sleep or other situations, as I have a plan to put in place to try out my medication myself. For example, having had two or three bad night's sleep I would take a sleeping tablet to ensure I get to sleep. If that fails after two or three nights then I would take some anti-psychotic drugs as it is likely to mean I am getting high.

Guy has also shown an understanding and awareness and appreciation of the uniqueness of each individual, and has always listened to the fact that the drugs come with side-effects and consequently has prescribed medication that suits my lifestyle. I have a short-acting sleeping tablet called Zaleplon. This enables me to get to sleep quickly but if I am woken in the night and need to attend to my daughter I am not dosed up. Guy has also encouraged me to take my medication early evening as well as at bedtime. This is to prevent what I call my hangover effect in the morning whereby I have got an excessive amount of drugs in my system, meaning that I find it really difficult to get up to attend to my daughter. The drugs dose is also weighted so that I have a higher dose in the evenings and less during the day as it is at night time when I feel I need greater amounts of mood stabilizer to help me sleep.

When I start to get high I take the drug Olanzapine that has the possible side-effect of causing weight gain. I explained my concerns to Guy that I did not wish to gain weight and asked whether there were any other drugs and he was able to find in my notes that a previous psychiatrist had recommended another drug which had anti-psychotic properties. It was unfortunate that this drug was even more sedating than the Olanzapine and consequently wasn't suitable for my lifestyle.

Guy appreciates the importance of multi-agency working. When I spoke with him over a year ago with my concerns about possible relapse and the consequences for my ability to care for Alison, whether she would reside with me permanently was in question. Guy was able to refer me to Eric to look at preventing relapse.

Eric

I started to do the early warning signs work with Eric about a year ago now. It has been very useful and has followed a logical pattern which has been very easy to work through (see Table 6.1). Eric has used a cognitive behaviour therapy approach in his sessions. This to my mind is a way of looking at thoughts and trying to understand what it is that lies behind them and possibly challenging some of those thoughts, i.e., whether they may be detrimental in some way or perhaps inaccurate. The first part of the work that I did with Eric was to draw up a timeline which recorded any significant event that happened during my life up until today (see Figure 6.1). It involved both positive and negative experiences that were of any significance to me personally. This was a very useful exercise that gave me the opportunity to reflect on my past and realise that many events had occurred, both positive and negative, that may have triggered a breakdown.

The one thing I found that was not looked at as much as it could have been, and that may have been useful, was the fact that there was a period of 10 years during my life, from when I was 16 to 26 that I remained well despite significant events occurring. It may have been useful to use a solution-focused therapy approach to try to identify what factors actually kept me well and happy during that period. I feel that would be a positive way of looking at the life event scale, as it would then look at drawing on the person's strengths and appreciating the aspects of their personality that they can draw upon at more difficult times that may lie ahead in the future.

However, set against this is to recognise that some of the stresses I have tried to deal with more recently have been of a much more intimate and psychologically demanding nature. For example, becoming a mother, then trying to manage a relationship break-up while attempting to sort out custody for my daughter. These have been significant factors in more recent complications with my bipolar disorder, so looking at structured attempts at problem-solving through the EWS work with Eric (and Guy) has had to take account of, and address, these significant life changes.

The early warning signs grid has been a really useful point of reference to come back to time and time again. I have found, given a year now of working with the EWS, that there are some aspects of it that are open to interpretation as to whether they are a symptom of stress or part of the disorder. However, I am aware that the increase in stress can cause a relapse and it is still useful to keep those signs and symptoms on my EWSG.

Most recently Eric and I reviewed the EWSG and came up with a list of a simple summary of the EWS that are now most significant to my life, as the other areas on the list I have somehow managed to either compensate for or are no longer an issue. This final list of six areas includes disturbed sleep, over identification of problems, increasing irritability, onset of voices and self-grandiosity. Heightened sensory awareness and stopping reading books except for the Bible are both crucial factors, indicating that I am in the middle to late stages of an onset and seriously need to consider altering my lifestyle and my medication regime.

Eric involved my parents in one session so they would be involved in the EWSG and make their own contributions. It was interesting to learn that my parents really cannot tell exactly when I am getting unwell: they just get a feeling for it and they are very much more dependent on me talking to them (which I often choose not to do) about how I feel and what I am thinking.

One aspect that was not specifically embraced by the cognitive behaviour therapy approach is the spiritual dimension. As a Christian, I strongly believe that each and every individual has a soul that is longing consciously or unconsciously for a relationship with God. It is God who has made us, so therefore He alone can provide us with the love and security we need, the value and sense of self-worth and also a purpose and significance that we have within our lives and that all this is essential for our souls to survive and thrive. This is not to diminish the work done by health care professionals; but further work on the role that God plays in my life in future could be of use.

Some organisational reflections

The fact that CBT and medication management for relapse prevention was available for Lauren has been helped by Gloucestershire Partnership NHS Trust (GPT) as an organisation. GPT has a track record of embracing psychosocial interventions (PSI), providing Thorn training and a range of other PSI-informed training modules (see also chapter 12).

In contrast, certain clinicians have reported barriers to clinical implementation of PSI (e.g. relapse prevention skills). These are probably due to a systemic shortcoming. On the one hand, it is possible that a 'critical mass' of PSI-trained clinicians has not yet been assembled. And on the other, GPT (like many other provider trusts within the NHS) faces challenges owing to the sheer scale and pace of health service reforms in the wake of the NSF (Department of Health 1999) and the national plan (Department of Health 2000) directives, and more recently, the requirement for financial book-balancing. Clinicians in some community mental health teams reveal that they have difficulty in applying their PSI skills because there is insufficient focus on psychosis, or that overall caseloads are too high, or that there is not enough time and/or that there are difficulties in obtaining clinical supervision. It is more likely that clinicians in GPT sited in specialist services such as assertive outreach and early intervention teams (like the first author), or crisis teams (like the second author), will have greater opportunities to deliver these evidence-based PSI.

Thoughts on staff who are service users

Lauren says:

For me personally, the hardest thing has been coming to terms with the fact that I have been diagnosed with a serious mental illness, and accepting this. To this day I do not feel I have truly accepted that I suffer with bipolar disorder, and I frequently lapse into distorted thinking and beliefs rather than acknowledge the severity of the illness I have. I have moved on from the stage where I didn't feel I could talk to other staff members about my illness, to a point where I will share with other colleagues about my illness if I feel there is a trust and friendship between us. By sharing this information it can become possible, slowly, to inform colleagues about the reality of my situation, and that recovery is possible. This might help reduce some of the stigma surrounding mental illness. However, it is still difficult to open up about my mental health needs as I constantly live in fear of judgement of others, which at times can lead to feelings of paranoia, e.g. believing that people are watching me and waiting for me to become ill or do something bizarre.

Eric says:

Working with Lauren has illustrated the difficulties associated with being a member of staff, while attempting to overcome mental health issues – in this case bipolar disorder. Perhaps the central feature of importance is the delicacy of the balance to be struck between the views of three professionals (Lauren, Guy and Eric), the user (Lauren), her family and the organisational requirements of GPT.

Thus, one of the first aspects of Lauren's care has been to recognise that Guy, Eric and Lauren all bring knowledge, skills and experience to bear. However, Lauren, in times of difficulty, is required not only to manage the challenge of diluting her professional status, but also to adopt the position of a service user, which can imply a status of 'passive recipient of services'. In turn, the challenge for Guy and me is to continue to remain collaborative, wherever possible, with Lauren, but also to act in her best interests at all times, which could mean implementing statutory treatment in extremis.

Also, the family component of the work with Lauren is important. Here the roles of adult daughter must be weighed against Lauren's parents' role. Lauren's parents are a source of support and also information. For example they provide pragmatic support for Lauren in being able to help look after her daughter. Also, they were able to contribute to her EWSG. But they may also need to request help if they become concerned about Lauren.

In addition, Lauren's right and choice to work need to be set against her professional responsibility to GPT as an organisation. Similarly, GPT as an organisation needs to be able to offer Lauren some flexibility in terms of working hours, and also in terms of managerial support and contact with the occupational health department (OHD). Lauren's position has been helped in GPT by having an honest, constructive and open dialogue with her manager, with prompt lines of communication to the OHD, helped with liaison from Guy. Another helpful factor for Lauren has been the delivery of ongoing clinical supervision in which her professional work is helpfully reflected upon in scheduled sessions from a suitably qualified colleague. This should be normal practice, but Lauren has not always received clinical supervision in the past.

Of relevance to Lauren's care is my relationship as consultant psychologist with Guy as psychiatrist. What helps is a mutual appreciation of team-working (between each other as well as with Lauren), and a clear commitment to person-centred, collaborative work framed against a 'realist-optimist backdrop'. Guy is able to embrace the fact that relapse prevention measures are useful and is also able to use the psychologically-informed practice of motivational interviewing. I appreciate that judicious medication prescription can be beneficial. Should differences in clinical management opinion arise, then they are discussed in an open manner. The danger of large professional differences is minimised by emphasising that Lauren's care remains central to our clinical efforts. In turn, this is helped by feelings of respect for Lauren, who has had the courage not only to negotiate her return to work, but also to write bravely about her experiences in this chapter.

Guy says:

People working in health care settings often have a very high degree of investment in their own health, particularly their mental health. This is deeply tied to their professional identity as a carer. The frequent corollary of this is a conscious or unconscious belief that only other people get ill: care needs are largely projected. Sam Shem famously made this the fourth law of his fictional hospital *The House of God* (1978): 'the patient is the one with the disease'.

This can make the journey from being a health care professional to being a patient a particularly difficult one. It involves letting go of fantasies of omnipotence and invulnerability and taking back projections of frailty, illness and disability. Stigma usually looms particularly large in the minds of this group of patients, who often have major concerns about confidentiality. Accepting care is often vigorously resisted because being a patient is often equated with being less of a doctor, nurse, occupational therapist or other professional. Scambler and Hopkins (1986) make the useful distinction between felt stigma and enacted stigma: *felt stigma* refers to the shame that goes with the diagnosis of a mental illness, and the fear of being discriminated against because of this; *enacted stigma* refers to actual discrimination. Often in this group, felt stigma is far more disruptive of lives and of a sense of well-being than enacted stigma. In particular, because 'patient' and 'health professional' are at some level often experienced as mutually exclusive, the stigma of mental illness can have a profound spoiling effect on professional identity. For those whose self-image is largely tied up in their professional affiliation, this can be a profoundly uncomfortable experience. As Goffman (1963, cited in Scambler 1997, p. 175) said, 'there is a constant quandary: to display or not to display; to tell or not to tell; to lie or not to lie; and in each case, to whom, how, when and where'.

For me, what makes this group of patients particularly gratifying to treat is that those who do complete the difficult journey from health care professional to patient often find the return journey richly rewarding. Their initial fears of being less of a doctor, nurse, OT, etc. are invariably confounded by the new knowledge they bring of life as a patient. This is not simply a matter of knowing at first hand the minutiae of what it means to be a patient, though this is important. What seems to be more transformative is a deeper understanding of their own self and the limits of their abilities and responsibilities. 'The wounded healer' is often an astute clinician with a sharpened ability to see the patient in front of them as a rounded human being – fallible and vulnerable but also a resourceful and able master of their own destiny.

Conclusions

This chapter has concentrated on the use of relapse prevention techniques for a staff member who is also a person with bipolar disorder. A brief consideration of policy directives and the evidence for clinical effectiveness of relapse prevention in bipolar disorder was presented. Lauren's experiences of this intervention were explored at length, together with some reflections regarding PSI delivery from an organisational perspective. Some observations of what it is like to be a staff member experiencing serious mental health issues were also discussed. In terms of challenging stigma, and promoting choice and recovery within mental health services for staff who are service users, the message remains consistent: wider opportunities are available if negative attitudes can be successfully challenged and some of the myths surrounding mental health are debunked.

Notes

1 A note on authorship: the name of the service user has been changed to provide anonymity, as have the names of her daughter (now 'Alison') and her ex-partner (now 'Jim').

2 See also chapter 7 on advance agreements and pre-emptive care planning.

3 See chapter 3: the use of these colours here are not synonymous with 'traffic lights' colours: in these EWS grids, having *no* colour means that there are no EWS: green denotes that there *are* problematic signs, although green ones are the mildest of these signs: hence the task is to stop even 'greens' from arising, but if they do, ensure that they do not lead on to amber or red signs.

References

Birchwood, M.J., Spencer, E. and McGovern, D. (2000) Schizophrenia: early warning signs. *Advances in Psychiatric Treatment*, 6, 93–101.

Colom, F., Vieta, E., Reinares, M., Martinex-Aran, A., Torrent, C., Goikolea, J. and Gasto, C. (2003) Psycho-education efficacy in bipolar disorders: beyond compliance enhancement. *Journal of Clinical Psychiatry*, 64, 1101–5.

Denney, J. and Davis, E. (2006) Integrated approaches to relapse prevention. In Gamble, C. and Brennan, G. (eds.) *Working with Serious Mental Illness*, 2nd edition, pp. 341–58. Edinburgh: Bailliere Tindall.

Department of Health (1999) *National Service Framework for Mental Health: Modern Standards and Service Models*. London: Department of Health.

Department of Health (2000) *National Health Service Plan*. London: Department of Health.

Department of Health (2001) *Mental Health Policy Implementation Guide*. London: Department of Health.

Goffman, E. (1963) *Stigma: Notes on the Management of Spoiled Identity*. New York: Prentice Hall.

IRIS [Initiative to Reduce the Impact of Schizophrenia] (2000) *Early Intervention in Psychosis. Clinical Guidelines and Service Frameworks*. www.iris-initiative.org.uk.

Jamison, Kay Redfield (1997) *An Unquiet Mind*. London: Picador.

Krawiecka, M., Goldberg, D. and Vaughan, M. (1977) A standardized psychiatric assessment scale for rating chronic psychiatric patients. *Acta Psychiatrica Scandinavica*, 55, 299–308.

Lam, D., Wong, G, and Sham, P. (2001) Prodromes, coping strategies and course of illness in bipolar affective disorder – a naturalistic study. *Psychological Medicine*, 31, 1397–1402.

Lam, D., Hayward, P., Watkins, E., Wright, K. and Sham, P. (2005) Relapse prevention in patients with bipolar disorder: cognitive therapy outcome after 2 years. *American Journal of Psychiatry*, 162, 324–9.

Lancashire, S. (1994) *Revised Version of KGV Scale*. Manchester: Department of Nursing, Psychiatry and Behavioural Sciences, University of Manchester.

Miklowitz, D., Richards, J., George, E., Frank, E., Suddath, E., Powell. K. and Sacher, J. (2003) Integrated family and individual therapy for bipolar disorder: results of a treatment study. *Journal of Clinical Psychiatry*, 64, 182–91.

Miller, W. and Rollnick, S. (2002) *Motivational Interviewing*. New York: Guilford Press.
Nuechterlein, K. and Dawson, M. (1984) A heuristic vulnerability-stress model of schizophrenic episodes. *Schizophrenia Bulletin*, 10, 300–12.
Perry, A., Tarrier, N., Morris, R., McCarthy, E. and Limb, K. (1999) Randomised controlled trial of efficacy of teaching patients with bipolar disorder to identify early symptoms of relapse and obtain treatment. *British Medical Journal*, 318, 149–53.
Rollnick S. and Miller, W. (1995) What is motivational interviewing? *Behavioural and Cognitive Psychotherapy*, 23, 325–34; and see: motivationalinterview.org/clinical/whatismi.html (accessed 1 August 2004).
Scambler, G. (1997) (ed.) *Sociology as Applied to Medicine*, 4th edition. London: Saunders.
Scambler G. and Hopkins, A. (1986) Being epileptic: coming to terms with stigma. *Social Health Illness*, 8, 26–43.
Scott, J. and Gutierrez, M. (2004) The current status of psychological treatments in bipolar disorders: a systematic review of relapse prevention. *Bipolar Disorders*, 6, 498–503.
Shem, Samuel (1978) *The House of God*. New York: Richard Marek Publishers.
Smith, J. and Tarrier, N. (1992) Prodromal symptoms in manic depressive psychosis. *Social Psychiatry and Psychiatric Epidemiology*, 27, 245–8.
Zweben, A. and Zuckoff, A. (2002) Motivational interviewing and treatment adherence. In Miller, W. and Rollnick, S. (eds.) *Motivational Interviewing*. New York: Guilford Press.

Chapter 7

Women's Experiences of Psychosis

Recognition of Gendered Difference

Vicky MacDougall, Karen Luckett and Megan Jones

Key Points

- There is starting to be an overdue recognition that different genders need different service responses.
- Early intervention services are predominantly used by young men. Women's experiences of mental distress are different than men's experiences.
- The caring role women have in our society, above all, has a bearing on their mental health well-being.
- Women appear to be invisible in bio-medical research settings.
- Women are asking to be listened to in order to ensure that services are genuinely sensitive to their needs and that they become integral to existing services and future service development.
- Women carry a much larger burden of personal abuse than do men; this needs to be identified and services developed in response to this.
- No dedicated first-episode for psychosis service exists locally for people over 35, yet 50 per cent of women are not diagnosed with schizophrenia until their mid-40s.
- Serious mental disorder may present its growing manifestation very differently in women than in men.

Introduction

This chapter will examine the general issues of women and schizophrenia, including the different aetiology of this disorder depending on gender, and women's experiences of their treatment. It will also examine policy statements about good practices in relation to women's services that are now beginning to be produced, after many years of campaigning by organisations such as Mind (e.g. 1994), and Good Practice in Mental Health (1994). These publications highlighted the need for different responses and services for women.

The impact of schizophrenia will be illustrated through the experiences of Karen and Megan, both of whom have a diagnosis of schizophrenia, with Megan also having a diagniosis of schizo-affective disorder. Karen has had a number of varying diagnoses, but her experience, as a young woman, of treatment during a first episode of psychosis, shows both similarities with and differences from the prevailing models of early intervention. Megan's experience illustrates the complexity of the multiple needs of a woman with children who undergoes a first episode of diagnosed schizophrenia and schizo-affective disorder.

Both of these experiences are in relation to first-episode psychosis, but what follows is pertinent to other women who have had a number of episodes of diagnosed schizophrenia. The issue is the recognition that different genders need different responses from services. On the other hand, however, women are not a homogenous grouping: as well as needing different services from men because they are women, they also have very different *individual* needs.

The conclusion of the chapter makes recommendations to help women with psychosis by recognising gender difference and the role that gender has in women's lives. Women should be recognised as having distinct needs of their own that are linked to the role women continue to have in society as care-givers. The emphasis of this chapter is on the need to *listen to women and to form services that they want*, a process which is highlighted in the recent documents: *Women's Mental Health: Into the Mainstream. Strategic Development of Mental Health Care for Women* (Department of Health 2002a) and *Mainstreaming Gender and Women's Mental Health: Implementation Guidance* (Department of Health 2003).

The Evidence

Gender differences

Kraepelin (1909) first observed that men were three times more likely than women to show the particular features of dementia praecox as a disorder featuring certain neurological abnormalities. Since then, much has been written about the increasing medicalisation of women's experience of serious mental health problems (Chesler 1972; Showalter 1987; Usher 1991; Barnes and Maple 1992; Doyal 1995; Russell 1995; Busfield 1996). This medicalisation highlights what Busfield (1996) calls a 'gendered landscape' in the relationship between the psychiatric profession and women: 'a distinctive patterning of diagnosed *disorder by* gender' (p. 14). However it has only been recently that the research agenda has acknowledged women and their different experience of psychosis and treatment, be it a first episode or the experience of living through many relapses.

Vicky says:

Schizophrenia is the most researched of the psychoses and this chapter will concentrate on women who experience schizophrenia, illustrated through the needs, experiences and stories of two women I have worked closely with: Karen and Megan. Other women have had many relapses; however, the underlying philosophy remains the same. My passion for this subject is grounded in my own experience as a practitioner who has frequently encountered women who have been the unheard voices of mental distress (MacDougall 1998), unheard as to their needs and their distress.

Policy Context

With the new millennium there arrived a series of policy statements suggesting that women's distinct mental health needs were going to be met. In March 2001, John Hutton, the Minister for Mental Health, announced a strategy for women that would:

> pull together issues of concern for women across the mental health framework and the NHS plan and link with work of other government departments; ensure that women are listened to and their views translated to those who currently provide valuable service for women in crisis.
>
> (Department of Health 2002a, p. 9)

The new Minister for Mental Health, Jacqui Smith, who stated that the Labour government was committed to addressing discrimination and inequality, took this further:

> The needs of women are central to the Government's programme of reform and investment in public services and to our commitment of addressing discrimination and inequality. Modernising mental health services is one of our core national priorities.
>
> (Department of Health 2002a, p. 5)

In 2003 Patricia Hewitt, at that time the Labour Secretary of State for Trade and Industry and Minister for Women, delivered the government's report *Delivering on Gender Equality* (Department of Trade and Industry 2003), which emphasised the initiatives that were being taken by the government to raise standards on gender.

Against this background and other Department of Health policies (including the removal of mixed sex wards in 95 per cent of NHS Trusts by 2002 (Department of Health 2000)) aimed at tackling inequalities, discrimination and disadvantage in the delivery of mental health services, the consultation document: *Women's Mental Health: Into the Mainstream. Strategic Development of Mental Health Care for Women* (Department of Health 2002a) was introduced. This document emphasises the many roles that women may have: within the workforce, the home, in child-care and caring for dependent family members. Also identified are women's experiences of low social status and value, social isolation and poverty. Women also experience the greatest level of childhood sexual abuse, domestic abuse and sexual violence. This complex interplay of distress has a great impact on women's mental health (Carmen, Rieker and Mills 1984; Finkelhor, Hoteling and Lewis 1990; Payne 1991; Beitchman et al. 1992; Faugier 1992; Mullen et al. 1993; Macran, Clarke and Joshi 1996; Goodman et al. 1997; Read 1998; Morrow 2002).

The consultation document also raises the importance of treating the underlying social causes of mental ill health in women, rather than just symptoms, which are the outcome of structural stress rather than random illness. Research has been available since the groundbreaking work by Brown and Harris (1978) that clearly linked stress, poverty and depression in women. The 2002a consultation document suggests that if women are given support in areas which have previously been ignored as being separate to their mental health problems (e.g. support with parenting) then their potential for recovery will be greatly increased. The consultation document clearly links mental disorder with unsupported stress (Merrill, Laux and Thornby 1990; Coverdale and Aruffo 1992; Coverdale et al. 1993; Zemenchuk, Rogosch and Mowbray 1995).

Biomedical Research

Women have long been critical of biomedical research, feeling that they have not benefited from it, owing to their lower rates of participation in clinical studies and research (Russo 1990), even though they are the main consumers of medication. Treatment with drugs also conveys the impression that the person who is prescribed them is sick or crazy and by implication that social and environmental factors are not relevant to the illness (McCarthy 1994).

Women appear to be invisible in biomedical research into schizophrenia, and this has huge implications for both their mental and physical well-being. Although this exclusion has been justified as being based on ethical grounds, owing to their child-bearing potential and possible foetal damage through any drug trials, it has in fact also excluded older women (Hambrecht, Maurer and Hafner 1992). Despite the evidence for different ethnic groups absorbing medication at different rates, and for women metabolising medication at different rates from men, and for the need for different medication treatments during both ethnic and white women's reproductive years, the evidence base for drugs usually relies on research undertaken on white men (Hendrick and Gitlin 2004).

This exclusion of women has meant that medical care is based on the presumption that treatments which have been researched and tested on men from one ethnic group can be generalised and then applied to all women, from both the same and other ethnic groups. In fact, the medical treatment that a woman may receive can cause catastrophic changes in her physical condition (Healy 1993). This gender blindness is also reflected in the psychiatric and psychological treatment of women (Hambrecht, Maurer and Hafner 1992; Good Practice in Mental Health 1994; Mind 1994; Doyal 1995; Johnstone 2002). The Department of Health's document laying out the priorities for the NHS for the 2003–6 period (Department of Health 2002b) sets treatment targets, but it does not even mention gender. We see this as an important omission, losing an opportunity to challenge and fully research the gender issues identified above.

Aetiology

Despite Kraepelin's early work, until recently very little research has specifically focused on the role that gender plays in the aetiology and course of schizophrenia. Schizophrenia is equally distributed across the genders in a lifetime, with first episodes manifesting earlier in men (14 to 25 years) (Castle, McGrath and Kulkarni 2000) than in women (21 to 30 years). The age distribution also shows first episodes in women having another peak, between the ages of 45 to 55 years (Goldstein 1988; Castle, McGrath and Kulkarni 2000; Takahashi et al. 2000). While recent early intervention for psychosis services are to be welcomed for men and women diagnosed at an earlier age, there is no dedicated service for those older women who experience a first episode after the age of 35. These women may have very different needs, suggesting that different service responses may be required from those offered to the early onset group.

There are two major summaries of the literature on gender differences in schizophrenia (Castle, McGrath and Kulkarni 2000; Seeman 2000). They conclude that recognition of gender differences is integral to the improvement of women's experiences of mental health services. What follows attempts to summarise some of their findings.

The occurrence of schizophrenia is more than expected in daughters whose mothers have been exposed to viral infections during the second trimester of pregnancy; obstetric complications have also been implicated as a risk factor in schizophrenia, occurring more often in mothers of sons who later go on to develop schizophrenia; this additional brain damage, resulting from the birth trauma, may explain the earlier onset in men and the greater ratio and severity of illness that occurs in young men (Castle, McGrath and Kulkarni 2000).

The pace of development of the left-hand side of the brain is faster in women than in men and this could be because of the release of testosterone in male foetuses. Normal brain structure asymmetry is often lost in men who have developed schizophrenia but not in women (Seeman 2000). Again the significance of this is not clear. In the general population, women have a more bilateral distribution of cognitive functions than men. This may be an advantage if one side of the brain is specifically impaired in schizophrenia. High resolution brain scanning has shown structural brain deficits in people with schizophrenia, compared with 'normal controls', particularly in frontal and temporal regions, as well as in the grey matter of the brain. These differences are more pronounced in men than women. After many years of the disorder, qualitative changes in attention, memory and judgement are present to an equal extent in men and women, although olfactory deficits, which can be markers of regional brain damage, remain less prevalent in women with schizophrenia until the onset of the menopause. The implication is that women may be protected from some of the severity of schizophrenia through some as-yet not understood, possibly hormonal, mechanism (Castle, McGrath and Kulkarni 2000; Seeman 2000).

A further issue related to the generalisation of male research onto the female population is that the categories for the diagnosis of schizophrenia may have been based on male case examples. There may be an inbuilt bias in the way that the diagnosis has been constructed. It is likely that there are two independent domains: behaviour which is perceived as dangerous; and depth of a psychotic disorder. It is argued that men may be more likely to have bizarre delusions and behaviours which are seen as dangerous. For example, men are more concerned with political conspiracies and undercover activities and have more grandiose delusions of power, royalty and divinity (Seeman 2000). Payne (1995) argues that because psychiatric beds are rationed, this rationing will mean that young men with behaviour that brings them to the notice of the psychiatric services owing to perceived dangerousness, will be more likely to be admitted and treated; whereas women, who might have similar levels of a psychotic disorder but who may not seem so dangerous, will be less likely to receive treatment.

This implies a response based on control, fuelled by public anxiety about perceived violence, rather than one based on care, motivated by a concern for those that have the most disturbing and distressing symptoms.

Another factor is that women are more easily cared for by the family at home because of their less bizarre presentation. This may mean those women are not receiving the best of professional help, early enough.

Women typically exhibit far less obvious signs of illness: for example, they may feel that their body is the wrong shape or exhibit concern about the way they look. This is often met with puzzlement by the treating GP, without this sign being seen as a possible prodrome of schizophrenia (although of course not every woman who presents to her GP who feels her body is the wrong shape may be suffering from schizophrenia!). Women may also show concerns with romantic preoccupations and false beliefs of pregnancy; these signs may be stereotyped as female behaviour rather than the signs of a developing serious disorder (Castle, McGrath and Kulkarni 2000).

A higher percentage of women experience hallucinations than men (Sharma, Dowd and Janicak 1999). Symptoms such as apathy; flattened affect; poverty of speech and social isolation with a consequent negative impact on relationships, are all more common in men than women (Vaughn et al. 1984; Seeman 2000). This could also be due to the earlier onset of schizophrenia in men as opposed to women: with a later onset, people may have already been able to develop long-lasting and loving relationships. Women with schizophrenia are seen to misuse alcohol and drugs less often than their male counterparts, but the severity of the substance misuse when present may not be very different from that of men (Castle, McGrath and Kulkarni 2000).

Women with schizophrenia generally display higher levels of function than their male peers in terms of social functioning; cognition; school achievement; and employment success. Women seem to recover more quickly and more completely than men, with a better social adjustment (Flor-Henry 1990). They stay in hospital for shorter periods and are often discharged on a lower anti-psychotic dose than their male peers (Angermeyer, Kuhn and Goldstein 1990). Women are more likely to comply with their prescribed treatment regime than men (Payne 1995). Female gender seems to predict a better outcome with respect to the rehospitalisation rate at 18 months, although up to 15 years after a first episode of schizophrenia, the relative advantage for women seems to disappear (Castle, McGrath and Kulkarni 2000).

In other words, schizophrenia, at least initially, interrupts women's lives to a lesser degree than it does men's. So, after hospitalisation, women may return to employment more quickly than men. They are more likely to marry and have a family, and develop and maintain larger, more intimate, social support networks. This may also be an indicator of a better outcome for women, as it implies they have a better quality of life then men who, with early onset, are more likely not to have developed long-term relationships. Men, owing to the course and symptomatology of the disorder, are more likely to have repeated episodes of hospitalisation and lose contact with their family.

The Case Studies – Two Individual Experiences

Editors' note: this chapter uses two different cases (Karen and Megan) to describe some of the issues particular to women's experiences of psychosis, and of how collaborative working between practitioners and service users can positively affect outcome.

Karen's story

Vicky says:

I first met Karen in 1997 when we were both presenting at a voice-hearers conference locally in Gloucester. Karen was a 24-year-old white woman who appeared bright and bubbly. She was co-facilitating a workshop about her positive experiences of psychosocial interventions for psychosis (PSI), from a patient's perspective. A community psychiatric nurse (CPN) who had recently completed the Thorn course undertook the PSI intervention being described and was also the co-facilitator. I attended the workshop and was struck by Karen's confidence and coherence. My contribution to the conference was to present, with two other practioners, the recent work we had been jointly undertaking with a group of voice-hearers. Karen attended this presentation and, along with other users of the services, challenged the stereotype of a person with psychosis through her experiences, actions and energy.

I had no further contact with her for five years. Unfortunately the PSI work she had been doing with the CPN had not been continued when the CPN moved to a new service. I met Karen again, coincidentally, when I was visiting another client, Megan, on an acute admissions ward in Gloucester in 2002. Karen told me she had been confined in hospital on a Section of the Mental Health Act (Department of Health 1983). My first impression was to double check that this was the same woman who had made such a lively contribution to the conference, five years before. Psychotropic medication had caused her to increase her weight enormously. Other side effects included agitation. Her physical appearance was worsened by her lack of self-care. She was also withdrawn, appeared isolated, and her speech was slow and slurred. Her explanation for her admission was that she was suicidal and had been self-harming by cutting her arms. She was also fearful that she was going to attack her father with a knife but couldn't explain why. I was shocked by the change in Karen.

Again I had no contact with her until I met her when I started supervising a hearing voices group which she was attending. She was doing a lot better, was out of hospital and living in rehabilitation accommodation. I started to work with her, doing presentations on self-harm and voice-hearing, recognising her particular skills as an expert in both areas. This was also a way of her being paid for her skills.

In 2003 I became involved with the Gloucestershire Partnership NHS Trust's 2003 Annual General Meeting. They were looking for users of the services to deliver the main speeches and to run workshops. I suggested Karen, who did both. She facilitated a workshop on the importance of hope, which (to her) had to come before choice, inclusion and recovery. Karen also undertook an exercise in facilitating her experiences of malevolent voices: this was an exercise undertaken with groups of four to six people. Two people take on the role of malevolent voices and the other people in the group try to carry on a normal conversation. The 'voices' talk through tubes into people's ears: this is to try to demonstrate what the malevolent voice-hearing experience is like. I'm not sure if this has ever been done before with such an eminent group of people that included a mayor, a chief executive, a director of social care, a director of nursing and a non-executive director of our local partnership trust!

Karen told the following story at the AGM as one of the main speakers: her story was about her mother and her journey into the mental health system.

Karen says:

[Mum's] death had a profound effect on me. I quickly slipped into a deep dark depression. Just two months after her death I found myself in hospital for the first time, because I was suicidal. Over the next couple of months I was in and out of hospital several times. I hated hospital because I was always heavily sedated and because it was always so noisy and chaotic. What I needed was peace and quiet. I found the mixed wards intimidating and threatening because I saw many violent incidents. It was at times 'a place of safety' but not a place of recovery. When I wasn't in hospital I was at home with my Dad. I lost my independence and if I am honest, I completely lost all hope. Over the next two years I was sectioned a number of times and although I had started bereavement counselling it wasn't helpful. I would have liked a different approach: perhaps using psychosocial interventions which recognise the need for a more holistic approach. At about this time I started to hear voices. They were very distressing and alarming, telling me I was evil, and that I deserved to die. It was like having someone screaming in my ear, very close much of the time. I shouted back at them and sometimes, because I was so frustrated, I banged my head on the wall. My whole world was caving in and devoid of all hope. I was so bad I didn't want to be treated in the community; I wanted to die in the community.

Three years after Mum died, my Dad and I moved to Gloucester and I was in hospital again. At about this time I started to use self-harm as a coping mechanism. It was a way of coping with overwhelming feelings and even now I still use it. It is crude and ultimately a self-destructive tool, but it gives me temporary relief from overwhelming pain and self-hatred. The release that self-harm gives me enables me to carry on even though the relief that self-harm brings only lasts for short periods. If this release had not been achieved I would have moved on to suicidal thoughts. For me this has resulted in a vicious circle of addiction to self-harm, which I am still struggling to break free from. I am a perfectionist and the voices make me believe that I am evil and worthless. Not a week goes by when I do not think about self-harm. When I am tempted, I think of my family because my self-harm emotionally cripples them.

After being in Gloucester, I began to improve. I was given the opportunity to leave hospital and go to a rehabilitation unit in the community and my recovery started there. The staff team in this unit were inspirational. It was a very small unit so they had plenty of time to talk and listen to me. They encouraged me to become more independent and I started to gain control over my life. I began to attend a voice-hearers group where other people had similar experiences.

So where am I now? I am living in independent accommodation with support from the assertive outreach team, completing a Certificate in Mental Health, doing voluntary work and undertaking research for the local Partnership Trust. I compare myself to a palm tree: it can live under the worst windy and dry conditions without being fed and yet it still exists and even thrives!

Vicky says:

My input with Karen has been on an ad hoc basis since this time. She is paid by the Trust to work with me, and by others to teach on voice-hearing and self-harm and also to co-facilitate a hearing voices group. She has also recently been involved in undertaking user-focused monitoring for our local 'supporting people' floating support service. Both Karen and Megan were trained to do this by the research and development section of the organisation. This is the first time that this department had done this for users of the service in this local Trust, and it has been 'worth its weight in gold': I and other practioners have learned from their expertise. Rose (1998) in *A Guide for Mental Health Service Providers, Users and Purchasers*, highlights the benefits of user involvement. Karen is now talking about a move to completely independent accommodation and is thinking about her future employment needs. Karen also continues to work with Megan, reviewing the floating support service.

Megan's story

Vicky says:

I met Megan in 2002 on the same ward as Karen as described above. Her main problem was hearing a malevolent voice, an area I had a particular interest in. Megan was a 47-year-old white woman: slim, intelligent, well spoken and well groomed. Once I began to talk with her, I became increasingly concerned with her troubled internal psychological world. She told me about a dictatorial male voice, whom she was convinced was God. This voice kept telling her to jump in the river because she couldn't give enough love to her children. She had been living in Spain with her male partner, where for many years she worked as a successful language teacher. She was the main wage earner and mother to their three children. Her partner had subjected Megan to years of domestic abuse. When the psychosis was becoming worse in Spain, she had been placed in a terrible dilemma of either choosing to get away from the abuse by entering a refuge, thereby losing custody of the children she so deeply cared for, or returning to the UK to the care of her family. She was advised to come back to England to be cared for by her family. On her return, she became more and more distressed as the malevolent voice became more commanding, reinforced by tactile hallucinations, experienced as God touching her. She described very powerfully being told not to move by 'God' and if she did, something awful would happen. This meant she was almost catatonic; and on disobeying, feeling her back was being flayed. At one point she thought she had disobeyed and felt she had been turned into a dog. I felt empathy towards Megan. My children were similar ages to hers; I could imagine how I might feel under the same circumstances with my children in another country, with a father whose job meant that the children were often left on their own.

At this time Megan was still on a section 3 of the Mental Health Act. Despite this and building on her strengths and with the support of the hospital staff and a community worker employed by a social services day centre, she was found a voluntary job working as a language teacher in a local school, teaching asylum seekers to speak and write English. Megan's mental health started to improve, but every time she was moved to supported accommodation she was ordered by 'God' to stop taking her medication and go and jump in the river.

Hospital, for Megan, was a safe place where she could negotiate with the voice of 'God', telling him that she couldn't go to the river, as she was expected in certain places at certain times. Hospital also allowed her to fulfil another command: to 'give to others through conversation'. Megan's interpretation of this was that she had to listen to people and give to them with her conversation. This could be by praising them. In the community there was no option to negotiate: she rapidly felt isolated and felt so weak that she could only obey the voice.

Megan was becoming increasingly distressed about the loss of her children and her lack of contact with them. At this point there was a very supportive team involved in her care that felt that if the children agreed to be in England with Megan, they could be better cared for and Megan's mental health would improve as she regained her parenting role. This was an inspired and calculated piece of risk-taking by the team and quite contrary to the frequent use of risk management that removes creative choices from the client and workers. I was one of the workers who supported this decision and was instrumental in offering the support of a community worker from the day centre. The children's father agreed that they could live with her; the children were ambivalent about the move but made the decision to try it for the duration of their school summer holidays.

With the support of the local accommodation scheme, a four-bedroomed house was found for Megan, and a local charity agreed to provide the airfares for the children (aged 10, 14 and 16). This charity also made a creative risk-taking decision to support a vulnerable woman, following extensive information from the care team, consisting of a CPN, myself (a manager of a social services mental health day centre), a support worker employed by the centre, and social services. We worked with Megan to put a care plan together to support the whole family, furnish the house and provide toys from our attics! It felt in some ways risky. We didn't know how the children would be, or if this intervention would prove positive. My own manager was not aware of the amount of input I was personally giving; and given the amount of red tape and policies in place to protect clients and staff that surround practioners work, I don't think this would have been fully supported.

The Department of Health in 2004 published a framework for the whole of the Mental Health services called *The Ten Essential Shared Capabilities* (Department of Health 2004). The aim of this document is to promote a shift in culture towards 'choice, person centeredness and mental health promotion' (p. 1). This is in response to users and carers continuing to report that they are not being listened to. The document clarifies the need for practioners to have 'essential capabilities' as part of their training. One of the identified essential capabilities for mental health practice is 'promoting safety and positive risk-taking: empowering the person to decide the level of risk they are prepared to take with their health and safety' (p. 7), which includes working with the tension between promoting safety, and positive risk-taking, including assessing and dealing with the possible risks for service users, carers, family members and the wider public.

Vicky says:

I find this helpful in reflecting on the work that was undertaken at this time. What we knew was that, up to that time, nothing else had worked. Whenever Megan had moved to supported accommodation, things rapidly fell apart, with Megan rapidly stopping her medication and isolating herself, resulting in her having to return to hospital. Megan continued to tell us of her distress and worry in being separated from her children. The care plan which was put together offered 24-hour care that included our home phone numbers. At this time, no after-hours crisis service or outreach services were in place in our Trust.

The care plan covered all aspects of Megan's care including how she would spend her days. This included occupation, and her attendance at the day centre to enable her to enjoy social activities and art, attend voice-hearing groups, and develop with her new skills, to enable her to work to her optimum. Weekly psychotherapy was also offered to Megan, which she found beneficial. She continued to work with asylum seekers with the community worker from the day centre. We worked closely with her family, who helped by offering her child-care and supporting the 24-hour-a-day programme.

In addition to Megan's support workers, the children had a Spanish-speaking social worker, especially important for the youngest child who could not speak English well. After the children arrived, members of the care team visited four times a day, including the evening, and met daily to discuss the plan. The amount of input reduced over the next few months as Megan's mental health improved, until Megan was only seeing her community psychiatric nurse fortnightly, for medication. Megan welcomed this, as she wanted to be a normal mother caring for her family. All involved, including the children, saw the interventions to have been successful.

The children did not go home after the summer, but stayed on in Gloucester, attending local schools. Megan went to the local college, undertaking an access course, a counselling course, and then going on to do a psychology degree. I moved on to another role during this time and lost contact, although I did hear that the children were doing well, one moving on to university and another coming first in a national exam.

However, one evening three years later, I saw her appearing to be heading off in the direction of the river with her head down and completely oblivious to what was going on around her. I stopped her and took her for a coffee. She told me that the voice of God had been telling her that she could not put off going to the river any longer. I discovered she had asked the children if they would now like to go back to live with their father, as his circumstances had changed, and they had agreed to this. Megan had stopped taking her medication, given up her studies and was thinking again about jumping in the river, although she was trying hard to resist. The next day I alerted her team that she was unwell again and I heard nothing further until two months later, when I learned from a staff member at the local hospital that Megan was in hospital on a section, feeling suicidal and having little or no contact with the children.

Given my knowledge of her capacity for research, I invited her to become involved with Karen and another service user in some user-focused monitoring groups. She did this over a period of months. Though it was difficult for her at times, she was supported by the other two women doing the research. I have now started to become involved again, working with her to help her resist her voices and help towards an understanding of them again; and I welcome this. With the support of her team she is also accessing voluntary work and using her skills as a linguist. She is still very troubled by her voices, but instead of encouraging her to resist them through the use of CBT, we are now discussing the idea of her undergoing a trial by God, in much the same way as did Jesus in the desert, the Buddah, and Christian in the *The Pilgrims Progress* (John Bunyan 1678/2003). Megan regularly travels to Spain to visit her children and understandably on her return her voice becomes more commanding. To support her particularly at these times she is writing a wellness recovery action plan (WRAP) (Copeland 1997).

What helped

Karen had the support of an assertive outreach team (AOT) when she moved to her independent accommodation and, like Megan, had a comprehensive care plan. There were again similarities with Megan: they both had a psychotherapist, which they saw as being invaluable, allowing them to talk about their feelings in a constructive way. This resource is not available to everybody but, given women's identification of the need for talking therapies, invaluable. Megan and Karen also attended a voice-hearing group and a number of community resources including The Club House where Megan is now teaching Spanish and feels again that she has a role. Tables 7.1 and 7.2 summarise the elements which both Karen and Megan found helpful and unhelpful.

Discussion

Women have long been critical of the measurements of 'mental illness', the diagnostic tools and language used by psychiatrists following the medical model. These devices are employed under the continuing belief that serious mental disturbance is a series of distinct diseases that can be classified and measured, without recognising the very different life experiences that women have had and are continuing to experience (Zubin and Spring 1977). It has even been suggested that such opposition and denial of their own locus of control can be so pathological to some particularly vulnerable women as to cause a psychotic episode (Zubin and Spring 1977). Clinical judgements of women tend to reflect the traditional stereotypes (Broverman et al. 1970). It would appear those clinicians' views of what constitutes normal health behaviour for women is influenced by stereotypical imagery and may well influence diagnosis, treatment and rehabilitation in many negative ways. Busfield however, in 1996, contradicts this somewhat, arguing that diagnostic biases are unlikely to be the whole explanation of the sex differences in diagnosis and that the explanation is far more complex. Data shows that there is an enormous variation in identified mental disorders, with men being far more predominant in some areas of diagnosis and women in others.

Karen and Megan's narratives show the different experiences that have led to their psychosis. Kessler and McLeod (1984) concluded that women are more vulnerable to environmental events than men, and in particular to events that happen in their close and family environment. While this can be a protective factor, it also carries the risk of being more distressing if there are incidents happening in their close family networks. This is not to ignore genetic factors; but both of them had taken on the roles expected of them by society as carers, Karen of her mother and Megan of her children. 'It is still portrayed as natural to care and unnatural not to do so' (Brown and Smith 1993, p. 187). This has come at an enormous cost for both of them, even though they both wanted and chose this role. For Megan

Table 7.1 What Karen identified in 2004 as having helped her

What helped	*What didn't help*
Talking about my Mum	People avoiding talking about my Mum's illness and death
Sharing my experience with other service users	Being put in hospital and not helped
Self-harm	Over medication to keep me quiet!
Hearing voices group	People doubting my experience – especially hearing voices
Some limited medication	Meaningless labels
CBT	
Being believed (about hearing voices)	
Psychotherapy – and learning how to express my feelings	
Continuity of care	
Being under assertive outreach team not a rehab. team meant more contact	

there was the double bind of being with a violent husband, yet wanting to stay with and care for her children. If Megan had stayed with her children in Spain she would have continued to have suffered at the hands of her partner, which was already having an impact on her mental health (although of course, leaving also put a strain on it). This strain appeared to result in an increase in Megan's voice-hearing, with the voice of 'God', telling her to care for her children and 'give more love'. For Karen, with the loss of her mother she also lost her role as carer. These events have had catastrophic results for them, with what they have described as tremendous feelings of guilt, reflected in their voice-hearing experiences and (for Karen) the developing of self-harming behaviour, while Megan developed compulsive suicidal behaviour.

Strong (2000) in *A Bright Red Scream* promotes the idea that self-harming behaviour is based on histories of past trauma. Karen and Megan have both suffered trauma. To ignore women's individual experiences of mental disorder is to ignore the complexity of their lives that may result in trauma, and a treatable or untreatable diagnosis. The literature suggests that the experience of men and women with severe and enduring mental health problems such as psychosis are very different. This is reflected in the case studies. The aetiology of such severe and enduring mental health problems is usually described in biological terms, yet there is little physical evidence for this being true in schizophrenia. Despite this, schizophrenia has a DSM category (Arnold 1994). There is also controversy in the diagnosis of other mental disorders, especially in the area of borderline personality disorder. Unfortunately, women seem to suffer particularly from this process of categorisation, having more disorders originating from social or environmental conditions than through biological factors (Brown and Harris 1978). Karen may be seen to have been lucky with her diagnosis of schizophrenia, receiving a range of interventions based on it. If she

Table 7.2 What Megan identified in 2004 as having helped her

What helped	*What didn't help*
My psychiatrist's quiet accepting attitude when I first came into contact with a psychiatrist in England.	One psychiatrist's dismissive, impatient attitude when the voice wouldn't disappear.
Going over my past notes, so that I could get a more sensible perspective on what I'd said previously and get in touch with my feelings.	Not being given enough consideration as a woman. Questions about motherhood and domestic violence weren't even asked.
Finding other people in a similar situation, and equally intimidated when I was first admitted to hospital.	The ward was over-crowded.
Having a named nurse, someone willing to spend a whole half hour listening.	Nurses in general not having enough time for patients.
Ward rounds offered limited help – just an update to check whether the medication type and amount was appropriate and general well-being looked all right.	Ward rounds were frustrating because there was too little time. It was the only time we saw the doctor and not enough time was spent on the human situation: a more holistic approach would have been preferable.
The caring atmosphere on the first ward. The generally shared 'philosophy' among patients that they can support each other and are all in the same boat.	Aggression that wasn't dealt with. People suffering from it were told 'he or she is ill' and that was all.
Other women to talk to, some of whom had also lost their children, too, although for different reasons.	
The well planned after care once I was back 'in the community' – a very human approach.	

had been diagnosed as having borderline personality disorder, which many of the existing symptoms could have suggested, she would have received a very different service, as until recently this has been seen as being untreatable (National Institute of Mental Health – England 2003),

At times both Megan and Karen have suffered from the side-effects of medication. Hendrick and Gitlin (2004) highlight the gender differences in the pharmacological treatment of women. They draw attention to the side-effects that are unique to women and suggest treatment considerations that recognise the menstrual cycle of women. Recent research undertaken by Cole on *Seeing Female Psychiatric Inpatients as Women* (2004) and presented at the Celebrating Women in Psychiatry conference concluded that '*illness*-based stereotypes and responses are powerful to the point that the chronically mentally ill are regarded as almost genderless by both researchers and clinicians'. This finding has been echoed by both Megan and Karen, neither of whom have any memory of ever discussing with their team at any point during their care, both in and out of hospital, their contraception or indeed if they needed any. We do know (again from Cole (2004) and other studies) that women with schizophrenia are at particular risk from pregnancy when unwell, owing to their impaired autonomy, which reduces their capacity to protect themselves.

Conclusion

Although the underlying philosophy of improving quality of life by moving from institutional care to community care was good, it has had and continues to have different implications for men and women. Women need to be recognised as having distinct needs of their own, as identified in the recent document, *Women's Mental Health: Into the Mainstream. Strategic Development of Mental Health Care for Women* (Department of Health 2002a).

Karen and Megan are very clear about what has helped and not helped, as shown in Tables 7.1 and 7.2. *Women's Mental Health: Into the Mainstream* (Department of Health 2002a) is clear as to how organisations need to change to meet the needs of women, by being sensitive to gender, ethnicity and specifically the needs of women at the planning stage, not as an afterthought.

In terms of these suggested changes and developments, Gloucestershire Partnership NHS Trust has a lot to celebrate: the appointment of a lead person for women's services; a number of women-only services across the Trust; training on the women's agenda; work being undertaken on the mental health and well-being of Gloucestershire women in prisons (at present this is solely with Eastwood Park, a women's prison near Bristol, but we hope to build on this work to include women coming from prisons across England back to Gloucestershire on release); groups for women survivors of sexual abuse; women-only hearing voices groups; inpatient and community women-only groups; and finally, the voluntary sector providing women-only accommodation for women and children who are at risk of domestic violence and who also have mental health problems.

The issue of domestic violence deserves particular mention. At present the costs to the NHS of domestic violence linked to women's mental health care is currently £176 million (Walby 2004). In response to this locally, the Trust is developing a training package to highlight the impact that domestic violence has on women's mental health. This is linked to Gloucestershire's Co-ordinated Community Response to Domestic Violence policy and part of a rolling programme of training to support the development of inpatient integrated care pathways (ICP). ICPs have been developed in response to the Department of Health guidance that each working age adult acute ward should have these. The pathways have been developed to look at patients' journeys from referral to discharge, with attention given to the standards in essence of care (Department of Health 2000), social needs, gender, etc. Locally there are good existing services that need to be built on – crisis teams/home treatment teams and early intervention teams.

The early intervention teams, though working with women with first episodes of psychosis under the age of 35, offer no specific services for older women who have their first episode in their mid-40s to 50s or older. This work is essential to improve the well-being of women and their families. A review of day services in our Trust was undertaken in 2005 and there is interest in commissioning women-only community services. This gives hope on behalf of the many women service users who have requested these services, which are identified in the document *Mainstreaming Gender and Women's Mental Health: Implementation Guidance* (Department of Health 2003). In response to the 2003 implementation guidance on the development of services for people with personality disorder (National Institute of Mental Health – England 2003), the Trust has developed a new team to respond to people with a diagnosis of borderline personality disorder across the county: this is predominantly a diagnosis given to women.

Vicky says:

Reflecting on my own role in working with Megan, I think now that I would have asked to have continued to be involved with her care over the last three years. The importance of workers following patients through their 'careers' is I feel still underrated, though research continues to highlight that the engagement of particular workers is what is important and not the particular therapies on offer (Svedberg, Jormfeldt and Arvidsson 2003).

On a final note, both Megan and Karen have (2005) been involved in training and facilitating user focus groups for the Trust. They were paid by the Trust to do the work and from this experience a research group is being initiated to support users of the services to undertake research that they see as being important. I never fail to be reminded of these women's courage in the face of adversity and to admire how they manage to keep going. Karen recently said, while she was teaching on deliberate self-harm to a group of workers at NHS direct, 'I may have the voices forever but I am no longer going to let them stop me getting on with my life'. That to me was very powerful and indicates how far she is on her pathway to recovery.

References

Angermeyer, M., Kuhn, L. and Goldstein, J. (1990) Gender and the course of schizophrenia: differences in treated outcomes. *Schizophrenia Bulletin*, 16, 293–307.

Arnold, L. (1994) *Understanding Self-injury*. Bristol: Bristol Crisis Service for Women.

Barnes, M. and Maple, N. (1992) *Women and Mental Health: Challenging the Stereotypes*. Birmingham: Venture Press.

Beitchman, J., Zucker, K., Hood, J., Da Costa, G., Akman, D. and Cassava, E. (1992) A review of the long-term effects of child sexual abuse. *Child Abuse and Neglect*, 16, 101–18.

Broverman, I., Broverman, D., Clarkson, F., Rosenkrantz, P. and Vogels, R. (1970) Sex roles and clinical judgements of mental health. *Journal of Consulting and Clinical Psychology*, 34, 1–7.

Brown, G. and Harris, T. (1978) *The Social Origins of Depression: A Study of Psychiatric Disorder in Women*. London: Tavistock.

Brown, H. and Smith, H. (1993) Women caring for people: the mismatch between rhetoric and women's reality? *Policy and Politics*, 21, 185–93.

Bunyan, J. (1678/2003) *The Pilgrims Progress*. Oxford World Classics. Oxford: Oxford University Press.

Busfield, J. (1996) *Men, Women and Madness*. London: Macmillan.

Carmen, E., Rieker, P. and Mills, T. (1984) Victims of violence and psychiatric illness. *American Journal of Psychiatry*, 141, 378–83.

Castle, D., Mcgrath, J. and Kulkarni, J. (2000) *Women and Schizophrenia*. Cambridge: Cambridge University Press.

Chesler, P. (1972) *Women and Madness.* New York: Doubleday.
Cole, C. (2004) *Seeing Female Psychiatric Inpatients as Women.* Paper presented at *Celebrating Women in Psychiatry* conference, Lancaster, 2004.
Copeland, M. (1997) *Wellness Recovery Action Plan.* Dummerston, VT: Peach Press.
Coverdale, J. and Aruffo, J. (1992) AIDS and family planning counselling of psychiatry ill women in community mental health clinics. *Community Mental Health Journal*, 28, 13–20.
Coverdale, J., Bayer, T., McCullough, L. and Chervenak, F. (1993) Respecting the autonomy of chronic mentally ill women in decisions about contraception. *Hospital and Community Psychiatry*, 44, 671–4.
Department of Health (1983) *Mental Health Act.* London: HMSO.
Department of Health (2000) *Safety, Privacy and Dignity in Mental Health Units.* London: Department of Health.
Department of Health (2002a) *Women's Mental Health: Into the Mainstream. Strategic Development of Mental Health Care for Women.* London: Department of Health.
Department of Health (2002b) *Improvement, Expansion and Reform: The Next 3 Years: Priorities and Planning Framework 2003–2006.* London: Department of Health. Available online: www.dh.gov.uk/assetRoot/04/07/02/02/04070202.pdf
Department of Health (2003) *Mainstreaming Gender and Women's Mental Health, Implementation Guidance.* London: Department of Health.
Department of Health (2004) *The Ten Essential Shared Capabilities: A Framework for the Whole of the Mental Health Workforce.* London: Department of Health.
Department of Trade and Industry (2003) *Delivering on Gender Equality.* London: Women and Equality Unit.
Doyal, L. (1995) *What Makes Women Sick: Gender and the Political Economy of Health.* London: Macmillan.
Faugier J. (1992) Taking women seriously. *Nursing Times*, 88, 62–3.
Finkelhor, D., Hotaling, G. and Lewis, I. (1990) Sexual abuse in a national survey of adult men and women: prevalance, characteristics and risk factors. *Southern Medical Journal*, 84, 328–31.
Flor-Henry, P. (1990) Influence of gender in schizophrenia as related to other psychological syndromes. *Schizophrenia Bulletin*,16, 211–27.
Goldstein, J. (1988) Gender differences in the course of schizophrenia. *American Journal of Psychiatry*, 145, 684–9.
Good Practice in Mental Health (1994) *Women and Mental Health: An Information Pack of Mental Health Services for Women in the United Kingdom.* London: GPMH.
Goodman, L., Rosenberg, S., Mueser, K. and Drake R. (1997) Physical and sexual assault history in women with serious mental illness: prevalence, correlates, treatment and future research directions. *Schizophrenia Bulletin*, 23, 685–96.
Hambrecht, M., Maurer, K. and Hafner, H. (1992) Evidence for a gender bias in epidemiological studies of schizophrenia. *Schizophrenia Research*, 8, 223–31.
Healy, D. (1993) *Psychiatric Drugs Explained.* London: Guildford.
Hendrick, V. and Gitlin, M. (2004) *Psychotropic Drugs and Women: Fast Facts.* London: W.W. Norton and Co.
Johnstone L. (2002) *Users and Abusers of Psychiatry*, 2nd edition. London: Routledge.
Kessler, R. and Mcleod, J. (1984) Sex differences in vulnerability to indescribable life events. *American Sociological Review*, 49, 629–31.
Kraepelin, E. (1909) *Psychiatrie ein Lehrbuch fur Studierende und Aertzte.* Leipzig: Barth.
McCarthy C. (1994) Historical background of clinical trials involving women and minorities. *Academic Medicine*, 69, 695–8.
MacDougall, V. (1998) Unheard voices. Unpublished MSc dissertation. Bristol: University of Bristol.
Macran, S., Clarke, L. and Joshi, J. (1996) Women's health: dimensions and differentials. *Social Science and Medicine*, 42, 1203–16.

Merill, J., Laux, L. and Thornby, J. (1990) Why doctors have difficulties with sex histories. *Southern Medical Journal*, 83, 613–17.

Mind (1994) *Stress on Women*. London: Mind.

Morrow, M. (2002) *Violence and Trauma in the Lives of Women with Serious Mental Illness*. Vancouver, Canada: British Centre of Excellence for Women's Health. Available online: www.bccewh.bc.ca/Pages/pubspdflist2.htm#mentalh (accessed 27 October 2005).

Mullen P., Martin J., Anderson J., Romans S. and Herbison P. (1993) Childhood sexual abuse and mental health in adult life. *British Journal of Psychiatry*, 163, 721–32.

National Institute of Mental Health – England (2003) *Personality Disorder No Longer a Diagnosis of Exclusion: Policy Implementation Guidance for the Development of Services for People with Personality Disorder*. London: Department of Health.

Payne, S. (1991) *Women, Health and Poverty: An Introduction*. Hemel Hempsted: Harvester.

Payne, S. (1995) The rationing of psychiatric beds: changing trends in sex-ratios on admission to psychiatric hospital. *Health and Social Care in the Community*, 3, 289–300.

Read, J. (1998) Child abuse and severity of disturbance among adult psychiatric inpatients. *Child Abuse and Neglect*, 22, 359–68.

Rose, D. (1998) *Getting Ready for User-focused Monitoring*. London: Sainsbury Centre for Mental Health.

Russell, D. (1995) *Women, Madness and Medicine*. Cambridge: Polity Press.

Russo, N. (1990) Overview: forging research priorities for women's mental health. *American Psychologist*, 45, 368–73.

Seeman, M. (2000) Women and schizophrenia. *Medscape Women's Health*, 5, 1–8.

Sharma R., Dowd. S. and Janicak, P. (1999) Hallucinations in the acute schizophrenic-type psychosis: effects of gender and age of illness onset. *Schizophrenia Research*, 37, 91–5.

Showalter, E. (1987) *The Female Malady*. London: Virago.

Strong, V. (2000) *A Bright Red Scream*. London: Virago.

Svedberg, P., Jormfeldt, H. and Arvidsson, B. (2003) Patients conceptions of how health processes are promoted in mental health nursing: a qualitative study. *Journal of Psychiatric and Mental Health Nursing*, 10, 448–56.

Takahashi, S., Matsuura, M., Tanabe, E., Yara, K., Konosuke, N., Fukura, Y., Kikuchi, M. and Kojima, T. (2000) Age at onset of schizophrenia: gender differences and influence of temporal socioeconomic change. *Psychiatry and Clinical Neurosciences*, 54, 153–6.

Ussher, J. (1991) *Women's Madness: Misogyny or Mental Illness?* London: Harvester Wheatsheaf.

Vaughn, C., Snyder, K., Jones, S., Freeman, W. and Falloon, I. (1984) Family factors in schizophrenia relapse: replication in California of British research on expressed emotion. *Archives of General Psychiatry*, 41, 1169–77.

Walby, S. (2004) *The Cost of Domestic Violence*. Leeds: University of Leeds.

Zemenchuk, J., Rogosch, F. and Mowbray, C. (1995) The seriously mentally ill woman in the role of parent: characteristics, parenting sensitivity and needs. *Psychosocial Rehabilitation Journal*, 18, 77–92.

Zubin, J. and Spring, B. (1977) Vulnerability: a new view on schizophrenia. *Journal of Abnormal Psychology*, 86, 103–26.

Chapter 8

Advance Agreements, Advance Directives and Pre-emptive Care-planning

Steve Brooks, Jo Denney and John Mikeson

Key Points

- 'Pre-emptive care planning' is a very simple and very sensible concept: that it is a good idea to have a plan, developed between service user, staff and family, as to what should happen if someone relapses into a serious mental health problem. The key issues are that:
  - The choices the individual would make for themselves should be considered in planning care.
  - People should be able to make such decisions for themselves if they are capable of doing so.
- Pressure from non-statutory organisations (for example, Mind), increased interest and legislation applied to civil liberties, and a review of mental health legislation, have all raised the profile of advance agreements.
- Outcomes from validated early warning signs packages are very usefully included in advance agreements.
- Clearly things may go wrong in such a plan, and every eventuality cannot be foreseen, but having an agreed plan must be a better idea than everyone acting in an unco-ordinated fashion.
- However, there is scarcity of research into how effective advance directives and advance agreements are, at improving outcomes for service users and carers.
- There is little consensus about what advance agreements should include.
- The plan exists to help people maintain/regain control over their lives rather than being controlled by the disorder. There is a recognition that some service users are more able to make use of this than others. The plan is about mitigating the extent to which control is lost when the disorder strikes.
- Most problems with such advance agreements and pre-emptive care plans seem to result from staff ignoring or forgetting about the plans or not being aware of them in the first place. Thus most problems are not a fault of the advance agreements/pre-emptive care

plans themselves, but of the way that they are implemented and supervised. Incorporating advance agreements within CPA documentation and planning may make it more likely that practitioners and service users will implement them.

Introduction

Indications recorded in advance by individuals about the healthcare that they would like (or not like) to receive are not a new concept. The most prominent example in the media which readers may have encountered is that of the controversy surrounding the legality of 'living wills'. Made by people with life-limiting conditions, such written arrangements are designed to record choices about the refusal of life-prolonging treatments beyond the point when an individual is able to express choice independently. High-profile court cases have supported the view that what choices the individual would make for themselves should be considered in planning care (Airedale NHS Trust v. Bland 1993) and that people should be able to make such decisions for themselves if they are capable of doing so (Miss B v. An NHS Trust 2002).

Another example of advance planning (more aligned to the expression of services which a person would prefer to receive rather than refuse) is the opportunity available in some areas of the United Kingdom for expectant parents to draw up a statement in advance with the maternity services about their preferred options for giving birth.

In mental health, too, there has been a debate about the rights of service users and carers to utilise their own (often extensive) experience of managing mental health problems and express their own informed choices about treatment during the care planning process. This chapter explores how far this idea, which seems so fundamental to any care system which claims to be collaborative, has been implemented and how effective a contribution it makes. It also looks at the extent to which policy is facilitative of this type of user/carer involvement and it examines our local experience in the Gloucestershire Partnership NHS Trust (GPT) of trying to implement advance planning in a 'real life' service setting.

Chapter 6 discussed how to work collaboratively in order to reduce the chances of relapse occurring; this chapter examines about how to work collaboratively to ensure that, if relapse does occur, the service user's wishes can still be taken into account.

The Evidence – A Summary

In the context of enduring mental health problems, recent recognition of the desirability of incorporating such statements into mental health care provision may be linked to a number of factors. Pressure from non-statutory organisations (for example, Mind), increased interest and legislation applied to civil liberties, and reviews of mental health legislation, have all raised the profile of advance arrangement. However, although the impetus to put them in place is evident from the literature, two major barriers to their implementation appear to exist: there is little consensus about what they should include; and a scarcity of research into how effective they are at improving outcomes for service users and carers.

Several types of advance arrangement are possible and have been interpreted in the context of mental health. The British Medical Association (1995) defines 'advance statements' as ones drawn up by the individual to reflect treatment preference or to provide an overview of personal philosophy designed to assist those trying to decide treatment preference. They may also nominate an individual to represent the individual's treatment preference, or contain a combination of the above. Such statements are not legally binding; this is in contrast to an 'advance directive', which contains a *refusal* of medical intervention or specific physical treatments, which may be legally upheld. Requests for treatment to be *included* in an obligatory way are currently not legally binding. However, although the advance directive is an option open to people with mental health problems in the same way as for people with physical health problems, it does not apply to treatment given under the Mental Health Act (MHA) (Department of Health 1983). Therefore advance directives cannot usually be enforced with respect to the interventions which adult mental health service users may most strongly wish to limit: those which are compulsorily applied when the service user is being treated under a section of the MHA.

A third option alongside unilateral statements and advance directives, and one that has made an impact in mental health services, is the 'advance agreement'. This is a statement of treatment preference as described above but one which is drawn up collaboratively with representatives of the mental health service. Such an approach has been criticised for introducing a dynamic which could disempower service users in the expression of their wishes. Further criticism relates to the possible dilution of agreement content to cover only preferences that the mental health service can easily meet. In addition, the lack of consensus among professionals that advance agreements can improve care planning can lead to inequalities over the extent to which service users are encouraged to draw up a plan, and services adhere to it. Despite these problems and criticisms, the social policy context favours joint planning, and most research into this area in the mental health context has been conducted on advance agreements.

Atkinson and colleagues (2003 a, b) have made an extensive and accessible study of the status of advance agreements nationally, which reveals the diversity of content possible even after the type of arrangement and its legal status have been defined. Examples given include refusal of a specified treatment, for example, electro-convulsive therapy (ECT), the wish for a particular treatment to be provided, for example, complementary medicine, or the request for planned social care provision, for example, nominated child-care.

One barrier to implementation of advance agreements relates to the comparative lack of research support as to their effectiveness. Studies which evaluate the effects of advance agreements are rare, and those which do exist do not reach the same conclusions. Backlar and McFarland (1996) conducted a survey of carers and mental health professionals (although not service users) in Oregon, USA, a state which has passed laws authorising the use of advance directives in mental health and which has developed an advance directives instrument. However, they found that the majority of carers and professionals were unaware of its existence, and it was therefore ineffective. On the other hand, where people did know about it and it had been adopted, service users' wishes had been respected and some had found this empowering, lending weight to the idea that it is not whether such plans make good sense or whether they are under investigation, but the way in which they are implemented and supervised that determines their usefulness.

This theme is picked up in a randomised controlled trial conducted by Papageorgiou and colleagues (2002), which measured whether having an advance directive (although in fact the 'directive' was more characteristic of an advance agreement in terms of this chapter) reduced the rate of compulsory readmission by improving the alliance between service user and services. The study demonstrated disappointing initial results as the trial showed that having an advance directive made no difference to readmission rates, and very few of the service users (13.5 per cent) identified them as useful.

The analysis which the authors make of these outcomes again highlights the importance of a comprehensive operational policy and a sincere commitment to implement it at all organisational levels, as they suggest a number of reasons for the low success rates: it may have been that service users were asked to complete the directives at the wrong time (for example, at the end of the previous stay in hospital), or that services were too under-resourced to implement them properly, or felt that they were already taking account of service users' wishes sufficiently. Lack of identification about who would be responsible for implementing and updating plans over time was also thought to have contributed to their lack of impact after a year. Furthermore the trial was only conducted with participants who had already been compulsorily detained and who may not therefore be representative of all those who might use an advance agreement. It was also not clear how far efforts to meet the requirements stated in these advance directives were met: the service users were asked only to express preferences, and amendments to the directives were made by professionals if the requests were deemed to be not locally practicable. This may have led to a sense of 'toothlessness', which could have served to reduce efficacy and service-user satisfaction with the plan: the study showed that only 40 per cent of service users would use advance directives again.

Further investigation into the outcomes of the study (Papageorgiou et al. 2004) led the researchers to recommend that the integration of the plan into both the care programme approach (CPA) documentation, and relapse prevention planning procedures, may improve its efficacy and perceptions of its usefulness.

In contrast, a randomised controlled trial by Henderson and colleagues (2004) found that those who had an advance agreement in place were detained compulsorily less often and spent fewer days detained under the MHA once they were in hospital. The study offered service users in the community with a diagnosis of psychosis the opportunity to complete an advance agreement in collaboration with one of the research team and (where desired) the mental health worker. The uptake by service users was lower than anticipated, but effective in reducing compulsory treatment. Although the outcomes of the study were less encouraging in affecting the number of admissions participants experienced or the total time spent in hospital, the study emphasises the use of advance agreements in reducing the amount of coercive care. This outcome is highly relevant to service users and their carers and congruent with recommendations made during the current review of the MHA.

Therefore although some evidence is available about what service users value in the content of such plans, how successfully they achieve their purpose, and how they should be treated by the organisation, the amount is limited, restricting the degree to which construction of advance agreements locally can be evidence-led.

The Case Study – Local Work and Its Impact

Editors' note: in the chapters so far in this book, one or more individual cases have been presented as 'worked examples' to demonstrate how the collaborative work has been undertaken. In this present chapter (and some of the following ones), the case or cases used are instead demonstrations of new ways of delivering and implementing therapeutic interventions, albeit still undertaken and written up as collaborations between users, carers and staff. Hence the case in this chapter revolves around how the work undertaken between Jo Denney (an occupational therapist within mental health services within Gloucestershire) and two users of local mental health services (John Mikeson and Steve Brooks) led to the development and implementation of the Rainy Day plan.

The inspiration for the Rainy Day plan (as it eventually became known) was provided during a clinical supervision session of one of the authors (JD). The supervisory issue was the difficulty of maintaining hope when planning care with a service user (JM) who had experienced many relapses and admissions. The supervisor helped identify the role which lack of control over any part of this cycle played in generating and maintaining hopelessness (Gilbert 1992). She recalled a training session at which a care plan generated by an innovative local service user had been presented. The plan had been devised specifically to ensure her preferences and pre-arranged support systems regarding the social and medical management of relapse so that these were known and implemented: although the details were missing and no copy of the plan was available to us, the information was enough to encourage us to attempt our own version, a process now described by John.

John says:

My name is John and I am aged 54. My parents died some years ago and my only relative is a younger sister. She has not offered me any support throughout my illness and we are not on speaking terms. When I was working I had plenty of friends. Sadly when I became long-term ill, they deserted me. Now I would say I have three very good friends whom I can rely on.

I used to have a responsible job in local government but started suffering from depression at the young age of 26. I eventually resigned my post at 29 and haven't been able to work since. I have in fact been told that I will never work again. I now live in sheltered accommodation and attend day centres for help and support. I have experienced care in the mental health services for 25 years and I often thought that I had knowledge that could be of use in helping to improve the service, but never thought anyone would want to listen. The creation of the Rainy Day plan is a small contribution from a service user.

I thought it would be useful if people could state their needs and wishes regarding treatment before they became very ill. I literally sat down with a blank sheet of paper and started writing headings which I gradually refined into a form. I thought the part of the form which allowed people to describe the signs of when they were becoming ill would be very useful in allowing professionals to pick up quickly when someone was becoming ill.

I felt there was a need for my own plan because often when I have gone into hospital I have been in a very distressed state and could not express my views on anything. I felt it would help staff because they would have a more personal perspective. Something simple like knowing the name the person likes to be known as could make it more friendly. Personally in my plan I wanted to make it clear that I only wanted ECT as a last resort. I was able to mention some physical problems which needed monitoring. With this plan in place I feel that, if I ever have to go to hospital again, my own personal views will be taken into account alongside my medical notes. Although the plan is not legally binding, it gives me assurance because I think it is inherently sound. The more it is used by professionals, the more it will become part of the system and will maintain its credibility. Giving a view from a user's viewpoint is, I think, very valuable. However, I feel that encouragement from senior management is needed to really make sure the plan is used throughout the Trust.

John's vision in realising that the idea of creating such individualised plans could help others, and be more effective if it was implemented organisationally, led us first to approach service users informally. This led to some changes in the headings we used within the plan. We then approached the local NHS Trust management. Approval was given for a pilot of the plan on the understanding that the Trust solicitors were able to clarify its legal status sufficiently to give us the 'go ahead'. Although they were not able to endorse a legally binding advance directive for reasons outlined in the previous section, they permitted the development of an advance agreement and a pilot of the plan was agreed. Figure 8.1 shows the headings and some of the further information used in these individualised Rainy Day plans.

The useful input of others regarding headings for the plan and the need to evaluate the pilot led to the development of a working party including service user volunteers, a representative of the Trust audit department, and a service user advocate from the National Schizophrenia Fellowship (now Rethink). This development was welcome in introducing formal reflection to the process of plan development, both on the underlying assumptions the plan makes about service users' ability to contribute to relapse management and on the scope of the plan.

The group first identified the philosophy underpinning the plan. This consisted of the following statements:

- The plan exists to help people maintain/regain control over their lives rather than being controlled by the disorder. There is a recognition that some service users are more able to make use of this than others. The plan is about mitigating the extent to which control is lost when mental disorder strikes.
- The plan is about recognising and recording patterns of wellness, illness and reaction in specific circumstances for individuals.
- There is an acknowledgement that in the past, service-user expertise on their own disorders has often been overlooked or under-used by professionals, and that developing individual plans/advance agreements is one way of achieving more active co-operation and collaboration. There is also recognition that future plans, in which service users have active participation and ownership, are an effective use of health care.
- One aspect of the plan philosophy is that it will allow for reappraisal of case histories.
- It may be reasonable to suppose that having a 'say' in the management of an episode of mental disorder would help promote self-esteem during the period of recovery.

Identifying the philosophy of the plan facilitated the development of its aims, which are that (continued on page 144):

Figure 8.1 Headings and information used within Gloucestershire Partnership NHS Trust Rainy Day plan

---

Rainy Day plan: a pre-emptive care plan for:

[Affix name and address label here]

This care plan has been written in advance to reflect your wishes either when psychiatric treatment is being planned or for an admission to psychiatric hospital. It is designed to help the team understand what is important to you and to provide some insight into any pattern of your illness. It will also help formulate care according to your considered wishes, when you are too ill to make a choice. This is not an advance directive, but a document to inform the psychiatric service of your past and present wishes and feelings.

What treatment I require:

- when I am well ....
- in the early stages of my illness ....
- when I'm becoming quite ill ....
- when I'm really ill ....

Where I want to be treated when I'm ill: ....

Medication:

- my view of my medication ....
- my experience of my medication to date ....
- things which I want to know about my medication in future and about any new treatment being considered ....

My view of other treatments and services (day centres, CPNs, alternative therapies) ....
....

If I have to go to hospital:

- people to contact and number/addresses ....
- practical matters to be attended to (pets, children, keys, money arrangements) ....
....
- observations regarding the care I will need (special diet, single room, shared room, etc.) ......
....

Any other comments ....
....
....

Signed .... Date ....

Accompanying Information

What is the 'Rainy Day' plan?

It aims to help you to use the times when you are well to make plans for the future, in case illness returns. This might mean:

- Making a distinction for others about what is 'you' – part of your individuality, and what may be a symptom of illness.
- Making a formal record in advance of the likely stages of your illness so that preventative measures can be taken in time.
- Recording your views, choices and past experiences of treatment, including medication and hospitalisation.
- Identifying practical steps you want taken if you do become ill – contacts to be made, child-care and pet arrangements, links with employers, social services or housing, for example.

Will it make any difference?

Recent reports from the government, professional bodies and user organisations all suggest that people's experience of their own illness is under-used by mental health services and that they should be more involved in planning care.

The care programme approach (CPA) care co-ordinator and named nurses aim to promote collaboration between you and staff in managing current problems but do not really address contingency or 'what if . . .?' issues, which can leave you and your family feeling unprepared, and professionals unsure about your wishes.

The mental health services are therefore trying out the jointly signed plan for one year to see if it does make a difference. During the year, feedback from all interested parties will be sought about whether the scheme is working, and whether changes need to be made.

How will it work?

- Start the ball rolling. Either you or your care co-ordinator, named nurse or community psychiatric nurse (CPN) might suggest that you could find a Rainy Day plan useful. All these staff can provide the paperwork, which is also available from:
  the leaflet rack at any resource centre
  the leaflet rack at day centres
  your care co-ordinator or named nurse.

- Fill in the plan. It will probably be most useful to do this with your care co-ordinator so they are aware of your views and can discuss them with you. You might also want to discuss it with family and friends.
- Store the plan. Keep a copy yourself. Your care co-ordinator will put a copy in your notes with your care programme (at the front) and send a copy to your GP if you think this is relevant.

What if my plan changes?

- Let your care co-ordinator know of any changes so that the plan in the notes or at the GP can be updated.
- Make an appointment with your care co-ordinator if you feel a complete rewrite will be necessary.
- At the time of your care programme approach case review, your care co-ordinator should check with you whether your Rainy Day plan is up to date.

Useful addresses

NSF Advocacy and Family Support, X XXX Road, Gloucester GLX XXX. Tel.: 01452 XXXXXX.
Carers' Network Tel.: 01452 XXXXXX

And finally . . .

- The plan is available for consideration by anyone who uses Gloucestershire mental health services.
- If you think that making a plan might help you, you don't have to wait for your care co-ordinator to suggest it.
- Gloucestershire mental health services support the philosophy of the plan and recognise it as an approved document. It does not, however, undertake to meet all the requests individuals might make, therefore the document should not be seen as an advance directive of care.

Developed by staff and users at the Memorial Centre from an original idea by Mrs Sally Blair and Mr John Mikeson.

- The plan functions as a means for service users to express their own wishes at times when they are not able to do so directly.
- The plan helps reduce anxiety and disruption in the lives of the families of mental health service users during periods of mental disorder.
- Completed plans provide reliable and accessible security that there is something to fall back on rather than purely relying on your own resources at the time of being unwell.
- The plan alerts staff to user arrangements and wishes concerning case management and facilitates inclusion in treatment.
- The plan provides a procedure and standard format currently not available for contingency planning.
- Blank plans and information on them are readily accessible through a variety of both user and service sources to both users and professionals.
- The plan is effective at reflecting common areas of concern but has the flexibility to accommodate individual need.
- The plan format is compatible with current Trust documentation requirements and formally included within this system.
- Where a pattern of wellness/illness is identified in advance, the plan allows some gauge of the degree of the problem within a personal framework and encourages preventative consultation where possible.

Introducing the Plan Locally – Awareness Raising

The next stage was to launch the pilot, which was planned to take place over a six-month period. A training session developed by the working party was then offered: it included orientation to the philosophy and the aims of the plan (described above); introduction to the plan format and operation; and a question and answer session. This was open to all service users and staff at the community mental health resource centre. Following this session blank plans and information about them were made freely available around the centre. The aim was that both care co-ordinators and service users would have equal access to the materials and either could initiate completion of a Rainy Day plan. The local inpatient facility was also informed, particularly targeting named nurses, who would be responsible for implementing the Rainy Day plan in the case of relapse involving admission to hospital.

The training session was well attended by service users but only one care co-ordinator/professional attended. When asked, the most commonly given reason for missing the session was lack of time: in retrospect more than one session could have been offered, particularly since those who had missed the session reported not feeling competent to offer the plan, a misperception since the procedure was simple and fully explained in a supplementary leaflet.

Although the plan was not diagnosis specific, the information supplied drew attention to the need for service users to have enough insight into their problems at the time of writing that it would accurately reflect their observations and wishes about individuals' patterns of wellness/illness and their management. Judgement about what constituted 'enough' insight was left to those involved in completion of each individual plan. Sayce (2000) describes the invalidation and exclusion engendered by the assumption of those not diagnosed as 'mentally ill' that illness adversely affects all functional capacity. Therefore although the working party briefly considered whether this could be quantified, to do so seemed operationally and ethically unworkable. Once the plan was completed, one copy of the Rainy Day plan was kept in the medical notes, one with the service user, and one with the GP where service users agreed to this.

Feedback from the pilot

At the end of the pilot, service users and staff members were asked to self-complete questionnaires designed to ascertain whether the plan was easy to use, whether it was in the right format and if it was effective. The staff questionnaire attracted a 50 per cent response rate and demonstrated that only two care co-ordinators had used the plan more than a few times with service users. Advantages of the plan which these two identified were that it was easy to use; that it helped to build a more equal relationship with service users and it raised staff awareness of service user perspectives. It provided a useful prompt for carrying out early warning signs work (an intervention designed to avert relapse by recognising the first indicators of returning mental health problems and putting a pre-arranged treatment plan into place, see chapter 6) and education about medication, it guided professionals' approach to management of relapse for individuals and it promoted understanding of service users' prior experience of the service and how this affected their current choices.

The majority of staff members, who had used the plan infrequently or not at all, identified a problem deciding who might benefit from having a plan, and many replied that it was not relevant to the people on their caseload. The second major problem staff reported was that the plan was time-consuming to complete and review and that, particularly because there was not a Trust requirement to complete it, it became a low priority for overloaded workers.

The service user questionnaire attracted only a 25 per cent response rate, much smaller than hoped for, although it was evident that service users who replied supplied many additional comments and had clearly spent time reflecting on their use of the plan. Most plans had been instigated by care co-ordinators although some service users had been encouraged by their peers to initiate a plan. All thought that the format was easy to use and should remain unchanged. Only three service users had tried to use the plan when they became ill. For two people this had been a positive experience; one found that early warning signs were detected and relapse averted, the other that the plan regarding management of hospitalisation was adhered to. The third service user had a less positive experience as the care co-ordinator did not use the information supplied by the plan during the service user's relapse and the service user was too ill to remind anyone of its existence.

Statistically, the response rate to both questionnaires was too low to claim confidently that it was representative of the views of all involved (a review by Robson 2002 suggests that at least a 70 per cent response rate is required for such a claim to be made). However, all service user respondents, whether they had operated the crisis part of the plan or not and whether it had worked in relapse for them or not, recorded that they liked the principle driving the plan and its format, and wanted it to continue, welcoming the opportunity to have greater input in their own care planning. As further data collection was not practically possible and because the service users who had participated had put time and effort into their responses, the decision was therefore taken to continue the project to the next stage of the process: organisational implementation. Further feedback on service users' experience of compiling a Rainy Day plan has been ongoing throughout the life of the project, validating many of the comments (positive and negative) which were originally received during the pilot and matching the experiences of service users more widely reported in the literature on advance agreements.

Steve says:

I am 33 years old and have suffered with mental illness for a period of time stemming back to my childhood. Following a compulsory admission to hospital in 1990, a diagnosis of manic depression was given. My stay was relatively short and I left, medicated and feeling stable. After a second relapse and a further six months in hospital it was recognised that I was a voice-hearer and required therapy and ongoing assistance in supported accommodation. I am still attending a day centre now. The first time I was ill I thought it would never happen again. The second time I realised that it would and that if you can be ill once you might be ill five more times: the illness is very potent. I have learned that increased stress and problems with my medication increase my chances of slipping back.

The Rainy Day plan was suggested to me at a relatively late stage of my recovery and was carried out very competently with me by a student nurse. The statements were orderly and structured. I liked the way that it started off with how my state of mind is when I am well and progressed through the stages up to when I am really ill. This complemented the early warning signs package (Smith 2000) which I also did; without both, many of my concerns regarding relapse would not have been addressed, causing an incomplete Rainy Day plan.

I felt the plan asked what view I had of the mental health service's attitude towards me and how I would like to be treated in future. I only hope that these statements of mine are considered seriously if I did relapse, as maybe a lack of beds might prevent this Utopian ideal presented to me from happening! I liked having the chance to state my experience and concerns about medication, especially future concerns over the side-effects of relentless tablet treatments. I noted my awareness of the help my mental health team could give me and encouraged them to keep working to maintain my recovery in mental illness: that attitude is very important to me in my local area.

Achieving Organisational Implementation

Following the local pilot, the Rainy Day plan was approved as a Trust document, which meant that it could be printed and distributed to service users and mental health workers in resource centres and inpatient units around the Trust area. However, although the plan was now recognised, resources to aid its implementation had not been considered, which meant that for many it remained an unfamiliar form, particularly where it had become separated from its explanatory leaflet. The plan sat outside the CPA documentation, so professionals were unsure whether to offer it, and many service users may have been unaware of its existence altogether. A merger with a neighbouring Trust to form GPT meant that further inequalities in knowledge and access to the plan arose, and the development of new, specialist teams made it difficult to keep abreast of new areas for implementation. Had the plan formed part of the CPA documentation at the time, there may have been a recognised requirement for a re-launch in the interests of redressing the geographical imbalance.

Another critical feature was the detachment of the plan from the control of service users and advocates at the point where it was adopted by the Trust. At the time the Trust employed no service users at management level to represent their interests and promote the plan, meaning that it ceased to be an agenda priority. This was compounded as the professionals involved in the original plan changed jobs or moved away.

In 2002 changes to the CPA made crisis and contingency plans a requirement. Through contact with service users and the CPA Association, the Trust lead officer for CPA implementation recognised that the Rainy Day plan offered a practice-led opportunity to implement and exceed what was required rather than merely comply with a policy-led requirement. Emphasising the service users' input and commitment to include the plan in the CPA as a voluntary supplement to complement the mandatory crisis plan reinforced the 'good practice' element of the issue rather than its compulsory nature. The service users' forum was therefore asked to make a choice whether to include the plan in the CPA, which they endorsed. The plan was then reprinted to conform with CPA documentation and is now available throughout GPT.

Advance agreements: the social policy context and the implications of review of mental health legislation

Non-statutory agencies representing service user and carer interests have been proactive for many years, both in advocating for individuals to make their wishes known to the mental health services and campaigning for improvements in rights at a national level. The statutory services' response to calls for greater inclusion for service users and carers in the decision-making process can be viewed as progressively more collaborative over the last 15 years. What is more contentious is the extent to which mental health law supports changing attitudes and practice, particularly when the service user is treated under the MHA (1983).

Care Programme Approach

The CPA was introduced in 1991 (Department of Health 1990) with the aim of improving collaboration with individuals and their carers living with serious mental health problems. The circular stated that individuals were to have a written plan of care, discussed with them by a representative of the mental health services, who would have responsibility for co-ordinating the delivery of the plan and its review, which would take place periodically. Although it was asserted at the time that these aims and activities would have a beneficial effect on the quality of care, Simpson, Miller and Bowers (2003) critically review the introduction of the CPA as a missed opportunity, a 'defensive administrative process' (p. 480) largely driven by bureaucracy and risk reduction. Their view is that these factors, coupled with a lack of positive models of case management at the heart of the new legislation, made it unpopular, unevenly implemented and ineffective for service users.

At the end of the decade the *National Service Framework for Mental Health* was published (Department of Health 1999a), setting standards which individuals and carers could expect of mental health services. The effectiveness of the CPA system was reviewed as part of this procedure (Department of Health 1999b) and some changes were made. One was in response to comments that the CPA was too bureaucratic; this resulted in an integration of the way in which health and social services planned care, designed to make its use more streamlined. Another responded to criticism that meeting the needs of service users and carers was not at the heart of the CPA and that refocusing on them was required. The review therefore built on previous legislation such as the Carers (Recognition and Services) Act (1995) (Department of Health 1995) to include formal procedures in CPA for assessing the needs of carers and taking account of their views.

In refocusing on service users' priorities, the review directed that care plans should be more collaborative, stating agreed treatment and goals. In addition, a key element of the revised care plan would be crisis and contingency planning for those with the most complex needs, a requirement later reiterated by *The NHS Plan* (Department of Health 2000). Crisis plans are more limited in scope than advance statements and agreements, in that they centre on the recognition and practical management of imminent or current relapse and may be service (rather than user) led, as a compulsory component of the CPA. However, the addition provided formal recognition of the benefits of thinking ahead and afforded the opportunity of including the more detailed and collaborative advance agreements as an optional supplement within the CPA, a position recognised as helpful in the literature about advance agreements in overcoming staff resistance to an 'unadopted' procedure by demonstrating organisational support.

Despite increasing recognition of the rights of service users and carers to have input into care planning and the inclusion of structures which facilitate their participation, the legal position regarding the enforceability of advance statements for users of the mental health services seems unlikely to change. As discussed in the first section, very little of what is included in an advance statement of care is legally enforceable and even refusals of treatment (the one stipulation which can be legally enforced) can currently be overridden by the MHA (Department of Health 1983)).

Mental Health Act Reform

The draft Mental Health Bill (Department of Health 2002, 2004), the result to date (2005) of the review of the Mental Health Act, makes little mention of advance agreements at all, despite promising early indications that the *Report of the Expert Committee* reviewing the 1983 Act would recommend their use (although not that of advance directives) in the reformed Act (Department of Health 1999c).

Summaries of the bill indicate only that treatment preferences may be recorded when well, and that the forthcoming code of practice will encourage mental health workers to facilitate this process. Where this results in an advance agreement between service user and mental health service, its content should be taken into account if a MHA assessment is required, the procedure by which a decision is made about whether an individual requires detention under the MHA. The most positive outcome envisaged of consulting the agreement would be to identify mutually acceptable interventions which avoid invoking the MHA altogether. Even if this were not possible, such an inclusion may result in the formulation of MHA orders which were more focused on individual need.

Such lack of inclusion is disappointing and suggests that there will be little change in the status of advance directives and that advance statements made by service users, but not agreed collaboratively with the mental health services, will continue to receive little recognition.

There has been criticism (see below) of this stance, which may be viewed variously as a sensible attempt to retain control over the treatment of the most unwell where individuals' own choices may compromise the health and safety of themselves or others; and also as the unjustified continuation of state-condoned oppression of a sector already marginalised in society. The Mental Health Alliance (2004) (an umbrella organisation representing the views of non-statutory organisations which advocate for service users and their carers) attacked the weakness of the proposals in their response to the Mental Health Bill (2004), calling for amendments which would oblige services to ensure service users had the right to make advance statements, that these would be included in the CPA procedure, and that they would be heeded. Such statements would be given the same status whether they were made by compulsory or informal service users. The Royal College of Psychiatrists (2004) has also generally criticised the emphasis on coercion in the revised Mental Health Bill and condemns the perpetuation of a system which places separate restrictions on mental health service users making treatment choices, even where the mental capacity to do so is unimpaired.

Other recent legislation provides some evidence that although real change in legal status is some distance away, the philosophical stance towards service users' involvement in advance planning is by no means consistent. The Mental Capacity Act (2005) (Department of Health 2005) is designed to strengthen the safeguards in place for service users who are not, temporarily or permanently, able to provide informed consent to interventions and are not in a position to resist them. It gives authority to advance statements because it establishes a principle of abiding by the service user's wishes where these are known: the associated Draft Code of Practice (Department of Constitutional Affairs 2004) puts the onus on practitioners to investigate the existence of any decision regarding future treatment refusal and consult with any nominated representative within it to try to find out the service user's wishes.

However, the code also reiterates the unchanged nature of the legally binding position of directives only applying to refusal of treatment. It indicates to practitioners that where the intervention falls within the scope of the MHA, this will continue to take precedence and could override the service user's preference, although documented justification for taking such action would be required.

Conflict between the principles established in the Mental Capacity Act and the lack of support for advance statements in the Mental Health Bill, coupled with the discriminatory nature of legislation which denies consideration of the wishes of detained patients, led the Scrutiny Committee (2005) to criticise the omission in the area of advance decisions. Optimistically for those trying to get advance agreements back on the agenda, the committee recommended legislation to enable people to make advance statements (both of treatment they wished to receive and reject) which were to be taken into account in clinical decision-making, although they once again reiterated that such arrangements would not be legally binding.

The current climate of policy reform and conflicting opinion about the extent to which service users and carers have the legal right to determine the care they receive is, to some extent, a barrier to the widespread adoption of advance planning systems. However evidence exists that, despite political dithering higher up the decision-making structure, at a local level systems inclusive of service user and carer views are being developed (Beevor 2002). The hope is that documenting such grassroots experience both disseminates strength and weakness in the process to other interested parties, and promotes the notion that it is *excluding* service users and carers from care planning which is now the anachronism.

Experience and Evaluation – Our Own Encounters

A weakness of the Rainy Day plan implementation (which is a further reflection of the lack of consideration originally given to maintaining it) is that there has been no formal evaluation of uptake of the plan or its effectiveness. Anecdotally the picture appears to reflect that which is found in the literature that, despite wide nominal availability, not many service users go on to complete a plan. This may demonstrate that lack of knowledge about the plan is as great a barrier as physical unavailability (the same conclusion as was reached by Backlar and McFarland in 1996): repeated promotion to professionals and users and carers remains a high priority. Local research (Crone et al. 2005) indicates that awareness of advance planning is a training issue, at least at community mental health team level.

Steve is not surprised by this finding:

As usual they don't recognise a good thing when they see it. The mental health system so often concentrates on things that aren't relevant to service users, especially long-term users. The Rainy Day plan helps to correct this imbalance and stops us feeling like numbers. It helps build your confidence to be asked about your wishes; that you are important enough to be asked.

Despite the ongoing organisational challenges of promoting the plan, feedback from service users remains positive. Although John has experienced the disappearance of the plan from his notes sometimes, he has had better experiences too:

John says:

My experience of using the plan has been good. It has been read by my consultant and care co-ordinator and has been kept on my file. The plan is looked at when my care plan is being reviewed. Staff at the day centre say how useful they find the plan. Being able to describe how my illness develops has enabled staff to refer me for medical help earlier and has, on one occasion, prevented me from going into hospital. I think it is good for the Trust to use the plan because it will show that it values input from service users and is prepared to accept new ideas. Perhaps having heard this idea was accepted, other service users will come up with other new ideas. Now the plan is accepted throughout the Trust, it means wherever you are, there is the same opportunity to express yourself. I would like to think that if other Trusts hear of this plan they might adopt something similar themselves.

Although Steve has not had to implement the plan in a crisis, he also regards the initiative positively, both for the reassurance it provides and the message that it sends about the relationship between organisation and service user:

Steve says:

I feel the Rainy Day plan was not intrusive into my privacy and was clear and concise. Having said this, the Rainy Day plan, like any form of questionnaire, does heavily rely on the user being open and honest. I had spoken to the nurse on several occasions prior to conducting the Rainy Day plan and therefore the rapport carried through and made the process a lot easier. From this point it would seem clear to me that user and nurse would benefit from meeting prior to the Rainy Day plan, helping the session to flow due to the added ingredient of mutual trust.

After noting my various points regarding the Rainy Day plan, it would seem to me that it is an essential part of the process concerned with intervention, should problems arise for the service user preceding serious relapse and hospital admission. To ensure that all service users can use the plan appears an intelligent approach, to prevent lack of insight from denying users their choices during the most intense periods of illness; I think if it had been around when I first became ill it would have helped my family too. To address the user and recognise his or her wishes and to reduce feelings of retribution when the plan was implemented would ease the minds of many and help develop a bond of trust between the service user and the mental health system.

The most important point I can make in this chapter is that the Rainy Day plan should certainly be standard procedure for all users with mental health problems who have or could enter hospital under adverse conditions. Without the Rainy Day plan, there is a far greater risk of the service user not being able to say what they want when their mental health is poor. The plan seems essential to maintain a consistent method of gauging and controlling your place in the mental health system, should problems arise.

Conclusion

We would like to finish with some final reflections on implementing advance agreements.

Although the legal position is complicated, some service users welcome the idea that there are opportunities for greater participation in joint care planning if they do wish to take them up, so perseverance is encouraged. Despite this, not everyone will want to draw up a plan: many people are unhappy about planning for the management of future adversity and the plan should remain voluntary; it is offering the opportunity that counts.

Outcomes from validated early warning signs packages are very usefully included in advance agreements. Our plan is not a validated package itself but it is a good place to record the main outcomes alongside the service user's preferences for management. To involve the Trust's lead officer for CPA implementation, and through that person incorporate the Rainy Day plan as a voluntary supplement to complement the mandatory crisis plan within CPA, was a key move which other organisations might wish to follow.

Although service users know that not everything on the plan will always be possible, plans can only be effective if services are making their best efforts to comply with them. Ignoring a plan in which the service user has invested effort and faith because of a lack of participation in its original construction or because of a member of staff's personal beliefs about their lack of effectiveness or a lack of time to adhere to it, is actually devaluing and promotes hopelessness for service users. There are therefore implications for service managers in implementing plans in terms of inclusion in the existing paperwork, planned project management, resource allocation and planned evaluation.

Acknowledgements

Jo Denney would like to thank Vikki Tweddle, Deputy Director of Nursing Services, Gloucestershire Partnership NHS Trust, for her comments on the chapter.

References

Airedale NHS Trust v. Bland (1993) 1 All ER 821.

Atkinson, J., Garner, H., Patrick, H. and Stuart, S. (2003a) Issues in the development of advance directives in mental health care. *Journal of Mental Health*, 12, 463–74.

Backlar, P. and McFarland, B. (1996) A survey on the use of advance directives for mental health treatment in Oregon. *Psychiatric Services*, 47, 1387–9.

Beevor A. (2002) *Advance statements in mental health*. Updates Research and Policy Briefings from the Mental Health Foundation 4 (4) The Mental Health Foundation. Available online: www.mental-health.org.uk/html/content/updatev04i04.pdf (accessed 12 October 2005).

British Medical Association (1995) *Advance Statements about Medical Treatment*. London: BMJ Publishing Group.

Crone, D., Heaney, L., Herbert, R., Wilson, J., Johnston, L. and MacPherson, R. (2005) A comparison of lifestyle behaviour and health perceptions of people with severe mental illness and the general population. *Journal of Mental Health Promotion*, 3, 19–25.

Department of Constitutional Affairs (2004) *Mental Capacity Bill: Draft Code of Practice*. London: HMSO. Available online: www.dca.gov.uk/menincap/mcbdraftcode.pdf (accessed 28 December 2005).

Department of Health (1983) *Mental Health Act*. London: HMSO.

Department of Health (1990) *The Care Programme Approach for People with a Mental Illness Referred to Specialist Psychiatric Services*. HC(90)23/LASSL(90)11. Joint Health and Social Services Circular. London: HMSO.

Department of Health (1995) *Carers (Recognition and Services) Act*. Policy Guidance. London: DoH.

Department of Health (1999a) *The National Service Framework for Mental Health: Modern Standards and Service Models*. London: HMSO.

Department of Health (1999b) *Effective Care Co-ordination in the Mental Health Services: Modernising the Care Programme Approach*. London: HMSO.

Department of Health (1999c) *Report of the Expert Committee. Review of the Mental Health Act 1983*. London: HMSO.

Department of Health (2000) *The NHS Plan: A Plan for Investment, a Plan for Reform*. London: HMSO.

Department of Health (2002) *Draft Mental Health Bill and Consultation Document*. London: HMSO.

Department of Health (2004) *Revised Draft Mental Health Bill*. London: HMSO.

Department of Health (2005) *The Mental Capacity Act*. London: HMSO.

Garner, H., Stuart, S., Patrick, H and Atkinson, J. (2003b) The development of potential models of advance directives in mental health care. *Journal of Mental Health*, 12, 575–84.

Gilbert, P. (1992) *Depression: The Evolution of Powerlessness*. Hove: Lawrence Erlbaum.

Henderson, C., Flood, C., Leese, M., Thornicroft, G., Sutherby, K. and Szmuckler, G. (2004) Effect of joint crisis plans on use of compulsory treatment in psychiatry: single blind randomised controlled trial. *British Medical Journal*, 329, 136–8.

Mental Health Act (1983). London: HMSO.

Mental Health Alliance (2004) *Draft Mental Health Bill. Memorandum from the Mental Health Foundation and the Foundation for People with Learning Disabilities*. London: Mental Health Foundation.

Miss B v. an NHS Trust (2002) EWHC 429 Fam.

Papageorgiou, A., King, M., Janmohamed, A., Davidson, O. and Dawson, J. (2002) Advance directives for patients compulsorily admitted to hospital with serious mental illness: randomised controlled trial. *British Journal of Psychiatry*, 181, 513–9.

Papageorgiou, A., Janmohamed, A., King, M., Davidson, O. and Dawson, J. (2004) Advance directives for patients compulsorily admitted to hospital with serious mental disorders: directive content and feedback from patients and professionals. *Journal of Mental Health*, 13, 379–88.

Robson, C. (2002) *Real World Research*. Oxford: Blackwell Publishing.

Royal College of Psychiatrists (2004) *College Response to the Revised Draft Mental Health Bill*. Available online: www.rcpsych.ac.uk/press/parliament/MHBill.htm (accessed 28 December 2005).

Sayce, L. (2000) *From Psychiatric Patient to Citizen*. Basingstoke: Macmillan Press.

Scrutiny Committee (2005) *Report on the Draft Mental Health Bill*, HL Paper 79 – I HC 95I.

Simpson, A., Miller, C. and Bowers, L. (2003) Case management models and the care programme approach: how to make the CPA effective and credible. *Journal of Psychiatric and Mental Health Nursing*, 10, 472–483.

Smith, J. (2000) *Early Warning Signs. A Self-management Training Manual for Individuals with Psychosis*. Worcestershire: Worcestershire Community and Mental Health NHS Trust.

Chapter 9

Recovery from Voice-hearing through Groupwork

Keith Coupland and Tim Cuss

Key Points

- Therapeutic work within a group is powerful because it combats social isolation and profoundly increases a sense of 'belonging'.
- Fellow group members can challenge unhelpful assumptions and behaviours in a way that is not possible for, but is complementary to the input of, mental health professionals.
- Effective groupwork is agenda-driven, but also flexible within a semi-structured framework broadly encompassing cognitive-behavioural principles.
- Gender issues are important and this may necessitate the formation of single gender groups.
- The use of structured assessments, shared with the service user, can help in problem identification and the measurement of change.
- Humour is a vital part of the process, while recognising that this remains respectful and appropriate.

Introduction

This chapter will explore the policy context and the evidence-base for the practice of groupwork for psychosis. To illustrate the impact of the groupwork on a participant, we have an extract from Tim's life story and how his perception of himself was transformed by the experience of dialogue with others through groupwork.

We will follow this by describing the practice-based evidence derived from our own experience of working with groups over the last eight years in Gloucestershire; including how the group was established within the organisation (initially east Gloucestershire, and since 2002 a county-wide combined health and social care Trust, Gloucestershire Partnership NHS Trust). The factors important in promoting recovery will also be explored.

The Evidence – Policy and Context

A variety of national and local policy drivers allowed us to develop our approach to groupwork. Nationally, a number of policy directives were emerging suggesting that there needed to be far greater access to psychological therapies, e.g., *Health of the Nation* (Department of Health 1992); *National Service Framework for Mental Health* (Department of Health 1999). Evidence was emerging that some therapies were more effective than others (e.g. Roth and Fonagy's 1996 book: *What Works for Whom?*), and there were increasing demands from service users for more alternatives to the use of pharmacological interventions alone, (e.g. Sainsbury Centre for Mental Health (1998, 1999). Our development of groupwork occurred within this national context, distilled locally through discussions with the manager of mental health services, Don Campbell, who argued that our Trust should implement the following 10 recommendations. It should:

1. focus interventions on those people in greatest need (i.e. people experiencing distressing psychosis)
2. provide interventions that service users want and need
3. provide quality therapeutic interventions based on good evidence and
4. be provided by multi-disciplinary collaboration, delivered by appropriately trained and supervised staff
5. evaluate the intervention and in so doing
6. provide an opportunity for service users to feed back their comments to improve the intervention
7. provide opportunities to form partnerships with service users to duplicate successful interventions elsewhere in the county
8. provide a value-for-money, effective, intervention
9. communicate and feed back the assessment and outcome of interventions to referrers and mental health teams
10. focus on the broader aims of recovery, rather than just amelioration of symptoms.

Translating Policy and Evidence into Practice

Our activities were based on these 10 policy points. The first author of this present chapter was a member of an interest group which planned the groupwork. Members of this group included nurses, social workers and psychologists. We had similar agendas for promoting work with persons with psychosis; in particular, we held similar values about the ability to improve people's quality of life through groupwork. We wanted to complement the use of medications, which are valuable but often become the only therapy that is valued.

Many of us had learned the basics of cognitive behavioural therapy (CBT) approaches to individuals with psychosis through the Thorn course (Gamble 1995). We were then keen to apply these techniques in a group setting, if possible, and with the benefit of multi-disciplinary care as suggested by the *Building Bridges* report (Department of Health 1995), which highlighted a lack of co-operation between agencies and suggested that services focus on the needs of those patients experiencing psychosis. In addition, the *National*

Service Framework for Mental Health (Department of Health 1999) for adults of working age espouses the importance of choice of intervention for service users, including psychological and social therapies, which are the core components of the groupwork.

We decided that the focus of our intervention would be on the phenomenon of 'voice-hearing'. We examined the evidence base and found that many people who hear voices find them helpful or benevolent (Romme and Escher 1993). Indeed, in a large study of 15,000 people it was found that there was a prevalence of 2.3 per cent who had heard voices frequently, contrasting with the 1 per cent prevalence of schizophrenia (Tien 1991). Sadly, for many people with a serious mental health problem, voice-hearing is distressing, and is often seen as a prime symptom of schizophrenia and other psychoses (American Psychiatric Association 1994). The prime focus of our intervention was therefore to reduce this distress.

Honig and others (1998) showed that the key differences between non-patients and patients hearing voices were in the content of what the voices said, not in the form of the voice-hearing (Honig et al. 1998). In other words, both the non-patients and patients heard voices both inside and outside their heads, but for the non-patients the content was positive, or the hearer had a positive view of the voice and felt in control of it. By contrast the patient group was more frightened of the voices and the voices were more critical (malevolent) and they felt less control over them. The experience of hearing these critical voices is often very anxiety provoking (Tibbo et al. 2003) and leads to high levels of depression and suicidality (Harkavy-Friedman et al. 2003). So our intervention was aimed at working directly with the voice and its content and at reducing anxiety, whereas conventional approaches in psychiatry to the problem of voice-hearing have been to ignore the meaning of the experience for the voice-hearer and concentrate on removing voices by the use of physical means such as medication (Romme and Escher 1989). Anti-psychotic medication is very helpful to many sufferers of psychosis (Fleischhaker 2002). Nevertheless, there is a significant proportion of people (at least 30 per cent) who still experience the 'symptoms' such as hearing voices (auditory hallucinations), despite very high doses of injected (and therefore non-compliance is not an issue) anti-psychotic medication (Curson et al. 1985).

The social psychiatrist Marius Romme suggests that anti-psychotic medication prevents the emotional processing (and therefore healing) of the meaning of the voices (Romme and Escher 2000). Indeed, for some people, voice-hearing is a protective phenomenon. As an example, one of the possible candidates for our group heard angels speaking to him, who offered useful suggestions to him about his art work. In fact, this potential participant declined the offer to join the group because he did not want this relationship with the angelic voice to be damaged. He also titrated his anti-psychotic medication to stop the majority of critical voices but allow some voices (including the angel's) to continue.

Traditional non-pharmacological practice, rooted in behavioural psychology, concentrated on either distracting the patient or ignoring references by the patient to the voice-hearing experience, with the hope that the patient would concentrate on 'real' experiences, the assumption being that the voice-hearing was a delusional belief or meaningless symptom. All of us who planned our groupwork approach had experienced this, as either practitioner or patient; one of the co-authors of this chapter, Tim, said at the time that instead of helping him focus on 'reality' it made him feel unheard and ignored.

Although groupwork has been reported to be a therapeutic medium by voice-hearers themselves (Baker 1995) there is little regular use of such groups by professionals treating psychosis. This may be because groupwork involves many skills and needs a low level of defensiveness on the part of the therapists in order to be able to learn from group members what is of most use to them (Coyne 1999). Alternatively it could also be because groupwork (alongside many other psychological approaches) has not been valued in work with psychosis, owing to the emphasis there has been on compliance with medication. This view may be founded on the work of May (1968), who found little evidence of psychotherapy being more helpful than medication alone, despite being a much more expensive intervention.

However, this view that psychotherapy is of little value in working with psychosis has been comprehensively challenged by Karon, who believes that the person with severe psychosis has a need to be understood, and that medication as a single treatment leads to long-term disablement despite a reduction in outward psychotic behaviour (Karon 1989, 2003). In fact, considerable research (e.g. Free 1999; Schermer and Pines 1999; White and Freeman 2000) has shown that given the right conditions, including a clear structure, clear boundaries, a here-and-now focus on specific issues, and an attempt to reduce anxiety at an early stage of the groupwork, then groupwork with persons experiencing psychosis can be successful in reducing 'symptoms' and distress and can provide an experience of being confirmed as a person through peer support.

The Case Study

Editors' note: the case here revolves around how the policy and evidence base discussed above could be used to create an effective group-based way of promoting recovery from voice-hearing. Keith Coupland, nurse consultant for psychosocial interventions in psychosis within the Gloucestershire Partnership NHS Trust, was key in developing the groups, and Tim Cuss was a member of an early group, who went on to develop and co-facilitate other groups. The case has three parts. First, some of the basic underpinnings (philosophy, training of facilitators) of setting up such a group are outlined; then Tim reflects on the experience of participating (and then co-facilitating) in them; and then a range of practical issues surrounding setting up such groups are explained.

Philosophy and theoretical underpinning

The explanatory/understanding framework for the voice-hearing which we used was an adapted form of the stress-vulnerability model. This model suggests there are many causative factors involved in the development of psychosis, including stress and trauma; and each individual has their own threshold of vulnerability or sensitivity (Zubin and Spring 1977; Nuechterlein and Dawson 1984). The original model had been criticised as being judgemental, mechanistic and with the suggestion of personal weakness being implied by vulnerability (Johnstone 2000). The new model emphasises the ongoing ability to cope, learn and evolve competency as well as being affected by disorder (Davidson and Strauss 1995).

The style of groupwork that we chose was the 'integrative approach to groupwork for psychosis' (Kanas 1996). This pragmatic and well-researched approach emphasises reduction in isolation by increasing social interaction between group members; learning to overcome the distress of symptoms (especially by sharing coping strategies); and being user led as to the content of sessions, as long as that is within the clear framework already negotiated. The facilitators are practitioners who use a directive approach to reduce anxiety, not passive observers of a group process, as may be the case when facilitators employ an analytic philosophy (Kanas 1999).

Training of Facilitators

Within east Gloucestershire, most of the facilitators had undergone specialist training in psychosocial approaches to psychosis and were skilled in working with groups. However, this training of staff in groupwork had taken a number of years. We developed the skills of other facilitators by combining the knowledge and skills of an experienced nurse, psychologist and social worker and pairing them with more novice workers (including service users) to develop emergent group facilitators. Other service users occasionally facilitate groups when they feel confident enough to do so.

The Perspective of a Participant: Tim's story[1]

Introduction

In this part of the chapter I will describe my personal pathway to recovering from psychosis and the part played by groupwork in that recovering.

In my experience, recovering seems to depend firstly on being in an accepting frame of mind so that, when one meets an important person on the road to recovering, one can accept the help offered. Secondly it is about feeling included and accepted by others and society, so that I feel confirmed as a person rather than limited by a diagnosis: a schizophrenic.

Symptoms, treatment and recovery

A group of people with the diagnosis of schizophrenia may have some similar symptoms such as hearing voices and often have similar treatment with medication, usually because their behaviour is so different from 'normal' that it has drawn attention. The medication sedates and may lead to more 'rational behaviour' for some people but this is not my idea of recovery!

The personal experiences of psychosis are not meaningless 'symptoms'. For example, an abusive voice, or 'auditory hallucination' heard by a person with schizophrenia may be a reminder of an abusive or critical parent. For another person a voice may seem like an angel and be very comforting and protective. However these and other 'symptoms' can often be overwhelming and may lead to a breakdown in social circumstances, leading to isolation and exclusion. One cannot access support from others because of the preoccupation with the psychotic experiences. Therefore, the asylum of being in society is lost and hospitalisation may follow; and then one becomes part of the society of the hospital, taking on the role of a patient with the accompanying drop in expectations of one's ability and often accompanied by giving up hope. This isolation may continue even with medication if there is no effort to reconnect to other people. Reversing this isolation process is required if recovery is to follow.

Services need to offer more choice in order for recovery to become more likely, particularly offering more psychological help, as 'talking therapy', and helping in the setting of realistic life goals.

The chance meeting

I see psychosis as a process of alienation from both society and myself. My points of reference became detached from what was really happening around me. This went on for years until a chance meeting with Steve Brooks,[2] a member of Milsom Street hearing voices group. When I was sitting in the common room, muttering to myself, Steve suggested I join this group and very gently encouraged me along. What I experienced was a revelation.

The hearing voices group allowed me gently to challenge my psychotic experiences and slowly detach them from me personally. What made the difference was the opportunity to discuss these experiences with other people with psychosis. I began to understand the 'symptoms' as having a personal significance yet without taking those 'symptoms' personally as I once did. I accepted the symptoms as an experience of mine. I then separated them from myself and then accepted myself. Before I discussed this in the group, I could not get any perspective, I became my symptoms, and my being was as a 'schizophrenic', one detached from reality and society. I felt these symptoms and I felt dejected.

This situation had lasted for decades. I had become the 'useless catatonic schizophrenic' described by my wife shortly before we divorced. I felt no one was listening and so I became mute; and remained mute as an inpatient for seven years. This separation from the symptoms, through groupwork, became a radical first step in reducing my alienation. I could actually feel the relief. I felt accepted by the group. Then I began to feel hope for my future.

The group gave me ideas that I started to practice for myself. The first thing I did was to learn coping strategies to deal with the voices and the anxiety they caused. I began to feel a sense of being effective in controlling firstly my symptoms (rather than simply eradicating them), then my understanding, my destiny and finally, myself.

Baseline 'measures'

The baseline measures for the groupwork involved answering the KGV (Krawiecka, Goldberg and Vaughan 1977; Lancashire 1994) questionnaire and having the results sent back to me. This was a baseline, a foundation. It was very important to know where I was, psychologically. I did not feel resentful about these assessments, as I did in the past, because they were not inquisitional! The results were produced with me. This was open, collaborative and different from the closed files of the hospital. This was the start of a dialogue. For example, I believed everyone heard voices but I was the only one that did not understand them! I then realised that these voices were symptoms of mental illness not mental sickness (disease). This distinction is important to me. Sickness or disease seems like a torpid, pallid, state that is more like a cancer that continues to grow. An illness is, to me, a process where you do not feel yourself: it is a temporary thing and something you might feel but can recover from. Although I believe that psychosis can be meaningful, I also believe that 'symptoms' or experience can be overwhelming and make you feel ill.

I became involved in the group. We began to share a deeper understanding. I noticed that my interactions with staff and other users changed. It was as if they knew and respected my progress through the group. The group promoted a logical discussion of psychosis in a friendly and open way that led to a real connection with others, a bonding. This is a very positive human and humanising experience.

There is a fear, in some people, that the discussion of psychosis will, in itself, bring about a breakdown. This is not at all the case in the hearing voices group where the discussion leads to build up of a person, not breakdown! The group is protective. You know it is there for you when you next need it.

In the past, the reaction of 'the public' to me made me feel stigmatised, alone and apart. This led to social withdrawal and I felt like I was being taunted and always alone or on the edge of a breakdown. In the hearing voices group, this does not happen. We all share this condition (of psychosis and voice-hearing) and therefore avoid stigma and prejudice between ourselves. This is helped by the safe boundaries we set in the group and the mutual respect for each other.

The group helps me to feel integrated and deal with the psychotic 'states' I had had in the past. Some people want to deny and escape their states of psychosis but I want to integrate those experiences after getting some perspective on them.

Changes in my relationships with people outside the group

Before the groupwork, I felt that when my father died (my last parent) I would end up, at best, in a home for the mentally ill. This is because my father had directed much of my life before he became terminally ill. However, as the roles were reversed and I became the carer, my relationship with him improved. We forgave each other and he prepared me to take over his bee hives, an enterprise that has thrived.

The group helped to put me in touch with researchers and lecturers and together we hope to further the understanding of psychosis. Collaboration with researchers allowed me to put ideas about recovery together: I became curious about mental illness instead of fearful.

Furthermore, people in the past looked at the difficulties of my psychosis but never concentrated on the ups, only on the downs and the relapses. Having learned to recognise these patterns myself, and with time and encouragement from the group members and others, I have not been hospitalised for years. I have become successful in the quite involved occupation of a bee-keeper as well as a part time lecturer on issues concerned with recovering from psychosis.

Trying to explain to the psychiatrist

The group helped me to understand my voices but my confidence in describing my experiences was set back when I was explaining to a locum psychiatrist how I deal with the voices. I went into some detail about my experience of the voices and the way I cope with it. The detail was such that the psychiatrist thought I must be suffering a relapse and increased my medication! Although this annoyed me, I used my coping mechanisms to deal with the anger and frustration by discussing the situation with the group again. They were supportive and I began re-negotiating the prescription. In fact, this led to a series of discussions with psychiatrists until I felt I was on the right dose of the kind of medication that had the least side-effects and was the most effective. I would not have been able to have this discussion without that support from the group. For many years the medications had left me feeling tired and as if I was not quite human, a person without a feeling of connection to others. Eventually, with active support from the psychiatrist, I was prescribed medication that allowed me to have my emotions again.

Trying not to repeat the past

When I was in hospital, dialogue was at best discouraged, or actively broken up. Since I found the group process so helpful, I wanted to develop the ideas in an inpatient setting so help could be available to others and much sooner than I experienced it.

I left the Milsom Street hearing voices group and wanted to help set up another group, like the one that had been a help to me, in hospital.

I worked with two psychologists in Gloucester and developed an inpatient group specifically for 'recovering'. We used the principles of 'dialogue' developed by William Isaacs (1999) as an alternative to debate in business and by Maurice Freidman (2003) as a therapy centred on connecting with and confirming the other as a person. Dialogue means a flow of meaning and togetherness and is not about scoring debating points from one another. Of particular importance is the idea and experience of 'hearing a voice', but this time my own voice – and of being heard – then being able to 'set the agenda', as for our group meetings.

Co-facilitating this group made me feel that I had come full circle from hospital to community to recovery and back to hospital but I was not back where I was all those years ago. I still experience psychosis but within this group, my experiences are what connected me to others rather than alienated me as they had in the past.

Conclusion of Tim's story

Recovering from psychosis is a personal and a social process of discovering a meaning and purpose in life again. It is about accepting psychotic experiences (symptoms), self and others. It is also about being accepted by others and being included by society. Social inclusion also involves developing work (paid or unpaid) that is meaningful and fulfilling. For me that was the bee-keeping, but I also enjoy the lectures and consultancy that developed from the groupwork. Then one needs to be resilient because not everyone will understand or welcome your recovery; and here one must be steadfast but flexible and see the road to recovery as having many twists and turns. It is a road worth travelling and it is very useful to have a band of companions from the group on the journey.

From my new facilitator's perspective, what is most powerful is seeing people who were previously 'written-off' and were disenfranchised begin to blossom again. Of specific importance is the fact that in my dual role of service user and facilitator, I can often positively challenge other service user's unhelpful thoughts or conclusions, in a way that would be difficult for staff members to do. This is where the medium of groupwork demonstrates its effectiveness in also reducing stigma and encouraging social re-integration.

The Process of Setting up a Group

The setting up of a group to work with voice-hearers in east Gloucestershire began by convening a multi-disciplinary team of interested practitioners who had support from their managers. We also invited Julia Caley, a CPN from Coleford in west Gloucestershire. Julia had already successfully begun a support group for people with psychosis in her catchment area and had had great success in enabling group members to be peer trainers to new members.

The planning group was fortunate to have a researcher, Kate Edgar, who kept minutes and evaluated the group (Davis et al. 1997). Eric Davis, a clinical psychologist in east Gloucestershire, supervised Kate and made the application to the Local Research and Ethics Committee (LREC) to obtain ethical approval. Vicky MacDougall, social worker, researcher and co-therapist of the group, ensured we included users in the planning, to ensure a stakeholding and ownership from early on in the process. The users, who included Steve Brooks (one of the authors of chapter 8 in this volume), proved to be a considerable asset in a number of ways. Steve influenced our basic philosophy, by asking us to review the stress-vulnerability model: he enabled us to see that stress could be relabelled as 'positive sensitivity' rather than the implied 'inability to withstand stress'. Steve and the other users also helped in gaining funds and giving presentations about the group: in particular, Steve was able to explain in detail how psychological approaches to psychosis, and especially those helping him to cope with malevolent voices, had proved crucial to him in preventing relapse. For example, he talked to members of a local charitable organisation, and we believe his input was critical in the group being awarded £5,000 as start-up monies to fund the evaluation and provide materials for the group. Our aim in the evaluation was to be pragmatic and demonstrate the value of this approach, so that later widespread adoption of groupwork in the organisation could occur.

Gender Issues

If women are present as group members then it is important that at least one facilitator is a woman (MacDougall 1998). Many people who experience voice-hearing have suffered childhood trauma including bullying, and sexual abuse is found more frequently in women than men (Read et al. 2001). This evidence suggests that separately-gendered groups may be required because of specific abuse issues (such as sexual abuse or domestic violence), which is now happening within Gloucestershire Partnership NHS Trust. The optimal group size is six to eight persons (Yalom 1995).

Inclusion criteria for group members

The group members were (and continue to be) chosen in relation to the first of the ten policy recommendations described earlier which the manager of mental health services had outlined: group members needed to:

- be distressed primarily from hearing voices, although they may also have other problems of psychosis

- want to work as a member of a hearing voices group and
- be aged between 18 and 65, the boundaries of the working age adult group of the Trust.

Other useful (although not all essential) inclusion criteria were that they:

- usually should have a diagnosis of psychosis/severe mental illness such as schizophrenia or schizo-affective psychosis
- usually will have tried a variety of anti-psychotic medication with little effect on the hallucinations/voices
- may have a contact who will liaise with the group facilitators, such as a care co-ordinator or key worker
- will already (where possible) be attending the centre where the hearing voices group or other group for psychosis is held, as this helps the person feel comfortable in the group. For some people it is very stressful to enter a busy day centre for the first time without knowing the people there. If they are not attending the day centre already, then a careful process of engagement may be needed, depending on the person.

Exclusion criteria for group members

The only exclusion criterion was (and still is): the continued misuse of substances such as amphetamines, heroin, etc., or large quantities of alcohol. We recognise that the group format can be very useful to deal expressly with dual diagnosis of psychosis and substance misuse and that such groups are effective; we excluded persons with these problems from the group because of the difficulty of dealing with the addiction problems alongside the psychosis. However, groups for people with co-existing problems could be offered as a separate intervention (Anderson 2001).

Referrals

We still use the referral process that we set up initially. Referrals are accepted from members of the multi-disciplinary team (MDT), who are alerted to the group being started and who are normally the care co-ordinator of the voice-hearer. However, referrals are also received from non-statutory sources and from voice-hearers themselves. The potential group users will receive a thorough assessment (see below), after which the appropriateness of group inclusion is discussed. Referrals from both statutory and non-statutory sources need to be in writing, including a brief psychiatric history and any details relating to risk. The voice-hearer should see the referral letter and agree its content before it is sent to the group facilitators. If a voice-hearer wishes to refer him- or herself to the group, the normal process is reversed in order to ensure the care co-ordinator is aware of the referral and is able to inform the assessment. Several group members have prompted the referral of voice-hearers who they know need help; this has been a very successful method of introduction. Most new referrals see the group video made by group members (Coupland and Jones 2002) and are encouraged to make an informal visit to the group before committing themselves.

Assessment

If the referral is accepted, the voice-hearer is asked to attend an individual assessment. If the voice-hearer does not feel ready to commit to this, then the referrer is notified and future re-referral is encouraged. It may be that individual work is found to be more appropriate, so this may be suggested instead.

If assessment is possible, the first strategy is to normalise the voice-hearing as a symptom of psychosis *and* human experience, especially as a reaction to stress. A careful and sensitive discussion surrounding the voice-hearer's experience in an unhurried and supportive fashion is essential. The assessment is quite lengthy and makes use of the Manchester symptom scale, also called the KGV after its original authors (Krawiecka, Goldberg and Vaughan 1977). The scale is very helpful in finding out how the voice-hearers experience their psychotic symptoms, as well as rating the anxiety, depression and suicidality that voice-hearing may cause. The scale has been revised many times by Stuart Lancashire (Lancashire 1994). The KGV is the preferred assessment tool because it is phenomenological in nature, thus allowing for voice-hearers to explain in as much detail as they are comfortable with, their lived experience of voice-hearing. However, being unable to complete a KGV does not necessarily preclude the sufferer from attending a group. A useful alternative is a very comprehensive assessment, known as the Maastricht interview, which is included in a book by Romme and Escher (2000).

Following the assessment we wrote back to the group member with the results, including a history of the voice-hearing, so that the voice-hearer can correct mistakes and co-create the final version of the assessment, a process that seems to increase the ownership of the experiences (Coupland, Davis and Gregory 2001). This co-created letter is sent back to the voice-hearer, with a copy to the care co-ordinator, explaining the outcome of the assessment and whether the person has been accepted at this point to join a group. An important part of the letter is identifying and reflecting back the coping mechanisms that the person already has, as well as a provisional formulation as to how the person is affected, and a plan of how the groupwork might help. Where possible, assessments are repeated every three to six months to evaluate and discuss changes.

Structure of the group

There are general guidelines (for example, Yalom 1983, 1995) that have been applied locally. These suggest that the group normally has six to eight participants and two facilitators, although some groups have preferred to have three facilitators who can form a rota to ensure there are always at least two present for each group. Feedback from our service users indicates that both these arrangements work well.

There is evidence for efficacy for short-term (six weeks) psycho-educational groupwork for voice-hearers experiencing psychosis (Wykes, Parr and Landau 1999), however our intuition (subsequently supported by our own research showing additional benefits of long-term work, such as building confidence for an experienced member, who is able to explain the process to new members (Coupland, Davis and MacDougall 2002)) was that a slower, longer-term group might be more useful. We therefore agreed that initially, the group would meet weekly for 12 sessions followed by a break for two weeks for evaluation. After a further 12 sessions, there would be another two-week evaluation period. The group met at a set time each week, at a time agreed by the group, who also agreed the ground rules. The group has continued with this 'slow open' style, with additional members joining the group from time to time and members leaving the group when they have jobs or move on for other reasons. Although regular attendance is one of the group's ground rules, group members sometimes need gentle encouragement over a long period to keep coming.

This style of group is also able to fulfil a training function within the organisation. For example, initially facilitators were chosen on the basis of one experienced and one less so, in order to foster learning and skill acquisition. Also, students and interested staff wanting to learn about the group have been welcomed as visitors by the group members, who feel valued by the external interest in hearing their personal stories. In turn, some group members feel less stigmatised, or set apart, owing to this external interest in their experiences.

Ground rules for groupwork

It is recognised that establishing ground rules is a useful means to create a safe environment in which a group can begin to function (Yalom 1983). This process began with the facilitators asking the group users what would feel reasonable in terms of the group's operation. It was hoped that this would foster a sense of mutual collaboration, ownership and confidence from the very beginning. This list, created by our group, may provide a useful point of reference to others:

- All participants need to have respect for the rules of the building, i.e. where smoking is permissible.
- There will be a break for tea, coffee and cigarettes after 45 minutes, followed by another 30 minutes of groupwork.
- Confidentiality: members and staff will not share information they hear in the group about members, with people outside the group, unless for risk management reasons or where permission is given for supervision or education.
- The group will start promptly each week at the agreed time.
- The group members can expect each other to attend regularly.
- The focus of the groupwork is the origin, content, meaning, understanding and ways of coping with the voices. This process helps us to be aware of how to deal with the voices.
- We will not criticise each other's contribution; we realise that what works for one person may not work for others.
- We aim to be supportive of each other in the group.
- Sharing is an important part of the groupwork.
- We will all be involved and take part in the group.
- Humour is an important part of the group, but laugh with us not at us.
- Facilitators are available for an agreed period of time after the group and are contactable at other times

Therapeutic process

The facilitators take an active role in running the group. They provide a high degree of structure by asking for and providing some agenda items, allocating time to provisional items, and connecting the group's business to previous groups, to ensure continuity. Research and experience has shown that this structure is very important for the early part of the group process, in order to reduce the anxiety that some people feel when they work in groups. New members are encouraged to offer agenda items for discussion but we recognise that it may take several sessions to build confidence, and initially there is likely to be a strong element of psycho-education, such as discussing what is meant by a hallucination, or a diagnosis of schizophrenia, to help remove the feeling of being under pressure to contribute and self-disclose. During this stage with its emphasis on learning, pamphlets about psychosis (Baker 1995; Downs 2001), as well as online leaflets such as those by David Kingdon (www.hearingvoices.org.uk/leaflet1.htm), can be offered to the group. The early sessions should also seek to establish the ground rules for running the group.

For some people the part of the groupwork that explores the voices is stressful and it is common to feel they are getting worse before they start to get better. It may be useful therefore, during these early weeks, to end the session with a relaxation exercise as a way of reducing anxiety. We have also found that several members are keen to tell jokes and this appears to be as helpful, as long as the jokes are not cruel or sexist! Fun and good humour seems to be as important as the depth of exploration of the voices.

We have found that the group members soon gain confidence to contribute, exploring what behaviour different members use when the voice-hearing starts and exploring what coping mechanisms are effective to combat the negative effects of the voices. Sharing this information seems to be very important, partly because many of the voice-hearers do not realise they have coping mechanisms and partly because it is useful to hear about other peoples' coping mechanisms in case this suggests new ways of coping to some participants.

As confidence grows in the group, an exploration of the origin of the voices can be made. This part of the group process needs extreme sensitivity and facilitators need to be very careful about the pace at which this exploration is made as some members relive past trauma. Facilitators will judge this by close attention to users' emotional status and by careful Socratic questions to aid the individual's journey of discovery. Socratic questions help the group member to give more information about their experience by suspending any judgements on behalf of the questioner and genuinely trying to understand the experience from the members' point of view. Such a question would be 'how does the voice actually sound to you, is it louder or softer than your own voice'?

As confidence grows, people often start to make changes both in their ability to cope with the voices and in the general quality of their lives because they are able to share experiences and feel accepted. This stage of the group provides a forum to examine the antecedents, behaviours and consequences of voice-hearing. In other words, the activating events, the associated thoughts, feelings, images or beliefs, and how each individual constructs their associated emotional and behavioural consequences. More effective ways of coping with the voices are then discovered and discussed within the group. A schedule that helped in this process was the cognitive assessment of voices interview schedule (Chadwick, Birchwood and Trower 1996). Despite being a complex process, the schedule was useful for each person to complete within the group process and this increased the members understanding of their own and others' experiences. Personal goal-setting and plans for the future may also be introduced at this stage.

As the group progresses, the beliefs about the voices can be further examined. This again requires great sensitivity as often very complex beliefs build up, over years of experiencing voices, where the person may not have been able to talk to anyone else about their voices in order to discuss these developing beliefs. Some beliefs take the forms that conventional psychiatry would call delusional. These beliefs may have very protective functions for the voice-hearer and should only be challenged if the overall benefit is a reduction in distress for the voice-hearer or the prevention of harm. However, a gentle, empathic, discussion about a belief by other group members often brings about changes much more quickly than a challenge from one of the group facilitators. It is important for the facilitators to 'suspend disbelief' as many voice-hearers have truly remarkable stories to tell (Kingdon and Turkington 1991).

Bringing in outside speakers to the group can also be very helpful. This can create new and stimulating perspectives on the voice-hearing experience, which encourages further reflection from users. Perspectives which have proved useful are those presenting an alternative theoretical viewpoint (such as a psychological one), or a different professional one (such as one from a psychiatrist, a clinical pharmacist or a clinical psychologist). Because such visits are planned, we find that users do not commonly find this disruptive.

Alternatively, the speaker could be a member of another hearing voices group and responses are usually very good as they are speaking from their own direct experience of the benefit of groupwork on their own lives. Some of the group members of the Gloucestershire hearing voices network are available to talk to new groups about their experiences of the recovering process.

We find it beneficial to include creative work as well as discussion within the group meetings; this may be especially useful as a means of engaging quieter group members. Each session incorporates an activity such as affirmation cards, drawing 'life-lines' and life-story-telling, which have all been well received. Affirmation cards take the form of a laminated card with a supportive statement in the present tense that can be carried around and viewed at times of potential stress e.g., 'I am a worthwhile person'. It is even more effective if there is a picture or photograph that is meaningful and uplifting on the reverse side of the card. Life-lines are another useful exercise that attempts to understand a person's history by linking salient or significant events to particular points in time. They are usually written down so as to form a document that can be used to inform intervention. Life-story telling simply involves listening carefully to the lived experiences of users. This work is based on the ideas of narrative therapy (Roberts and Holmes 1999) and self-acceptance (Dryden 1998).

The nature of the groupwork changes with time. In our experience, a more narrative style develops that involves facilitators and group members co-operating in forming and reforming members' life stories and how they perceive their 'scripts' or unchallenged assumptions of their limitations (Vassallo 1998; Roberts and Holmes 1999; Roberts 2000). The story-telling may be aided by artwork; one of our groups has made a formal art therapist-led section a part of their group process.

The last session of each 12-week block is spent as a celebration with a meal in a pub! This is to celebrate the value of the group as a means of increasing confidence, reducing distress and fostering a sense of hope. For the staff members, there is great value in seeing users' confidence and hopefulness grow. As users' recovery gathers pace, new opportunities emerge. For example, users can contribute to the actual running of the group, and this is both powerful and moving to see.

Supervision

There was weekly post-group supervision, provided by Eric Davis, clinical psychologist. This supervision was an essential part of building our confidence in the early days when there was little literature on groupwork for psychosis. As the group developed, we were able to help set up groups in other parts of Gloucestershire and every month the facilitators met as a group for supervision, usually for two hours, rather than after each group. This had the extra advantage of sharing ideas between groups.

Evaluation

Initially, we evaluated the group formally, using a series of measures of social functioning (Birchwood et al. 1990); psychopathology (Lancashire 1994) and beliefs about the malevolence of the voices (Chadwick and Birchwood 1995). We found some evidence for a reduction in anxiety, depression and voice-hearing (Davis et al. 1997) and, in the long term, three members stopped hearing voices and returned to full time work. A qualitative evaluation showed that members appreciated the ability to share their experiences; and that users felt less isolated and more accepted (Coupland, Davis and MacDougall 2002).

Some members seemed to be transformed by the process and either reduced voice-hearing or increased their resilience to the voices. However, at the evaluation after 12 weeks, most of the members did not experience a drop in the amount of voice-hearing or the nature of the voice (if it was critical, it remained critical). The second evaluation took place at 24 weeks: the situation was the same with voice-hearing, but there was an increase in feeling in control and a reduction of anxiety and depression. We did not measure quantitatively the concept of 'feeling accepted' or the relief of sharing experiences, which were the most important outcomes on the qualitative evaluation. Among the facilitators, there was also a high degree of satisfaction in working in a group format and seeing changes taking place in members in a mutually supportive atmosphere.

On the other hand, some members felt the group process too stressful and left, demonstrating that despite our careful assessment process, it is not always possible to identify users who may not gain from using the group. Timing may be particularly important if users are too unwell to attend a group: close contact with the individual's care co-ordinator can ensure they are encouraged to return when they are less poorly. The timing also relates to the confidence of the voice-hearer to talk to others about their experience.

Conclusion

In our different roles as facilitator and member, we believe that the groupwork has been mutually beneficial. We have both increased our understanding of voice-hearing and both experienced the way the group brings about a feeling of being connected to others. We have gone on to work together in teaching about groups, and the combination of facilitator and member views of what happened has proved to be very helpful.

Some members have been asked to assess and support other voice-hearers on the hospital wards; this has been a mutually positive experience. If you are considering starting up a group for voice-hearers, we may be contacted through our Gloucestershire hearing voices web site: http://www.hearingvoices.org.uk/ where we have a number of downloadable resources.

The national Hearing Voices Network has much to offer, including information on local user-led hearing voices groups and self-help groups and an excellent newsletter *Voices Magazine*, Hearing Voices Network, 91 Oldham Street, Manchester M4 1LW. Tel./fax: 0161 834 768. Website: http://www.hearing-voices.org/.

Notes

1 Tim was a member of one of the groups.

2 Steve is one of the authors of chapter 8.

References

Aderhold, V., Agar, K., Argyle, N. and Read, J. (2003) Sexual and physical abuse during childhood and adulthood as predictors of hallucinations, delusions and thought disorder. *Psychology and Psychotherapy*, 76, 1–22.

American Psychiatric Association (1994) *Diagnostic and Statistical Manual of Mental Disorders*, 4th edition. Washington: American Psychiatric Association.

Anderson, A. (2001) Psychoeducational group therapy for the dually diagnosed. *International Journal of Psychosocial Rehabilitation*, 5, 77–8.

Baker, P. (1995) *The Voice Inside*. Chester: Handsell Publications.

Birchwood, M., Smith, J., Cochrane, R., Wetton, S. and Copestake, S. (1990) The Social Functioning Scale: the development and validation of a scale of social adjustment for use in family intervention programmes with schizophrenic patients. *British Journal of Psychiatry*, 157, 853–9.

Chadwick, P. and Birchwood, M. (1995) The omnipotence of voices II: the beliefs about voices questionnaire (BAVQ). *British Journal of Psychiatry*, 165, 773–6.

Chadwick, P., Birchwood, M. and Trower, P. (1996) *Cognitive Therapy for Delusions, Voices and Paranoia*. Chichester: Wiley.

Coupland, K., Davis, E. and Gregory, K. (2001) Learning from life. *Mental Health Care*, 4, 166–9.

Coupland, K., Davis, E. and MacDougall, V. (2002) Group work for psychosis: a values led evidence based approach. *Mental Health Nursing*, 22, 6–9.

Coupland, K. and Jones, C. (2002) 2.2 *Overview of Groupwork for Psychosis. On Working with Psychosis* [video and multi-media pack]. Cheltenham: Gloucestershire Partnership NHS Trust.

Coyne, R. (1999) *Failures in Group Work: How We Can Learn from Our Mistakes*. Thousand Oaks, CA: Sage.

Curson, D., Barnes, T., Bamber, R. and Weral, D. (1985) Long term depot maintenance of chronic schizophrenic outpatients. *British Journal of Psychiatry*, 146, 464–80.

Davidson, L. and Strauss, J. (1995) Beyond the biopsychosocial model: integrating disorder, health, and recovery. *Psychiatry*, 58, 44–55.

Davis, E., Coupland, K., Edgar, K. and MacDougall, V. (1997, December). *A Study to Investigate the Psychological Impact of a Voice-hearer's Group*. Paper presented at the London conference of the British Psychological Society, London.

Department of Health (1992) *Health of the Nation Key Area Handbook: Mental Illness*. London HMSO.

Department of Health. (1995) *Building Bridges: A Guide to Inter-Agency Working for the Care and Protection of Severely Mentally Ill People*. London: Department of Health.

Department of Health (1999) *The National Service Framework for Mental Health: Modern Standards and Service Models*. London: HMSO.

Downs, J. (2001) *Starting and Supporting Hearing Voices Groups*. Manchester: Hearing Voices Network Publications.

Dryden, W. (1998) *Developing Self-acceptance: A Brief, Educational, Small Group Approach*. Chichester: Wiley.

Fleischhaker, W. (2002) Pharmacological treatment of schizophrenia: a review. In M. Maj and N. Sartorius (eds.) *Schizophrenia*, 2nd edition. pp. 75–113). Chichester: Wiley.

Free, M.L. (1999) *Cognitive Therapy in Groups: Guidelines and Resources for Practice*. Chichester: Wiley.

Friedman, M. (2003) Martin Buber and dialogical psychotherapy. In R. Frie (ed.) *Understanding Experience: Psychotherapy and Postmodernism*. London: Routledge.

Gamble, C. (1995) The Thorn Nurse Training Initiative. *Nursing Standard*, 9, 31–4.

Harkavy-Friedman, J., Kimhy, D., Nelson, E., Venarde, D., Malaspina, D. and Mann, J. (2003) Suicide attempts in schizophrenia: the role of command auditory hallucinations for suicide. *Journal of Clinical Psychiatry*, 64, 871–4.

Honig, A., Romme, M., Ensink, B., Escher, S., Pennings, M. and Devries, M. (1998) Auditory hallucinations: a comparison between patients and nonpatients. *Journal of Mental and Nervous Disease*, 186, 646–51.

Isaacs, W. (1999) *Dialogue and the Art of Thinking Together*. New York: Currency.

Johnstone, L. (2000) *Users and Abusers of Psychiatry*, 2nd edition. London: Routledge.

Kanas, N. (1996) *Group Therapy for Schizophrenic Patients*. Washington DC: American Psychiatric Association.

Kanas, N. (1999) Group therapy with schizophrenic and bipolar patients. In Schermer, V. and Pines, M. (eds.) *Group Psychotherapy of the Psychoses: Concepts, Interventions and Contexts* (pp. 129–47). London: Jessica Kingsley.

Karon, B. (1989) Psychotherapy verses medication for schizophrenia: empirical comparisons. In S. Fisher and R. Greenberg (eds.) *The Limits of Biological Treatments for Psychological Distress*. New Jersey: Lawrence Erlbaum.

Karon, B. (2003) The tragedy of schizophrenia without psychotherapy. *Journal of the American Academy of Psychoanalytic and Dynamic Psychiatry*, 31, 89–118.

Kingdon, D. (undated) *Understanding Voices*, an online leaflet produced by Dr David Kingdon. Available online: www.hearingvoices.org.uk/leaflet1.htm (accessed 15 October 2005).

Kingdon, D. and Turkington, D. (1991) The use of cognitive behavior therapy with a normalizing rationale in schizophrenia. Preliminary report. *Journal of Nervous and Mental Diseaases*, 179, 207–11.

Krawiecka, M., Goldberg, D. and Vaughan, M. (1977) A standardised psychiatric assessment scale for rating chronic psychotic patients. *Acta Psychiatrica Scandinavica*, 55, 209–308.

Lancashire, S. (1994) *Revised Version of the KGV Scale*. Manchester: Department of Nursing and the Behavioural Sciences. University of Manchester.

MacDougall, V. (1998) *Unheard Voices*. Unpublished MSc, University of Bristol, Bristol.
May, P. (1968) *Treatment of Schizophrenia: A Comparative Study of Five Treatment Methods*. New York: Science House.
Nuechterlein, K. and Dawson, M. (1984) A heuristic vulnerability-stress model of schizophrenia. *Schizophrenia Bulletin*, 10, 300–12.
Read, J., Perry, B., Moskowitz, A. and Connoly, J. (2001) The contribution of early traumatic events to schizophrenia in some patients: a traumagenic neurodevelopmental model. *Psychiatry: Interpersonal and Biological Processes*, 64, 319–45.
Roberts, G. (2000) Narrative and severe mental illness: what place do stories have in an evidence based world? *Advances in Psychiatric Treatment*, 6, 432–41.
Roberts, G. and Holmes, J. (eds.) (1999) *Healing Stories: Narrative in Psychiatry and Psychotherapy*. Oxford: Oxford University Press.
Romme, M. and Escher, A. (1989) Hearing voices. *Schizophrenia Bulletin*, 15, 209–16.
Romme, M. and Escher, S. (1993) *Accepting Voices*. London: Mind.
Romme, M. and Escher, S. (2000) *Making Sense of Voices*. London: Mind.
Roth, A. and P. Fonagy (1996) *What Works for Whom? A Critical Review of Psychotherapy Research*. London: Guilford Press.
Sainsbury Centre for Mental Health (1998) *Keys to Engagement*. London: Sainsbury Centre for Mental Health.
Sainsbury Centre for Mental Health (1999) *Report on User Focused Monitoring Project*. London: Sainsbury Centre for Mental Health.
Schermer, V. and Pines, M. (1999) *Group Psychotherapy of the Psychoses: Concepts, Interventions and Contexts*. London: Jessica Kingsley.
Tibbo, P., Swainson, J., Chue, P. and LeMelledo, J. (2003) Prevalence and relationship to delusions and hallucinations of anxiety disorders in schizophrenia. *Depression and Anxiety*, 17, 65–72.
Tien, A. (1991) Distributions of hallucinations in the population. *Social Psychiatry and Psychiatric Epidemiology*, 26, 287–92.
Vassallo, T. (1998). Narrative group therapy with the seriously mentally ill: a case study. *Australian and New Zealand Journal of Family Therapy*, 19, 15–26.
White, J. and Freeman, A. (2000) *Cognitive-behavioural Group Therapy for Specific Problems and Populations*. Washington: American Psychiatric Association.
Wykes, T., Parr, A. and Landau, S. (1999) Group treatment of auditory hallucinations. *British Journal of Psychiatry*, 175, 180–5.
Yalom, I. (1983) *In-patient Group Psychotherapy*. New York: Basic Books.
Yalom, I. (1995) *The Theory and Practice of Group Psychotherapy*, 4th edition. New York: Basic Books.
Zubin, J. and Spring, B. (1977) Vulnerability: a new view on schizophrenia. *Journal of Abnormal Psychology*, 86, 103–26.

Chapter 10

Recovery through Sports in First-episode Psychosis

Sean Adams, Lydia Bishop and Jane Bellinger

Key Points

- Social integration is an essential part of recovery and can help combat stigma.
- Mental health service users have higher rates of physical ill health, much of which could be ameliorated by exercise.
- Some treatments can contribute to health problems.
- There is a growing evidence base for the positive effects of physical activity for many mental health problems.
- Less is known about the effects for psychosis, but empirical findings indicate significant benefits.
- There are many hypotheses about the relationship between exercise and mental health: of these, theories relating to distraction, social interaction, self-efficacy and mastery are particularly relevant in overcoming psychosis.
- Social development is often disrupted by first-episode psychosis (FEP).
- Groups offer therapeutic benefits to service users and an opportunity to assess progress for clinicians.
- Although clinicians may have been slow to embrace exercise for its psychological benefits, service users find it both acceptable and valuable.

Introduction

It is hard to get up and go. Some mornings I can't move with worry and inside my head I feel lost. I feel overwhelmed by my thoughts and think that I can't do anything and that stops my motivation, but sport generally eliminates all that. I think it might have prevented the need for me to go back on anti-depressants. It's far better than Prozac for me and I don't get the side-effects. I think that it's the only thing that is keeping me sane at the moment; it's amazing how different you feel.

(Lydia)

Context

The following chapter is written from the perspective of a new early intervention in psychosis team based in the southwest region (Gloucestershire Recovery in Psychosis – GRIP team). The pilot team (comprising one consultant clinical psychologist, three mental health nurses and an administrator) operates out of a partner non-statutory youth agency – Cheltenham Community Projects (CCP) – based in Cheltenham town centre. We aim to assess and treat people between the ages of 14 and 35 experiencing or at risk of first-episode psychosis using a bio-psychosocial approach and an assertive outreach team caseload model (see www.gripinitiative.org.uk).

This chapter is an account of how the GRIP team launched first a well attended sports group for service users and then started a carers' sports group. More importantly it highlights some of the opinions and experiences of participating users of our service (carers and people with psychosis). In the chapter, the terms 'exercise' and 'physical activity' are used fairly interchangeably; 'sports' generally will refer to more organised competitive team games with rules (loosely enforced in our case!)

The Evidence and The Policy – Fighting Social Exclusion and Ill Health, with Activity

The problem of stigma and social exclusion

> Poor mental health is sustained by social exclusion and discrimination.
>
> (Rankin 2005: 9)

The socio-economic consequences of mental health difficulties are often devastating for many people. Social withdrawal is a common problem for people with psychosis. Initially this withdrawal may be a way of coping with distressing and confusing thoughts for the individual. Later, even if paranoid thoughts and distracting hallucinations are less problematic, a residual loss of confidence often prevents participation in community activities. Isolation can be perpetuated by a number of factors: pervasive community discrimination; barriers to participation, both practical and psychological; the lack of clear responsibility among mental health professionals for promoting social and vocational outcomes; and the labelling with a psychiatric diagnosis itself (ODPM 2004).

In recent research, improved access to recreational activities was deemed by service users as necessary to improve their social inclusion: over a third identified a desire for more leisure activity (ODPM 2004). Leisure contributes to building social networks and promotes a sense of social well-being (NIMHE and Mentality 2004) and physical activity also produces social benefits: 'Through the development of community groups, confidence building and social cohesion, physical activity has been considered a key element of neighbourhood regeneration programmes and a particularly useful mechanism for addressing social exclusion' (Grant 2000: 14).

Figure 10.1 offers a diagrammatic representation of how sports and leisure activity can promote social inclusion, by filling the 'social isolation gap'. There are other benefits too: exercise has a positive impact on *physical* health and there is growing evidence indicating a

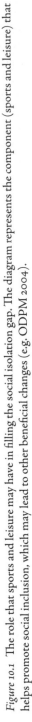

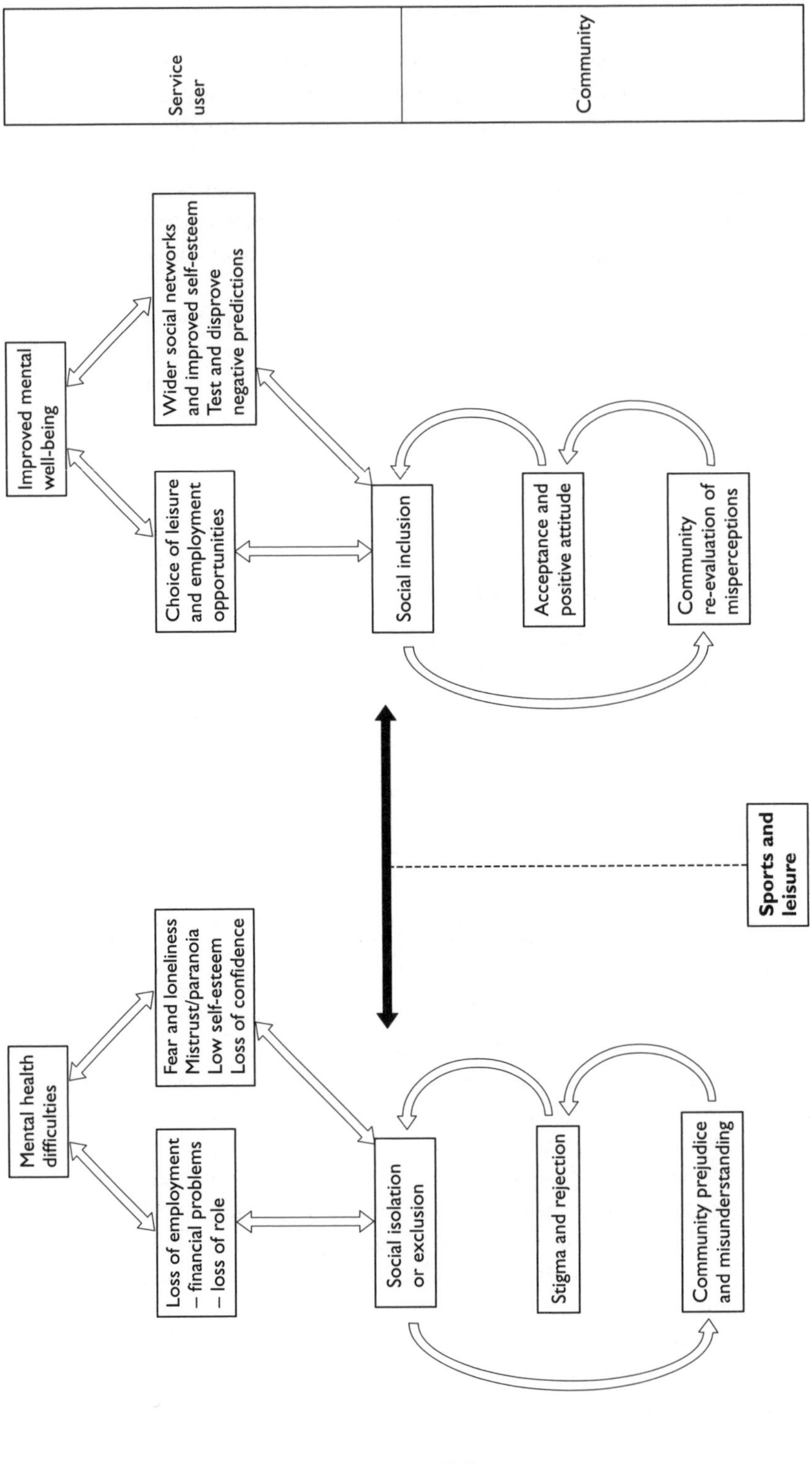

Figure 10.1 The role that sports and leisure may have in filling the social isolation gap. The diagram represents the component (sports and leisure) that helps promote social inclusion, which may lead to other beneficial changes (e.g. ODPM 2004).

correlation between physical activity and *psychological* well-being. Among all the improvements in medication and psychological therapies, exercise as an intervention seems disarmingly simple. In reality of course, sport is not a magic wand nor a universal panacea; but it has demonstrated some effectiveness in reducing symptoms of schizophrenia. In the remainder of this chapter we will first look at some of the research demonstrating the positive impact of physical activity, and then outline our local experience which shows how the careful introduction of physical activity can make a positive impact on the quality of life for some clients using mental health services and how it can act as a bridge towards greater social inclusion.

Mental Health and Physical Activity

Obviously, the physical benefits of activity to people with mental health problems are similar to the benefits to those without such difficulties. This is particularly important because:

- people with mental health problems have higher rates of physical illness, and shorter lives than the general population (e.g. Harris and Barraclough 1998)
- the incidence of coronary heart disease and respiratory disorders is at least doubled or trebled for mental health service users (Brown, Inskip and Barraclough 2000, Phelan, Stradins and Morrison 2001)
- type 2 diabetes has been reported as two to four times higher among people diagnosed with schizophrenia (Mukherjee et. al 1996)
- physical illnesses are often detected late, since people with mental health problems are less likely to access primary care.

Limited finances, social isolation, low self-esteem, reduced motivation and poor housing are more likely than lack of knowledge about health risks to be factors in perpetuating their problems (NIMHE and Mentality 2004).

Lack of occupation is also likely to be a factor, as is admission to psychiatric hospital. In my (JB) recent experience, it is not uncommon for young people to complain of loss of fitness even following a fairly short admission. Boredom and lack of physical activity are often cited as contributing to weight gain and increased smoking. Medication side-effects are also a problem: many anti-psychotics promote an increase in appetite while inflicting drowsiness that makes it more difficult to participate in exercise.

Since physical activity has a preventative effect on developing chronic physical illness, and participation in sport has a beneficial social impact (DCMS 2001), there is a very persuasive argument in favour of the routine use of exercise early on in the recovery of all those with serious and enduring mental health problems. There is, moreover, exciting evidence for exercise contributing to the psychological well-being of service users.

Government targets related to exercise of particular interest to mental health early intervention services include reducing obesity in young people and halting the declining mental health of adolescents. The encouragement of physical activity in younger populations through initiatives to promote partnership working between health workers, the local community and sports providers is seen as one route to achieving this.

Evidence for Mental Health Benefits from Physical Activity

> 85 per cent of people . . . with a severe mental illness who take physical exercise find it to be of therapeutic benefit.
>
> (Rethink 2002)

The evidence supporting 'exercise therapy' as a valuable intervention in mental health recovery is impressive (Biddle, Fox and Boutcher 2000; Grant 2000), with a large body of evidence relating to problems of anxiety, depression and low self-esteem. Hence for anxiety and stress:

- exercise has at least a low to moderate effect on reducing anxiety (Grant 2000), with the largest effects being in unfit and highly anxious people (Department of Health 2004)
- physical activity can reduce short-term physiological reactions to brief stress and improve recovery (Grant 2000; Taylor 2000) and may increase people's resilience in coping with psychosocial stress (Department of Health 2004), although some anxiety disorders such as panic disorder with agoraphobia or social phobia may not benefit from this therapy (Grant 2000).

With depression:

- exercise is effective in reducing clinical symptoms of mild to moderate depression, with several studies finding it to be at least as effective as some forms of psychotherapy (Grant 2000; Mutrie 2000)
- physical activity programmes can be as effective in treating depression as medication (Department of Health 2004): even a cautious meta-review of randomised controlled trials recommend exercise prescription alongside standard treatment (Lawlor and Hopker 2001)
- there is some support for exercise providing a degree of protection from developing depression (Mutrie 2000; Department of Health 2004).

With self-esteem problems:

- physical activity can promote a person's perceptions of physical self-worth, as well as specific physical self-perceptions such as body image; for some people these changes are linked with improvements in self-esteem (Fox 2000)
- the most positive effects of exercise are likely to be experienced by those with initial low self-esteem (Fox 2000; Department of Health 2004).

There is limited research investigating the effects of exercise on schizophrenia (although a Cochrane review is underway). Faulkner and Sparkes (1999) express concern that the over-emphasis on rigorous 'scientific methods' of research has led researchers to avoid studies with people with psychosis. This is due to factors such as the heterogeneity of symptoms in people diagnosed with schizophrenia, the variety of medications used, the prevalence of co-morbidity (e.g. depression and anxiety) and the small numbers available for study; all of which make comparison and generalisation of results difficult. Also, it is only recently that the effects of exercise in psychosis have begun to be recognised as being of potential therapeutic benefit. Their exclusion from this research activity, however, tends to increase their marginalisation and to exclude them from potential benefit (because new services have to be 'evidence-based' and if people with psychosis have been excluded from the trials, then there is no evidence of effectiveness from which to argue for their inclusion in such new services).

However, some work has been done with people with psychosis. Studies by Chamove (1986) and Pelham and Campagna (1991) reported that physical activity programmes were associated with:

- fewer psychotic symptoms
- improved mood
- increased energy
- reduced anxiety
- improved concentration and
- increased social interaction.

Plante (1993) suggested that it was the alleviation of co-existing (co-morbid) problems which improved the quality of life, rather than a reduction in the actual psychotic symptoms. Faulkner and Sparkes (1999), however, argued that exercise *does* have the potential to reduce positive symptoms. Yet even *if* improvements were *only* noted in mood and stress, this would still be of enormous benefit for people with psychosis on two counts: first, we know that stress increases vulnerability to psychosis (Zubin and Spring 1977); second, depression and anxiety are prevalent co-morbid problems with psychosis (Jackson, Hulbert and Henry 2000).

Despite the paucity of rigorous research, the benefits of a physically active lifestyle are being championed as a self-help measure in a number of countries: Mind in the UK promotes exercise in one of its information booklets (Mind 2004); the Canadian *Early Psychosis Intervention Program* endorses physical activity for managing stress (Fraser Health Authority 2005) and, in Australia, sport forms an important part of the group programme for the renowned Early Psychosis Prevention and Intervention Centre (EPPIC 2000). There is also service user feedback: studies have highlighted that service users rate exercise therapy more highly than many standard treatments (Daley 2002).

Sean, one of the co-authors of this chapter, says:

When you focus on the exercise activity, it breaks the pattern of behaviour, breaks up your thoughts. You can think a lot of nonsense if you've got a lot of time so that you dwell on thoughts like being monitored. When I was in hospital I found that it (exercise) broke the pattern of those sorts of thoughts for the duration of the exercise and then for about half an hour after.

How Much and What Sort of Exercise?

The considerable research relating to the type, duration, intensity and frequency of exercise required for various health benefits (dose-response) is outside the scope of this chapter. It would seem likely that forms of exercise which are non-isolating, such as team sports, would be more beneficial for social inclusion than activities such as solitary jogging.

However, Sean highlights the intensity of exertion as an important factor:

For myself the intensity needs to be such that I perspire and get out of breath . . . I think that the effects of exercise last longer than other social activities . . . where the distracting effects only last for the duration of the activity. The physical effort is more taxing and breaks the pattern more . . . Walks help unclutter your head when you are feeling OK, but were no good initially when I thought I was being monitored, as thoughts were triggered by things I saw.

Lydia, another of the co-authors of this chapter, suggests the optimum frequency and duration of exercise which has helped her to cope as a carer:

Ideally I think every day would be good, but I'm not as focused on it at weekends. No longer than two days between. The feeling of well-being lasts on average two days before a top-up is needed . . . Twenty minutes swimming is very beneficial, but even five minutes and building up slowly according to fitness would be fine. Perhaps if you're very fit you may need increased levels of exercise to get the benefits.

Professional Resistance?

Given the low cost implications and obvious benefits of exercise, it is surprising that the NHS has not whole-heartedly adopted the routine use of physical therapy in mental health. A study by Faulkner and Biddle (2001) on psychologists' views about exercise and mental health concluded that exercise was rarely prescribed for a number of reasons: lack of awareness of the evidence, a perception that it was incompatible with psychological models or that it was just too simple!

The Case Study – Policy into Practice

Editors' note: as with chapters 8 and 9, the case here revolves around how the work undertaken led to the development and implementation of a new way of delivering a part of a service: in this case, a sports and exercise group. Jane Bellinger is a case manager/community development worker for the Gloucester early intervention in psychosis service, and Sean Adams and Lydia Bishop have both benefited from exercise, Sean as a user of mental health services, Lydia as a carer.

Jane says:

The review above of national policy and of the evidence base suggested that the running of a sports or exercise group could be beneficial for service users. This was further reinforced by local county-wide research. Prior to our service, 65 per cent of young users with psychosis had no opportunity to take part in leisure activities organised by the mental health services and a larger proportion (74 per cent) did not receive help in accessing community-based leisure activities such as sports clubs or adult education (Davis and Morgan 2004). Local research into the longer-term health of 'serious mental illness' service users indicated lower levels of activity and higher levels of unhealthy lifestyle behaviours than in the non-clinical population (Crone et al. 2005).

However, it was remarks from service users that actually prompted me to set up this sports initiative. Early on, several of the service users that I met were expressing dissatisfaction at weight gain and loss of fitness following a period of hospitalisation. Our client group at that time predominantly consisted of young men. Sport gave us the opportunity to engage them, where traditional 'talking therapy' and community mental health resources failed to appeal. Thus the sports group was born. There was still a key consideration: should we use an existing community-based sports group or form our own?

Community Group Versus Service Users' Group

Clients may be inhibited from using a mainstream community facility for personal, social or practical reasons, including:

- loss of self-esteem
- anxiety
- diminished motivation
- stigma
- lack of community acceptance (both real and perceived)
- transport difficulties and poverty.

Jane says:

From the outset, I have been mindful of the tensions between providing the recommended familiar, non-threatening and supportive environment for exercise, (Grant 2000, EPPIC 2000) and the risk that this will perpetuate the social segregation that we are so desperate to avoid. I firmly believe that non-stigmatising/non-institutional community resources are the ideal; but, not all of our clients are ready for this step.

Bates (2005) advises mental health workers to proceed with caution when considering abandoning mental health user groups in favour of mainstream groups. He cites benefits including peer support and a sense of belonging as key assets of service user groups. In a paper on social inclusion, Rankin (2005) describes two functions of mental health day services: 'bonding' and 'bridging'. She suggests that the shared experiences and confidence-building that can occur in a secure environment are valuable, but that building bridges to mainstream community activities should not be ignored. Both authors agree that the best approach for an individual should be tailored to meet their needs and stage of recovery.

Jane says

I asked Sean why he, or anyone, might use our group rather than a community group. He thought that it was because our group confers the advantage of not having to explain about personal mental health difficulties, nor worry what people will think. I [JB] have taken the stance that good recovery-based practice would be for case managers to channel sports interest towards mainstream community facilities as a service user's confidence grows. Meanwhile, there is sufficient evidence for the benefits of exercise that, I believe, it would be neglectful to omit it until people are ready for community groups.

The sports group seems to have been a catalyst for some of our clients to resume or commence sports interests outside the group.

- Sean's fitness has improved over the past year, and he has recently found the confidence and motivation to join a local badminton group independently.
- Mike (pseudonym), a talented basketball player with an interest in athletics, has joined a gym in order to resume the fitness training he once enjoyed. He is also considering joining a basketball club and future work in the fitness industry.
- Simon (pseudonym) has taken advantage of cheaper membership at a different local gym to accompany his mother on some of her visits.
- Jason (pseudonym), one of our most skilful football players, has decided to pursue academic goals and has commenced a sports science degree.
- Ricky (pseudonym) developed some impressive badminton skills, was given a racquet as a Christmas gift, and has used it since at the weekly sports group.
- On the other hand, when I met Amy (pseudonym), her confidence had dipped following hospitalisation and so she had taken a break from regularly playing women's hockey. In her case it was more appropriate to support and encourage her to return to her mainstream hockey club rather than replace it with our service users' group. She recently signed up again to play hockey next season.

Sean articulates the benefits of the group that he has experienced relating to both peer and staff sensitivity on the one hand, and the 'normalising' approach on the other:

[people are] more understanding if someone is unwell . . . [it is a] more forgiving environment. People don't over-react [to slight changes in mental state] whereas work [colleagues] might panic that changes signify a permanent relapse; at the group, people recognise it might just be temporary.

Avoiding stigma

Jane says:

One of the challenges in setting up the group has been the need to minimise costs through negotiating preferential rates, while trying to avoid clients being 'marked out' as different. Since stigma is so damaging for this client group, I have endeavoured to meet key personnel (at facilities that we use on a frequent basis) to ensure that negative misinformation and any concerns are addressed at the outset. From then on we have been able to agree that participants are just booked under the team acronym which is fairly anonymous.

Identifying allies

Jane says:

As a member of a fledgling team with limited staff resources, it was clear that although I might be able to initiate the group, I would need help and support to sustain and nurture it. An important early step was to identify stakeholders and allies. (The stakeholders and allies within the local area whom Jane found helpful are outlined in Figure 10.2.)

User-led or staff-led groups

Jane says:

Although the group was set up by staff members, there is now little evidence of traditional group facilitator roles or hierarchy. The group has evolved a culture of mutual respect and responsibility and many of the group tasks (e.g. deciding on game timings, breaks and teams; requesting and returning equipment) are in fact done by service users.

On one occasion staff commitments meant that the group would have to be either cancelled or user-led. Although not able to commit himself to a regular organisational role, Sean facilitated the group on this occasion and so was able to make some comparisons.

Sean says:

The group ran as usual with the exception of omitting the cool down stretches. However, I prefer that staff are present at the group: I feel reassured that this gives staff the opportunity to monitor people's mental health in a low key way and intervene as necessary if someone was not well or was relapsing.

Jane says:

Demonstrable benefits in terms of user engagement helped with gaining commitment from colleagues to continue the sports group. We were fortunate in that all members of the GRIP

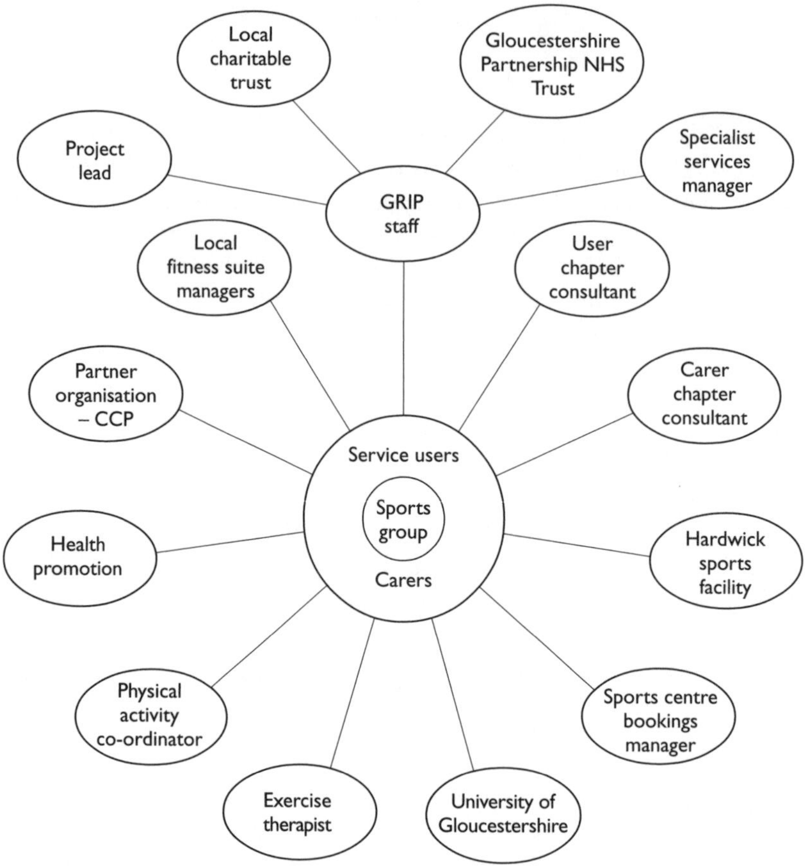

Figure 10.2 Local stakeholders and allies found helpful in developing these sports groups.

team enjoyed some form of sport or exercise – even if they were a bit rusty! Latterly, the secondment of a qualified sports therapist for one session a week has been a considerable asset: co-facilitating the group, and bringing additional benefits of continuity and specialist expertise. Staff members involved in the group participate fully, modelling the acceptability of playing, regardless of sporting prowess! This has undoubtedly contributed to building rapport and the patient–therapist alliance. There have been unexpected benefits for staff, too, with positive effects on fitness and job satisfaction.

Sean liked the opportunity through the group to meet other members of the staff team informally and to hear their viewpoints. He liked the fact that staff were not seen to be coaching or supervising the group.

Sean says:

[staff] don't need to be excellent ... [it] would be more competitive, like us against them, against authority, if staff were very competent and [it would] reverse the whole point ... [He saw] staff participation as a great leveller: ... more social ... like big children ... [you] get to know people [staff] ... not like an official brick wall.

Venue and transport

Jane says:

I was fortunate in being able to negotiate the free use of a nearby university sports facility [Hardwick] which promoted local community participation. Although this facility has been superseded by a more modern complex, it retains links with the university and offers a large multi-purpose sports hall which has been a great youth-friendly base for the group.

A number of our users are not yet sufficiently confident to travel to Hardwick using public transport. As a team we have decided that the benefits of picking up some of the group members outweigh the risks of creating dependence. Car journeys can often provide a surprisingly fertile ground for engagement and interaction. Often young people seem to find extended eye-contact unsettling, and this is true of many of our service users: the car journey allows them to talk while legitimately avoiding eye-contact with their driver/therapist. However, transporting clients is undeniably time-consuming, so we are exploring other options including a local taxi contract or appropriately insured volunteer drivers who could transport clients living in the community who are well engaged and on the road to recovery.

Cost

The group is free of charge to users: because the team was able to negotiate free use, no sports hall hire charges are incurred, and in view of the considerable evidence base, it can be seen as an essential part of our clients' treatment package. On occasions when other facilities have had to be used, monies have been found from within the GRIP budget, or through the financial support of a local charitable trust that supports mental health initiatives.

Aims

The initial aims for the group were modest. Through the medium of youth-friendly recreation and physical activity we aimed to:

- enhance engagement
- promote enjoyment
- improve well-being and
- provide a first step to more challenging group environments (e.g. local community sports group, or more traditional 'talking therapy' type groups).

However, as the sports group has evolved, many more benefits have become apparent: informal health-education, peer group support and social interaction are among the most obvious.

Local research (Davis and Morgan 2004) indicated overwhelmingly that early intervention service users did not want to participate in more traditional psychological group therapy. One might speculate that this could be related to the stigma associated with 'therapy'; denial; relative inexperience and discomfort associated with talking about feelings (especially for young men); or any number of individual prejudices. The recreational groups however, are not only more acceptable, but have afforded staff informal opportunities to offer psycho-education during breaks, where members often congregate around the vending machine to exchange views on their experiences, medication and life circumstances. In this informal, unpressured setting, service users are often more receptive to staff suggestions and advice. Here too, they can reveal as much or as little as they like about their difficulties, and have them validated and 'normalised' by their peer group – a powerful influence.

Jane says:

The familiar faces in a small group setting have been an advantage in developing interaction and social confidence for our service users. I confess to being both surprised, and delighted, at the level of mutual encouragement and support between group members: this has helped to make it a safe place to use humour and gentle teasing. This setting also provides a useful initial venue for some *in vivo* exposure and reality testing for those with paranoia.

Stage of recovery

The sports group offers something for people at various stages of recovery. Relief from boredom, fun and physical 'release' appealed to those attending from the wards and provided useful continuity with the team and service users on discharge. For those further along the road to recovery, the group offers an opportunity to socialise and to build on strengths and interests, with people regaining old sports skills or learning anew. Continued attendance also assists in maintaining well-being. Sean has stated that he wishes to continue attending the sports group for the reasons he has outlined above. He suggests that as people recover they will be able to make their own way to the group as he and some of the others do. However, he also thinks that offering information, support and encouragement to join community groups is important as well.

Jane says:

On reflection, I can see that the presence of people who are recovering well from their difficulties could offer hope, guidance or inspiration to group members who may be struggling with their first episode of psychosis. This would seem to benefit both groups, and has led me to ponder on how best to incorporate early intervention 'graduates' without 'squeezing out' new participants or stifling social inclusion.

Practicalities

Group membership and usage

At the time of writing (June 2005) we are regularly inviting up to 18 people a week (just under half our caseload) to the sports group. Two or three of these people may be inpatients, possibly detained under the MHA (1983) but with section 17 leave. The remainder will be service users living in the community who will have been on our caseload for anything between one week and two years. Currently, an average of one-third of those invited attend any one session, although well over half of our invitees will probably have attended at least once in the past month.

The group meets for two hours every Friday. We have found that the afternoon is the best time, as it allows late risers on our caseload to attend (and as a bonus, red-faced and exhausted staff have only another hour at work before slumping off home to nurse their aches and pains).

To date we have not needed to stipulate group rules, but have dealt with issues relating to clients wishing to bring friends or relatives on a case by case basis. So far we have been lucky in not needing to address issues such as being under the influence of alcohol or street drugs, discrimination or aggression, but this is a task we will be undertaking soon as it would be advantageous to be clear about such boundaries before problems arise.

Participation criteria, feedback and group size

Ours is an 'open' sports group, i.e. membership is fluid. Some people choose not to attend for reasons including work or child-care commitments, not feeling comfortable in groups, or just not enjoying physical exercise. Any client can attend as long as there are no physical health contraindications, and they are able to cope with some group interaction. We have not found the need to have specific referral forms; plans to introduce someone to the group are discussed at the weekly clinical meeting. New introductions are limited to two per sports group in order to ensure that sufficient attention can be given to first timers. Initially, we recommend that they come with their care co-ordinator, to observe or participate for part of a session, which helps overcome initial anxieties.

Weekly verbal feedback is reinforced by a simple form we have developed. This records an individual's attendance at the groups and how they got on; and is integrated with case notes on completion.

Group size would ideally be around eight service users to two facilitators. This number would optimise the group dynamics (and opportunities for five-a-side!) We have, however, held groups with as few as three service users, and would argue that this still represents good use of staff time. Over a period of around 12 months since the sports group's commencement we have established a core of around nine clients who attend. Each session will usually have around four to six keen participants, a considerable proportion of our small team's caseload. The increase in attendance underlines the value that service users place on the sports group: many of them cite the group as a key element in their recovery.

Pre-group planning: weekly checklist

Each group will have its own checklist; ours goes something like this:

- Which staff members are co-facilitating the group?
- Are there any changes to the venue/time?
- Which service users are attending this week?
- What information do we need to pass on about strengths/difficulties of new or existing participants?
- Who needs help with transport?
- Have we got the sports equipment (including plastic cups for drinks)?
- Who will write up the group notes/feedback?
- Are there any messages to pass onto otherwise difficult-to-reach clients?

Fitness to exercise

Pre-sport health checks present us with a dilemma. These young people are generally physically well, and could choose to participate in sports independently without any health checks. However, we have a duty of care to ensure that risks are calculated and minimised. The commonest health problems that we encounter are hay fever, asthma and loss of fitness often associated with heavy smoking or obesity. Currently, any health concerns can be flagged up at our clinical meeting; meanwhile, work is underway on developing a basic pre-exercise screening tool. This is specifically designed to take account of the medication and health issues pertinent to this user group. Over time these measures should provide us with some useful data on physiological changes for any future research or audit, and could be developed to form part of a physical health promotion session.

Choice of activity

The content of these groups has largely been consumer led and reflects the interests or strengths of members, and has naturally favoured team sports over more solitary physical activity such as jogging. After a warm up which might involve throwing Frisbees around the hall, we have evolved a loose programme of badminton, basketball and indoor football. Although a struggle, we have recently been able to implement an 'uncool' cool down and stretch at session end.

Jane says:

Despite our chosen sports being essentially non-contact, a fair degree of good natured tackling can take place. While a referee would be horrified, as a facilitator, I interpret it as a positive sign of growing confidence and comfort with sharing body space, if only for the duration of the match. Another observation is participants' increased physical tolerance over time of the inevitable minor knocks and bumps sustained during play.

Team sports have proven to be very popular, fostering alliances, social interaction and friendly competition which seem to increase motivation and energy levels. Team-work also means that there is no one winner or loser – success or 'coming second' is shared. Thus we have found that with racquet sports, doubles matches are more popular than singles. On the other hand, Sean questioned how important winning or losing at sports was: his personal experience was that it didn't matter as long as he was playing and putting the effort in. We have experimented with a variety of methods whereby service users determine team selection through blindly picking numbers, (which can result in very unevenly matched teams), or an agreement that staff members are chosen last.

Modest goal setting within the group can help with participation and motivation: the person who lacks fitness or confidence and would otherwise sit out, may respond well to an individual challenge (e.g. scoring three baskets) as long as efforts are recognised and reinforced.

Early emphasis on enjoyment and participation rather than skill has enabled some of our 'less sporty' service users (and staff!) to persevere, resulting in an observable increase in fitness and stamina for those who attend regularly.

Alternative Exercise

Alternative activities we have tried include outdoor tennis, archery, indoor climbing wall and swimming. A few clients have also participated in outdoor adventure run by the Prince's Trust or our partner youth agency (CCP), and a couple of people have tried mountain biking. Few service users have utilised the gym (a fairly solitary form of exercise), despite gym staff being very amenable. We plan to develop an outdoors sports programme, but have not yet done so.

Carers

We have recently commenced our first carers' group. Anecdotally, they appreciate the regular activities offered by the GRIP team as helpful in tackling the poor motivation and social isolation often associated with psychosis, even in recovery. However, another bonus is the time for themselves. Lydia has used some of her free time to exercise:

Lydia:

It's very important as a carer to do something for yourself . . . Now I'm trying to be disciplined and organise my work diary and other commitments around my swimming. As a carer the time element is important, so I try to go early in the morning while [my son] is still sleeping. Swimming helps me manage my own situation. It gives me inner strength to keep coping and I find it easier to get going . . . Time out from the home situation is really important. It regenerates you, like a coastal walk. I like walking too but that takes longer so can be difficult.

One of the most difficult things for any would-be exerciser is getting around to it. Lydia offers this tip: 'I've got into the habit of getting my kit ready the night before: that really helps, I can put my costume on first thing without having to think about it then.'

Evaluation of the Groups

We have sought the views of people who use the sports groups, using a combination of anonymised questionnaire, a ranking exercise and informal group and individual discussions with up to eight of the dozen or so service users who have regularly attended the sports groups.

Overall, for those who attend, the sports groups were valued as one of the most helpful interventions that the team offered, echoing the findings of Martinsen and Medhus (1989). Written feedback from participants indicated satisfaction with the groups, with requests to increase sports groups. While this is clearly not evidence for the effectiveness of any intervention over another, it does demonstrate the acceptability of these groups to clients.

Football and basketball were initially the most popular of the sports activities, although as participants have gained racquet skills, many now enjoy badminton doubles. Although Lydia, the co-author who is a carer, found swimming helpful, it was least enjoyed by the majority of our young male service users. The evidence base might suggest that this is because leisurely swimming is a less focused, less competitive and a lower intensity exercise, and lacks the social structure and shared purpose temporarily provided by team games, thus providing fewer mental health gains.

What helps and why: group participants' views

While indepth analysis of why service users value the groups has not been attempted, we did learn that 'getting out of the house and doing something' was considered really important by group members. Some valued it as a return to normality '[to] get back to the things I used to do'. Others appreciated the socialising element: meeting with people they wouldn't usually see and discovering that they got on well with other group members. Improved motivation, fitness and stamina were also rated by group members to be helpful, as was getting into a routine.

Some see the distraction/focusing nature of sports as beneficial.

Sean says:

It gets you out of the routine of having to think [about it] over and over again, [it] breaks the pattern of panic.

Jane says:

Mike told me that the sports group eliminated his disturbing intrusive thoughts for the duration of the activity, and that he felt better after it; although he acknowledged difficulty in overcoming low motivation and negative thoughts to attend. Oliver told me that sports helped reduce the bad thoughts, and focusing on something like a team game gave a break from the voices, and was (he thought) better than therapy or medication.

It is encouraging to note that our clients say overall that our group programme is 'fun', and that it helps by 'making me feel better about myself'.

Collaboration with Organisations: Partnership Working

Without a generous financial contribution from a charitable organisation towards our set-up costs and a booster grant for our sports and social groups, our team would not have been in business so early, nor been able to sustain the weekly events for service users. No wonder then that we have a positive attitude to working with other agencies!

From the outset, the GRIP team has had an ethos of partnership working. We are based in a local non-statutory youth organisation which has a positive 'can-do' attitude and the tag line of 'helping young people realise their potential'. Thus we are closely allied with an organisation, with an optimistic outlook that matches our recovery focused service. Building on the expertise and local knowledge of CCP, we have been able to make links with other youth and community organisations that promote outdoor education. Another successful example of sports partnership working is our link with the sports science department at the University of Gloucestershire.

While we are grateful to the organisations we are working with, partnership implies that we would offer something in return. Training on mental health in general, and psychosis in particular, is something that we have been able to offer to youth workers such as CCP and Connexions, fitness instructors and college staff. This training has been well received and also helps in dispelling stigma and improving understanding.

From within our NHS Partnership Trust, exercise therapists and health promotion staff have been particularly helpful in offering advice and support.

Reflections on Co-authorship

Jane says:

As a nurse rather than an academic I am still surprised that I find myself contributing to this book. More astonishing perhaps is the shift in my approach. Like many mental health professionals I used to think that sports groups were recreational at best, too simple to be therapeutic, and peripheral to my work. How wrong I was!

This is a co-authored chapter, but the reality is that I wrote much of it. Sean and Lydia both reflected on their experiences, but they preferred to use interviews and consultation as the way to add their comments. I agree it would have been even better for them to have more of a voice, but they had other priorities. In fact, I found it both liberating and a little intimidating to share authorship with Sean and Lydia. The concerns I had that it might have been too challenging for them have been disproven and serve as a caution not to underestimate our 'customers'. However (for me at least), writing is a lengthy process, and I think that we should recognise that our service users have other lives as well. I have been appreciative of my co-authors' patience, and Sean's gentle prompts that I should stop procrastinating and get on with it!

Lydia commented that the process of consulting on and reading through the chapter gave her an opportunity for reflection. It has reinforced her commitment to and belief in exercise, and she has recently added walking to her physical activity strategy.

Sean had not found contributing problematic and said that in fact he had gained confidence through the realisation that he could concentrate long enough to read through Jane's overlong (!) initial drafts. He thought it was good to be involved, and found it useful to read a carer's perspective on psychosis.

Jane says:

If we were to work jointly on another project, one of the things Sean and I agreed we would do differently would be to recruit a second service user. The two of them would then be able to discuss ideas and it would make any dissent with the other authors easier to verbalise.

Conclusion

This chapter has primarily related a clinician's experience of starting a sports group, the comments of service users recovering from first-episode psychosis, and of a carer who has used exercise as a coping strategy. As demonstrated by the literature review, there is little research on exercise and schizophrenia, and we found no studies specifically looking at first-episode psychosis. Although it could be argued that one should not commence an intervention without favourable randomised controlled trials and meta-reviews, there is, however, plenty of evidence illustrating positive effects of exercise in treating the depression, anxiety and low self-esteem that often accompanies psychosis. This alone is reason enough to promote this activity. Furthermore, the positive evaluation of service users and the evident benefits to them are the most powerful indicators that some element of the group is effective.

Jane says:

There were lots of things that I think we did right, although there are a number of things that I would do differently if starting again:

1 An elementary mapping exercise to determine what sports resources and contacts were available both within the Trust and in the local community. I have now met many good allies, but it would have been good to have the advice from the start.
2 I would find the time to secure long-term funding for the groups, making the case for a share of the NHS budget or researching available grants.
3 I would explore transport options early on. Although the groups clearly appeal to service users, getting them to the venue can be problematic.

Our 10 top tips for starting a mental health sports group are shown in Table 10.1.

It is hoped that in the future more will be known about the mechanisms and optimal dose–response relationship of exercise, and its type, required to speed the recovery of people with psychosis. Meanwhile, I would urge practitioners and service users to be bold in publicising their experiences of developing and evaluating sports initiatives, no matter

Table 10.1 Ten top tips for starting a mental health sports group

1. Be prepared to start small with two or three interested service users.
2. Consider demographics – sports resources will vary, outdoor adventure may be more feasible in rural locations.
3. Identify allies among your colleagues and in the local community.
4. A session from a sports therapist and/or strong links with an academic institution will help maintain credibility and momentum.
5. Use a persuasive evidence base to justify using a portion of meagre NHS budget for sports.
6. Service user testimonials can be very powerful when applying for grant monies from charitable organisations.
7. Talk to local sports facilities – many are very willing to help.
8. Offer something in return to your partner sports organisations: information and training sessions can be helpful in combating discrimination.
9. Evaluate the sports group regularly in conjunction with service users to keep it relevant.
10. Don't forget health and safety: consider ground rules, insurance, qualifications, risks and benefits.

how unscientific, since every contribution adds to this body of knowledge through gathering evidence.

We don't yet know exactly how physical activity works: what we do know is that it is simple, empowering, acceptable, inexpensive, side-effect free and effective for people recovering from mental health problems. If you haven't tried it already, do!

Acknowledgements

Jane says:

I would like to thank the past and present participants of the sports groups who have provided invaluable feedback on the service, demonstrating that some of the interventions least researched are in fact the most valued by service users, thus giving me something to write about. I would also like to thank allies in local sports and exercise facilities for their generous assistance, the local charitable trust who enabled us to buy sports equipment, and colleagues who made helpful suggestions on early drafts of this chapter.

References

Bates P. (2005) *Accidents at the Inclusion Traffic Lights*. National Development Team. Available online: www.ndt.org.uk/ETS/ETILT.htm (accessed 16 October 2005).

Biddle, S., Fox, K. and Boutcher, S. (eds.) (2000) *Physical Activity and Psychological Wellbeing*. London: Routledge.

Brown, S., Inskip, H. and Barraclough, B. (2000) Causes of excess mortality of schizophrenia. *British Journal of Psychiatry*, 177, 212–17.

Chamove, A. (1986) Positive short-term effects of activity on behaviour in chronic schizophrenic patients. *British Journal of Clinical Psychology*, 25, 125–33. Cited in Faulkner, G. and Sparkes, A. (1999) Exercise as a therapy for schizophrenia: an ethnographic study. *Journal of Sport and Exercise Psychology*, 21, 52–69.

Crone, D., Heaney, L., Herbert, R., Wilson, J., Johnston, L. and Macpherson, R. (2005) A comparison of lifestyle behaviour and health perceptions of people with severe mental illness and the general population. *Journal of Mental Health Promotion*, 3, 19–25.

Daley, A. (2002) Exercise therapy and mental health in clinical populations: is exercise therapy a worthwhile intervention? *Advances in Psychiatric Treatment*, 8, 262–70.

Davis, E. and Morgan, J. (2004) *Mental Health Service Response to First-episode Psychosis in Gloucestershire*. Gloucester: Gloucestershire Partnership NHS Trust. Available online: www.gripinitiative.org.uk (accessed 16 October 2005).

DCMS (2001) *Building on PAT 10: Progress Report on Social Inclusion*. London: Department for Culture, Media and Sport. Available online: www.culture.gov.uk/PDF/social_inclusion.pdf accessed 16 October 2005).

Department of Health (2004) *At Least Five a Week: Evidence on the Impact of Physical Awareness and Its Relationship to Health. Chief Medical Officer's Report*. London: Department of Health.

EPPIC [Early Psychosis Prevention and Intervention Centre] (2000). *Working With Groups in Early Psychosis*, no. 3 in a series of Early Psychosis Manuals. Victoria Australia: Mental Health Branch, Human Services.

Faulkner, G. and Biddle, S. (2001) Exercise and mental health: it's not just psychology! *Journal of Sport Sciences*, 19, 433–44.

Faulkner, G. and Sparkes, A. (1999) Exercise as a therapy for schizophrenia: an ethnographic study. *Journal of Sport and Exercise Psychology*, 21, 52–69.

Fox, K. (2000) The effects of exercise on self-perceptions and self-esteem. In Biddle, S. Fox, K. and Boutcher, S. (eds.) *Physical Activity and Psychological Wellbeing*. London: Routledge, pp. 88–117.

Fraser Health Authority (2005) *Early Psychosis Intervention Program*. Downloads. British Columbia Canada: Fraser Health Authority. Available online: www.psychosissucks.ca/epi/pdf/@lifestyles.pdf (accessed 16 October 2005).

Grant, T. (ed.) (2000) *Physical Activity and Mental Health: National Consensus Statement and Guidelines for Practice*. London Health Education Authority.

Harris, E. and Barraclough, B. (1998) Excess mortality of mental disorder. *British Journal of Psychiatry*, 173, 11–53.

Jackson, H., Hulbert, C. and Henry, L. (2000) The treatment of secondary morbidity in first episode psychosis. In Birchwood, M., Fowler, D. and Jackson, C. (eds.) *Early Intervention in Psychosis: A Guide to Concepts, Evidence and Interventions*. Chichester: Wiley, pp. 213–35.

Lawlor, D. and Hopker, S. (2001) The effectiveness of exercise as an intervention in the management of depression: systematic review and meta-regression analysis of randomised controlled trials. *British Medical Journal*, 322, 763–7.

Martinsen, E. and Medhus, A. (1989) Adherence to exercise and patient's evaluations of physical exercise in a comprehensive treatment programme for depression. *Nordic Journal of Psychiatry*, 43, 411–15. Cited in Daley, A. (2002) Exercise therapy and mental health in clinical populations: is exercise therapy a worthwhile intervention? *Advances in Psychiatric Treatment*, 8, 262–70.

Mind (2004) *Mind Guide to Physical Activity* (booklet). Available online: www.mind.org.uk/information/booklets/mind+guide+to/mindguidetophysicalactivity (accessed 16 October 2005).

Mukherjee, S., Decina, P., Bocola, V., Saracini, F and Scappicchio, P. (1996) Diabetes Mellitus in schizophrenic patients. *Comprehensive Psychiatry*, 37, 68–73.

Mutrie N. (2000) The relationship between physical activity and clinically defined depression. In Biddle, S., Fox, K. and Boutcher, S. (eds.) *Physical Activity and Psychological Wellbeing*. London: Routledge, pp. 46–62.

NIMHE [National Institute for Mental Health] and Mentality (2004) *Healthy Body, Healthy Mind:*

Promoting Healthy Living for People Who Experience Mental Health Problems. London: NIMHE. Resources available online: www.shift.org.uk/index.cfm?fuseaction=main.viewSection&intSectionID=27 (accessed 16 October 2005).

ODPM (2004) *Mental Health and Social Inclusion – Social Exclusion Unit Report.* London: ODPM Publications.

Pelham, T. and Campagna, P. (1991) Benefits of exercise in psychiatric rehabilitation of persons with schizophrenia. *Canadian Journal of Rehabilitation*, 4, 159–68. Cited in Faulkner, G. and Sparkes, A. (1999) Exercise as a therapy for schizophrenia: an ethnographic study. *Journal of Sport and Exercise Psychology*, 21, 52–69.

Phelan, M., Stradins, L. and Morrison, S. (2001) Physical health of people with severe mental illness. *British Medical Journal*, 322, 443–4.

Plante, T. (1993) Aerobic exercise in prevention and treatment of psychopathology. In P. Seraganian (ed.) *Exercise Psychology* New York: Wiley, pp. 358–79. Cited in Faulkner, G. and Sparkes, A. (1999) Exercise as a therapy for schizophrenia: an ethnographic study. *Journal of Sport and Exercise Psychology*, 21, 52–69.

Rankin, J. (2005) *Mental Health and Social Inclusion: Mental Health in the Mainstream. Working Paper* 2. London: Institute for Public Policy Research.

Rethink (2002) *Doesn't It Make You Sick?* London: Rethink. Available online: www.rethink.org/research/pdfs/Doesn%27t-it-make-you-sick.pdf (accessed 16 Ocotober 2005).

Taylor, A. (2000) Physical activity, anxiety, and stress: a review. In Biddle, S., Fox, K. and Boutcher, S. (eds.) *Physical Activity and Psychological Wellbeing.* London: Routledge, pp. 10–45.

Zubin, J. and Spring, B. (1977) Vulnerability: a new view of schizophrenia. *Journal of Abnormal Psychiatry*, 86, 103–26.

Chapter 11

Employment, Mental Health and PSI

Occupation is Everyone's Job

Sarah-joy Boldison, Rosie Davies, Hilary Hawkes, Christiane Pacé and Ruth Sayers

Key Points

- There is a need for health and social care services to engage fully with people's lives where work is central: a basic human need.
- There are very strong economic and humanitarian reasons for wanting to assist people with a mental disorder to access work and meaningful occupation.
- During developing crises, most services focus on immediate medical and intra-psychic needs, to the exclusion of wider networks and longer-term employment and other needs.
- Instead what is needed is early intervention across primary and secondary care, including the wider systems of support that make up people's support networks, and incorporating effective care co-ordination, to provide skilled assessment of needs and holistic care-planning that makes best use of community and individual networks and resources.
- Access to job retention and vocational schemes, and skilled occupational therapy advice, provided in collaboration with primary care, is key.
- Many issues relating to occupation remain to be tackled, including stigma and discrimination, the benefits system, widening the responsibility for issuing sick notes, and the potential for using direct payments.
- Clear guidelines for best professional practice are needed, as is effective leadership, multi-disciplinary team-working and dedicated resources.
- The complex issues relating to occupation are being increasingly acknowledged, and a clearer agenda for action has emerged.

Introduction

'The absence of occupation is not a rest;
a mind quite vacant is a mind distressed.'
Will Cowper, poet, detained in an asylum in the eighteenth century (http://en.wikiquote.org/wiki/William_Cowper (accessed 22 October 2005))

Boredom and monotony are not good for our health. Many people with severe mental health problems may never have established any secure foothold in work or may have lost work. Such losses damage people's confidence and self-esteem, and often devastate future plans and expectations. However, as the Office for the Deputy Prime Minister's *Mental Health and Social Exclusion* report shows, 'People who experience periods of mental disorder want to work or to be occupied with things they enjoy, and have the same broad aims and aspirations as everyone else. The longer people do not work, the harder the transition into paid employment becomes' (ODPM 2004a, p. 52).

Employment and occupational issues are fundamental to everyone being included in our communities – to social inclusion. 'People are saying they want a life and not a Care Plan' (Repper and Perkins 2003, p. 145): these views reflect a need for health and social care services to engage fully with people's lives.

The Evidence

The latest statistical evidence from the Social Exclusion Unit (SEU) is that people with mental health disability:

- exhibit the lowest employment rate of any other disability group – 21 per cent
- are twice as likely to lose their job
- experience a significantly higher rate of financial problems and debt
- are more at risk of homelessness and rental problems
- are three times more likely to be divorced.

The economic costs are £77.4 billion, of which more than half is due to shortened and lowered quality of life, the rest being accounted for by loss of employment and state benefits. This figure includes £540 million in prescription costs, plus £5.3 billion, the staggering cost of suicide from mental health problems.

The *Labour Force Survey* (Office for National Statistics 2003) shows that 628,000 adults of working age in Britain regard mental disorder as their main disability. There are therefore obvious strong economic and humanitarian reasons for wanting these figures to improve dramatically.

We, as the authors of this chapter, are a mixed group of health professionals and service user researchers (one of whom also works in the voluntary sector providing intensive home support). We were invited to collaborate by using our various experiences to create a joint chapter. But we became aware that the word 'collaboration' has a dual meaning – 'to work with another or others on a joint project' *and* 'to work traitorously with the enemy' (*Collins*

English Dictionary 1992). We were working together, but were we enemies? This often seems to be the anticipated set-up, or the defensive position to which both service user and professional groups retreat when things go wrong.

We know from our own experience that getting occupation on the agenda is difficult, and many people do not receive services which address occupational issues. Improving this situation requires us to join forces to genuinely learn and develop, seeking out what is effective and discarding practices which are not. This chapter illustrates the implications of this omission and presents ways to address the problems.

In this chapter we are particularly drawing on material presented in two reports in which we were involved. They are significant because they illustrate both personal experience and what a service can deliver, as well as illuminating the challenges. The two reports are:

- *Life's Labours Lost*, which focuses on the impact of loss of occupation. People who experienced this loss undertook this research, which was part of the Strategies for Living programme run by the Mental Health Foundation (Bodman et al. 2003).
- *Getting Back Before Christmas* (Thomas, Secker and Grove 2003), which consisted of an extensive literature search and a review of the job retention pilot that took place in Bristol. This was jointly funded by the Department of Health and Department of Work and Pensions. This report resulted in the birth of the first public-private partnership which focuses on building networks not buildings, and pools resources across a wide range of organisations (Work Life Partnerships, www.wlp.uk.com). This organisation continues to support the growth of the national job retention network. For more information about Work Life Partnerships and the job retention network look on the website above.

All the authors were involved with one or other of these projects, so our shared learning and indeed some shared frustrations have driven our work and our current thinking.

Our hope and desire for improving practice and provision of occupational services is reflected in the action plan (chapter 9, pp. 94–113) of the *Mental Health and Social Exclusion* report mentioned earlier (ODPM 2004a). This report assesses the impact of lack of employment/meaningful occupation linked with mental health problems. It outlines an action plan to drive change that has government commitment across a wide range of departments. It fills us with hope that renewed attention will be given to the value of occupation; and that co-operative action will be taken to implement, and fund, its recommendations. We hope the imaginative use of modern technology will enhance and hasten the implementation of its vision.

The Case Study – Kim's Stories

From the two project reports mentioned above (Bodman et al. 2003; Thomas, Secker and Grove 2003) we have created a composite case study that illustrates how services can influence the relationship between mental health problems and employment during a person's journey through mental disorder. The boxes in Figure 11.1 identify key points at various stages.

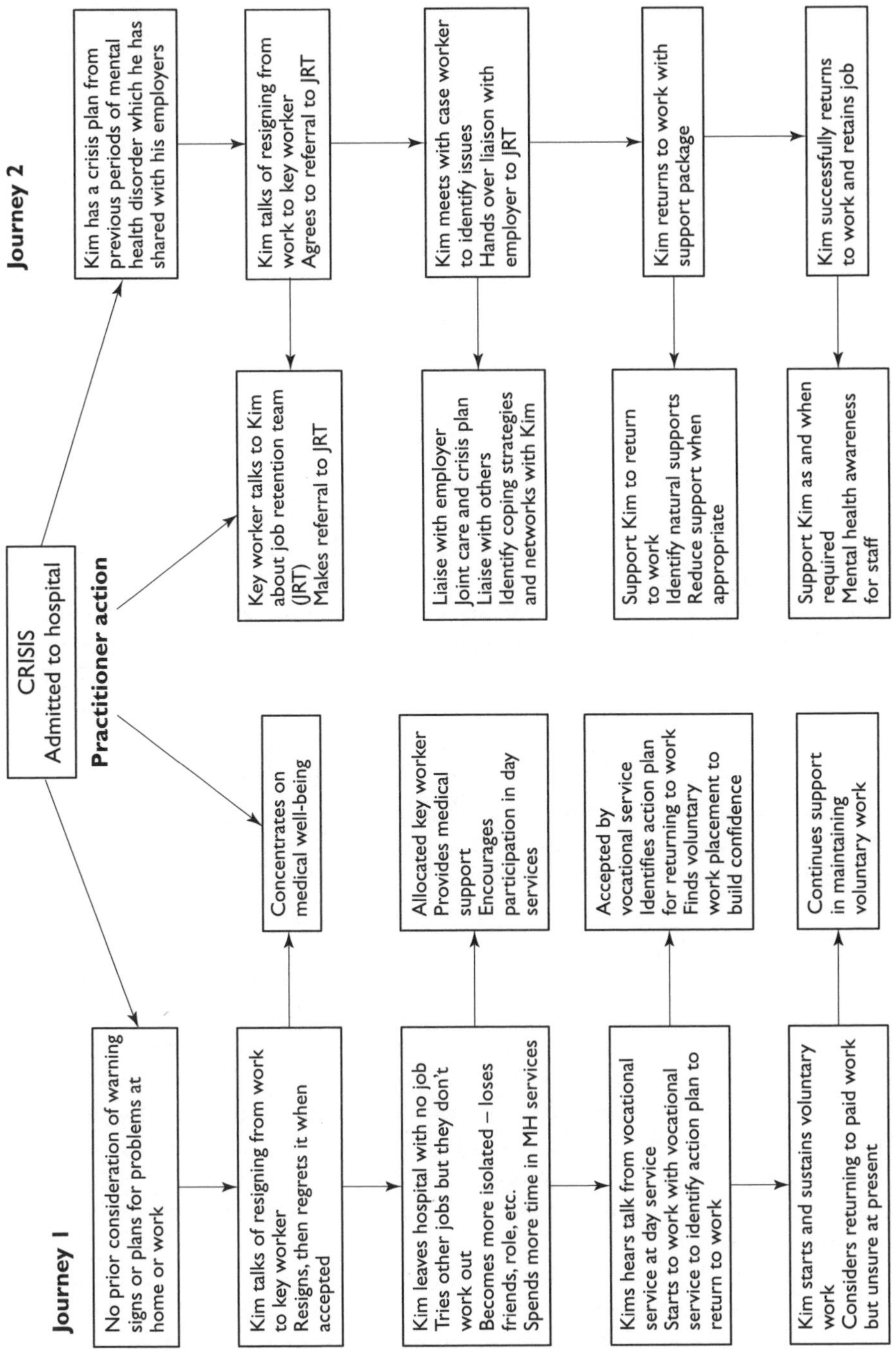

Figure 11.1 Kim's two journeys

Kim is a primary school teacher with a diagnosis of bipolar[1] disorder. He has had three episodes of this disorder (with corresponding sick leave) over the last 18 months. Kim is 35 and has a partner.

The following stories show two different paths that Kim could take and identify key aspects of each journey. The two journeys are shown diagrammatically in Figure 11.1.

Story 1

The previous episodes of the disorder have resulted in Kim feeling that his colleagues are now keeping their distance and expecting further difficulties. Kim feels alone, ashamed and stigmatised, and continues to feel very stressed and pressurised at work. Kim is highly anxious, not sleeping, and is working very long hours. He is unable to discuss these problems with anyone. Kim's relationship is also suffering.

Kim has not disclosed his diagnosis at work, fearing stigma and discrimination and generally lacks support. The implications of Kim's disorder have not been considered and no plans are in place for any difficulties. Kim is not clear about the warning signs for the disorder and does not seek help. Kim does not have a care plan, and there is no focus on the impact of his problems on his occupation.

Kim's problems escalate when the head teacher criticises his work with two children in the class who regularly behave badly. She wants him to stop referring the children to her and she wants Kim to deal with them more effectively in class. Over the next few days Kim works frantically and veers from anger to distress. The pupils' behaviour in his classroom deteriorates. Kim shouts at a colleague who tries to intervene and is asked to go home. That evening he has a major row with his partner who is tired of disruptions and problems, and of Kim's instability, and who threatens to leave if Kim cannot cope better.

Kim continues to deteriorate, becoming more manic. Kim refuses to go to the GP or psychiatrist, and his partner leaves to stay with a friend. The police detain Kim after he threatens a member of staff in the local supermarket. As a result Kim is sectioned and detained in an acute mental health ward. After a few days in hospital, Kim talks to a member of staff in the ward about the problems at work and his wish to leave the job. The staff member suggests he focuses on getting better. However, the next day Kim writes a letter of resignation while on the ward. When Kim returns home, he finds a letter accepting the resignation.

Doctors and nursing staff focus on medical well-being, and are not aware that Kim resigns while on the ward. Acute staff do not ask about employment issues on admission, and fail to discourage Kim from making decisions while he is unwell. There are no named staff on the unit with responsibility to link with vocational services or be aware of the available resources. There is no awareness of the job retention service and nothing is done to liaise with the school about Kim's situation.

Kim's manic episode is followed by several months of deep depression. Kim regrets resigning from work, and feels resentful of the swift acceptance. Kim feels the school just wanted him out. Kim also feels ashamed and does not want to meet ex-colleagues or parents. Kim splits up with his partner and does not go out much. Kim cannot face applying for benefits and runs up debts on credit cards. Eventually Kim registers to do supply teaching, but feels panicky at the first school when the children behave badly. Kim does not go back on the second day. Kim makes another attempt a few weeks later, but this is not a success. Although Kim gets less depressed, he has no confidence and feels his life is unravelling. The GP prescribes anti-depressants and continues to sign Kim off sick.

There is little contact with mental health services on discharge from hospital and a delay in being allocated a community psychiatric nurse. The psychiatrist focuses on medical symptoms and treatment, the GP provides sick notes. Once allocated, the CPN helps with application for benefits and encourages Kim to participate in day services. Lack of support and practical plans, on top of isolation, exacerbate Kim's problems. Kim has the motivation to try to work, but cannot sustain it. Each failure reinforces problems and further decreases Kim's confidence.

Despite depression Kim applies for a job running an after-school club part-time. However, this job is in a local school. Kim suspects that the teachers will know his history and worries about their attitudes. This makes him feel anxious and stressed at work. In the third week a child has an accident on a climbing frame; the parents are angry. Kim feels he cannot cope and resigns after six weeks.

Kim becomes more isolated and loses friends. He feels inadequate, lost and a failure, without any identity, hope or sense of purpose. Kim increasingly sees himself only as a mental health service user, and staff attitudes reinforce his own low expectations. Kim is taking mood stabilisers, but still feels depressed and puts on a lot of weight. He has little energy, feels unattractive and unfit.

Kim now identifies himself as a service user and is unable to work. Kim is increasingly socially excluded. Day services fill up time, but do not help Kim to build his support or interests in the community. Kim does not know about a local self-help group, or the national organisation for people with bipolar disorder.

A year later Kim hears a talk at the day centre about a local vocational service; he had no idea such a service existed. Kim eventually makes contact. The vocational service agrees to work with Kim, and starts to develop an action plan for return to work. This includes finding a voluntary work placement to build confidence. The first does not work out, but at the second Kim's role is to help children with reading problems and he starts to enjoy this. Nonetheless, Kim feels it is very unlikely that he will ever be able to cope with doing paid work again.

The vocational service starts to help Kim to rebuild some kind of working life. However, this is a long, slow process. Kim begins with a very low level of confidence and self-esteem, and has to find a way to believe that his life could change for the better. Rebuilding a meaningful life will take Kim a long time and he will need a lot of support to sustain his journey.

Story 2

Story 1 was not inevitable. This alternative story starts at the same point that Story 1 did.

Following Kim's last episode of bipolar disorder he was referred by his GP to a self-management programme,[2] which included developing a personal crisis plan. Part of that plan involved Kim confiding in some trusted colleagues at school, including the head of year. Signs of mania are therefore recognised by his colleagues, and this helps them to take appropriate action.

Kim has been increasingly disorganised at work, has become very over-talkative and enthusiastic but is not producing the work to his normal high standard. As well as this, there have been three incidents where Kim has made inappropriate sexual innuendoes to colleagues and parents. The head of year recognises these as early warning signs of a bipolar episode and requests that Kim sees his GP.

Access to a self-management programme enabled Kim to create a crisis plan. He shared the plan with some colleagues who could then identify early warning signs of the disorder and encourage him to see his GP. Kim therefore sees his GP early, and prompt action reduces the severity of the episode.

The GP refers Kim to the specialist mental health service. It is agreed through the crisis plan that, in order to get Kim's sleep pattern settled, he will have a very brief inpatient stay and will then be supported at home by the Crisis and Home Treatment team. This includes a course of medication to reduce the mania. As the surgery has links to the local job retention team (JRT) network Kim is immediately referred to the case worker. The surgery also lets the ward staff and the Crisis and Home Treatment team know that this has been done.

The primary care occupational therapist based at the surgery is linked to a vocational network which brings together specialist information. In this case Kim is referred to a job retention case worker. This means Kim gets access to appropriate employment services immediately. There is co-operative working and information sharing between health professionals in different services. There is good liaison with crisis and acute services.

The case worker finds Kim extremely concerned about being away from work, the effect on his students and what they and other colleagues will be told. Kim is considering resigning as he feels his colleagues see him as inadequate and irresponsible, and he is unsure of his own stability.

Kim's wish to resign is discussed with the case worker and deferred. The case worker seeks Kim's written permission to liaise with the school, the Teachers Support Network[3] and the GP, thereby relieving Kim of responsibility while he is unwell. This agreement will be reviewed after four weeks.

After eight days in hospital Kim's progress is good and he is more settled and sleeping well. The case worker is encouraging and holds the hope that Kim will return to his job despite his current loss of confidence. The case worker begins to work with Kim on naming what the challenges were at work.

Immediate occupational issues are addressed. Kim's wish to resign is discussed with the case worker and deferred. Kim is encouraged and support systems are strengthened. The case worker takes on liaison with employers. The case worker takes responsibility from Kim in the short term and evolves a shared plan of action.

The case worker meets Kim and the Crisis and Home Treatment team before discharge from hospital to negotiate a holistic care plan which includes a return to work strategy. The care plan also agrees that Kim will go swimming with his best friend three times each week to help with the excess energy and resettle his sleep pattern. Kim also uses his support network to spread the load so that he is not so reliant on his partner. Kim's partner has been included in most of these negotiations, only being omitted by agreement or because of time restraints, and stress in the relationship is discussed and addressed.

In addition he will access the Teachers Support Network's counselling service to explore his feelings about his colleagues and his own abilities. Kim had already identified his most supportive colleague and agrees to invite him to a joint meeting with the case worker. It is agreed that the care plan will be reviewed in four weeks time.

The care plan is holistic, includes his relationships, and incorporates a return to work strategy which identifies both support networks and coping strategies.

Kim's progress continues and at the review his medication is reduced. It is planned that Kim will go back to work after half term: this allows him another three weeks to enable further recovery.

Following the review, the case worker and Kim meet with the head of year and together they implement the plan for his return to work. This includes Kim returning part-time initially and having regular meetings with his supportive colleague and the case worker. The head of year agrees this plan and arranges a further meeting to discuss progress.

The transition back to work is planned. Colleagues are informed and involved in the process.

The job retention team also run an 'awareness of mental health' training for the school governors who have become aware of their lack of knowledge and skills to manage mental health well. This results in a new policy for managing mental health issues in the school. Kim is delighted that this is happening.

Feeling supported and pleased that he has learned to take positive action if the mania returns, Kim now has more tools in his survival kit. Kim feels confident in returning to work after his eight-week absence. He is reassured that the case worker offers ongoing support (by telephone or ad hoc meetings) for the next six months if needed.

Kim's episode of disorder has increased his awareness of how to cope with stress at work. His confidence, self-esteem and ability to cope have been improved. Ongoing support is available.

Awareness has been raised among colleagues and governors. This results in an improvement in the school's ability to manage mental health issues in the workplace. There is also a new policy in place to support Kim and others in his position.

The National and Organisational Context

The national context for occupational issues has been shaped by many influences, including the disability rights movement and the equalities agenda. The report *Saving Lives – Our Healthier Nation* (Department of Health 1999a) identified social exclusion as a key issue to tackle in improving health. This prepared the ground for the national service frameworks (e.g. Department of Health 1999b) and the modernisation agenda. In turn these laid the foundation for the *Mental Health and Social Exclusion* report, which presents a vision 'of a future where people with mental health problems have the same opportunities to work and participate in their communities as any other citizen' (ODPM 2004a, p. 100). These are welcome words.

The *Mental Health and Social Exclusion* report presents a comprehensive and evidence-based appraisal of the causes of social exclusion and progress to date. It sets out a 27-point action plan that aims 'to bring together the work of government departments and other organisations in a concerted effort to challenge attitudes, enable people to fulfil their aspirations, and significantly improve opportunities and outcomes for this excluded group' (ODPM 2004a, p. 6).

Addressing these issues implies a broader focus of service provision, with more emphasis on the whole person and the wider impact of mental health problems alongside the current emphasis, which tends to be on mental health crises and symptoms. The *Social Exclusion Unit Report* explores and develops these points.

The lack of coherent planning and leadership has also been identified as a problem; this has resulted in fragmented services pulling in different directions with significant gaps. Importantly therefore, leadership and implementation roles have been clarified in this Social Exclusion Unit report. There is a cross-governmental team, based within the National Institute for Mental Health in England (NIMHE), which holds national responsibility for transforming the action plan into practice. The regional offices of NIMHE, the strategic health authorities and the regional development agencies, hold regional responsibility. Locally, the Primary Care Trusts and the local authorities hold joint responsibility to lead implementation.

Another significant background document is the vocational rehabilitation framework (Department for Work and Pensions 2004). This attempts to address the gaps in practice, guidelines and standards. The framework provides governmental commitment to draw together a wide range of stakeholders and pool expertise in this field. They will produce nationally agreed guidelines and tools for practice. This document is important because it recognises that many government departments are involved in taking the action plan forward (for example the Department of Health, the Department for Work and Pensions, the Department for Education and Skills, as well as the non-statutory sector). The need to work together to provide an effective and equitable service is recognised.

These aspirations link to the Affiliates Network[4] that is being established as part of the *Action on Mental Health* guide (ODPM 2004b). There is wide-ranging evidence on the connection between participation and mental well-being. This is well presented in the New Economics Foundation's manifesto for well-being (2004). The Foundation is a new member of the Social Exclusion Unit's Affiliates Network.

All of the reports cited describe strategies to tackle occupational issues, but the strategies need to include a number of different players (see Figure 11.2). Together they create an agenda for change. It is clear that partnership working and the creation of a 'whole system' approach has become a key challenge given the number of organisations involved and the need to integrate different agendas. Health care organisations, local government departments, employers, voluntary organisations and user and carer organisations all need to be included, as well as government departments. However, currently they all have different aims and ways of working. The emerging agenda implies crossing boundaries between previously separate services.

Effective ways of working together need to be forged. Information must be shared so that good practice in different fields is understood as widely as possible. These organisational challenges go hand-in-hand with the need for further development of multi-disciplinary approaches between different practitioners in health and social care. For example, workers in housing organisations, employment and benefits agencies, carers and users all contribute

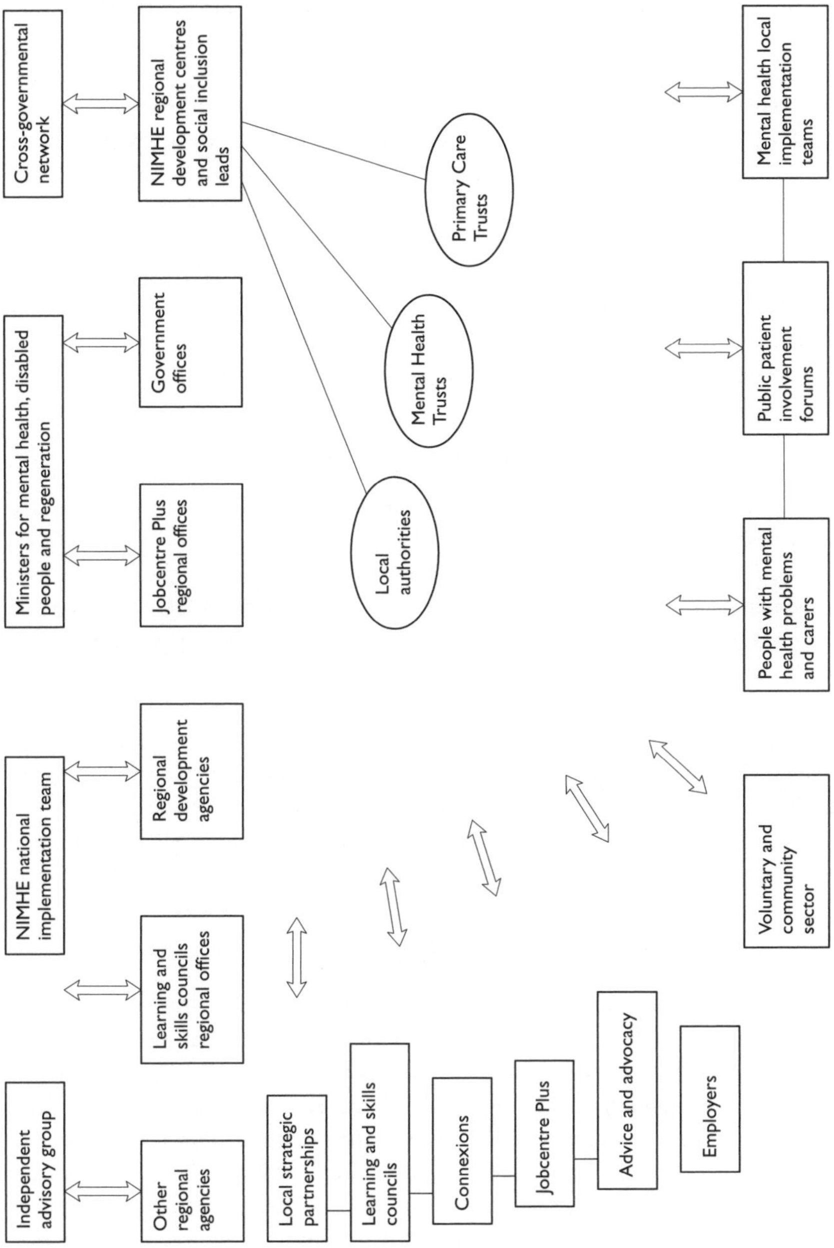

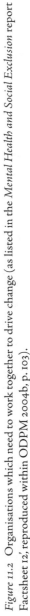

Figure 11.2 Organisations which need to work together to drive change (as listed in the *Mental Health and Social Exclusion* report 'Factsheet 12', reproduced within ODPM 2004b, p. 103).

to the whole picture. Shared objectives and language need to be developed to facilitate such changes.

However, thinking creatively about new ways of offering more integrated and flexible services which emphasise vocational aspirations can trigger major concerns about change, job losses and redeployment. Fear of cuts and loss of services by both service providers and users can also stifle organisational and service development. Efforts to establish new and desirable services can run into the sand. At all levels, organisations need to consider these challenges and how best to support and sustain change.

In the past, serious mental health problems have too often resulted in very significant social exclusion. If people are to regain some hope and start to build meaningful lives within their communities, two other major issues must be tackled. Stigma and discrimination, and the benefits system, are still significant barriers to better access to work.

Stigma and discrimination

Stigma and discrimination need to be viewed from three perspectives. The first is discrimination in society as a whole, including employers. Fewer than four in 10 employers say that they would consider employing someone with a history of mental health problems (Factsheet 1 on stigma and discrimination in *Action on Mental Health: A Guide to Promoting Social Exclusion* (ODPM 2004b)). Urgent action is needed. This guide suggests many different ways things could be improved. Second, health and care professionals tend to have low expectations relating to work. These attitudes are now being challenged by the 'recovery' approach. Third, people with mental health problems have often lost confidence and hope, and fear change. Many people have given up and tried to reconcile themselves to a marginal existence with low expectations. However, as well as the guide referenced above, NIMHE has written a five-year plan to tackle stigma and discrimination, called SHIFT (www.shift.org.uk). Implementation of this plan is essential to improving vocational opportunities.

The benefits system

There have been some improvements in benefits provision – for example, the provision of payments to help people back into work, and the linking rules which maintain entitlement to benefit should people be unable to sustain paid work. But in general the benefits system is still inflexible, and particularly discourages people with severe mental health problems who fear recurring episodes of disorder. The system tends to see people as either well or ill. It needs to acknowledge that many people experience frequent changes in their mental health; some people may only be able to stay well and work with ongoing financial support. Although Incapacity Benefit accommodates some work through permitted work arrangements, Housing and Council Tax benefits operate under different rules that create serious financial disincentives to attempting paid work. The permitted work rules are very short-term, and thus unhelpful for people with serious and ongoing mental health problems. Our experiences as service users confirms that many aspects of the benefits systems still act as a disincentive to work. There are specific actions to address this in the *Mental Health and Social Exclusion* report (ODPM 2004a), but these still need to be actioned. A new website keeping us updated on progress was launched in autumn 2005 (www.socialinclusion.org.uk/home/index.php).

Improving access to direct payments can also provide a mechanism for people to address a wider range of needs and become more empowered by enabling them to buy the services they want. These payments could help people to get more vocational support. So far, however, people with mental health problems have the lowest uptake of direct payments of any of the eligible groups. Service users are not told about direct payments, or how to access them. Not enough practitioners know about them or understand the choices they might open up. Very few are trained in how to support people to apply for and manage the payments. However, accessible information is now being provided by the NIMHE Knowledge Community.[5]

Effective Services

The *Mental Health and Social Exclusion* report (ODPM 2004a) includes many examples of good practice, and the other reports and initiatives we have described also show helpful ways forward. In our experience there is still a need for greater clarity about the co-ordination of activities at the practitioner and service delivery level. However evidence is emerging on what effective services look like and how they can be best delivered.

There needs to be practice-level interventions for people in work, so that they do not lose their jobs as a result of mental health crises.[6] The job retention service, referred to in Kim's second story, is an excellent model for such services. It is based on case workers and involves working in flexible ways both with employers and employees. We firmly believe that sustaining and developing access to employment is dependent on a national commitment to, and development of, some kind of job retention service accessed from primary care. Indeed the *Social Exclusion Unit Report* recommends vocational leads within GP practices. These ideas grew out of the vocational services within the mental health services in Bristol which had won a Beacon award and were cited in the *National Service Framework for Mental Health* for adults (Department of Health 1999b) as an example of good practice. Work with the employment service showed that people did not receive appropriate help early enough. Delays often exacerbated difficulties and often lead to loss of work, as reported in *Life's Labours Lost*. The evaluation of that service resulted in *Getting Back Before Christmas* (Thomas, Secker and Grove 2003); since then more job retention services have been established across the country.

One major development which could be undertaken, however, would be for the NHS to set a good example by employing more service users. The South London and Maudsley Trust is doing this in its vocational services strategy, which is based on individual placement and support (Crowther et al. 2004). This is evidence-based, to support individually tailored placements in a real place of work within the Trust. All NHS Trusts could develop these initiatives.

The job retention services need to be supplemented by services which help people whose social exclusion includes an absence of occupation, to develop activities, skills and confidence so that they can regain a place in society and have some kind of meaningful occupation. Such people are currently often the clients of rehabilitation services. If health professionals are to become 'holders of hope' and support higher aspirations for service users, they need to work effectively in broad partnerships that enable a wider range of needs to be addressed. This shift is being evolved in the 'recovery' approach. If this is a new idea to you we urge you to find out more about it and how to apply the ideas in practice.[7] Professionals themselves need support, training and resources to challenge the current attitudes and assumptions in order to embrace this new thinking.

One way for all mental health teams to develop and maintain awareness of employment and occupational issues would be to develop a vocational network, where every team would have one vocational specialist. The network as a whole could develop and share expertise, and the individual practitioner in each team could then act as a link into other services as appropriate. Developing vocational networks can also help individual staff members who may otherwise feel isolated and marginalised in their attempts to develop more holistic practice. The South London and Maudsley Trust is setting a good example in its commitment to develop such a network.

Early intervention is just as important in vocational services as in other aspects of health care. As well as improving medical outcomes, it can help people retain jobs and stay connected to their communities. People who have serious mental health problems, including psychoses, arguably need *more* access to support in maintaining good mental health and to develop relapse plans to respond to early warning signs of recurring disorder. Effective interventions to develop and maintain social inclusion and access to occupation, as well as practical crisis planning, are also likely to be cost effective. These kinds of interventions become more accessible and 'fit' better if they are delivered in the primary care setting.

More focus on services in the primary care setting would bring services to people earlier, with all the potential benefits of preventing problems escalating and multiplying. However, given their workload and time constraints, GPs are unlikely to be able to deliver broader services. They need to be able to refer promptly and easily to other mental health workers who are based in primary care.

The care plan approach must play a central role; however we have found that plans, where they exist, are not holistic. Yet care plans have the potential to provide a tailored person-centred plan for each service user. Facilitating better access to a wider range of services depends on everyone having a care plan. This should automatically include consideration of occupational issues, alongside housing and finance, social networks, and access to leisure activities. The current focus of care plans on medical needs must be shifted to include these areas of everyday life.[8]

For care planning to develop its full potential, staff who take on the role of care co-ordination need to be skilled in assessment across the whole range of possible needs. Meeting these needs includes liaison with and referral to a huge range of potential 'service providers', which should be expanded outside conventional health and social care, including, for example, more mainstream community activities, or voluntary work.

One approach would be to have more occupational therapists (whose training is focused on holistic assessment of needs) working as care co-ordinators in primary care. They could potentially also take on the provision of sick notes for people with mental health problems and liaise with and supervise the new graduate mental health workers. This new role is described in the National Institute for Mental Health, North West Development Centre's enhanced services specification for depression guidance (NIMHE-NW 2004a) and their guide to the new graduate worker in mental health role (NIMHE-NW 2004b). It includes improving access to self-management approaches. The new graduate workers have the potential to evolve into a much broader role than currently exists.

Mental health workers in general need to have a more holistic role across disciplines, although to date this has not yet been adequately addressed in the Department of Health's *The National Mental Health Workforce Strategy* (Department of Health 2004). Training needs to include input from service users and carers.

People with psychoses are also likely to enter the health care system with acute needs, via crisis intervention services and admission to acute mental health wards (Clark 2004). The previous comments about effective and holistic care planning apply across the board, and the understandable emphasis on medical issues in acute services needs to be supplemented by broader considerations. All secondary and tertiary providers therefore also need to increase their focus on occupational issues.

Conclusion

We introduced this chapter by describing the consequences of an absence of vocational focus for individuals with severe mental health problems. Our exploration includes the personal experiences of both service users and professionals. The current state of affairs is shown in the bleak statistical evidence on employment and its link to social exclusion. These highlight the high personal and economic costs to all of us, whether we use services, provide them, or just pay taxes. There has been an absence of focus on occupation as a basic human need, of clear guidelines for best professional practice, and of leadership or dedicated resources. Disillusionment and suspicion has built up between users and practitioners within mental health services. The first version of Kim's story is an individual illustration of this. In resolving these issues we all face a major challenge.

In the last five years these complex issues have been acknowledged in the reports cited in this chapter. They have generated a clearer agenda for action to increase access to occupation and support people's participation in their communities.

In order for these agendas to make a difference, the wide range of organisations identified in these reports' action plans need to work together as never before. This amplifies the need for effective leadership, multi-disciplinary team-working, and a commitment to improving people's everyday lived experiences. The diagram in Figure 11.2 illustrates the organisations involved in driving these changes to service provision. The local action plans which will detail work to be done in each locality will be available via www.socialinclusion.org.uk/home/index.php.

We have identified a number of other major issues that need to be tackled: stigma and discrimination, the benefits system and widening the responsibility for issuing sick notes. The potential of using direct payments also has yet to be fully explored.

Kim's second story describes the individual benefits of early intervention across primary and secondary care, including the wider system of support that makes up Kim's support network. This includes care co-ordination that provides skilled assessment of needs and holistic care planning that makes best use of community and individual networks and resources.

Table 11.1 Key advice about employment and mental health, for individuals, practitioners and organisations.

Advice for individuals

- Make sure you, or your loved one, have a care plan that includes occupation among a wide range of your needs.
- Talk about your hopes and aspirations as part of this plan.
- Learn to use your network, direct payments and advance directives to support your needs.
- Learn more about how others have coped

Advice for practitioners

- Ask all service users about occupational issues and the impact that their mental health problem might have on them.
- Assess your own practice and attitude in relation to the recovery agenda.
- Make sure you are well networked to the vocational and employment services in your patch.
- Use available tools of practice and resources to support service users.
- Help get the recovery of hope messages across in your daily work.

Advice for organisations

- Make sure there is occupational focus within all aspects of service provision.
- Include focus on occupational issues as part of staff continuing personal development plans.
- Keep up to date with latest occupational research evidence.
- Make a commitment to networking with local, national and international occupational service organisations.

In writing this chapter together as service users and practitioners we have explored our different views and perspectives. Working together has not felt like 'collaborating with the enemy'. In fact we feel remarkably united, both in our views of what is *not* happening, and in what *needs* to happen to achieve more effective services. This collaboration has in fact led to creative working and shared learning, demonstrating effective cross-boundary partnership. We have reached agreement on our key points for practice and organisational change, and these are summarised in Table 11.1.

We have seen that effective services can lead to a situation where an episode of serious mental health difficulties might help a person develop confidence, build awareness of coping strategies, and strengthen and develop support networks. If Kim gets the services he deserves, we can see that a different picture appears across all facets of his life. If tackled across the whole system, then there really is hope of service improvements.

We share the same dream – that Kim's second story will become a possibility for all. We will only achieve better outcomes for everyone entering mental health services (at whatever level) if we all work to seek solutions to make our key advice a reality. We all need to play our part and make sure that 'occupation becomes *everyone's* job'.

Notes

1 Or manic-depressive psychosis, as it is also often known.
2 One programme is run by MDF The Bipolar Organisation (http://www.mdf.org.uk/index.asp?o=1649) and includes mapping out support networks.
3 The Teachers Support Network is a national body which addresses stress for staff in teaching: see http://www.teachersupport.info/.
4 This is a network of 60 organisations which are joining forces to implement *Action on Mental Health. A Guide to Promoting Social Inclusion* (ODPM 2004b).
5 The NIMHE Knowledge Community was launched in June 2004 as the online resource for sharing good practice and debates on all aspects of the mental health agenda. It is accessed via www.nimhe.org.uk.
6 See chapter 6 where Lauren is helped to retain her occupational role by the very processes advocated within this chapter.
7 See chapter 1 for more on the recovery approach.
8 See also chapter 8.

References

Bodman, R., Davies, R., Frankel. N., Minton, L. Mitchell, L., Pacé, C., Sayers, R., Tibbs, N., Tovey, Z. and Unger, E. (2003) *Life's Labours Lost: A Study of the Experiences of People Who Have Lost Their Occupation Following a Mental Health Problem*. London: Mental Health Foundation. Available online: www.mentalhealth.org.uk/html/content/lifes_labours_lost.pdf (accessed 22 October 2005).

Clark, S. (2004) *Acute Inpatient Mental Health Care: Education and Training and Continuing Professional Development for All*. London: NIMHE/Sainsbury Centre for Mental Health.

Collins English Dictionary (1992) London: Collins.

Crowther, R., Marshall, M., Bond, G. and Huxley, P. (2004) *Vocational Rehabilitation for People with Severe Mental Illness. (Cochrane Review)*. The Cochrane Library, issue 1.

Department of Health (1999a) *Saving Lives – Our Healthier Nation*. London: Department of Health.

Department of Health (1999b) *The National Service Framework for Mental Health: Modern Standards and Service Models*. London: Department of Health.

Department of Health (2004) *The National Mental Health Workforce Strategy*. London: Department of Health.

Department for Work and Pensions (2004) *Building Capacity for Work: A UK Framework for Vocational Rehabilitation*. London: Department for Work and Pensions.

New Economics Foundation (2004) *A Well-being Manifesto for a Flourishing Society*. London: New Economics Foundation.

NIMHE-NW [National Institute for Mental Health, North West Development Centre] (2004a) *Enhanced Services Specification for Depression under the New GP Contract: A Commissioning Guidebook*. Hyde, Cheshire: NIMHE-NW. Available online: www.nimhenorthwest.org.uk/archives/docs/nGMS.pdf (accessed 22 October 2005).

NIMHE-NW [National Institute for Mental Health, North West Development Centre] (2004b) *Primary Care Graduate Mental Health Workers: A Practical Guide*. Hyde, Cheshire: NIMHE-NW. Available online: www.nimhenorthwest.org.uk/archives/docs/PCGMHW.pdf (accessed 22 October 2005).

ODPM [Office for the Deputy Prime Minister] (2004a) *Mental Health and Social Exclusion – Social Exclusion Unit Report*. London: HMSO. Available online: www.socialexclusionunit.gov.uk/downloaddoc.asp?id=134 (accessed 22 October 2005).

ODPM [Office for the Deputy Prime Minister] (2004b) *Action on Mental Health*. London: HMSO.

Available online: www.socialexclusionunit.gov.uk/downloaddoc.asp?id=300 (accessed 22 October 2005).

Office for National Statistics (2003) *Labour Force Survey*, Quarterly Supplement, no. 22, August 2003. Crown Copyright. Available online: www.statistics.gov.uk/downloads/theme_labour/lfsqs_0803.pdf (accessed 22 October 2005).

Repper, J. and Perkins, R. (2003) *Social Inclusion and Recovery: A Model for Medical Practice*. London: Balliere Tindall.

Thomas, T., Secker, J. and Grove, R. (2003) *'Getting Back Before Christmas' Evaluation of the Avon and Wiltshire Mental Health Partnership Trust Job Retention Pilot.* Final report to the Department of Health and Department for Work and Pensions. London, Institute for Applied Health and Social Policy, King's College London. Available online: www.healthaction.nhs.uk/upload/public/attachments/4/Job%20retention%20pilot.pdf (accessed 22 October 2005).

Useful Web Links

SHIFT: www.shift.org.uk

NIMHE Knowledge Community: www.nimhe.org.uk; and also see NIMHE North-West: www.nimhenorthwest.org.uk

New Social Inclusion site: www.socialinclusion.org.uk/home/index.php

Work Life Partnerships: www.wlp.uk.com

Mental Health Foundation: www.mhf.org.uk

Social Exclusion Unit: Mental Health section: www.socialexclusionunit.gov.uk/page.asp?id=257

Chapter 12

Using Effective Management Strategies to Facilitate the Delivery of PSI

Debbie Furniss and Eric Davis

Key Points

- The presence of a senior manager who thoroughly understands the clinicians' perspective of delivering psychosocial interventions (PSI) helps to implement these interventions in routine practice. This position in the management hierarchy between team leaders and board members seems a particularly good place from which to effect change.
- An effective training programme such as the Thorn course is important, not just because of the knowledge and skills that it imparts, but because of the opportunities it presents to help promote wider organisational change.
- A sense of urgency needs to be displayed by senior managers and clinicians in order to begin any change process (Kotter 1995).
- Although one sector of an organisation can usefully begin change efforts, the wider organisation needs to understand the nature of required change if this is to be successful in the long term (Waterman, Peters and Philips 1980).
- Policy direction, in this case the *National Service Framework for Mental Health* (NSF) (Department of Health 1999) and *Mental Health Policy Implementation Guide* (MHPIG) (Department of Health 2001), plays an important part in creating the climate for change.
- In order to safeguard a culture in which change is welcomed, the organisation needs to be able to engage in 'corporate reflection' in order to remain open to innovation.

Introduction

This chapter describes how a senior manager (Debbie Furniss) and a senior clinician (Eric Davis) worked together as part of a wider team to implement up-to-date psychosocial interventions (PSI) approaches, through effective management processes. This includes their impact on services received by individual service users and their families, as well as their influence on the design of new services that support the delivery of PSI in routine practice.

As described in chapter 1, there is a robust evidence base that demonstrates the effectiveness of PSI (Department of Health 1999). Comprehensive assessment procedures, assertive case management, family intervention and cognitive behavioural approaches to psychosis are all known to improve service outcomes for individuals coping with psychosis, and their families and carers. The use of such techniques produces high levels of user and carer satisfaction (for example, see Baguley and Baguley 1999). The importance of providing PSI training for staff is clearly stated within such reviews.

The need for training in PSI has also been recognised within government policy. The *National Service Framework for Mental Health* (Department of Health 1999) specifies the importance of a 'national programme of focused education and training to address initial skill gaps, including competencies, strategy and psychosocial interventions' (p. 111) in its education and training guidance.

This position is reinforced by the *Mental Health Policy Implementation Guide* (MHPIG) (Department of Health 2001) which specifies that 'restructuring the mental health service and adding new resources to the mental health service will not achieve the intended results without a sufficient workforce with the right skills . . .' (p. 104).

However, despite the policy and guidance, it is often rather more problematic actually to ensure that staff do have this training and acquire the necessary competencies (Department of Health 2004), and then to develop the management frameworks within everyday services such that staff have the time and support (such as effective supervision) to use these skills. Indeed, there is evidence that, in the absence of significant management support, implementing PSI is very problematic (Kavanagh et al. 1993; Brooker et al. 1994; Fadden 1997). This mirrors a more general issue: the problems of implementing evidence-based practice within routine clinical practice, where the mixture of good training in the new skills, practitioner support for change (including local ownership and the development of local champions), active middle management support, and high level (e.g. board/chief executive) approval for implementation, are all necessary to effect such developments (Rogers 1995; Waddell 2001; Smith and Velleman 2002; Velleman et al. 2002).

This chapter will describe how we developed an appropriate system to train staff within our NHS Trust in these necessary PSI competencies (using the Thorn model, recognised and evaluated as an evidence-based training programme for this purpose (Brooker et al. 1992; Baguley et al. 2000)) and how we then put in place the management systems such that these trained practitioners could start to use their skills and implement PSI within routine practice.

The Case Study

Editors' note: the case study in this chapter is somewhat similar to those in chapters 8, 9 and 10, where new ways of delivering and implementing therapeutic interventions were demonstrated, although here the example is one of management change and implementation instead – the case here is not a service user and a family, nor a group, but rather a part of a major NHS Trust.

History and Context of the Thorn Course and Its Corporate Application

Eric says:

The Thorn course (see Baguley and Baguley 1999) has been absolutely central to the managerial/clinical vision embraced by myself and Debbie, with colleagues, to implement PSI approaches within Gloucestershire Partnership NHS Trust (GPT). This central vision espouses the routine implementation for service users with psychosis and their carers of the latest, most clinically effective, PSI measures, including:

- comprehensive assessment
- assertive case management
- family intervention (FI)
- cognitive behaviour therapy (CBT) for psychosis[1]

It was in 1995 that the journey to develop a Thorn course in Gloucestershire started. In order to begin the process of implementation it was necessary for me to enhance my existing skills. I obtained clearance from my manager (Don Campbell, senior manager in the earlier east Gloucestershire NHS Trust) to attend the Thorn course, with a nurse colleague, Keith Coupland; the course we attended was in Manchester, as this was the closest provision at that time.

Immediately after completing the programme, Keith and I set to work devising our own Thorn course that would run in collaboration with our local education provider (see Rolls, Davis and Coupland 2002). All plans were developed with the backing of senior management colleagues who recognised that the routine implementation of PSI was central to modernising services within Gloucestershire. In order for services to change, local clinicians needed the skills and knowledge that could be acquired through the Thorn programme. These skills and knowledge would also help clinicians to challenge certain negative perceptions and attitudes that may have developed in connection to working with psychosis (for example, that recovery cannot be achieved for people with psychosis).

As more comprehensive PSI approaches began to be implemented, more successful outcomes for service users began to be observed; these included, for example, service users talking openly about managing their voice-hearing experiences and co-facilitating groups (see chapter 9). Keith and I would routinely feed such information back to service managers, who by this time included Debbie, and she was able to ensure that such messages were relayed to the GPT executive board. (GPT was formed in 2002 from a merger between east Gloucestershire NHS Trust and Severn NHS Trust.) Therefore, the initial outcomes of clinical work obtained from implementing PSI approaches within routine practice settings gave credence to the original managerial vision and meant that local Thorn training became valued and viewed as an integral part of the GPT corporate strategic and operational framework.

Debbie says:

When I first began working with Eric, the key responsibilities of my post included line-managing community mental health team (CMHT) leaders and managers of community and residential rehabilitation homes, service development and contributing to both the operational and strategic agenda. Figure 12.1 shows the organisational chart that details my position within the hierarchical structure (specialist services manager).

Since 1998 I had been supporting staff in undertaking the Thorn course in addition to working with those individuals who teach and facilitate the course. During this time the benefits to both service users and clinicians from the use of specific PSI in everyday practice were becoming apparent. However, those who had completed their training were limited in their scope to apply their skills owing to large caseloads and sometimes unsupportive team leaders. This led to thoughts about how individuals could be best supported from a managerial perspective in implementing, post-graduation from Thorn, the PSI skills they had gained.

During a conversation with Keith Coupland about potentially useful management techniques to facilitate the development of family work services to co-ordinate the delivery of family interventions (FI), an offhand comment was made – that it was a shame that I had not undertaken the course myself. We agreed that my having first-hand experience of the course would be useful in developing structures and systems that support implementation of PSI in routine practice.

We agreed that my developing a more sophisticated understanding of what it is that clinicians actually do to deliver frontline services would increase not only my theoretical knowledge but would also help me to understand how the interventions worked in practice. I would gain an insight into the barriers that clinicians were facing, which would help me to provide well-informed managerial support and enable me to foster an enabling operational framework.

I undertook the Thorn course in the academic year 2002/3. Full support was given from GPT in releasing me from my normal duties to attend the course and from the Workforce Development Confederation (WDC) which funded my student fees. An agreement was reached between myself and my line manager that enabled my full attendance at the course, which included completing the pre- and post-course multiple choice questionnaire. I aimed to gain the practice skills needed to deliver FI by working with one family (rather than the two usually required to demonstrate competence), but did not attempt to work with any individuals. The other components I omitted were the written assignments. Instead, through writing this chapter, I have outlined the benefits of attending the Thorn course from the management perspective. Although it was understood that, owing to the course, there might be meetings, etc. that I would not attend, my actual workload did not alter – the specialist services still needed to be managed. In effect therefore, attending the Thorn course was 'an extra', something which needed to be done on top of an already busy job. What helped me was my enduring passionate interest to see PSI approaches implemented within GPT.

I was able to attend approximately 85 per cent of the 40-day course which gave me a comprehensive overview, and some indepth understanding of its four main components. Other students were interested that a senior manager should invest such commitment in attending the course.

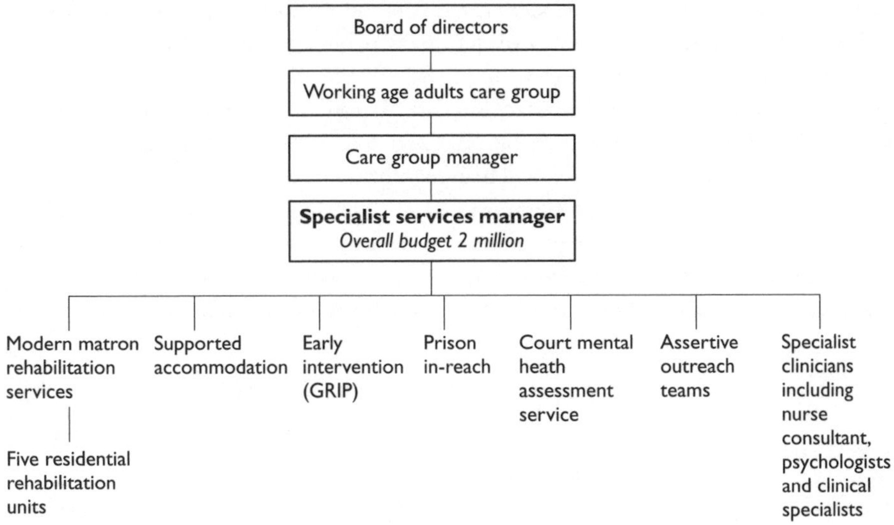

Figure 12.1 Organisational structure, Gloucestershire Partnership NHS Trust (2005)

Eric says:

Having a senior manager undertake the Thorn course in 2002 was particularly helpful as it showed that the degree of corporate commitment from the newly-formed GPT towards further PSI implementation remained as high as in the previous organisations. Debbie now recognises that effective PSI work requires more clinical time than traditional interventions which have a questionable evidence base. Consequently, she has been able to support some clinical team leaders in their initial efforts to reduce overall individual clinical caseloads to give Thorn-trained clinicians time to deliver effective interventions.

Debbie says:

Prior to attending this course I had a relatively superficial understanding of activity monitoring and recording clinical data. Attending the Thorn course increased my appreciation of the range of ways in which clinicians could work with people, and therefore the recognition that for activity recording to be meaningful, it had to be more than just a number exercise. I was able to see the value of working not just with symptoms but in a more holistic way, for example, taking account of a service user's social situation when discussing an experience of paranoia. I also recognised that, in order to promote recovery, clinicians need to spend more time with users and carers than had been possible previously with traditional CMHT caseloads. Team managers need to recognise that a decrease in the numbers of service users seen can result in the time spent with individuals being used much more productively. It highlighted that good case management is not about seeing more people, as this may have the effect of decreasing effectiveness so could be viewed as a false economy.

I recognise that the small caseloads (12 to 15 per full-time staff member) advocated by the MHPIG (Department of Health 2001) for assertive outreach and early intervention teams should enable workers in these teams to provide PSI to all service users. Unfortunately, as yet there is no such template for staff in CMHTs to determine the size of caseload that would allow them to use their skills best in relation to assessment, FI and CBT for psychosis. More accurate data collection will help to inform this debate.

Having clearly understood the importance of acquiring the knowledge and skills delivered through a rigorous training programme such as the Thorn course, and with my detailed knowledge of what the interventions entail, I can now make the case within management forums more strongly for GPT to embrace these approaches and make them happen.

Organisational implementation

Eric and Debbie say:

We realised that organisational change was required in order to stimulate interest in developing training and services which would facilitate the delivery of PSI across all clinical areas. Through supervision which we provided, and from management meetings and informal conversations, it was apparent that workers who had completed the Thorn course were still experiencing difficulties in implementing the interventions with as many service users and families as they would wish. The barriers they described mirrored those found in other organisations (Smith and Velleman 2002).

We decided that if PSI implementation was to become 'the way we do things around here' and become part of routine GPT operation, then it was important to devise a coherent management strategy. In this, the work of Kotter (1995) was helpful in guiding our efforts to bring about the change. Kotter suggests that there are a number of management steps that need to be taken in order to ensure that organisational transformation efforts do not fail. We would recommend these points as representing a transferable template to help others in terms of change efforts. His suggestions are numbered 1–8 below with our commentary upon how these suggested efforts were achieved within GPT:

1 Establishing a sense of urgency

We realised that the *availability* of the local Thorn training meant that GPT was in a sound position to capitalise upon the earlier management decision to improve PSI skills. Opportunities were afforded by both the NSF (Department of Health 1999) and MHPIG (Department of Health 2001) for us to create a more modern and responsive mental health service. Conversely, doing nothing was not an option, given that the government was pushing user and carer choice through its policy agenda. Through a number of meetings with senior managers and clinicians, and also the Executive team, PSI implementation was adopted with sufficient urgency to begin to promote change.

2 *Forming a powerful guiding coalition*

Since the creation of GPT in 2002, Debbie has ensured that Eric, alongside Keith Coupland and Jo Denney (the current Thorn course leader), has continued to help devise strategy and shape operational service responses. In Kotter's words, she has ensured that we have remained part of a powerful guiding coalition. This has meant that we have been engaged in informed dialogue and also delivered formal presentations to the GPT executive board to ensure that service development and the overall 'direction of travel' remains congruent with the delivery of evidence-based practice, and in particular the delivery of PSI.

The organisational merger in 2002 could, theoretically, have resulted in development difficulties. For example, working relationships between senior clinicians and managers can be disrupted in times of wider organisational change. Further, key decision-makers may also physically relocate, or become more geographically remote from each other. In reality, no such difficulties have arisen. Indeed, Debbie's input has been very important, promoting and capitalising on further potential service development opportunities. To some extent, relationships had to be built and/or renewed: Debbie has been instrumental in ensuring that key decision-makers from the Executive Board and the Training, Education and Continuing Professional Development Steering Group remained in close contact with Eric, Keith and Jo.

3 *Creating a vision*

Through our input, the vision for GPT was (and remains) to implement effective PSI strategies for service users with psychosis and their carers in *everyday practice*. The importance of routinely using comprehensive assessment procedures, an assertive case management model, FI and CBT for psychosis was forged at the level of the GPT executive board who took the final decision to endorse the PSI strategy, as well as having the support of those creating the Trust's training strategy.

The strategy for implementing the vision could then rely upon both 'top down' executive endorsement and 'bottom up' influence from the increasing number of Thorn-trained workers graduating each year, who could then be strategically deployed in front-line clinical services.

4 *Communicating the vision*

The vision to implement PSI approaches as standard practice was communicated at all levels of the organisation, including corporate strategy documents, formal presentations and informal conversations between interested parties. This ensured that funding remained available via the WDC to continue training sufficient staff so that a 'critical mass' was achieved. Users and carers were also involved and were informed of the vision through formal 'recovery-based' workshops arranged by GPT and through other user- and carer-focused self-help groups.

As discussed earlier, the attendance of Debbie on the Thorn course was a powerful practical and symbolic reminder of the importance that GPT attached to PSI implementation. In essence, Debbie was modelling new behaviours that could be adopted by other managers in order to support evidence-based practice, by setting an example from the guiding coalition.

5 *Empowering others to act on the vision*

Because working effectively with service users and their families coping with psychosis was prioritised by GPT, this meant that some resources (staff) were redeployed to respond to service demand. This included the creation of a new team: the emergence of the early intervention team (see chapter 2), and the crisis and assertive outreach teams meant that the provision of limited caseloads in these teams became an operational priority, creating the necessary capacity to implement PSI skills.

As well as the creation of the newer teams helping PSI implementation through their greater corporate focus both on psychosis and smaller case-loads, a number of risk-taking and non-traditional ideas, activities and actions was promoted. User and carer choice in terms of mental health treatment were explored through a series of recovery-focused workshops. This revealed an emphasis upon creating more 'talking therapy'. An emphasis on valued occupation was explored through planned contact with users and carers which examined ways of achieving this. Because the use of comprehensive assessments has revealed that users and carers often have unmet needs that cannot be satisfactorily resolved through recourse to traditional services, a number of partnerships are being developed with the non-statutory sector to promote recovery through training, employment and leisure schemes. The recent appointment of user and carer development workers will help explore further options.

6 *Planning for and creating short-term wins*

Visible performance improvements have already resulted for GPT. Denney (2001), in an unpublished audit regarding implementation of Thorn/PSI approaches, has shown that users and carers benefit from enhanced knowledge and skills acquired by mental health professionals, in terms of their clinical outcomes. Also, professionals derive satisfaction from their increased acquisition of skills and knowledge. There is some evidence that a more optimistic outlook and attitude also results for staff attending the course.

However, one of the drawbacks that have been identified is that certain staff experience difficulty in being able to implement Thorn/PSI approaches fully, owing to pressure from large caseloads. More specifically, this appears to be a difficulty for those staff in CMHTs who are trying to apply such skills. We return to this theme in point 7 below.

Conversely, other staff have purposefully moved to other clinical teams where such skills can routinely be used (e.g. assertive outreach, early intervention, crisis) and posts in some traditional teams (CMHTs) are in the process of being redesigned to facilitate PSI implementation.

7 *Consolidating improvements and producing still more change*

The role of workers within CMHTs will probably develop further, as wider organisational changes are implemented. For example, the recent enhanced development of primary care services means that users with more common mental health problems such as anxiety and depression now receive their care from this part of the system. Similarly, the new teams will see people with psychotic problems at various stages of their disorders (e.g. the GRIP early intervention team caters for the first three years of people's psychosis – see chapter 2; assertive outreach teams will deal with people who are difficult to engage and suffer from serious mental disorder; and crisis teams deal with acute mental health difficulties). As these changes filter through, this should lead to a degree of increased capacity within CMHTs for the care of those people with psychosis; and as more time becomes available within more traditional CMHT services, so staff will be able to respond to (and utilise their PSI skills with) those service users and their families with longer-term needs associated with psychosis.

Also, the increased expansion of these newer assertive outreach, early intervention and crisis teams will consolidate PSI implementation. Increasingly these teams and services are recruiting staff who are Thorn trained, given the recognition that these skills are well suited to the specific demands of these jobs.

Developing a menu of service options for users is important. The most recent service improvements involve the creation of the Family Work Steering Group, designed to extend behavioural family work across the Trust for users with psychosis, and the building of the rehabilitation unit for users with long-term and enhanced needs.

Further change is accruing through partnership working between GPT and the non-statutory sector. This is because an emphasis on recovery demands that service users and their carers receive more holistic intervention. This cannot be achieved by the health service alone, so contact with, among other groups, employers, educational establishments and leisure providers in the community is being vigorously explored to ensure access to a wider package of care and life chances. (See chapters 10 and 11 for more discussion about leisure and vocational initiatives.) A number of connected research projects will hopefully demonstrate improvements for users by changing the model of service delivery.

Further improvements to services can also be expected if service users who are recovering, and carers, can be employed by GPT. They bring unique insights to service operation. This process has just started and is expected to accelerate.

8 *Institutionalising new approaches*

The actual and planned changes described above are articulated within the GPT strategic blueprint for how services are expected to develop in future. Progress in terms of the GPT annual report means that progressive PSI implementation is widely disseminated among various stakeholders such as mental health professionals, users, carers and decision-makers within GPT, but also other powerful performance management monitors such as the Strategic Health Authority (SHA) and Primary Care Trusts (PCT) which commission and therefore oversee relevant service developments.

If the whole-service systems redesign being implemented by GPT works effectively as envisaged, this will have important future implications for how GPT itself as an organisation will be configured and as to how its services are paid for through the commissioning process. Effective throughput of service users is important for clinical reasons and also because the government is proposing a system of payment by results (PBR). It is anticipated that PBR will be introduced within the mental health arena by 2008. The idea of PBR is that Trusts will be paid according to predetermined levels of effective clinical activity, although many of the exact details associated with this proposed mechanism of payments for mental health have not yet been fully worked through.

A further factor relevant to the future corporate success of GPT is the potential decision to apply for Foundation Trust (FT) status. FT status will only be granted to those organisations that hold three stars, are financially viable, and can demonstrate sound management and governance arrangements. If FT status is achieved for GPT, then one of the potential major rewards will be the ability to raise significantly more finance to develop future mental health services. This is of clear importance in ensuring wider corporate success, which will also underpin and include the delivery of PSI implementation. In turn, leadership development and succession planning for PSI implementation could be significantly affected by the outcome of such a major corporate decision, although the precise implications are difficult to predict at this stage. However, in the widest sense, greater corporate autonomy for any Gloucestershire foundation mental health service would be anticipated to work in favour of still more progressive PSI implementation change efforts.

Debbie says:

The philosophy and principles underpinning the Thorn course have been instrumental (alongside the MHPIG (Department of Health 2001)) in the design of new teams, service modernisation and strategic service development within GPT.

I am using the '7Ss' model described by Waterman, Peters and Philips (1980) shown in Figure 12.2 to illustrate the seven aspects of the organisation which have been adapted within GPT to facilitate the delivery of PSI work. This model is used in addition to Kotter (1995), because its emphasis is slightly different. Whereas Kotter places more emphasis upon the *process* of change management, the 7 Ss model, in contrast, also examines how an organisation is *actually* organised as well as the process of change. By this is meant that the seven factors need to be clearly harmonised, integrated and 'pointing in the same direction' if the organisation, in this case GPT, is to be successful in sustaining its change efforts. Also, the 7Ss model could be said to be clearer in specifying the desired components necessary to facilitate the achievement of the corporate outcomes described below.

Examples are cited below from assertive outreach, early intervention and rehabilitation services. These illustrate progress in developing services within this model. A further factor which occurs to me, but is not contained within the original '7Ss' model is that of 'surroundings'. The value of considering this factor, in addition to the original seven, is that this enables a description of a capital development scheme for the design of a Specialist Rehabilitation unit which facilitates further PSI development. I have added this final 'S' below as 'S8'.

S1: structure

The assertive outreach, early intervention and rehabilitation services teams, the Thorn course, clinical psychologists, PSI clinical specialists and the nurse consultant for PSI are

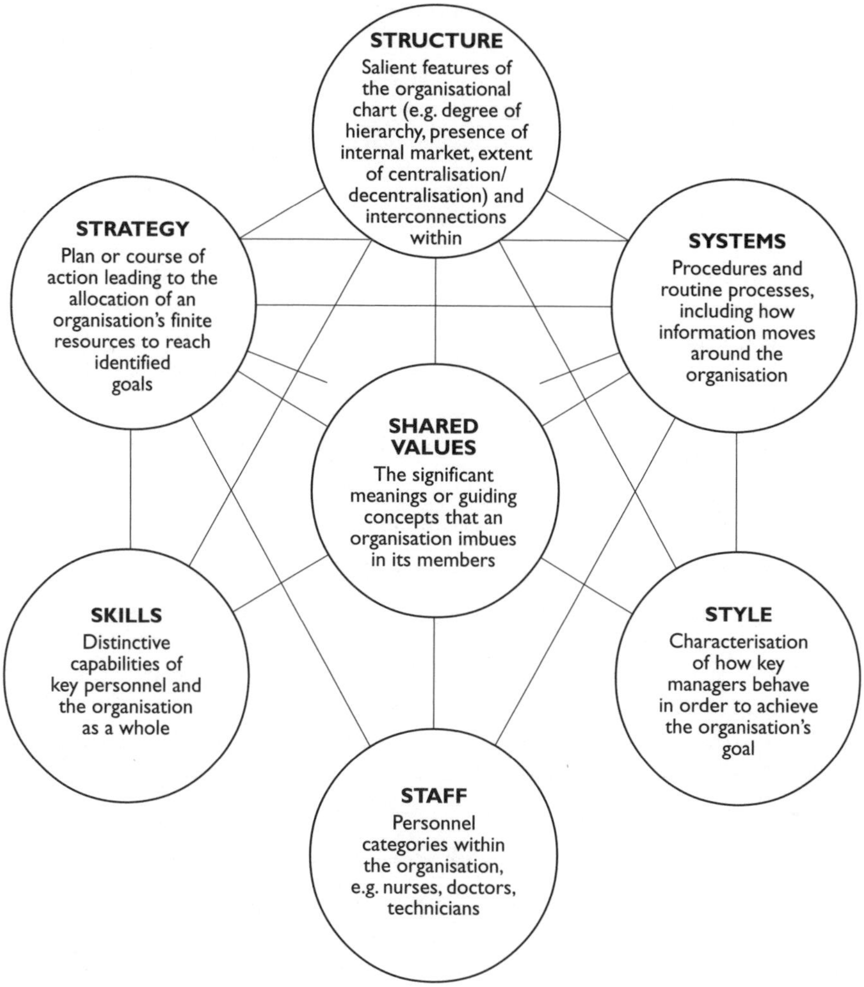

Figure 12.2 The 7 Ss model, adapted from Waterman, Peters and Philips 1980

managed by me (Debbie Furniss) within specialist services in a care group which serves working age adults across the county. This enables close working relationships between service delivery, planning and education, through joint working between senior clinicians and managers. There have also been benefits resulting from creative working relationships with non-statutory organisations for users, for example, joint working to meet service users' social and leisure needs. The decision to base these teams/individuals within specialist services was influenced by the desire to develop a concentration of skills and ability. Additional benefits to this model are described by Barrowclough and Tarrier (1997) and include increasing the possibility of initiating change; an increase in the profile and value of PSI service providers; it enables staff to enhance their careers as a result of developing specialist skills;

and training can be delivered to small numbers of individuals meeting their specific needs, so reducing 'patchy absorption' of skills learned. The implementation of PSI is more effective owing to the structural features, in that specialist services serve all the working age care group across the county. A useful feature of my role within this is that it enables me to facilitate PSI implementation within defined service areas throughout the Trust.

S2: strategy

The strategy is to have a core of PSI workers delivering services within a defined locality and supporting colleagues in service delivery and development through joint working, education and supervision. The aim is to prompt service planning (through myself as specialist services manager): to focus on the nature of interventions to be delivered in both local clinical practice and strategically through service development and redesign; to address obstacles that can hinder successful implementation; and to integrate PSI work into routine practice.

S3: style

The approach adopted is embedded in my belief that all stakeholders can make a valuable contribution to services and that practice can be greatly enhanced through supportive approaches involving a variety of individuals. Collaborating with, and empowering (or at least ceasing to disempower) users, carers and staff at all levels is encouraged within all aspects of service delivery and planning in specialist services. Examples of this inclusive approach are in the work surrounding the modernisation of two residential rehabilitation homes, which is discussed below, and in the Family Work Steering Group.

S4: skills

There is a core of Thorn-trained staff who deliver PSI and supervise others in their clinical practice. Their role also extends to include sharing practice and encouraging others to undertake the training through role modelling, sharing expertise, and evidence of improved outcomes for users.

They also undertake work with course lecturers to clarify the competencies required by individual professions to enable them to deliver PSI effectively and encourage staff to undertake shorter skills-based courses (for example, medication management training) as an alternative for those individuals who do not want to commit to the Thorn course. This has been in response to feedback from individuals who have not been able to commit to the full 40-day Thorn course but still wanted to develop specific psychosocial skills.

S5: systems

Information systems which have the capacity to collect data relating to clinical interventions and outcomes are being explored through the trust pilot of a workload management system, and locally within each service. Bespoke systems are also developed to capture specific information for identified projects. We have used audit as a tool for doing this: for example, the implementation of psychosocial interventions audit (Denney 2001) was used to identify where Thorn graduates and those who are trained to deliver family work are working within the Trust, and whether these graduates are practicing and receiving supervision. There are routine processes in operation in the form of regular, planned meetings within specialist services which facilitate the sharing of information and good practice and which aim to enable a move towards fully integrated services. This is supported by the availability of specialist clinical supervision across the services. I facilitate the use of supervision through encouraging team leaders to view it as an integral part of care delivery. We aim to build regular sessions into work planning and assist individuals to identify an appropriate supervisor.

S6: staff

Specialist teams are set up with one team leader and a number of designated named workers which include CPNs, OTs, social workers, psychologists, support workers and medical staff. Caseloads are small with each full-time staff member holding a maximum number of 12 cases. Some posts are generic where the professional background is less relevant than the clinical competencies individual workers possess. Locally, we have had good experiences in employing more generic workers, who are not trained in traditional ways (i.e. holding mental health qualifications), but who bring life experience and positive attitudes towards working with people with mental health problems. Their role is to complement more mainstream-trained staff.

Partnership working is encouraged to increase the ability to deliver all aspects of PSI work, through joint working with staff from other services. Aligning with other interested individuals in order to deliver services has proved to be particularly beneficial when delivering family work.

S7: shared values

A shared vision between myself as the manager, and colleagues within specialist services, is encouraged, aiming to promote, develop and deliver evidence-based approaches to meet the needs of users and their carers. The recovery approach (Anthony 1993) underpins all current service provision; and future developments are based on the 'strengths model' which involves identifying and building on individuals' strengths, from which coping strategies can be developed.

S8: surroundings

Recent work related to the development of a rehabilitation unit (the Honeybourne Specialist Rehabilitation Centre), which opened in September 2005, provides a good example of this factor. The vision was to replace two traditional rehabilitation homes with a building designed to meet the needs of contemporary rehabilitation service users whose care/treatment is underpinned by the recovery model. The design was informed by the recommendations outlined by Whittaker and Welch (1996) in their proposals for service development for those individuals who require 24-hour nursed care.

It comprises 10 24-hour nursed beds to meet the needs of those users with severe and enduring mental disorder who, while not requiring hospital treatment, do need 24-hour nursed care owing to the sustained and severe nature of their disability. One bedroom is designed to meet the needs of those users with physical disabilities. The original population to be served by this development was 245,000 but the merger which formed GPT has meant that it will now be part of a wider 24-hour nursed care rehabilitation service for the county (population 564,000). The staff comprises 1 unit manager, 1 deputy manager, 8.5 registered nurses, 8 health care assistants, 1 activity co-ordinator, 1.4 housekeepers, 0.5 occupational therapists and sessional input from psychology, pharmacy, nurse consultant, social worker and medical staffing.

There are four flats attached to this accommodation which are for the group of users who still require 24-hour nursing support but have sufficient living skills to live more independently. These service users will continue to receive ongoing assessments and work will aim to address the strengths they possess in order to identify further life opportunities. We recognise that it can be a huge leap for individuals to move from inpatient services to independent living: this accommodation is designed to enable a period of time to establish skills and confidence within a community setting.

The aim is to provide a service that enables users to progress towards greater independence. A typical user journey for someone requiring longer-term nursed care such as this would start in the hospital, move on to the 10-bedded unit, then to one of the flats, and then to independent accommodation, probably in the local community. The model, however, is being designed to have enough flexibility to respond to changes in user needs so, while it is anticipated that most will progress through the unit to independent living, there is sufficient flexibility to allow for individual care pathways to take them to and from all areas within the model. There is one bed set aside for respite, which would be pre-planned for a specific period of time. Beds will also be available for short-term admissions for specific interventions such as Clozaril management, where an individual might require admission to an inpatient facility for Clozaril treatment but who would not require a bed in an acute hospital.

Residents will have personal individual space where they can spend time with, or without, staff, in privacy for any purpose, including PSI work. They will also have personal storage space to keep records of any work they are doing safely.

The facility is located within an urban setting with good infrastructure including public transport, GP surgeries, day centres and local amenities. A wide range of therapeutic interventions will be available to the users of this service (Honeybourne Draft Operational Policy: Gloucestershire Partnership NHS Trust 2005) but there will also be an emphasis on encouraging individuals to engage with local community resources. As usual, families and friends will be included in service users care through the care programme approach. (Figure 12.3 illustrates the proposed care pathways.)

Conclusion

This chapter has described the process of an organisational attempt to promote PSI changes, mainly though the introduction of Thorn-inspired working practices: the institu-

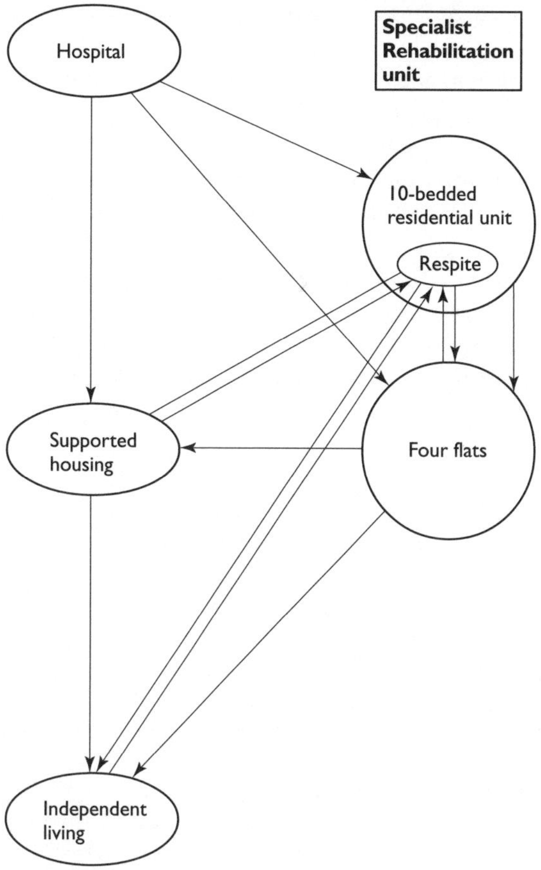

Figure 12.3 Illustration of proposed care pathways for the new rehabilitation unit

tional embedding within GPT of comprehensive assessments, assertive case management, family work (see chapter 3) and CBT for psychosis.

This process was discussed and analysed through the prism of Kotter's (1995) model regarding the process of organisational change, and Waterman, Peters and Philips' (1980) 7 Ss model of institutional organisation.

We are sure that this drive to implement newer working practices has been helped by the availability of a core number of senior clinicians and managers, working well together, with energy and commitment, and with a clear vision in mind. In addition, the policy drive contained within both the NSF (Department of Health 1999) and MHPIG (Department of Health 2001) helped create the platform for these efforts. These together, however, have meant that the initial impetus for this work has developed and expanded, from being something that the specialist services sector of GPT was attempting to undertake, to its present position where it has influenced current and future operations within the wider adults of working age care group.

There are, of course, tensions and debates in this endeavour. Although clinical effectiveness is improved and hence longer-term outcomes are better, undertaking PSI work involves more time from staff, which in the short term costs more or which means that fewer people are able to be seen. There is therefore a tension between the demands of more traditional and newer services. GPT is of course not the only organisation grappling with this dilemma (NHS Confederation and Deighan et al. 2004). The challenge therefore for the future for GPT will be not only to safeguard and enhance up-to-date clinical practices but also, just as crucially, to create the necessary organisational structures and systems upon which further service modernisation will continue to prosper, while still working within the Trust's financial constraints. Given our progress to date and the support we have developed across all levels of the organisation, we are confident that this challenge will be met.

Note

1 All these elements have been described in earlier chapters in this book.

References

Anthony, W. (1993) Recovery from mental illness: the guiding vision of the mental health service system in the 1990s. *Psychosocial Rehabilitation Journal*, 16, 11–24.

Baguley, I. and Baguley, C. (1999) Psychosocial interventions in the treatment of psychosis. *Mental Health Care*, 2, 314–17.

Baguley, I., Butterworth, A., Fahy, K., Haddock, G., Lancashire, S. and Tarrier, N. (2000) Bringing into clinical practice skills shown to be effective in research settings: a follow-up of Thorn training in psychosocial family interventions for psychosis. In Martindale, B., Bateman, A., Crowe, M. and Margison, F. (eds.) *Psychosis: Psychological Approaches and Their Effectiveness*. London: Gaskell, chapter 5, pp. 96–119.

Barrowclough, C. and Tarrier, N. (1997) *Families of Schizophrenic Patients: Cognitive Behavioural Interventions*. Cheltenham: Stanley Thornes.

Brooker, C., Barrowclough, C. and Tarrier, N. (1992) Evaluating the impact of training community psychiatric nurses to train relatives about schizophrenia. *Journal of Clinical Nursing*, 1, 19–25.

Brooker, C., Falloon, I., Butterworth, A., Goldberg, D., Graham-Hole, V. and Hillier, V. (1994) The outcome of training community psychiatric nurses to deliver psychosocial intervention. *British Journal of Psychiatry*, 165, 222–30.

Denney, J. (2001) Implementation of psychosocial interventions. An audit of uptake and experience among graduates of a local training initiative in east Gloucestershire NHS Trust (unpublished).

Department of Health (1999) *The National Service Framework for Mental Health: Modern Standards and Service Models*. London: Department of Health.

Department of Health (2001) *Mental Health Policy Implementation Guide*. London: Department of Health.

Department of Health (2004) *The Ten Essential Shared Capabilities: A Framework for the Whole of the Mental Health Workforce*. London: Department of Health.

Fadden, G. (1997) Implementation of family interventions in routine clinical practice following staff training programmes: a major cause for concern. *Journal of Mental Health*, 6, 599–612.

Gloucestershire Partnership NHS Trust (2005) *Honeybourne Specialist Rehabilitation and Recovery Centre: Operational Policy*. Gloucestershire: Gloucestershire Partnership Trust.

Kavanagh, D., Clark, D., Manicavasagar, V., Piatkowska, O., O'Halloran, P., Rosen, A. and Tennant, C. (1993) Application of cognitive behavioural family interventions for schizophrenia in multidisciplinary teams. What can the matter be? *Australian Psychologist*, 28, 1–8.

Kotter, J. (1995) Leading change: why transformation efforts fail. *Harvard Business Review*, Mar/Apr 73, 1–20.

NHS Confederation and Deighan, M., Cullen, R. and Moore, R. (2004) The development of integrated governance. London: NHS Confederation. Available online: www.cgsupport.nhs.uk/PDFs/debate3.pdf (accessed 24 October 2005).

Rogers, E. (1995) *Diffusion of Innovation*, 4th edition. Toronto, Ontario: The Free Press.

Rolls, E., Davis, E,. and Coupland, K. (2002) Improving serious mental illness through interprofessional education. *Journal of Psychiatric and Mental Health Nursing*, 9, 317–24.

Smith, G. and Velleman, R. (2002) Maintaining a family work for psychosis service by recognising and addressing the barriers to implementation. *Journal of Mental Health*, 11, 471 – 479.

Velleman, R., Heather, N., Hay, L. and Kemm, J. (2002) Dissemination and implementation of research findings. In Alcohol Research Forum (eds.) *100% Proof: Research for Action on Alcohol*, London: Alcohol Concern, pp. 124–33. Available online: www.alcoholconcern.org.uk/servlets/doc/615 [20031016_100027_Research forum Vell heath hay kemm.pdf]

Waddell, C. (2001) So much research evidence, so little dissemination and uptake: mixing the useful with the pleasing, *Evidence Based Mental Health*, 4, 3–5.

Waterman, R.H. Jr, Peters, T. and Philips J. (1980) Structure is not organisation. *Business Horizons*, June 1980, 14–26.

Whittaker, N. and Welch, P. (1996) *24-hour Nursed Care for People with Severe and Enduring Mental Illness*. Leeds: NHS Executive.

Chapter 13

Carer–Practitioner Collaboration in Research and Evaluation

Willm Mistral, Michael Drage, Gina Smith, Siobhan Floyd and Nicola Cocks

Key Points

- UK public services have a duty to consult carers and involve them in the planning and development of relevant research and service activities.
- This chapter gives as an example a carer-led action research project which set out to develop a tool to measure the effects of family intervention for psychosis.
- Good action research is *participatory*; seeks to contribute to *human emancipation and flourishing*; and strives to develop *practical knowledge* useful in everyday life.
- Involving carers in research requires provision of a supportive environment and real cognitive and emotional engagement by all stakeholders.
- The power relationship between professionals and both service users and carers can be visualised in terms of a 'ladder of participation'.
- The present research process has been a learning journey for all involved.

Introduction

The chapter begins with an overview of the political context within which carers are becoming more involved in health service research. Then follows descriptions of the experiences of different members of a collaborative research team, brought together in a carer-led action research project to develop a tool to measure the effects of family intervention for psychosis (FI). This collaboration in the service of a set of shared values has created a whole most definitely greater than the sum of the individual parts.

The Evidence

The politics

Health research agendas change according to changes in society and political fashions (Carrick, Mitchell and Lloyd 2001). By the 1990s, the notion of health service users as customers or consumers was gaining ground (Peck, Gulliver and Towel 2001). Over the last 15 years, the role of health and social care professionals has come under increasing scrutiny, and all public services now have a duty to consult the people who use these services (e.g. The NHS and Community Care Act 1990; The Patients' Charter 1992; *The NHS Plan* (Department of Health 2000)). Further to this, the *National Service Framework for Mental Health* (NSF), Standard 6, states that service providers should consult carers about services, and involve them in the planning and development of these services (Department of Health 1999). There is, however, a world of difference between *involvement* and *consultation*. Involvement implies 'included, concerned in, emotionally engaged with' as opposed to simply being asked for information or advice (Baulcombe et al. 2000, p. 6).

Research is conducted in the social world where the dynamics of power affect everyone (Parker 1994). There is an obvious imbalance of power between professional researchers and both carers and service users. Professionals have specific training, they have resources and they represent agencies with statutory powers and duties (Baulcombe et al. 2000). While all stakeholders might agree that service planning and development should be based upon appropriate research evidence (Sackett et al. 1996), there can be dispute about what constitutes 'appropriate' evidence in various contexts. Many social researchers might agree that 'for those of us who work with a variety of communities and stakeholders, the temptation is to please one (usually the most powerful) and say that our work is good for the others' (Rappaport 1994, p. 15).

A type of professional closed circuit can operate in health care research which excludes the views and, especially, the involvement, of those people for whom the services are supposedly developed. Professionals have a body of knowledge and experience which they express in a language initially difficult for laypeople to understand. Professional researchers also often seek to distance themselves from research participants. There are at least two reasons for this. The first may be in the pursuit of 'objectivity', which is a basic tenet of some branches of modern scientific methods. However, as argued by Kuhn (1962), a scientific community cannot practice without a set of widely shared received beliefs – a shared subjectivity in fact – and these shared professional beliefs are difficult for non-professionals to challenge. Professionals may also distance themselves as a form of protection against the sometimes unpleasant realities of people's lives and their experiences of the services with which they are provided.

One result of this professional closed circuit is that many carers, service users and other laypeople understand very little about the research process, and this in itself can be taken as a further reason not to attempt to involve them. All these factors have contributed to a situation where consultation is a relatively easy option, while real involvement is not. As a reaction to this, Stewart and Bhagwanjee (1999), in a paper promoting group empowerment through participation, argue for more collaborative research to demystify the research process, which traditionally remains unexplained and incomprehensible to research participants. Professional researchers need to be continually aware of, and respect, the context from within which both they and the users or carers are coming to the research. Arnstein (1969) illustrates this as a *ladder of participation*. At the lowest level of the ladder, an individual or group is being manipulated, at a higher level they are being informed, then being consulted, then forming partnerships and, finally, they hold managerial power. Arnstein's model has subsequently been adapted, for example by Wilcox (1994), in terms of:

- information giving
- consultation
- deciding together
- acting together
- supporting independent community interests.

Action Research

The term *action research* has been used with reference to a wide range of methodologies and research practices. Reason and Bradbury (2001) argue, however, that good action research is fundamentally different from much traditional academic research. Good action research is *participatory* in that it is *with* and *by*, rather than 'on', people; it seeks to contribute to *human emancipation and flourishing*; it is *emergent*, in that it is an evolutionary, developmental process which cannot be defined in terms of fixed methods and outcomes; and it strives to develop *practical knowledge* which is useful in everyday life.

It can be argued that the foundation of action research is a participative worldview (Reason and Bradbury 2001). Reason (1998) argues that participation is not merely a 'methodological nicety' about engaging the people who are being researched, but is founded on at least four imperatives:

- the *political imperative* that people have the ability and right to be included in decisions which affect them
- the *epistemological imperative* that tells us there are many different types of evidence and ways of knowing
- the *ecological imperative* that derives from a belief that if we fail to understand our interdependence with our fellow creatures and our environment, we will destroy both, and ourselves and
- the *spiritual imperative* that leads us to recognise the essential community of all humanity.

These imperatives influence the choices that action researchers need to make with regard to their research practices, and which in turn have implications for the quality and validity of their inquiries (Reason and Bradbury 2001).

The Case Study

Editors' note: the case study in this chapter is again somewhat unusual compared with the rest of the book – here the case is a research project; but again a central issue has been carer–practitioner collaboration, coupled with carer leadership of the project.

The project

We, the writers of this chapter, first came together in 2002 at the family work for psychosis service (FWS) office at the Mental Health Research and Development Unit (MHRDU – an R&D unit run jointly between the Avon and Wiltshire Mental Health Partnership NHS

Trust (AWP) and the University of Bath) on the campus of the University of Bath. Our task was to examine current family intervention practice being undertaken within AWP and to discover why this specific intervention appeared to work so well for families where at least one member had a diagnosis of psychosis. The hope was, and still is, that eventually this small research team might develop an evaluation tool that would indicate clearly what worked for families, what did not, and why. Such information would then improve training and services through deepening and broadening the evidence base. As it turned out, the task was bigger than it looked.

The success of the FWS had already been recognised within the NHS. It had been awarded government Beacon site status in 1999 and over the next three years many practitioners and carers came from other areas to discuss how the service had evolved and how they might try to emulate it. In an article published in the *Journal of Mental Health* (Smith and Velleman 2002) the main architects of this service declared that, although families were clearly benefiting, no one was really sure which ingredients made the service so effective. It was this uncertainty that prompted the setting up of a research project within the MHRDU. In line with government initiatives involving carers and users in service development, for example the NSF (Department of Health 1999), and the recommendations of Wooff and colleagues (2003), this research team was to be carer-led, and would be advised by a steering group comprising clinicians and researchers.

The core research team comprised Michael Drage, a carer-researcher; Siobhan Floyd, a researcher with the mental health R&D unit; and Nicola Cocks, an undergraduate placement student with the FWS. Support was provided by Gina Smith (nurse consultant) and Willm Mistral (research manager).

It was originally considered that the evaluation tool would be developed over a one-year period, funded through the AWP small grant scheme, which secured the team a research budget of £5,000. However, we soon accepted that, as there was no existing literature to build on, the project was going to take much longer. Our current vision, which is to extend the research process over a further two-year period while remaining faithful to the original research aims, has been born from a commitment to develop a robust questionnaire, rigorous in its methodological design, able to produce both valid and generalisable data, which will contribute to the evidence base. This reflects both the team's growing confidence in using research skills, and our faith in the working alliance we have established.

The carer-researcher

Having been in this job for nearly two years I now feel in a position to reflect. First walking through a strange university campus, at the age of 66, clutching my old briefcase, was a novel, challenging and disturbing experience. All these very young people breezing through this vast campus space, intent on learning and exploring and romancing and all this noise, colour, idealism and movement, reminded me of my Cambridge days so many years ago. Although so little seemed to have changed, I knew I certainly had: older, slower, sadder, half traumatised, perhaps wiser. Should I really be here? What did I have that apparently made me valuable?

When two of our five children developed schizophrenia (and see chapter 4 for more detail on this), I stopped teaching psychopathology and registered with the Open University for an MSc in psychology. I took every brain module available and did a bit of research methodology; but without a thought that this might lead to future research. I did not really believe then that the trauma my wife and I had barely survived with the help of the FWS was worth very much to anyone else. I now realise that it was the combination of these experiences that had made me a possible candidate to be a carer-researcher. Real research with real people, real practitioners and real traumatised families, in a non-virtual university campus, however, was something else. It felt like a different existence and I was curious as well as slightly frightened. I also knew that I would be a curiosity to the people in the MHRDU and the research team that I was supposed to lead! Self-doubt and false attributions abounded. I nearly walked back home there and then. But, I didn't.

In my view the more puzzling and complex a concept is, the more likely it mirrors the nature of reality. Wittgenstein (1953/1967) once wrote, 'We find certain things about seeing puzzling because we do not find the whole business of seeing puzzling enough' (1953 edition, p. 212). I think, therefore, that it is probably correct to find the concept 'researcher-carer' puzzling, even more perhaps than the concept of an objective researcher. How can a person who is a carer, set out to research carers and their families in any slightly objective, useful way? I now realise that it can be done, provided the approach is deliberately reflexive and open, and provided quite a bit of help is on offer. Given these, the old tensions and apparent conflicts between older positivist, empirical approaches to the social sciences (asserting that facts and values are separate), and more recent approaches which stress the socially constructed nature of reality, the intimate relationship between researcher and researched, the situational constraints that shape inquiry, and its value-laden nature, can be used to advantage. The philosophy and hence the methodology of action research as outlined previously in this chapter capture the essential paradox of the latter type of research rather well. But it is one thing to describe and explain this research as a celebration of human subjectivity, which 'makes no claim to be value free [and] acknowledges the value-laden nature of human research activity' (Morton-Cooper 2000, p. 9) and quite another to practise and fund it collaboratively. I can now give full marks to the MHRDU for being a pioneer in this field.

When I first came to the MHRDU I was not prepared for what was to come. Although I did not tell anyone, I needed ongoing help and reassurance, in particular with the following areas:

- That it really was OK to be me; that I had something to offer, for example, my years as a carer, teacher, husband, father and priest and my academic background in psychology. Of greater relevance perhaps was our family's experience of mental health services, both before family interventions, during intervention and afterwards.
- Comprehensive information about what happens in a university R&D unit and the philosophy of this one in particular, including information about the support and training structures it employs.
- Relevant information about any physical base for me within the MHRDU and information about payment, insurance and expenses.
- Some ongoing guidance through the dense thickets of research governance processes, including help to comprehend research protocols, research governance approval procedures, ethics reviews and funding constraints.

- An understanding of the level of the 'ladder of participation' which other people thought I was on, and the levels they thought I might eventually occupy. In those early days I did not see myself as a lead researcher of the project or even much of a researcher, although I tend to give people the impression that I am more capable than I truly feel! Looking back, there was a need to share assumptions, attributions and expectations.

The above needs were eventually met thanks to the kindness and wisdom of this unit's practitioners under the management of Willm Mistral, and in particular our small team, that I have gradually come to know and appreciate. But the transition period should have been a period of fixed, purposeful and organised conversion to the world of research and to this particular kind of research in this university department. In order for this introductory phase to happen I needed a steering group who understood what they were getting with me! A very few painful and embarrassing moments need not then have taken place. I blame no one. It was new to all. I could and would even argue that the way it *did* happen built the enriching, supportive, collaborative relationships that I now value immensely and that mature daily. However, so much was seemingly left to chance. With another group of people in other circumstances, it could have completely collapsed.

If then, in mental health research, suitable carers of severely mentally ill relatives are to be invited to be collaborative research partners, it is essential that at least three things are done by research and development units:

1 They develop a thorough programme of induction within a fixed transition period. Carers looking after a severely mentally ill relative are very vulnerable people recovering from an agonising trauma peculiarly their own and in many ways are their own worst enemy (Mohr, Lafuze and Mohr 2000).
2 They ensure that the steering group and team not only meets frequently but also fully understands the situation of the invited carer. For most sufferers, schizophrenia does not go away, there are relapses and continuing hospitalisations and this inevitably will have implications for the carer/researcher and their family, for example: mental and physical exhaustion, depression and sudden absences, and thus implications for the research project itself.
3 They provide ongoing one-to-one support with a research/carer mentor. It was this last provision, in the shape of Gina and additionally members of the core research team (Siobhan and Nicola), that saved the days for me when it rained heavily.

Perhaps the best moments in the past two years have been when our small team engaged, set-up, met with, and analysed the deliberations of carer focus groups. In trying to understand and share their stories and their experience of intervention we were helped in understanding and sharing our own stories. At times it was indeed a 'celebration of subjectivity', a place where certain elusive ingredients could be and were found, and there was a real sense of equal expertise, involvement and partnership which still goes on.

The undergraduate student (NC)

I came to the project as a mature undergraduate psychology student on placement with the FWS. At first I felt a little out of my depth. My research experience had been largely theoretical, I was not an expert in family work and had no idea what it was like to be a carer, although I knew a little of Michael's history and had listened to stories from other carers who had used the service. Given the national recognition that the FWS had received, I very much wanted to be involved but was not quite sure what I could contribute. As a result, when I first met Michael I was less than confident about my own knowledge and skills. I was surrounded by people who were experts in their field and I looked to them to take the lead. My age, even though I was approaching the time when life begins again, did not seem to help my confidence – I was the new girl, out of my depth.

Michael, in contrast, struck me as knowledgeable and confident but with the weight of the world on his shoulders and an urgent message to tell. He spoke about his life with a passion and it was impossible to listen without being deeply moved. I found it particularly poignant that someone who had gone through so much and had experienced such trauma was willing to make things better for others rather than just bury his head in the sand. He was an inspiration to us all and I assumed, with his experience of research methods, caring and life experiences, that he would take on the role of lead researcher. To me, a newcomer, the apparently revolutionary idea that a carer should also be a researcher seemed wholly appropriate. Once I understood its novelty and got to know Michael better, I began to appreciate the enormity of his commitment. I also learned how important it is to support fully anyone brave enough to take on this role.

As our relationship grew and the three of us (Michael, Siobhan and myself) became a team, my feelings of self-doubt lessened. I think in the early stages we all felt a little like fish out of water and each of us was looking to the others for guidance. We all had our own areas of expertise but none of us, except perhaps Siobhan who was confident in her research skills, had yet realised where our strengths lay. With support and encouragement I found that I did have something to contribute but that it was different from that of Michael or Siobhan. As we naturally gravitated towards our respective strengths, our roles became more clearly defined. I was able to contribute by becoming the anchor and administrative support for the team by combining my pre-student day administration and life skills with the newly acquired knowledge I had learned at university and on placement. In the end it was our complementary skills that enabled the project to progress. As well as pulling together towards the same goal, we began to understand what that goal meant to each one of us, what our own areas of expertise were and where our vulnerabilities lay. Only when this level of openness was achieved was it possible to achieve true collaboration. It was an extremely rewarding experience.

In retrospect, I've come to understand that building a good relationship between the three of us was key to the success of the project. When a group of people come together with a common goal there is an assumption that this will act as sufficient impetus to bond them as a team. When Michael, Siobhan and I first started working together this was indeed the case and we all worked hard and to the best of our abilities to make the project a success. However, building relationships between people with such disparate backgrounds takes time. It is one thing to organise focus groups and recruit participants to meet timescales, but it is quite another to be able to understand each others' strengths and weaknesses and have the confidence to be open and honest about roles and expectations.

I was very sad to leave the project. We had successfully carried out two focus groups and managed to secure funding for phase 2. I left with a great sense of pride and achievement and felt confident that I had played a valuable part. My final contribution was to transcribe the focus group tapes. It is now two years since I have taken an active role but I am still in contact with both Siobhan and Michael and can appreciate how much their relationship has developed. Finally, I feel I cannot have done too bad a job because the door has always been left open for me to return.

The researcher (SF)

My story starts when I was asked to collaborate on the development of an evaluation tool for the FWS. This ongoing project is distinctive in its concern for the 'carer burden' associated with severe and enduring mental illness, and specifically with the efficacy of FI in reducing the impact of this burden. I was excited by the opportunity, yet I was unsure of my potential role within the small research team. Concepts such as 'consultation', 'supervision' and 'mentor' were offered to describe and help me define this remit but they left me feeling a little intimidated. I certainly did not consider myself an expert in this field, yet I embarked upon the project trusting I would find my place, and with a determination that I would contribute all I had to offer. My involvement and contribution in the research team over these two years has demonstrated how, in real-world research, one's personal as well as professional experience must never be underestimated.

By research team, I refer to the original triad of Michael, Nicola and myself. I arrived a little way into the research, and in other circumstances this may have triggered feelings of intrusion. To the contrary, I was welcomed quite literally with warm and open arms, and I relished the challenging discussions we dived into almost immediately, a forum to both learn and educate. Nicola, who in my eyes held the project together during phase 1, became a dear friend. The research team lost a valued member as Nicola's placement came to an end; we are, however, colleagues again on the MSc in Mental Health Practice course at the University of Bath. Currently Michael and I form the core research team and it is this relationship upon which I hope the following description shines a light.

I have been collaborating with the team in designing, implementing and managing the project. I have brought to the team both generic and specialist skills acquired from three years experience of working in the MHRDU. I have contributed knowledge and experience of using qualitative methodologies, data collection through focus groups, and the analysis of complex data sets using grounded theory (Strauss and Corbin 1990). My understanding of ethical and research governance requirements has been essential, as increasingly high scientific and ethical standards are demanded in all (and especially NHS) research. Involvement in the project has also afforded me the opportunity to develop a number of research skills, working collaboratively on a grant application to fund phase 2, for example. As a research team we have now become confident in seeking guidance and support from outside professionals in the local Research and Development Support Unit (RDSU), in this case for their specialist knowledge of questionnaire design. Early in the process, we felt we needed a certain level of competence to understand these specialists. This assumption has since been challenged by the excellent person-centred service offered by the RDSU, to both novice and experienced researcher alike.

As collaborative partners we have established a working alliance where we are able to make our own individual contribution to the research process. The essence of our shared experience, however, is our inter-relationship. For me the value of this alliance transcends any individual gains, much akin to the Gestalt concept of the unified whole being greater than, or different from, the sum of its parts. This is illustrated in a quote attributed to Fritz Perls, who co-founded Gestalt Therapy with his wife Laura: 'The 'We' doesn't exist, but consists of 'I' *and* 'You', and is an ever-changing boundary where two people meet. And when we meet there, then I change and you change, through the process of encountering each other' (cited by Hycner and Jacobs 1995, p. 7).

I have been transformed (a strong word, but that is often how it feels) through my relationship with Michael in particular. We normally meet every Wednesday from 11 am until 2 pm and I have learned to protect this time, a difficult task in a busy research unit where I am accustomed to responding reactively to work needs. Maintaining this clearly defined boundary is an important aspect of our working alliance, partly because time is precious, and also as a way of showing respect to one another. We have also learned the importance of developing work schedules, and to clarify the tasks we will undertake each session. This has become essential in keeping the project on track, and ensuring a continual reflection on both short-term and long-term goals. Indeed, when I find myself becoming entrenched in the mechanics of the research process, it is Michael who ensures I maintain a vision for what we hope to achieve ultimately.

However, the paradox of our working relationship is that despite a desire to maintain consistent boundaries, flexibility is essential. As a carer, Michael faces demands that have an importance and priority far exceeding the requirements of the project. Our working approach is responsive to the unpredictability of caring responsibilities, and this flexibility ensures the continuity of the research process. On occasions we may choose simply to meet on a different day and time, or work individually on tasks prescribed by our work schedule while keeping in regular telephone contact.

Last year, Michael took a period of leave when he experienced a combination of a family crisis and dissatisfaction with his researcher role. I was concerned for, and missed working with, Michael during this time. I engaged myself in placing the research 'on hold'. The AWP research and development office, which funded this project, was extremely supportive in recognising the resource implications of Michael's unforeseen absence, and was willing to allocate further funds to cover the additional costs incurred to facilitate the completion of phase 1. Thus, in developing a model for good practice in carer-led research, experience teaches us that understanding and flexibility from all levels of the research partnership is integral to developing a successful and rewarding collaboration.

To move forward in a truly equal partnership means learning to make decisions collaboratively, to analyse, to compromise and to synthesise. This has been achieved through rigorous discussion, where all assumptions, beliefs and ideas were respected as valid, yet open to challenge, until a shared understanding was reached. This process enables joint ownership. Thus, through working with Michael, I have broadened and deepened my knowledge, not only about the experience of being a carer, but also as a researcher. Perhaps it is true that one learns best when teaching and supporting another. Sharing my research experience has required that I be methodical in my explanations, breaking down learning into bite-sized pieces and using language that is appropriate. I have found inspiration in working outside the comfort of a researcher discourse.

I have come to believe that it is essential in any carer-researcher collaboration to uphold the three core conditions advocated by the person-centred approach to counselling (Rogers 1957). *Empathy* (understanding from another's own perspective), *unconditional positive regard* (non-judgemental acceptance) and *congruence* (warmth and genuineness) are mutually held values that have allowed the relationship between Michael and I to flourish. These are necessary for the development of a trusting, respectful and open relationship, for growth, and for change. For myself, this brings a sense of being truly valued. Alongside this, the boundaries that have been established, and a commitment to confidentiality, ensure a safe place for us both. As we have learned, however, regularly exploring and monitoring individual expectations within the research team is integral to protecting the well-being of all. Thus the provision of a safe space allows the relationship to develop in the same way that ensuring a supportive and inclusive working environment allows a carer to feel integrated within the wider research team.

As Michael's experiences of being a carer have had a profound impact upon both his identity and character, I hope so will his developing expertise as a carer-researcher. Since Michael's return to the project, our working relationship has recreated itself. His confidence in using research skills has grown and his enthusiasm and willingness to confront the increasing demands of research governance has been of huge support to me. In my eyes Michael has truly embraced the role of lead researcher with commitment and dignity.

The nurse consultant (GS)

Winning the NHS Beacon award in 1999 meant that we had many visitors asking both how we set up the FWS and how we evaluated it. The former question was easy to answer (Smith and Velleman 2002), but the latter always left me feeling that I was making excuses. We did, of course, measure the impact our service had on hospital admissions, and were able to report that in our first year of operation no one that we had worked with had been readmitted to hospital. But others and I have always felt that relapse and hospital admission are far too clumsy as measures of whether or not all family members have benefited from FI. It was this dissatisfaction that led me, with Willm's help, to apply for a small research grant from AWP to try to devise a useful measure.

When applying for the grant it was always my intention to employ a carer with research skills to lead the project. I was delighted when Michael accepted the job and it was only with hindsight that I realised that he doubted that Willm and I really meant that he should take the lead; he appeared so self-assured and knowledgeable. He started in the job soon after Nicola joined the FWS on a year's undergraduate placement. I felt she was ideally placed to help Michael orient himself to the University of Bath and all the facilities it had to offer. I realised later that this had omitted a proper orientation to the MHRDU, which left Michael feeling rather unsure of his position and somewhat unknown as far as other researchers were concerned. His discomfort and his ability to articulate it has ensured that carer-researchers who follow him will receive a proper induction programme!

When Michael felt he needed to take a break from the project, he and I maintained contact with each other through my role as family worker (see chapter 4). It was then that he explained how he had felt unconfident in leading the research, and I was able to apologise for not picking this up sooner. We both acknowledged that he had given the impression that he was more confident than he actually felt and that I had been convinced that his confidence was real; this affirmed for me the importance of avoiding making assumptions, and explicitly checking that each member of the team is secure within their role and responsibilities. This needs to be done with great sensitivity, which I feel I am gathering through feedback from Michael, to help the carer move effectively from being a client in receipt of FI to the role of colleague.

Through this project I am gaining a deeper understanding of how carer-led research demands from me an ability to balance my expectations of Michael as a researcher and my offers of support to him in recognition of his caring responsibilities. We have now learned to discuss the necessary ongoing adjustment of his workload on a regular basis and accept the limitations without question. This means we need an unusual degree of flexibility within the research governance framework and in this respect we have benefited greatly from the support and understanding of AWP's Research Director, Tony Soteriou, who succeeded Richard Velleman when he left the Trust board in 2003; I am sure without this tolerance the project would have foundered months ago. Nevertheless, we have always kept to the required ethical standards and informed the local ethics committee when appropriate. As others have said, our confidence as a collaborative research team is growing and I feel honoured to be part of such an important piece of work.

The research manager (WM)

The MHRDU, at any time, can have 20 or more varied research projects underway. I hold overall responsibility for ensuring that these projects are completed to a high standard, within the time and money available. Initially, to me, this project was just one of many, and a small one at that. When Michael first came to the unit as a carer-researcher, I treated him as I would any other professional researcher. I held assumptions about his sense of competence, his level of confidence and his feelings of comfort in this environment. I came to understand that this was a mistake: he was not, and is not, any other professional researcher. Whatever or whoever he may be in the many and varied aspects of his life, in this context he is first and foremost a carer, and only secondarily a researcher. In these circumstances I found that the research environment needed to foster a culture of inquiry into its own processes, as well as to maintain a focus on the research project itself. I believe that this engendered almost a therapeutic community for all involved (Mistral, Hall and McKee 2002), facilitating self-discovery, learning, caring, collaboration and a democratic, de-institutionalised approach to research.

I came to learn, however, that when researchers and carers work together in this way, more time has to be allowed than when working in an exclusively professional situation:

time for induction, for training, for discussion, for recovery from misunderstandings and for caring! And increasing the time spent on one project means decreasing the time spent on another. As a manager I continue to find this problematic as the research team has to operate within clearly defined resources and deadlines. There is no simple solution to this problem, but I believe that where the political, epistemological, ecological and spiritual imperatives outlined above (Reason 1998) are accepted as being at least as important as timetables and balance sheets, solutions can be found. Not only can solutions be found but also research can become more useful, more meaningful and more humane.

Conclusion

This research process has been a journey of learning for all involved. A brief summary of the conclusions we have reached (so far) on this learning journey are that carers are needed in research but, on the other hand, not all carers, even if suitably academically qualified, should attempt this kind of activity. The horrible times are relived and an adequate support network is essential.

It is also the case that many researchers do not really understand the particular agony of looking after and looking at a much loved relative with severe mental health problems. Those without this understanding need help to develop the attitudes and skills which would allow them to acknowledge and value the carers' experiences, while protecting themselves from becoming overwhelmed by it.

It is also important to recognise and respect the difficulties that co-workers might experience when first faced with the prospect of equal collaboration with each other. All members of the team (carer-researcher, research worker, research manager, etc.) may find it equally difficult to accept equality, albeit for possibly different reasons.

Induction of the carer into research processes and to working in the professional research environment is essential. An induction pack, an individual post tray, access to computer, information about accessing library and database facilities and an individual mentor are all needed. Similarly, integration into the wider research group is equally essential – introductions at researcher's meeting and invitations to team social events.

It is not all about 'official' things: the evolving inter-relationships among people that occur during the research process should be valued. In fact, what we have really discovered is that the process of this kind of research is equally important as (or perhaps even more than) the outcome of an evaluation tool. The first usually gives birth to the second and therefore has to be of first-order quality.

Our final conclusion is that it is difficult, but it is worth it!

References

Arnstein, S. (1969) A ladder of citizen participation. *American Institute of Planning Journal*, July, 216–24.

Carrick, R., Mitchell, A. and Lloyd, K. (2001) User involvement in research: power and compromise. *Journal of Community and Applied Social Psychology*, 11, 217–25.

Baulcombe, S., Edwards, S., Hostick, T., New, A. and Pugh, H. (2000) *Asking the Experts: A Guide to Involving People in Shaping Health and Social Care Services*. Grimsby, northeast Lincolnshire,

UK: The Community Care Needs Assessment Project (CCNAP). Available online: www.rsmh.se/vardagsmakt/askingtheexperts.pdf (accessed 30 December 2005).

Department of Health (1999) *The National Service Framework for Mental Health: Modern Standards and Service Models*. HMSO: London.

Department of Health (2000) *The NHS Plan: A Plan for Investment, a Plan for Reform*. HMSO: London.

Hycner, R. and Jacobs, L. (1995) *The Healing Relationship in Gestalt Therapy*. New York: The Gestalt Journal Press.

Kuhn, T.L. (1962) *The Structure of Scientific Revolutions*. Chicago: University of Chicago Press.

Mistral, W., Hall, A. and McKee, P. (2002) Using therapeutic community principles to improve the functioning of a high care psychiatric ward in the UK. *International Journal of Mental Health Nursing*, 11, 10–17.

Mohr, W., Lafuze, J. and Mohr, B. (2000) Opening caregivers minds: National Alliance for the Mentally Ill's provider education programme. *Archives of Psychiatric Nursing*, 14, 235–43.

Morton-Cooper, A. (2000) *Action Research in Health Care*. Oxford: Blackwell Science.

Parker, I. (1994) Reflexive research and the grounding of analysis – social psychology and the psy-complex. *Journal of Community and Applied Social Psychology*, 4, 239–52.

Peck, E., Gulliver, P. and Towel, D. (2001) Information, consultation or control: user involvement in mental health services in England at the turn of the century. *Journal of Mental Health*, 11, 441–51.

Rappaport, J. (1994) Community psychology and politics – commentary. *Journal of Community and Applied Social Psychology*, 4, 15–20.

Reason, P. (1998) Political, epistemological, ecological and spiritual dimensions of participation. *Studies in Cultures, Organizations and Societies*, 4, 147–67.

Reason, P. and Bradbury, H. (2001) *Handbook of Action Research: Participative Inquiry and Practice*. London: Sage.

Rogers, C. (1957) The necessary and sufficient conditions of therapeutic personality change. *Journal of Consulting and Clinical Psychology*, 21, 95–103.

Sackett, D., Rosenberg, W., Muir Gray, J., Haynes, R. and Richardson, W. (1996) Evidence-based medicine: what it is and what it isn't. *British Medical Journal*, 312, 71–2.

Smith, G. and Velleman, R. (2002) Maintaining a family work for psychosis service by recognising and addressing the barriers to implementation. *Journal of Mental Health*, 11, 471–9.

Stewart, R. and Bhagwanjee, A. (1999) Promoting group empowerment and self-reliance through participatory research: a case study of people with physical disability. *Disability and Rehabilitation*, 21, 338–45.

Strauss, A. and Corbin, J. (1990). *Basics of Qualitative Research: Grounded Theory Procedures and Techniques*. Thousand Oaks: Sage Publications.

The NHS and Community Care Act (1990) London: HMSO.

The Patients' Charter (1992) London: HMSO.

Wilcox, D. (1994) *Participation Guide*. Brighton: Partnership Books.

Wittgenstein, L. (1953/1967) *Philosophical Investigations*. Oxford: Blackwell.

Wooff, D., Schneider, J., Carpenter, J., Brandon, T. and Schneider, J. (2003) Correlates of stress in carers. *Journal of Mental Health*, 12, 29–40.

Chapter 14

Changing Practice

Gina Smith, Michael Drage, Eric Davis and Richard Velleman

Key Points

- This book has shown, through detailed case descriptions, that psychosocial interventions can and do work in practice.
- The chapters have also demonstrated the fact that a unique, personal recovery approach is both highly effective and within the reach of every person who suffers from mental disorder, or who suffers owing to a relative's disorder.
- Other key themes in this book have been the importance of the social context to people's lives; the taking of an holistic perspective; practitioners being active; the integration of new ideas into existing frameworks and structures; the therapeutic ideas of stress-vulnerability and early warning signs work; the importance of motivational interviewing, relapse management and other cognitive behaviour therapy (CBT) ideas; and the needs for independent housing, developing a larger social network, work/meaningful occupation, sorting out finance/benefits and medication management; and the importance of integrated working – between teams, between practitioners, and between these and users and carers, which requires training and both middle *and* senior management involvement and support.
- There is a bias towards publishing evidence-based practice (EBP) and against practice-based evidence (PBE); and yet basing practice purely on quantitative research is self-limiting. Case studies and qualitative work are needed to develop PBE.
- Practitioners learn most from seeing what works in practice and developing their skills so that they can replicate such good practice.
- Personal stories (case studies) are also key to breaking down the stigma associated with mental disorder.
- Government policy demands that service providers work collaboratively with service users. Every chapter in this book has been a demonstration of such successful collaborative working.
- Professionals need to be willing to operate beyond their professional boundaries in order to promote recovery. Learning and change are possible when we work effectively together.
- Mental health recovery is not only about effective therapies; it is also about the importance of the social context (families, relationships, friendships, employment, leisure and meaningful activity) in people's lives.
- This book does not cover everything: a second volume of collaborative case studies may emerge which will address some of the remaining areas.

Gina Smith, Michael Drage, Eric Davis and Richard Velleman

Looking Back

When the idea to write this book was conceived, it was our intention to write about a broad range of experiences which would demonstrate psychosocial interventions (PSI) in practice. We wanted to do this to help others learn from our experiences of putting policy into practice, sharing the lessons we had learned. Two years on we are in a position to look back and reflect on how well we achieved our aim.

Our major reflection is that the book has done what it set out to do. Each chapter has demonstrated the workings of PSI in practice. Each chapter has been the result of a close working collaboration between practitioners, and either service users or carers, and sometimes both. These chapters demonstrate well that the various policy documents emanating from 'on high' which outline both the need for more PSI work, and the importance of partnership working between the users of services and the providers of these services, can be translated into effective practice. Providing better quality services and implementing policy into effective and routine clinical practice, does not have to be a vague dream: these 12 chapters of real case studies (chapters 2 to 13, book-ended as they are by an introduction and this summing up by us as editors) demonstrate reality.

On the other hand (and with the benefit of hindsight), it is now possible to see how ambitious this project was. That does not mean it has not been an enriching process for the authors: it has been striking how co-writing the chapters has deepened and strengthened the links and friendships between the practitioners and the service users or carers who have collaborated so well on them (and some of them, e.g. in chapter 10, have written about the process of collaborating). Even so, to write collaboratively, to gather all sides of a story into one coherent whole, was far more time-consuming than we anticipated, both for each chapter's authors and for ourselves as editors.

It was not simply a question of time, of course. Writing about mental health problems with people who have these problems provided its own challenges. For example, one chapter which was planned for this book concerned using PSI with paranoia. However, the service user working with us on that chapter (who suffered with paranoia – that was why he was going to co-author the chapter) regrettably relapsed and his paranoia increased, so he decided that he did not wish to proceed. Another planned chapter was on the importance of involving users of services in training mental health personnel: this also had to be postponed because of mental health difficulties for both a staff member and service user collaborating on this work. This underscores the variability of outcomes associated with psychosis, although we would hope that the service users in question might wish to work with us again in the future, health circumstances permitting. In other cases the outcomes for this book were better: some other service users relapsed during the writing of their chapters, and they and their co-authors needed to wait until they felt able to continue before completing their work.

Co-writing between users and providers of services throws up challenges other than relapse. Writing such material requires levels of openness and clarity, and of trust, between the writers, all of which are hoped to exist in good therapeutic relationships, but which are often not there at this hoped-for level, where power relationships between practitioners and their 'patients' often get in the way. The chapters in this book demonstrate extremely strong therapeutic relationships, and ones where trust and openness is shared in both directions.

Emerging Themes

Looking back over the work described in these chapters, which reflect the input of 37 disparate and varied authors, we see one major common theme emerging. This is the *therapeutic and optimistic belief* that a unique, personal recovery approach is within the reach and power of every person who either suffers from mental disorder, or who is a family member of such a person. These chapters demonstrate that this healing pathway is most attainable when *all care stakeholders (users, carers, practitioners) work closely together, as equals, over time.* In this way every salient interconnection is then employed. Such a belief is demonstrated at work in practical terms in every chapter but especially so in chapters 2, 3, 4, 11, 12 and 13.

Chapters 6, 7, 10 and 13, though their subject matter is diverse, all reflect an important commonality: comparatively, all four have had to grapple with what could be called 'the professional closed-shop' syndrome, with varying degrees of frustration and success. Here again, the reluctance to use all available interconnections, echoes the parable of the farmer and the village described later. If outcomes in psychosis are to be changed beneficially, then the relevant professional and scientific closed supermarkets, along with the media ones, have got to be brought to significant change.

Other key themes in this book have been:

- The importance of the *social context* to people's lives. This came out extremely strongly in the chapters where both users and carers spoke about their interacting lives (e.g. chapters 4 and 5, and also in the chapters where either service users or carers described the impact on family life (e.g. chapters 2 and 3); but it was also strongly demonstrated in the chapter on sport and exercise (10) and especially in chapter 11, describing the importance of employment and meaningful activity, and the lack of help in retaining it, that so many users experienced in the past.
- An *holistic perspective:* although it is excellent to have vocational rehabilitation services, or AO or FI services, in reality they do not work optimally on their own. People need person-centred services, where help is offered in an *integrated* way *according to need.* People do not need services based on organisational constraints or theoretical ideas which take on a life of their own and which are not responsive to and creative with respect to people's needs.
- *Practitioners being active:* many chapters describe the powerful impact that practitioners can have when they *act,* as well as listen or talk: in chapter 5 for example, an ECS support worker would regularly provide John with transport to and from his supported employment and would sometimes have lunch with him; in chapter 7, Vicky actively intervened with Megan, providing toys from her attic, and intercepting Megan on her way to the river; and there are many other examples.
- *Integration of new ideas* into existing frameworks and structures. As but one example, chapter 8 showed that the integration of the Rainy Day plan into both the CPA documentation and relapse prevention planning procedures, led to improved efficacy and perceptions of its usefulness.
- A number of *therapeutic ideas* have run through most of the chapters: these include the stress-vulnerability models (Zubin and Spring 1977; Nuechterlein 1987), early warning

signs work, the importance of motivational interviewing, relapse management and other CBT ideas; and a wide range of non-CBT ones such as the needs for independent housing, developing a larger social network, work/meaningful occupation, sorting out finance/benefits and medication management.
- Finally, all the chapters have supported *integrated working* – between teams, between practitioners, and between these and users and carers. Also, these chapters have shown that integrated working requires (and therefore has large implications for) training, middle management and senior management involvement and support. The utility of having 'project champions' has also been reinforced throughout as a way of ensuring that all these integration issues are taken forward. It is vital, though, that the project champion is of sufficient status and is sufficiently competent to impact on services and organisations at the required levels (Smith and Velleman 2002).

Evidence-based Practice and Practice-based Evidence

The *National Service Framework for Mental Health* (NSF) (Department of Health 1999a) synthesised the available research evidence to guide its evidence-based clinical framework. EBP means that one's practice should be guided by the use of the best available evidence. The logic is that evidence is generated from research trials and that practitioners need to look at these trials and at the evidence produced, and alter their practice accordingly, so that they work in ways which have been shown by research to be effective. Similarly, policy-makers should set policy direction on the basis of the best evidence of 'what works'. We say more about EBP below, before contrasting it with Practice-based Evidence (PBE): evidence which is drawn from practice; findings that come from the direct experiences of service users, carers and practitioners.

EBP uses a hierarchy of evidence:

- *Type I evidence* – at least one good systematic review, including at least one randomised controlled trial (RCT).
- *Type II evidence* – at least one good RCT.
- *Type III evidence* – at least one well designed intervention study without randomisation.
- *Type IV evidence* – at least one well designed observational study.
- *Type V evidence* – expert opinion, including the opinion of service users and carers.

EBP also states that some types of evidence are 'worth more' than other types: the closer the research findings are to Type I evidence, the more weight they are accorded in subsequent decision-making by policy-makers. Thus meta-analyses or systematic reviews of various approaches would be expected to influence strongly those charged with policy-making, resource allocation and service development.

While there is undoubtedly merit in pursuing such a systematic approach with its in-built appraisal of available evidence, it is not without drawbacks. These include:

- The final recommendations or conclusions of any meta-analysis are dependent upon the quality or otherwise of the research trials upon which it is based. The pooling of poor

Type II trials (and many of these do get published) could lead to poor practice and service recommendations.

- Unconscious experimenter bias can confound and weaken Type I and Type II evidence. Adequate randomisation and counterbalancing of research studies may not be achieved. There may be difficulties around blinding and drop out: in RCTs 'double blind' means that both experimenters and participants ought not to know who is receiving what treatment. In trials of new drugs, this is relatively easy: the experimental drug and the control (placebo or inert) drug can be made to look identical. But in psychological and social studies such 'blindness' is exceptionally difficult to achieve. (It is extremely difficult to get a 'control' psychological intervention to look similar to the 'experimental' psychological intervention: if it looks similar enough, it then *becomes* the experimental treatment!) This, in turn, has implications owing to the importance of expectancy effects in psychological research: people who provide or receive the 'experimental' intervention may have greater expectations that it will work; and those providing or receiving the 'control' condition may be more likely to drop out of treatment. In fact, drop-out rates are often extremely large: if a RCT begins with 100 participants, but 70 drop out (as sometimes happens), it could be suggested that the remaining 30 participants are not sufficiently representative to enable sound conclusions to be derived from the research – yet such studies are still published and entered into Type I reviews.
- As well as methodological limitations, there are also limitations stemming from the nature of statistical analysis. Research findings are not either 'proved' or 'disproved': they are always linked to the probability of any result being a 'chance' finding; and sometimes this leads to errors. So sometimes researchers and readers will consider that a result actually *was* due to the impact of whatever it was that was being studied, when in reality the effect was simply a random or chance one; and, in other cases, an effect will be considered to be the result of chance variation when in reality it actually *is* due to the impact of whatever it is that is being studied.
- There are also publication biases: it is much easier to get research published if large numbers of participants are involved, or if the results are highly 'statistically significant', even if the results have a low potential for clinical applicability; whereas research which may demonstrate effects which are clinically important but which have only statistically modest results may remain unpublished. It is also much easier to get research published if they report 'unexpected' results; whereas research which demonstrates that current practice works well may not get published, precisely because it is not exceptional.
- The bias towards Type I and II research, towards tightly controlled RCTs, also pushes researchers into studying simpler problems (i.e. ones that can be more tightly controlled). It is far easier to study the effect of a new drug, or the effect of a contained and specific PSI, than it is to study much broader but potentially much more important areas such as the role of employment, sport or gender and their influence upon mental health outcome. This bias means that much more RCT-type research is funded, undertaken and published in these 'simpler' areas; correspondingly, when research is reviewed, policy formulated or new practice introduced on the basis of RCT-type evidence, there is far less work related to these vital social-context areas.
- There are further difficulties for Type I and Type II evidence because of the way that

psychosis is conceptualised in this type of research. For example, schizophrenia in this type of research is often regarded by researchers as an entity: someone either has or does not have schizophrenia, and the research looks at the impact that a drug or a PSI has on their schizophrenia. However, as was discussed in chapter 1, there are many cogent criticisms which have been made about fundamental issues of reliability and validity associated with the aetiology, diagnosis and prognosis connected to schizophrenia (see Bentall 2003 for a fuller discussion). Instead, a symptoms-based approach to research is suggested, combined with attempts to understand the underlying meaning of psychosis.
- Most research is undertaken by research teams who are highly focused, well-resourced and keenly interested in the area that they are researching and trained to a high degree in terms of practitioner ability. EBP suggests that research findings should translate into changed clinician practices and hence into more effective practitioners. But expecting research automatically to translate into clinical effectiveness in real-world clinical settings is unduly optimistic: as much effort needs to be devoted to the dissemination and implementation of research findings as to the original research itself. It involves considerable investment in practitioner training, service development and management support; even then, it is not clear whether the results obtained from highly enthusiastic research practitioners will always translate into changed practice from stressed, tired, overworked and sometimes 'burnt-out' workers.

In certain respects, Type III, IV and V evidence suffers from converse criticism associated with Type I and II evidence. Such research may be viewed as offering more descriptive rather than exploratory findings. It cannot say how effective one treatment is compared to another and it is less sophisticated in that experimental variables cannot be manipulated with the degree of specificity achieved by RCTs. However, precisely because of much of the nature of Type III, IV and V research (for example, single-case studies, observational studies and expert opinion) the clinical applicability of such findings can appear easier to see. Also, this type of research can benefit from research questions derived and analysed from a qualitative perspective. Unlike RCTs, this research can unearth themes or topics that may connect to user and carer experience in a more direct way than more quantitative research can appear to manage.

Our view is that this 'hierarchy of research' is associated with inherent difficulties. We think that there are great merits to quantitative RCT-type research. But we think that there are equal merits associated with findings that come from the direct experiences of service users, carers and practitioners. This is PBE: evidence which is drawn from practice.

Our view is that, certainly, practice should learn from quantitative research evidence: the idea of EBP is an excellent one. But equally, we believe that practice should learn from other practice (i.e. from case and observational studies); and also that PBE ought to inform EBP. New research questions are often developed at Type V, IV and III levels, which may go on to inform larger research studies. They may begin (and continue) in qualitative fashion, but be expanded also into a quantitative domain which could lead to new RCTs. Clinicians, users and carers may generate new research ideas, with high real-world relevance at Type III, IV and V levels.

There is an associated issue (which is further explored in chapter 13) of who sets the research agenda. The implicit assumption has been that it is the province of trained professionals. Our view is that users and carers, who could be said to be 'experts-by-experience' (Department of Health 2001a), should be able to influence the research agenda; and indeed, that their ideas and insights are vital to ensure that research produces relevant and appropriate findings. Indeed, effectiveness is not the only area which should be being examined: research and evaluation needs to get users and carers to express their satisfaction or not with the type of service that they are receiving. There are some avenues for this to occur: Type V evidence includes 'expert opinion' from users and carers as well as professionals, and Type IV case-study material (such as that presented in the chapters in this book) can also contribute to setting the research agenda. Hence research and evaluation could continue to include more traditional questions such as the effects of medication upon symptoms; but it could also include an examination of wider influences, such as the role of employment or sport and their impact upon mental health outcomes.

Crawford and colleagues (2003) and Perkins and Repper (1998) both suggest that user involvement is important in service audit, evaluation and research. Perkins and Repper argue for user expertise in defining relevant service goals and suggest appropriate measurement methods. Crawford and colleagues too emphasise user-derived goals and subsequent measurement. They also examine a range of factors that help and hinder this process. Helpful factors for user involvement include:

- managerial support
- national policies supporting user involvement
- user groups possessing the required skills and expertise
- the project is clearly conceived
- service users considering the project a priority
- jargon is avoided during discussions.

Obstacles to user involvement include:

- trust concerns that users are not representative
- trust staff resistant to involving services users
- current legislative framework limiting the role of user involvement
- too few users involved
- staff not trained on what meaningful involvement requires
- trust mergers reducing the influence of user groups.

Gathering Practice-based Evidence

Frank Burbach and the Carter family note in chapter 5 that FI and AO are rarely offered together. This does not reflect the experience of work in the Avon and Wiltshire Trust (AWP). However, what is the case is that these workers within AWP have failed to write about it. Work which is not written up, no matter how innovative it is, cannot appear in a literature search, which makes it effectively invisible to everyone beyond those with whom these service providers have personal contact. This serves as a useful example of the need for people in touch with mental health services, including academics, to be prepared to notice innovative practice and encourage its publication.

Traditionally, clinical psychologists have taken a 'scientist-practitioner' or 'research-practitioner' role within which they have developed EBP (Orford 1992), although some medical practitioners are also very obviously research-active. Community psychology is changing this agenda (Nelson and Prilleltensky 2005) and challenging researchers, not just to create new knowledge but also to 'change social conditions' (p. 6).

Within this challenge the researcher-practitioner role is being extended. This includes graduate mental health workers (Department of Health 2000) who may carry out research; and nurse consultants (Department of Health 1999b) who have research responsibilities (as well as teaching, leadership and clinical practice) firmly established within their job descriptions.

Two chapters within this book demonstrate the value of a mental health trust (in this case Avon and Wiltshire Partnership NHS Trust) investing in a Mental Health Research and Development Unit (MHRDU). Chapter 4 describes FI that would not have been available to the Drage family had the Trust not invested in a development project to learn how to get FI into routine practice. Similarly, it is unlikely that the action research project described in chapter 13 would have ever begun without the manager of the MHRDU being available as a resource to local mental health practitioners.

Challenging Stigma and Reducing Discrimination

Getting to know individuals who have experienced serious mental health problems is a very effective way of reducing the stigma associated with mental disorders (Penn et al. 1994). Yet many people are fearful of letting it be known that they have a diagnosis of schizophrenia or bipolar disorder (personal communication between service users and each of the editors). Sadly, this fear has been reflected by some of the authors of this book, with a number of the service users or carers choosing to remain anonymous rather than risk the impact that open acknowledgement could have on future ambitions for themselves or other family members.

However, there is growing evidence that more people in high profile positions are willing to reveal their personal experiences of mental disorder. For example, Alistair Campbell (while in post as the prime minister's Director of Communication and Strategy) wrote:

> It was a 24-carat crack up and I'm proud of the fact that I got through it, rebuilt myself, did OK as a journalist and went on to do what I do now ... being tough-minded, focussed, mentally and physically fit. I feel the breakdown and the recovery played a big part in all that.
>
> (*Sunday Times Magazine* 2002)

Other examples include Dr Mike Shooter, president of the UK Royal College of Psychiatrists, who has spoken publicly about his recurrent depression, which he has experienced for the past 30 years (Meriden 2005, p. 11); the Nobel prize-winning economist John Forbes Nash Jr (schizophrenia); actress Patty Duke (bipolar disorder); writers Kay Redfield Jamison, PhD (bipolar disorder), Art Buchwald (depression) and William Styron (depression);

sports personalities such as Dame Kelly Holmes (self-harm) and such public figures as Tipper Gore (depression) and Kitty Dukakis (depression, substance misuse).

Allott and Loganathan (2003) argue that Kraepelin's view of schizophrenia (put forward over a century ago) as an illness with an inevitable poor prognosis was responsible for the persistent negative perceptions and ongoing stigma associated with mental disorders. We hope that it will not take another hundred years for the knowledge that recovery is possible to dissipate this stigma fully. Indeed, we are hopeful that a changed culture with regard to an open acceptance of mental disorders will be noticeable if there is a second volume of case studies, in that fewer or no authors will feel the need to adopt a pseudonym.

How quickly the public perception of schizophrenia will change remains to be seen, but in the light of EBP there is no excuse for workers to operate a 'mental health system in which negative beliefs and attitudes provide little or no hope of recovery' (Allott and Loganathan 2003, p. 2). In this review of the recovery literature there is a central theme, the necessary interconnectedness between services users, workers and the wider community, the importance of another person who can convey hope. It appears that when professionals populate this hope-inspiring position they take on more than is required of them by their professional role: 'They break the rules to form a reciprocal relationship' (p. 10).

This description fits the way many of this book's authors have described their experience of writing their chapter(s). The open reflection between service users and workers that the collaborations have demanded would (or could), in the past, have been judged as unboundaried poor professional practice. Within a recovery philosophy it is acceptable to break the rules in order to allow mental health workers to show their feelings.

Collaborative Working

Barriers to collaboration

> Once upon a time there was a farmer who owned a small arable farm of about a hundred acres; it was very close to a village. The farmer was a newcomer to the area. For a number of undiscovered reasons he became obsessive about protecting the boundaries of the farm: previously permitted footpaths were closed, new high barbed fences (some electrified) appeared round the perimeter and 'Keep out – no entry' signs warned the public not to cross onto his land. Numerous closed circuit TV cameras were strategically placed on high trees and the farmyard itself was guarded by three fierce-looking dogs.
>
> The farmer had a pretty wife and three school-aged children. It was noted that the family went everywhere by four-track vehicle and never shopped in the village nor used the village school. It was rumoured around the village that there was something mentally wrong with the farmer and with one of his daughters, but nobody knew for sure.
>
> Anyway, as a result of this exercise of power the farmer succeeded in keeping people away from his farm and also in creating many strangers. As he always refused to take any advice his crops did not amount to much and the few livestock he had did not live very long.
>
> It was seen one morning that all the family drove away leaving their three dogs in

> the yard behind very large locked gates. That same night the farmhouse and barns caught fire and were burnt to the ground for no one could get in; all three dogs perished in the fire. The family never returned.
>
> On the night following the fire, a villager in the local pub referred to the fire and was heard to say, 'What a tragedy; if only they'd realised how interconnected they really were!'
>
> This story/parable appears pertinent to the present task of drawing together what we have learned and what we would now like to share; like most parables, the sad tale of this farmer and his family lies very close to a real event. While the detail of the parable will mean different things to different people, the main message or moral of the story, and this book, is hopefully very clear and it is this: when we allow barriers or boundaries based upon prejudice, false attribution and fear into the human condition, the result is always the impoverishment of that same condition. The farmer and his family were not solely to blame for what happened; equally the community around that farm must share part of the responsibility for the tragedy that ensued.

Within any mental health service, as in any human activity, there are abundant opportunities for unhelpful boundaries and barriers to emerge (Hannigan 1999) in the form of varying texts, classifications, institutions, contested spaces, policies and discourses; strangers are created, imprisoned and disempowered (Sayer 1992). But equally, there are opportunities to rethink 'circuits of knowledge' (Smith 1998, p. 310), to co-operate, to consult, to interconnect, to involve and to empower and recover; unhelpful barriers can be dissipated, unhelpful boundaries need not be drawn (Smith and Velleman 2002).

One major obstacle in the provision of mental health services today is the reluctance of the many disciplines involved, to share resources and expertise more fully, both inter-professionally and with the people in their care. Owing to our professional and natural conditioning, sharing to this extent is hard, especially in mental health where the perceived stigma, risk count and issues of confidentiality are both complex and high. New initiatives are now inviting professionals to experience collaborative working (Douglas and Machin 2004) so that recent UK government policies can be implemented (Arksey 2003).

Policy that Promotes Collaboration

The thrust of government policy over the past few years has been towards increasing consumer choice (www.mhchoice.org.uk), with the concept of choice applied across the whole range of mental health services. It is recognised, however, that the choices for mental health service users are likely to embrace rather different domains from those opted for by those requiring physical health care. This is usefully captured by the suggestion that, for those with a physical health problem, *where* and *when* the treatment is provided are likely to be the most important considerations, whereas mental health service users and their carers are likely to be more concerned by *what* and *how*.

That choice adds value is the philosophy underpinning this policy initiative. To achieve this aim it is recommended that mental health services consider themselves within two broad categories: those that are *relieving* in their purpose and those that are *enabling*:

- Those in need of relieving services may have lost capacity to make immediate choices or be so acutely unwell, that choice may be overwhelming. In such cases, adhering to an advance directive (or Rainy Day care plan like the ones described in chapter 8) will ensure that the service user's predetermined choices are embraced.
- An example of an enabling service is the hearing voices group described in chapter 9, facilitating social inclusion, reducing stigma and promoting recovery. Chapters 10 and 11, focusing on sport/exercise and employment, also fit this category.

Almost certainly, the collaborative relationships described throughout this book are enabling in themselves. However, most services, and indeed most of our case studies, will embrace elements intended both to relieve mental distress and to enable improved functioning and satisfaction with life.

Service Choice and Consumerism

An extension of the argument for greater service user involvement therefore lies in giving users (or 'consumers' or 'customers') greater choice. Sir Terry Leahy (2005), chief executive of Tesco, argues that it is the *lack* of choice facing users of NHS services (including mental health) that can potentially compromise the quality of services that are delivered. He acknowledges critical differences between the private and public sector. For example, unlike the NHS, Tesco does not have to deal with 'command and control' strictures issued by ministers from the Department of Health or with massive NHS organisational change imposed on a comparatively frequent basis, or with measurements of service activity that can distort real-world clinical priorities. Further important differences are that users or consumers often cannot easily 'shop around' for mental health services, because of the difficulty of obtaining good-quality information about different mental health services; or, because of referral patterns which are inflexible and occur because of system(ic) rigidity. A trickier difficulty, of course, arises when the consumer cannot make a valid choice because of mental ill-health or disorder (and may even need to be sectioned). But, even in this instance, mental health services would need to work as effectively as possible to promote recovery.

As Debbie Furniss and Eric Davis write in chapter 12, the changing face of the organisational environment for the NHS may allow for more future valid consumer choice including mental health services. With the advent of mental health foundation trusts being promised in the next few years (e.g. Gloucestershire and a handful of others) greater economic liberation from centralised government will happen. Foundation trusts therefore should be able to exercise greater control over expenditure and their core business, so the advent of better consumer choice is, in theory, made more practicable. Payment by results (PBR) is supposed to be in place by 2008. PBR is probably more accurately conceptualised as payment by activity (PBA), because it is the throughput, of (e.g.) bed occupancy of wards, that will determine the level of finance available to the newer mental health foundation trusts. Potentially, service benefits to 'customers' will accrue if commissioners (currently Primary Care Trusts) are clearer about what services are being delivered (e.g. by foundation trusts), and to what level of service specification – thereby ensuring assurance of quality. However, there are also some threats: certain mental health services may be seen as less attractive or difficult-to-commercialise, so that certain clinical services could end up receiving levels of investment that would call into question their viability. 'Better' services may attract more 'customers', with the implication being that other poorly performing services might even struggle to survive.

Politically, this would cause difficulty if certain areas and/or clinical functions could not offer *any kind* of service and presumably would be deemed unacceptable. A further difficulty has arisen for certain trusts who have built new facilities in partnership with the private sector (private finance initiatives) and then been unable to meet repayments specified in financial contracts. However, these potential threats may have been resolved (for mental health trusts) by 2008 when PBR is scheduled to commence, as this proposed mechanism currently lies in its infancy.

Ensuring Staff Are Well Trained

Since its publication of the NSF (Department of Health 1999a) and *The NHS Plan* (Department of Health 2000), the government has commissioned work to explore the abilities of the mental health workforce to deliver modern services that can offer service users the promised choices (Department of Health 2004). What has been developed is a list of the 'capabilities required to achieve best practice for education and training of all staff who work in mental health services' (p. 1). These capabilities are exemplified in this book:

- *Working in partnership* – this encourages workers to develop and maintain constructive relationships with service users and their families, as well as with their colleagues and the wider community. This forms the core of collaborative working and is thereby embraced by all chapters.
- *Respecting diversity* – through the writing of this book, all authors have demonstrated their respect for a range of diverse views and opinions. This capability will be more overtly covered in our proposed second volume (see below), by case studies that will demonstrate practice that explicitly takes into account culture, race, disability, age, gender (one aspect of which is covered in chapter 7), sexuality and spirituality.
- *Practising ethically* – recognises the power differentials and strives to minimise them wherever possible. All chapters have been written with this value in mind.
- *Challenging inequality* – almost all the chapters have addressed the consequences of stigma. An acknowledgement that a major cause of stigma is related to a lack of personal connection to someone experiencing a mental health problem was part of the impetus to write this book. We now feel that the case studies speak for themselves.
- *Promoting recovery* – tackling mental health issues with optimism and promoting hopefulness is a central philosophy of this book. There is an understanding that recovery is not about being cured, but rather of self-determination and empowerment.
- *Identifying people's needs and strengths* – this is closely related to working in partnership; it has a particular focus on helping individuals to recognise not just their problems and needs, but also their strengths and how these can be employed to best effect. Chapters 8 and 13 demonstrate this well.
- *Providing service user centred care* – this involves clear communication to negotiate mean-

ingful goals for service users and their families. All chapters provide examples of this in action.

- *Making a difference* – this is closely related in this instance to 'challenging inequality'. All contributors to all chapters will be able to celebrate having achieved this capability!
- *Promoting positive risk-taking* – this involves empowering service users and their families to decide for themselves the level of risk they are prepared to accept. Openly acknowledging the value of taking a risk was central to the work described in chapter 4.
- *Valuing personal development and learning* – this entire book is about the value of personal development and the promotion of learning, both in its creation and as a resource for others.

Looking Forward

Although this book covers many areas, there were omissions, and these have led us to begin to think about writing and editing a second volume of such collaborative case studies. What would such a second volume contain?

There are, of course, the two chapters mentioned at the start of this chapter, on working with *paranoia*, and on *training*, which we had originally planned to include. We had also originally wished to have a chapter on *medication management*. But there are also other areas we would like to see written about in a similar way to this first volume. These areas include:

- contributions from *black or minority ethnic* service users or carers: we know that PSI is effective with populations from many countries and cultures – for example, family intervention (FI) has been found to be equally effective worldwide (Pitschel-Walz et al. 2001); and similar findings have been found for other interventions such as assertive outreach (AO)).
- case studies from *child and adolescent* mental health services, *learning disability* services, services for *older adults*, and *forensic* mental health. In these areas the RCT-related evidence for PSI is less clear, so recording individual's experiences is vital in order to begin to build a body of literature on which to base practice. We hope that this book will inspire practitioners working in these services to contribute to the process.
- cases focused on the role of *spirituality* within recovery from psychosis. 'Lauren' in chapter 6 specifically mentions the importance of her faith and spiritual beliefs in helping to promote her recovery from psychosis. Deegan (1988) who we cite in chapter 1 also alludes to the importance of a spiritual dimension as being of clear psychological importance in terms of her recovery. Related to this, it would be good to have cases relating to *sexual and relationship issues, including sexuality* within recovery in a second volume.
- case studies where people have both psychosis and a substance misuse problem. Such *co-existing problems* are increasingly being seen as a major area of work, with substance use being a triggering factor for the onset or relapse into psychosis, or being a form of self-medication, or simply with the two problems co-existing independently (Baker and Velleman 2007).

If there is a second volume, we will actively seek to redress all of these areas.

Conclusion

This book is about the presence of psychosis in the human condition, and those who suffer directly or indirectly from its symptoms; it includes the experiences of people with psychosis and their carers, families and friends. It is also about professionals from a variety of disciplines who have seen it as their calling and duty, within the framework of local resources, research evidence and UK government policy, to attempt to ameliorate the mental ill-health of those who have been referred to them. The practice described within this book occurred in southwest England, and is ongoing. This area consists of a typical composite of cities, towns and a host of rural communities, so we would expect our findings to be applicable in other parts of the UK and possibly worldwide.

This book amply describes the great benefits of collaboration. We believe we may have played a part in promoting collaboration as the norm and that we will soon see the next paradigm shift, where mental health service users and their carers really are, as government intended (Department of Health 1999a; 2000; 2001a, b), at the heart of service planning, development and delivery.

We offer these case studies, not as a guidebook of easy steps for others to follow, but in the spirit of sharing our learning, in order that others may learn from our experience. Because the work described has taken place in real-world, routine clinical settings, we think that other workers could also employ these approaches given the necessary working conditions. We hope that others may be inspired by reading this volume to wish to contribute to the second volume: if so, get in touch with us. Planning for this book has commenced. And finally . . . 'Although the problems [may be] intractable, both learning and change are possible when we work together effectively' (Attwood et al. 2003, p. 29).

References

Allott, P. and Loganathan, L. (2003) *Discovering Hope for Recovery from a British Perspective: a Review of a Sample of Recovery Literature, Implications for Practice and Systems Change*. Birmingham: Mental Health Resource Centre, Centre for Community Mental Health, University of Central England in Birmingham. Published online at: www.nuts.cc/almanack/lit/gov/nimhe/central/recovery.html (accessed 2 January 2006).

Arksey, H. (2003) Scoping the field: services for carers of people with mental health problems. *Health and Social Care in the Community*, 11, 335–44.

Attwood, M., Pedler, M., Pritchard, S. and Wilkinson, D. (2003) *Leading Change: A Guide to Whole Systems Working*. Bristol: The Policy Press.

Baker, A. and Velleman, R. (eds.) (2007) *Clinical Handbook of Co-existing Mental Health and Drug and Alcohol Problems*. Hove: Bruner Routledge, in press.

Bentall, R. (2003) *Madness Explained*. London: Penguin Allen Lane.

Crawford, M., Aldridge, T., Bhuik, Rutter, D., Manley, C., Weaver, T., Tyrer, P. and Fulop, N. (2003) User involvement in the planning and delivery of mental health services: a cross-sectional survey of service users and providers. *Acta Psychiatrica Scandinavica*, 107, 410–414.

Deegan, P. (1988) Recovery: the lived experience of rehabilitation. *Psychiatric Rehabilitation Journal*, 11, 11–19.

Department of Health (1999a) *The National Service Framework for Mental Health: Modern Standards and Service Models*. London: Department of Health.

Department of Health (1999b) *Making a Difference: Strengthening the Nursing, Midwifery and Health Visiting Contribution to Health and Healthcare*. London: Department of Health.

Department of Health (2000) *The NHS Plan: A Plan for Investment, A Plan for Reform*. London: Department of Health.

Department of Health (2001a) *The Expert Patient Programme*. London: Department of Health.

Department of Health (2001b) *Mental Health Policy Implementation Guide*. London: Department of Health.

Department of Health (2004) *The Ten Essential Shared Capabilities: A Framework for the Whole of the Mental Health Workforce*. London: Department of Health.

Douglas, S. and Machin, T. (2004) A model for setting up interdisciplinary collaborative working in groups: lessons from an experience of action learning. *Journal of Psychiatric and Mental Health Nursing*, 11, 189–93.

Hannigan, B. (1999) Joint working in community mental health: prospects and challenges. *Health and Social Care in the Community*, 7, 25–31.

Leahy, T. (2005) Like Tesco, the NHS must accept the consumer is king. The *Guardian*, 5 February, p. 18.

Meriden (2005) *Meriden Newsletter*, 2 (5), July 2005. Available online: www.meridenfamilyprogramme.com/documents/newsletters/Meriden%20July%202005.pdf (accessed 2 January 2006).

Nelson, G. and Prilleltensky, I. (2005) *Community Psychology: In Pursuit of Liberation and Well-being*. Basingstoke: Palgrave Macmillan.

Nuechterlein, K. (1987) Vulnerability models for schizophrenia: state of the art. In Hafner, H., Gattaz, W. and Janzarik, W. (eds.) *Search for the Causes of Schizophrenia*. Heidelberg: Springer Verlag, pp. 297–316.

Orford, J. (1992) *Community Psychology: Theory and Practice*. Chichester: John Wiley.

Penn, D., Guyman, K., Daily, T., Spaulding, W., Garbin, C. and Sullivan, M. (1994) Dispelling the stigma of schizophrenia: what sort of information is best. *Schizophrenia Bulletin*, 27, 73–92.

Perkins, R. and Repper, J. (1998) *Dilemmas in Community Mental Health Practice: Choice or Control*. Edinburgh: Radcliffe Medical Press.

Pitschel-Walz, G., Leucht, S., Bauml, J., Kissling, W. and Engel, R. (2001) The effect of family interventions on relapse and rehospitalisation in schizophrenia: a meta-analysis. *Schizophrenia Bulletin*, 27, 73–92.

Sayer, A. (1992) *Method in Social Science: A Realist Approach*, 2nd edition. London: Routledge.

Smith, G. and Velleman, R. (2002) Maintaining a family work for psychosis service by recognising and addressing the barriers to implementation. *Journal of Mental Health*, 11, 471–9.

Smith, M. (1998) *Social Science in Question*. London: Open University/Sage Publications.

Sunday Times Magazine (2002) 6 January.

Zubin, J. and Spring, B. (1977) Vulnerability: a new view of schizophrenia. *Journal of Abnormal Psychology*, 86, 103–26.

Author Index

Subject Index

Note: page references in *italics* indicate table and diagrams.